To - m...

We are so proud of your
children, and what you have
meant to them. Thank you
for your personal contribution.

Applause for the speaking and work of Dr. Frank W. Hale, Jr.

You were terrific. You managed to inspire the faculty and staff as well as the students in the audience. I hardly ever see faculty enthusiastic about a keynote address or speaker.

Dr. Jean Girves
Associate Director
Committee on Institutional Cooperation
Champaign, Illinois

Thank you for participating in our conference. Your oratory was splendid as usual! The participants thought so, too. I have just summarized the post conference evaluations and yours were unanimously excellent.

Dr. Rosetta Taylor Moore
Assistant Dean, Graduate School
St. Louis University
St. Louis, Missouri

I want to thank you for the absolutely superb presentation made to the members of the Council of Black Graduate Schools. Your knowledge, expertise, and experience were evident, as were your interest and commitment. Several of the deans, many of whom are seasoned veterans of the speaking circuit, commented on the excellence of your presentation.

Ms. Carole D. Slaughter
Program Administrator
Educational Testing Service
Director, New Jersey

Your commencement address was magnificent—the best I've ever heard at Ohio State.

Dr. L. H. Newcomb
Professor and Chair
Department of Agricultural Education
The Ohio State University
Columbus, Ohio

Please accept our sincere thanks for the fantastic speech you gave during the annual salute to our Ph.D. graduates. The campus is still buzzing with excitement about your visit.

Johnetta G. Davis
Associate Dean
Student Relations
Howard University
Washington, D.C.

Everyone is still talking about how enlightening and motivating you were without notes. I am proud to say, each time, that you have done that for years.

The Honorable William F. Bowen
State Senator
Columbus, Ohio

I can certainly understand why you are in demand as a speaker and as a consultant all over this land of ours.

Dr. John Wagner
Former President
Union College
Lincoln, Nebraska

We were indeed blessed with your presentations, but in addition to that you provided the necessary 'eye openers,' the necessary history, the necessary context, and the necessary motivation for continuing to forge ahead with definite measures towards attending to the needs of diversity on our campus.

Dr. Newton W. Hoilette
Vice President for Student Affairs
Andrews University
Berrien Springs, Michigan

You make everyone associated with Ohio State proud! Your message (commencement address) was clear and valued, your presentation uplifting and dazzling.

Dr. Roy A. Koenigsknecht
Dean, The Graduate School
The Ohio State University
Columbus, Ohio

Angels Watching Over Me

Angels Watching Over Me

The Autobiography
of
Dr. Frank W. Hale, Jr.

James C. Winston
Publishing Company, Inc.

First printing

PUBLISHED BY JAMES C. WINSTON PUBLISHING COMPANY, INC.
Trade Division of Winston-Derek Publishers Group, Inc.
Nashville, Tennessee 37205

Library of Congress Catalog Card No: 95-62385
ISBN: 1-55523-781-9

Printed in the United States of America

For my endearing parents, Frank and Novella, though now deceased, live on!

———•+•+•———

For my beloved family: Ruth, my wonderful bride of forty-eight years who has never wavered in times tough and tender and who, with consummate integrity and with clean hands and a pure heart, has always maintained dignity and majesty; my cherished daughters, Ifeoma (Jim) and Sherilyn; my stalwart son, Frank III (Irene); my gorgeous grandchildren, Renene (James), Frank IV, Christina, and Charles; and my flowering great grandchildren, Ryan and Jordan. Each member of my immediate family, in her and his own way, has added to the glue which has helped to keep me together during all of my days of toil.

———•+◆+•———

I dedicate this story, too, to my ninety-seven year old aunt, Mrs. Isy D. Young, who over the years has been a guiding light and monstrous pillar of support as the family matriarch.

———•+•+•———

Cousins Susie, Georgette, Charlotte, Marian, Elfleda, Corinne, and Ludy have always been there, as have Madge, Glo, Corloyd and Thomas.

———•+◆+•———

I am indebted, too, to those relatives, friends, colleagues, and *student wonders* whose motivations and memories flourished even before my writing burned the indelible impressions of their influence upon the pages which follow.

Contents

Preface

This book has been in the making for sixty-eight years, but it has been under the inspiration of my pen for nearly a year. My life has been full, filled with mountains and valleys—seldom plateaus, for I am far too kinetic to remain unoccupied.

The idea of writing an autobiography was not my own. My children suggested some time ago that I should share my various experiences with others, particularly young people. Their lives are sometimes changed in a positive direction when they have dared to embrace the views of those who have resisted oppression, and who, by opposing it, have gained a greater freedom for themselves, as well as others. My life has been sandwiched between slices of a substantial African-American cultural heritage and a sterling spiritual genealogy as reflected in the lives of my Christian parents.

My story is both personal and historical. It recounts my unwillingness to accept things as they are on matters of race. It focuses most heavily on my educational sojourn and my experiences in black and white educational settings as an educator who happens to be black.

The book does not in any way reflect the full scope of my life, my personal victories and failures. I have neither the gall nor indiscretion to tell everything because, like others before me and now, I have often taken leaps into the irrational and absurd. Life can be humbling if you dare open your heart to the ambiguities of your own frailties. I find myself constantly challenging God to not let me become divorced from the roots of my own reality. My story has been one of discovery and rediscovery—a challenge of confronting both my past and my destiny.

The shadow of vulnerability and mortality looms ever larger as the years multiply behind us and diminish before us. We, all of us, tend to point outward and away from ourselves when we are confronted with the problems of life. We are only as heroic as our willingness to look inward, and in the words of David say, "Search me, O God, and know my heart: try me, and know my thoughts; and see if there be any wicked way in me, and lead me in the way everlasting." (Psalms 139:23–24)

I hope that those who read this book will note that I have seldom failed to face an issue squarely or fairly, and with the kind of balance and perspective that is demanding of both intellectual and spiritual maturity.

I have come to know more and more that the object of life is not just to know the truth, but to be it. To this end, it is my hope that this story will reflect in me an unconquerable human spirit bolstered by the knowledge and faith that God, all through the years, has sent His protecting angels to watch over me.

Acknowledgements

———◆—◆—◆———

It is difficult to imagine to what extent my life and writing have been influenced by the thinking and scholarship of others. Were it possible to pay tribute to all who have helped to shape my understanding of issues that require probing beyond what any one person can absorb, the list would have become too voluminous for reader consumption.

This volume reflects genuine milestones in my life that go far beyond the scope of my experiences in higher education. It was Ms. Luvada Lockhardt who, after my earliest teachers had given up on me, "made a way out of no way" by loving and nurturing me to the fullest in the fourth grade. It was she who provided the "touch of immortality" that set me on the high road of self-confidence, towering ambition, and the rejection of anything that would seek to strangle my spirit or initiative. I had the privilege of having Dr. Winton H. Beaven as my teacher and adviser at Union College (Nebraska). He, as a white professor, dared to synthesize the insights of tradition and the black predicament on an all-white campus and became a pivotal mentor and friend, when I might have become a dropout in a sea of isolation and alienation. It was because of him that I chose the field of communication as my major discipline.

It was the members of the Hub of Harmony who formed the tie that bound us together in Christian love and support when we needed it most.

I learned much from Elder Frank L. Peterson. It was he who offered and gave me my first professional opportunity as college teacher, as well as the privilege of becoming the first faculty member to earn the Ph.D. while teaching at Oakwood College.

Doctors Arliss Roaden, Keith Brooks, and Albert Kuhn opened the doors of opportunity for me at The Ohio State University. Dr. William J. Holloway, my "brother," paved the way in his precious and dedicated commitment to students of color. Dr. Edward H. Jennings, former Ohio State University president, demonstrated courage and generosity during a time when interest concerning issues of diversity had begun to flounder. He provided the glow and recognition that stabilized my faith in my final years at Ohio State.

My very special thanks go to Joycelyn Wilson, who through the months has given hours on end in typing the manuscript and in making the appropriate emendations for final review. Hers has been a labor of sacrifice and dedication. Deneene Merchant and Cristine Range also gave fine assistance in the latter stages of this manuscript.

For those who have given of their diligent best in proofreading this manuscript, they are Pastor Ifeoma Kwesi, my daughter; Ms. Leslie Slaughter, and Ms. Jacqueline Parris.

Dr. Jannith Lewis of Oakwood College made her files available to me, an important courtesy for which I am very grateful. I wish to express my indebtedness again to Leslie Slaughter who made it possible for me to make certain vital additions, even after the manuscript was completed, with her expeditious and expert typing.

When my spirits were low and my body was wracked with fatigue, I could always gain support by telephoning Mr. Vertis Barnes, Jr., Mr. Henry Griffith, Mr. David Harmon, Dr. Jannith Lewis, Mr. Robert Lewis, Dr. and Mrs. Roy Malcolm, Dr. Gaines Partridge, and Dr. and Mrs. Jon Robertson.

I owe much to all of them who have given me the inspiration which made possible this personal adventure.

Introduction

It was an afternoon that I will long remember. Anticipating the inevitable, I had headed toward downtown Columbus, Ohio, to pick up a photograph of my father at Chick's Camera Shop on Sabbath, April 27, 1991, when my car phone rang. It was the voice of my son, Frank III, on the other end, declaring in a distressful tone, "Dad, Chief has just passed." My wife, Ruth, and I had just left his apartment a few minutes earlier to procure an enlarged portrait of one of our favorite images of him. We had sensed the rapidly diminishing vitality in his final fight with cancer, and we wanted to have that picture before the store closed for the weekend. It was a painful journey that we took over the next few blocks before we acquired the large eleven by fourteen-inch black and white photograph that would be the focal point of his memorial service.

My father and I were very close. I enjoyed making him and my mother happy. My dad was incredibly proud of my accomplishments. No matter what successes I had, great or small, he lost little time in telling his friends and associates. Restive, lovable, creative and compassionate, his whole life revolved around making people happy. He was a marvelous blend of Christian commitment—strong, independent, and self-assured on one hand, and yet, tender, ministering, and at one's call on the other.

I studied him carefully through the years—how he suffered and, at the same time, confronted the racial indignities of his time. He used to say, "People can't stop you if you have it (grit, I assumed) in you Frank; they can only slow you up." And to drive his point home, he would follow his admonition with the words of the old Negro spiritual, "So don't you let nobody turn you 'round." I took those words to heart, and braced myself for the years ahead—years that would challenge the racist society in which I was born. The pageant of African-American people, undulating though it is, has been imbued with the belief that America will ultimately fulfill its obligation to breathe life into the meaning of democracy for all of its citizens.

Just a belief offers only a faint hint of hope for those of us whose existence predated the *Brown v. Topeka* decision of the Supreme Court. The difficulties of democratization seemed so far removed that we never anticipated even the progress, however minimal, that we see today. The negative images still remain. The inadequate facilities that saturated our segregated schools—the battered desks, shattered shades, and the worn, torn, soiled and hand-me-down (from the white schools) textbooks. Then there were the eating establishments that either refused to serve blacks or which served them only in separate dining areas. Everything was, in fact, separate. It was American apartheid. This caste arrangement had extended itself into all aspects of our lives. White America has had a complete paralyzing monopoly on the lives of African-Americans. Notwithstanding the nation's espousal of the ethics of Jefferson's democracy and a Judeo-Christian tradition, it nevertheless has found unreasonably convenient means for rationalizing and perpetuating a caste system that has become the core of racial tension and hostility since its establishment.

So, as a child, I experienced a wilderness of walls. Everything was separated by walls of prejudice and discrimination—restaurants, hospitals, schools, buses, neighborhoods, trains, hotels, churches, city parks, funeral homes, rest rooms, and even cemeteries. Anywhere there were people—black or white—dead or alive, there were walls. Similarly, each occupation carried its stigmatizing label and approval of dehumanizing rank categories based solely on race as the more servile jobs in maintenance, in maid and domestic service, in garbage collection, in kitchen and waiting chores at hotels and restaurants were reserved for black people. A few blacks gained lower-middle-class status as mail carriers and railroad waiters and porters.

It was very early in life that I observed my father's response to the unfortunate position in which blacks were born. While blacks were born into a position which society had predetermined as their lot—a position which was as automatic as the process by which they had inherited the color of their skin—my father never acquiesced to the notion that he was either inferior or foredoomed to failure. He escaped from the troubles and discomforts of his racial predicament by dreaming, speculating and aspiring to a higher order in the social scale because of the strong grip by which he was grounded in his understanding of God and a history of African civilization.

Dad always reminded me of who I was—a child of God and of rich African ancestry. He had an insatiable curiosity about African history. While all of us had been raised on European history and had been taught to think of Europe as the center of the civilized world, he alerted me to the fact that Europe was an outpost of civilization when Africa was experiencing a renaissance with the extraordinary contributions of brilliant black Egyptian scholars, mathematicians, engineers, philosophers, artists, scientists, embalmers, architects, and poets. Dad introduced me to the magnificent and breathtaking temples, pyramids and statuary of those Egyptian master builders of more than thirty-three centuries past whose genius remains unparalleled and unrivaled.

It was during the summer of 1992 that my wife and I, while celebrating our forty-fifth wedding anniversary, were able to confirm all that my father had taught me as we cruised the Nile and visited such great wonders as the Karnak Temple near Luxor, the Pyramids of Giza, the Mohamed Ali Mosque, Philae, the Sphinx, the Temple of Hatsheput, and the Valley of the Kings, Queens, and Nobles.

It is no wonder that Herodotus, that noted historian who visited Egypt in the fifth century B.C., wrote that "nowhere are there so many marvelous things, nor in the world beside are there to be seen so many things of unspeakable greatness." There is absolutely no doubt in my mind that the earlier advances of African civilization had a monumental impact on and foreshadowed the emergence of modern science, art, and philosophy of the later Greek, Roman and European civilizations. The fact of that having been ignored, for the most part, in American historiography in no way dimmed my sense of somebodiness.

I learned early in life not to rely on the traditional historians. I garnered strength and affirmation from black historians and scholars like Carter G. Woodson, W. E. B. DuBois, and Charles H. Wesley. As I read of the splendid and awe-inspiring accomplishments of women and men of African descent, I became more and more determined to plunge into those desperate and perilous situations that so often engulfed my defenseless people with the exalted simple faith and willingness to believe that, with God's help, I could move mountains.

My mother, as well, played no small part in my healthy sense of self and destiny. I recall one magical moment when she wanted to confirm the magnificence of God's future plans for me by sharing an experience which transpired when I was only an infant. It was only six months after I was born that my mother's eldest brother, Uncle Lloyd Banks, died. My mother took a train during that month of December to attend his funeral in Washington, D.C. Poised on the seat next to her in the passenger car, I joined her in deep sleep amidst the rocking motion of the train as it proceeded down the railroad tracks. Mother was awakened by the jarring of the train at about two o'clock in the morning only to discover that her infant son was no longer on the seat beside her. In desperation and in panic, she cried out in despair while awakening and alarming other passengers, "Where is my baby!?!" Jumping to her feet and heading toward the front of the coach to summon the porter, her fears were immediately dispelled when she observed her robust baby in the middle of the aisle, snoring heavily with unwavering staccatos of breath-taking inhalations and exhalations and totally oblivious to his new place of rest. It must have been a treacherous and dangerous lurching of the train that had tumbled me into this terribly dangerous interlude. My mother's fears were now matched only by her gratitude to God for sparing me of any serious injury. She later told me that as the trains went down the track, and as she held me tightly in the grip of love in her lap, she began to quietly sing, "All night, all day, angels watching over me, my Lord." It was an old traditional spiritual that was to become, to a great extent, my legacy and my future fortune.

Chapter 1

Born to Move Mountains

———⫍⊃⊙⊙⊂⫎———

The historical pageantry of many Americans, whose ancestors were European immigrants and who sailed into New York Harbor with great expectations and visions of freedom upon viewing the Statue of Liberty, was lost on my parents Frank and Novella Hale. Their roots reached back into the subsoil of an African people; consequently, they suffered the anti-black attitude of the prevailing culture which existed when I was born in Kansas City, Missouri, on March 24, 1927. Kansas City, despite its midwestern location and orientation, had its own tradition of resentment and hostility toward blacks, a hostility that was widened by the fact that I was born in General Hospital Number Two. General Hospital Number One was reserved for white folks. It was clear that the system had invented one more mechanism for keeping blacks and whites quarantined from each other, even in matters of health, as General Hospital Number One was reserved exclusively for white patients in another part of town.

There can be no doubt that the great exodus of blacks from the South to the North between 1914 and 1920 had an impressive impact on urban communities like Kansas City. As blacks sought to take advantage of greater job opportunities during the war, higher wages and educational opportunities, their presence deepened the insanity of the white working class who became resentful of their new competition. When the war came to an end with millions of soldiers being discharged into a shrinking labor market, racial rivalries became more intense. As tensions rose, economic motivation among blacks became stronger.

Kansas City was a vigorous example of what was taking place. In addition to the traditional middle and upper-class cluster of mail carriers, barbers, and dining car waiters, there a were few black business and professional persons whose clientele were mostly white prior to and during the war. After then, racial tension had the redeeming virtue of developing a spirit of race pride, self-help, and a sturdy core of merchants, professionals and politicians who were undergirded and supported by people in the black community.

My father, being the energetic and ingenious person that he was, gave up his job as a substitute mail carrier and opened up a five and ten cent store on the corner of Eighteenth and Vine. Even before the infusion of black southern immigrants, the black citizens of Kansas City—seized with a desire for black independence, a thirst for entrepreneurship, and a boundless faith in their own potential—began to undertake the kinds of business and professional ventures only faintly considered or embarked upon in earlier days. Kansas City boasted such black businesses as Street's Hotel, Johnson's Pharmacy, and a host of barber shops, beauty parlors, grocery stores, barbecue houses, restaurants, auto repair garages, and branch offices of black-owned insurance companies like Atlanta Life Insurance and Supreme Liberty Life. T.B. Watkins Funeral Home met the needs of the bereaved black community. The *Kansas City Call*, with its publisher, C.A. Franklin, and its manager, Roy Wilkins, dominated the black journalistic scene and was the most influential enterprise, along with the National Association for the Advancement of Colored People (NAACP), in exposing the well-established pillars of segregation and discrimination.

Kansas City, stained by its involvement with the corrupt Pendergast political machine, had for years been a haven for blacks who had come up the Missouri from Alabama, Tennessee, Louisiana, and Mississippi. I remember the days when my parents would visit friends in Kansas City, Kansas. I always hated to cross the Lewis and Clark Viaduct, going from the Missouri side to Kansas, and to return because of the stench that came from the gigantic stockyards that fed the meat-packing industry. Kansas City, alongside Chicago, was one of the most highly industrialized meat-packing centers in the nation. My only escape on such trips was to pinch my nostrils in order to protect myself from the shattering odors that emerged from the stockyards and slaughter houses.

At age eight, I earned a little spending money every Friday by selling copies of the *Kansas City Call* on busy street corners as black people got off from work with their weekly paychecks. My pleading sales chant was: "One for a nickel,/Two for a dime,/Forty-five cents/will bring you nine." It was at that juncture in my early life that I unwittingly became a proponent of equal opportunity and fair play for my people.

Gifted writers such as Langston Hughes, Countee Cullen, Alain Locke, Arna Bontemps, and Claude McKay focused on black culture and social inequalities in those days. Kansas City, at the crossroads of America, was a source of both pain and pride to its black inhabitants, who knew and endured many of the intolerances generally associated with southern states, but who at the same time isolated themselves against the destructive winds of segregation and discrimination by clinging to their cultural tradition, their hopes, and went on living, surviving and dying in their own traditional ways.

My parents were a loving and a humbly-dignified couple. Because they knew who they were, I always knew who I was—that is to say—God's child. My parents went out of their way to keep me ever reminded that I was somebody! They taught me to fear no man or, for that matter, any situation. The gospel of self-esteem was a part of their practical day-to-day theology. When I was three years of age, they arranged for my first public appearance. Though slightly bewildered at first, I sang "Jesus Loves Me" before the congregation of Paseo Baptist Church, the largest Baptist church in Kansas City, then pastored by the Reverend D. A. Holmes, who was considered the dean of black Baptist preachers in the country.

As long as I live, I shall cherish the memory of my childhood days in Kansas City. Although there were only three of us—my mother, my father, and me—we were a very, very close family. While a good part of my early childhood was spent in the depths of the Great Depression, my loving, generous, and sacrificing parents spared me of much of the misery that they certainly must have encountered on a daily basis. Nevertheless, though I was born during those vicious days of the depression to Novella Banks Hale and Frank Hale, Sr., I was especially blessed to have been born to a beautiful young couple who were defiant of the jaded culture that quarantined American blacks from the paths and opportunities afforded their white counterparts. Like many blacks, my parents worked, scraped, and sacrificed to make life comfortable and meaningful for me as a child. They, like many others of African ancestry, exhibited such wonderful attributes as industry, perseverance, enthusiasm, congeniality, and a striving for excellence in whatever they pursued. It was not that they were necessarily involved in performing some great activity, but they lived each day earnestly and consistently.

My mother, Novella, was one of five girls (Georgette, Ida, Gladys, and Isy) and four boys (Lloyd, James, Malachi, and Howard) born to Richard H. Banks and Irene A. George Banks on the family farm in Surry, Virginia. My grandfather, Richard, was an enterprising gentleman of quiet nobility, and my grandmother, Irene, possessed a warm personality of enormous magnitude. Before the turn of the century, around 1880, less than two decades after the Emancipation Proclamation of 1863, and only fifteen years after General Grant's crushing defeat of General Lee and the Confederate army at Richmond and Appomattox Courthouse in 1865, my grandfather, Richard, purchased several hundred acres of rich farmland in Surry County and built the home that would later house his large family. It is of note that Grant's Virginia campaign culminated at a point only miles from the family homeland, which we still own, and within the shadow of the James River where my grandparents on my mother's side, my mother, and all of her brothers and sisters were baptized into the membership of Mount Nebo Baptist Church.

My father, Frank, was one of two children born to Paul and Maude Hale. He and his brother, Harold, who was two years his senior, were born in Athens, Ohio, a small city located about sixty miles southeast of Columbus, Ohio, the state's capital. Athens had little to offer, except that it was the home of Ohio University, one of the state-supported institutions of higher education. I had little knowledge of my paternal ancestors, only that my grandfather, Paul, and his father, John, my great-grandfather, were born in Oberlin, Ohio. In recent years, I have developed a readiness to pursue my lineage on that side of the family.

I suppose it was my family heritage on mother's side that satisfied my sense of what families should be all about. Mother constantly kept me abreast of family history and was always promoting and inquiring about the successes and failings of contemporary family members. She remained in constant touch with her siblings, their children, and with any trace of ancestry that would undergird her background of her forebearers. While not born to royalty, Mom identified with those aristocratic tendencies that promoted spirituality, literacy, and fluency as the minimum essentials of civility among all family members.

Mom and Dad were a handsome couple. Mother had a sweet, oval face with liquid brown eyes, and she spoke with a soft voice that could be raised to the appropriate level when confronted with "careless behavior" or insufficient improvement in my studies as evidenced by my grade card following the last grading period. Dad had definitive features—a broad nose, thin lips, and penetrating eyes. His manner was direct and dynamic. Both of my parents were unwilling to compromise on moral principles.

My father was an ambitious, resourceful man. There was an overpowering independence in his makeup that bolstered his desire to personally direct the day-to-day activities of his own life. His every action demonstrated that he considered self-reliance as absolutely indispensable to his well being.

After a short period of working as a family domestic and then doing a short stint as a substitute mail carrier, he opened his small five and ten cents store. He instinctively knew how to relate to the public because of his warm and friendly manner. There are few men blessed with the magnetic and obliging personality so characteristic of my father. His voice and laugh and his hale and hearty approach to life enlarged those around him, and in due time, his little store was bulging with patronage.

Although there were only a few public places where black people were welcomed or could enjoy themselves, my parents made every imaginable opportunity available to me. I clearly recall our visits to the Swope Park Zoo, our weekend picnics, our auto tours through those plush neighborhoods with manicured lawns and geometric gardens and with restrictive covenants that barred black people from ownership. With my parents, I enjoyed a very delightful and intimately personal friendship, through all my childhood and later years. This was similarly characteristic of my relationship with with Mr. and Mrs. Vertis Barnes and their son Vertis, Jr., who became "my brother" for life.

Vertis and I, along with another good friend of ours, Curtis Burton, formed an inseparable triune. We skated together, played ball together, rode bicycles together, and played follow the leader together in various and precarious ways. We made extra money parking cars together when the Kansas City Monarchs, a black baseball team, came to town. Vertis and I lived on 24th and Brooklyn, only two blocks from the Kansas City Blues Baseball Station. The Kansas City Blues was a white farm team of the New York Yankees. Those were the days before black players, like Sachel Paige, who was with the Monarchs, could play on white teams. Nevertheless, we made nickels and dimes parking cars in the lot next to our apartment building for people who attended the games. Early in life, I was somehow made conscious of the value of money to the extent that I began saving a portion of my earnings from selling papers and parking cars.

While I had heard the saying, "God protects the ignorant and the innocent," I became more convinced of its validity as I grew older. Because of our close-knit relationship, Vertis and I as children would often—at each other's daring—do very foolish things. Only because of God's mercy were we spared of tragedy time after time. There were times when we would get on our bicycles and sandwich ourselves between two streetcars, each going in the opposite direction, defying the dangers of entrapment, of being crushed or mangled beneath uncompromising wheels of steel. One occasion during the winter, we rode our bikes across the ice-covered surface of Troost Lake and watched, horrified, as the ice cracked in perforated patterns just behind us as we managed to safely cross this thirty-foot deep abyss. Our mothers' prayers unquestionably had followed us despite our youthful irreverence.

I remember the day when I was sent to Campbell, Ohio, to live with Dr. and Mrs. William P. Young, my aunt and uncle. My mother had become ill and had to be hospitalized indefinitely. It was a sad, sad day for our family. Yet I was fortunate to be able to live with my mother's sister, Aunt Isy, and her husband, Uncle William. Uncle William had just begun his medical practice a few years earlier in this small, remote steel town, not far from Youngstown, Ohio. My uncle had his practice on the second floor of a building that overlooked the steel mills, and we lived down the hall from his office. Naturally, I was fascinated as I looked at the large steel furnaces that were always ablaze, day and night. Having already completed the first grade in Kansas City, I was enrolled in the second grade in the Campbell Public Schools. Up until that time, I had enjoyed the acceptance and stimulation which I had received in an all-black school.

In my new environment, I felt lost in space. I had no friends, and no one seemed anxious to befriend me. Because I was new, I naturally hesitated to take any initiative at the beginning because I was a total stranger and felt isolated as the only black student in my class. Most of the students had long and unfamiliar last names. My teacher's name was Slovosky. I had become familiar with one and two syllable names in the black community—names like Jones, Smith, Johnson, Harris, and Cantrell. I was puzzled, frustrated, and abandoned. What was I to do? My earlier sense of confidence was stretched beyond my ability to cope. Because I received little or no encouragement to participate in the classroom or the playground, I withdrew. It was a dark, dark period in my early life. The clouds in my mental sky increased with each new day.

My aunt and uncle were beautiful people, and they gave abundantly of their love and time. It was with Aunt Isy that I spent most of my time when I wasn't in school. It was her attentiveness that propped my ego, at least temporarily, when I was outside of the classroom. I remember when she gave me a hug or took me to the ice cream parlor to console me after I had endured another dastardly day at school. The weekends offered me an exodus from the tensions and frustrations of school life. I have never forgotten the auto excursions that we took to nearby Warren, Struthers, Youngstown, and Cleveland to visit my aunt's and uncle's friends. Well connected socially because of their professional standing and reputation, Aunt Isy and Uncle William often spent their weekends in the company of some of their closest friends, as well as with some of their most intimate personal acquaintances. I have golden memories of those eventful sojourns which I found exceedingly enjoyable because there was always an abundance of good food that was available to satisfy my unquenchable and insatiable appetite. The emotions of my run-away cravings were always tempered by a penetrating glance from my aunt. One such look awakened all of my sensibilities concerning good manners and the need for me to let moderation govern my wide-eyed temptation to be greedy in the presence of such delicious and sumptuous cuisine. It was dangerous being naughty on such occasions because the palms of my uncle's hands, which I had experienced on other occasions, were enough to both envelope and blister my derriere apparently beyond repair, at least for the moment.

There were many variations of those weekends. At one extremity, we attended dog races. It was exciting to observe the powerfully sleek greyhounds, running at incredibly swift speeds in pursuit of those electric rabbits which always managed to outdistance them, even if only by a hair. Staunch gamblers manifested little restraint as they exhausted and emptied their pockets to satisfy their thirst for fortunes that, in most cases, were never realized. Thanks to their sense of self-restraint, my relatives made no secret that they were there to observe the races and to enjoy the excitement which the competitive contests induced as the springy greyhounds rivaled each other for positions and prizes. At other times, I was exposed to the artistries of top black musicians. The image of Cab Calloway, honed in his all-white outfit—white suit, white shirt, white big brim hat, white bow tie, white socks and white shoes—is still finely etched in my memories. He sent the audience into uncontrollable thrills with his unabashed antics, singing and dancing in his rendition of the popular jazz tune, "Minnie the Moocher."

I don't remember the Great Depression in terms of what I felt at the time. After all, I was a child, and parents and relatives—in fact, grown-ups generally—have a way of attempting to protect children from the suffering perplexities that plague adults. Except for enduring the normal pangs of early childhood—having my tonsils removed and having my first tooth extracted by Dr. Tate, who was a partner in my uncle's office—I had little knowledge of the tribulations that older people suffered in the 1930s.

It was in June of 1936 that I completed—barely completed—the requirements for passing the third grade. I received all E's on my report card. An E didn't mean *excellent* in those days. E was the grade between D and F in the grading system. It represented a *pass* with reservations. I sagged with embarrassment as I took my grade card home and presented it to my aunt and uncle. The grades telescoped my blanket of academic deficiencies. I cannot say I learned anything at all during that school year. I couldn't read, add, subtract, spell, or write very well. After all, because I had felt unwanted in school, I fidgeted, day-dreamed, looked out the window, doodled, and reluctantly looked at the teacher while instantly blocking out and ignoring whatever she was saying or demonstrating. I managed to exhibit sufficient decorum so as not to be disruptive, but I am sure that my behavior telescoped my disinterest and displeasure. My third grade experience left a deep negative imprint on my psyche in terms of what school was all about. I left Campbell, Ohio, to return to Kansas City, with no chance of surviving educationally at all, except for my providential encounters with my fourth grade teacher, Luvada Lockhardt.

I was happy enough to find a bronze-colored, statuesque young woman with a glowing smile standing at the door of Beacon Light Seventh-day Adventist Church School, greeting each of the students as they began their first day in school. My parents had seized the opportunity for me to be enrolled in a small church school where, hopefully, I would get the necessary attention and encouragement that would address the academic deficiencies with which I was plagued. As my turn came, Ms. Lockhardt clasped my hand firmly and looked warmly into my eyes. Her manner registered the magnetic assurance and simplicity that envelops all true teachers.

My parents never elaborated on the details of what they had told my new teacher about my need for special help. Obviously, they did not need to, because my dreadfully unsatisfactory report card was confirmation enough. Knowing my loving parents, I am certain that they did not stand by impassively and patiently, hoping that things would work themselves out. Instinctively, as I look back, I can imagine my parents taking the initiative to place me in a school where I would receive personal attention, a school that promulgated the Christian training and values which they so fervently espoused.

The school was not really much of a school physically. It was a muddle of contradictions. The walls carried a tone of cold bleakness, with paint flaking to the floor at the slightest provocation. Yet Ms. Lockhardt exuded a warmth that revealed, in great measure, the extent to which she relished her profession and really loved children. It is more than a little remarkable that, though there were about fifty children—all of us seated in one large room in grades one through six, our teacher always seemed to have had total control of the entire class and of each student individually, as she steered us, one by one, helping us to recognize the capability within each of us to discover truth. Even as she moved from one grade to the next, often there was an interconnectedness between what was being discussed or assigned at one grade level and what was occurring at another grade level. So, during the period of a full day, every pupil in the classroom was exposed to all six grades of instruction. Though the student-teacher ratio was 50 to 1, Ms. Lockhardt's congeniality, good humor, personal attention, and sincere dedication and commitment neutralized what some teachers might have considered an impossible situation. She continually defied the law of educational gravity. Such a catalogue of incongruities might have discouraged others, but Ms. Lockhardt was more than just a teacher, she was a teacher *par excellence*!

Not long after I had begun my fourth grade adventure, I began to sense that my new teacher wanted to help me, that she was interested in my growth and development, that she wanted me to improve, and that she was willing to go to great lengths to help me succeed. She took time with each of us as we needed it. She praised us when we did well, and she helped us to set more realistic goals when we failed. Occasionally, she pampered us with extrinsic rewards like peanuts and red hots for minor accomplishments and candy bars for significant ones. I will always remember the day that I received three Mr. Goodbar's for winning first place in a spelling bee. *Encouragement, encouragement, encouragement* seems to have been the important mainstay in her arsenal of love, because she was always on hand to give assistance through difficult periods. And of course, encouragement and motivation were just what I needed, given my experiences over the previous year and a half.

Ms. Lockhardt made every possible effort to keep my parents informed of her expectations, as well as of my progress in school. At the end of the school week, my mother was handed a stack of books that contained supplementary assignments for me to complete before returning to school on Monday. My parents, recognizing the importance of an active partnership between home and school in the development of a child, scheduled appropriate study time for me and monitored my homework to make sure that I understood the assignments before turning them in to the teacher. As a result of the cooperative relationship with the teacher and my parents, I developed a real zest for learning during my fourth grade year. I developed the capacity to enjoy school with Ms. Lockhardt's occasional pat on the shoulder and generous compliments for work well done. Her imprint was reflected in the fact that, at the end of the year, I averaged a grade of ninety percent or more in each of my subjects. I was on the way to achieving my maximum potential for my grade level because of Ms. Lockhardt's commitment as a teacher. She was the embodiment of the concept that *teaching is a touch of immortality*. From that fourth grade experience alone, Ms. Lockhardt's influence lived on in my life at every stage of my educational development thereafter.

Chapter 2

Our Move to Topeka

It was in June of 1937 that, at the beckoning of friends, Byron and Marthella Spears, my parents moved to Topeka, Kansas. They were challenged by the prospect of furthering their business aspirations and achieving a greater degree of economic independence. In responding to an inner daring, desire and faith to make a better life for themselves, they uprooted themselves with a singularity of purpose that needed no urging.

Located approximately seventy-five miles west of Kansas City, Topeka, the capital of Kansas, enjoyed some semblance of prosperity. The state was remarkably resourceful. It supplied one-fifth of the nation's wheat, and it provided sufficient staples for its citizens by growing an ample supply of corn, oats, alfalfa, beef and poultry. The boom in its farming was aided by its ability to purchase mechanized farming equipment and by the focus it gave to modernizing its highways, bridges, and waterways—all vital in transporting the state's products to major markets.

My dad, a man of incurable optimism, found in Topeka a city of opportunity and, with his handyman resourcefulness, eagerly turned his efforts toward seeking ways in which he might establish his own business. He was determined to break free from the traditional clutches of doing domestic day-work or other menial chores for whites. Distress was acute and widespread in the black community. As was the case throughout the country, blacks were left out in the cold when professional, semiprofessional, managerial, clerical, and white collar jobs were concerned. Most black workers were victims of ills not of their own making. Though honest and hard-working people, few owned their homes. Their employment, by and large, was restricted to domestic services, janitorial positions, and odd jobs in service stations, garages, restaurants, and hotels. Blacks who held positions in the post office or as mail-carriers or who worked as porters, dining car waiters, or as railroad men were considered middle class.

As Dad rehearsed in his thinking the stock market crash of 1929 with its overreaching climate of misery and gloom, he was determined to stake out an economic venture that would spare him from the indignities of bread lines, soup kitchens, or peddling wares on street corners in order to survive. From time to time, he would attempt various pursuits. Once, he launched into a bottle and jar washing business with Byron Spears. They purchased used bottles, washed them, and then resold them to companies that packed pickles, salad dressing, catsup, drinks, and a variety of other foodstuffs. They rented an old building and stocked it with huge galvanized tubs that were used to wash and rinse their glassware, after which they were dried before they were boxed in cardboard cartons prior to delivery. The venture required a breathless tempo to keep abreast of the orders. Lacking the initial capital to purchase the machinery that would have increased production and lightened their twelve to fifteen hour a day load, they were forced to abandon their exhausting enterprise in order to save their health and salvage the remainder of their investment before being completely devastated financially in the face of a floundering future.

A new era in business began for Dad in 1938 when he began working at the Pioneer Wastepaper Company. It proceeded to be a fascinating opportunity. The company purchased old newspapers, magazines and books. As a consequence of the nightmarish depression, people were forced to do whatever they could to make ends meet. Tens of thousands of people were jobless, and although the government was experimenting with new initiatives to stimulate economic recovery, consumers—overburdened and crippled by their circumstances—sold their home furnishings, clothes, and even family heirlooms in order to minimize the suffering that had reduced their provisions to rock bottom.

It was in such a climate that my father noticed that many books were being salvaged, along with newspapers and magazines, as people brought thousands of pounds of wastepaper to the company each day. At the time, the company was paying a cent a pound, or $1.00 per one hundred pounds, for the wastepaper.

The possibility of starting a bookstore, with a minimum of capital and with a substantial volume of good books, captivated Dad's mind as a distinct possibility. He was working as a sorter in the warehouse, and he offered the owner, Glenn Brown, two cents a pound for the books and magazines which he would select as marketable items. Mr. Brown agreed to the proposition, and in less than a year Dad had enough books and magazines to rent a space between Fifth and Sixth on Kansas Avenue where he opened Hale's Book Store. From the very beginning, it was a flourishing success.

Sales surged as people got word of the valuable volumes that were available at moderate prices. Flushed with uncommon creativity and energy, Dad built his own bookcases from orange and apple crates and labeled them according to subject areas such as *Art, Decorating, Education, Engineering, Health, History, Humor, Jurisprudence, Mental Health, Philosophy, Religion, Sports, Travel,* etc.

Incomparably more important, perhaps, than his collection was Dad's personality. He was a self-educated man. What he read, he remembered, and he read everything. Customers marveled at his breadth of knowledge, and more so at his sparkling and effusive personality. His manner was such that he was so comfortable with himself that even those who might have at first glance halted because of his race were inspired and won over by his warmth and unaffected demeanor. He knew no strangers, and it is also significant that he took a back seat to no one. He was determined to provide a better life for me than he had experienced as a young boy.

Under the encouragement of highly visible and respected people in the Topeka community, the bookstore became a chosen and desirable fixture in the city and state. Governor Alfred M. Landon, a wealthy oilman, visited the bookstore with regularity and advised us of particular books which he wished to add to his library. Dr. Karl Augustus Menninger, the world famous psychiatrist, was among a group of celebrated notables that were frequent customers. Reverend Charles Sheldon, the author of *In His Steps,* spent hours browsing among books in the sections on philosophy and religion. Surrounded by such eminent devotees of his wares, Dad lost little time in replenishing his stock. In addition to his connection at the wastepaper company, he purchased books from customers and made visits into some of Topeka's foremost homes to purchase books at the time of moving sales, auctions, and estate sales.

Because of the store's reputation, the Topeka Board of Education designated the store as one of the few stores that were approved to sell new textbooks for those children who attended the city schools. This new opportunity injected vigorous new blood into the day-to-day operations of the store, especially during the summer months prior to the opening of school. Children and parents were often lined up a half block or longer outside the store as they anticipated purchasing their supplies. During this season of the year, it was necessary to employ six to ten clerks in order to handle the booming business.

My parents had, meanwhile, been aware of this vast storehouse of knowledge and what it could mean to my personal development if I took advantage of it. Therefore, I worked there in the afternoons after school, on weekends, and full time during the summers. Whenever I wasn't serving customers, I was expected to take advantage of the many books that were available. In the process, I gained a liberal education. It was not uncommon for me to devour five to ten books during a week.

Prior to my parents entering the book business, one of their first transactions was getting me enrolled in school. The school that I was to attend was Buchanan School, but enrollment was not as easy a proceeding as one might think. Having completed the requirements of the fourth grade at Beacon Light Seventh-day Adventist School in Kansas City, my parents assumed that admission to the fifth grade at Buchanan would simply be a perfunctory happening. My enthusiasm for entering the fifth grade immediately lost much of its early momentum when the principal of Buchanan School, Mr. Morgan Maxwell, advised my mother that I would have to repeat the fourth grade because he could not locate Beacon Light School in any of his directories of certified schools.

My dear mother lost no precious moments in pleading in my behalf. So confident was she of my ability that she saw no need to squander my potential on repeating what I had already covered. She insisted with powerful ethos, "Just give him a chance. Put him in the fifth grade and let his performance speak for itself." Taking this stance, she felt sufficiently girded by her faith in God and in all of the effort that she, my dad, and Ms. Lockhardt had invested in me the year before. Her calm assuredness and urging played directly into the hands of Maxwell, who was a man given to honesty and fairness. "All right," he responded, "we'll give him a chance and see how he does, but you must understand that, if he has too many deficiencies, we will have to put him back." After the brief conference was adjourned, my mother, in walking down the hall, quietly exclaimed, "Thank you, Jesus; thank you, Jesus." At that point, even as a ten year old, I knew that, in a way of speaking, the monkey was on my back. I had to produce or else. Nevertheless, I felt certain that angels were watching over me.

I was aware immediately that, if my success was to be, it was up to me. I soon learned that my previous year's experience in the fourth grade under Ms. Lockhardt had prepared me well for my initial encounters in Ms. North's fifth grade class at Buchanan School. Although I was only ten, I was caught up in the intense rivalry that is particularly characteristic of those children who have come from homes where education has been stressed as an avenue to success. During my first few days in class, I became aware that there were children there who made very good grades and who were prepared to recite on any subject that had been assigned. My earlier experiences in school, along with my parents' encouragement, had taught me the importance of self-reliance. As an only child, I had no sisters and brothers to turn to for help with my studies. I was forced to rely upon my own resources and to think for myself. It was also important for me to learn the importance of grit and courage. After all, I was the new kid on the block, as it were, and the class and playground bullies lost little time in testing my mettle.

Fortunately, I had parents who had supplied me with a high degree of self-confidence. I had no doubts about my abilities, having survived my second and third grade misfortunes and making a dramatic academic comeback in the fourth grade.

"Frank, do you know your multiplication tables?" Ms. North inquired during my first week in her class. I responded quickly, "Yes, Miss North. I can recite them all, from the one's to the twelve times tables." She nodded gingerly, and urged me, "Go right ahead." By the time I had whizzed through the eight times tables with zest and enthusiasm, I could tell that I had already captured the attention and respect of my new classmates, who were observing the whole scenario in rapt attention and who were echoing such interjections as My! and Wow! When I got to the end of my rapid fire sequence with the final pronouncement of "12 times 12 is 144," the teacher exclaimed, "That was wonderful, Frank!" as she led the class in the kind of generous applause that signaled the fact that I was fast becoming appreciated and respected. This approval encouraged me to take all of my subjects seriously and be prepared each day because I never knew when I would be called upon to demonstrate my knowledge of an assignment.

Within a few weeks, my mother was summoned to the school and was advised that I would not need to continue in 5A, and that I would be skipped to the 5B because I had already mastered the material that was being covered in the first half of the curriculum. That evening my parents expressed their approval of my advancement and expressed their gratitude to God during evening worship which was a part of their daily routine after each dinner meal.

Mom was a disciplinarian who never let up. When I came home from school, I was required to lie down for a half hour's rest, followed by a light snack before undertaking the assignments that had been meted out by the teacher that day. There was a vacant lot next door to our house at 1008 Woodward where the neighborhood boys would play ball each day almost immediately after they came home from school. Mother would say, "First things first. After you finish your assignments and I check them, then you can go out and play ball." Oh, how I hated the fact that I did not enjoy the delicious freedom that my friends had. It was difficult for me to immerse myself in my subjects as I listened to the clamor and excitement of what was taking place outdoors. I felt cramped and discontented. As my friends knocked at my door, wanting me to join them in their frolicking, they were summarily advised, "Frank will join you when he finishes his lessons." As a consequence, I was initially teased and jeered as a *mommy's boy*. Children can be incredibly cruel and unflagging in their ridicule. Fortunately, when I was released from my mother's unwavering commitment to my training, I was able to establish instant credibility with my turn at bat. My eye and hand coordination was such that I could knock the daylights out of any softball that came within the proximity of home plate. I soon learned that, even though my schoolwork was a priority to be accepted among the boys in the neighborhood, we had to demonstrate vigor, strength, and superior athletic skills as well. It was common practice to exaggerate the value and qualities of physical powers above brain fiber and mental acumen. Thank God I had parents who had a sufficient understanding of life to deal with it symmetrically and not from any one-sided all-absorbing perspective.

I was especially blessed to have had a superior crop of teachers at Buchanan School. Vivian Washington, my sixth grade teacher, was a striking and attractive lady with a mine of musical talent that she would unearth at a moment's notice. She had such a passion for music that she could call out the best in her students, especially when we sang the school song, "Shine on Buchanan." As she played the piano with unbridled rhythmic gusto, our singing became infused with the demonstrative fervor of her enthusiasm.

It was my stalwart, towering and gangling seventh grade teacher, Mamie Williams, who was so intimidating because of her imposing stoic manner, her thorough knowledge of her subject matter, her demands for efficiency and exactness, and her instinctive and prompt resistance to any behavior that even slightly departed from her precise expectations. On the other hand, she was quick to acknowledge and reward good work with words of approval and approbation. She kept just enough pressure on us to promote self-reliance, to sense and accept personal responsibility, and to make conditions in the classroom ripe for the kind of classroom competition that kept our minds honed and clear enough to begin recognizing that knowledge is power. Ms. Williams, while covering the basic subjects, was always attuned to the day-to-day affairs of the world. Consequently, she helped us to explore the world of ourselves and the world outside of ourselves. Her class was so well-organized that we elected class officers, dramatized stories and poetry, gave speeches on subjects of our interest, and competed for prizes in English, mathematics, music, social studies, art, and spelling. I was sufficiently stimulated and excited to the point where I won top prizes in English, music, math, and spelling at the All-School Recognition Program at the end of the school year. By the time I left Ms. Williams and passed to the eighth grade where Mr. Morgan Maxwell, the principal, was my teacher, I had already begun to think of myself as a good student, thanks to the skilled and dedicated black teachers under whose tutelage it had been my privilege to sit. In reflection, I feel certain that they had committed themselves to a special measure of allegiance in educating black children, who had little else offered, since the conservative educational system in the community gave no quarter in their behalf. The separate but equal doctrine was just as embedded in Topeka's elementary schools as it was in any deep south community.

I cherish the memory of every one of my teachers at Buchanan School, as well as the two principals, Mr. Morgan Maxwell, who taught me the first half of my eighth grade year, and Mr. J. B. Holland, who taught us the second half of the eighth grade after Mr. Maxwell moved to Arizona. I revere their memory because they were very charming people—encouraging us at every step, perpetually challenging us to have race pride. We were introduced to the achievements of outstanding black heroes and heroines year round, not just during Black History Week. We enjoyed special assemblies where we sang and memorized "The Star Spangled Banner" and all three verses of James Weldon Johnson's Negro National Anthem, "Lift Every Voice and Sing". It pains me today to see that many young African-Americans need to sing this beautiful freedom hymn from printed song sheets. I am convinced that the sweep for integration has, to some extent, divested us of some of our most prized ethnic treasures.

Fortunately, it was not necessary for me to rely solely upon the assistance of my teachers for personal growth and enhancement. My community was well-stocked with caring neighbors. The propensity to look out for other people's children was a way of life on Woodward Street where I lived. There was a kinship of unspeakable unity that existed among families. There were the Browns, the Carpers, the Austins, the Cropps, the Paces, the Sawyers, and many more. Any adult not only had the right, but also had the responsibility, to correct any child in the neighborhood who got out of line. When, as children, we had to be corrected by an adult who was not a member of our immediate family, we made every effort to appease the one whom we had offended. We begged for mercy so that the incident would not be reported to our parents. We were indeed subject to double jeopardy when it had become apparent that we had been misbehaving when our parents weren't around. Corporal punishment was not off limits during those days. Neither did parents question the reproof of their children by those whom they realized had more than a cursory notion of what good citizenship entailed.

On several occasions, Mr. Daniel Sawyer, who lived across the street, would invite some of us as youngsters to join him on his front porch during the summer. He had a great zest for governmental affairs. He discussed in detail with us the Constitution, elections, representation in the House of Representatives and the Senate, and the composition of the Supreme Court. We would all sit around this wonderfully patient man and drink in so much of what he was able to share with us in terminology that we could enjoy and understand. But it was Buchanan School that made such an indelible impression on the lives of so many of us that it was no accident or wonder that in later life we could point to the influence that it had in contributing to the professional successes of the likes of Mahlon Bunch, Howard Morehead, Maxine Turner, Ira Hutchinson, Marian Jane Brown, George Hayden, Leonard Pryor, and scores of others including myself. Knowledge is inseparable from dedication in the classroom, and the quality of education which black children received from their black teachers in Topeka was underscored by the fact that, at two of the four black elementary schools in town, more of the teachers held masters degrees than at any of the eighteen white elementary schools.

It was not until I entered the ninth grade at Curtis Junior High School that the Jim Crow system of education began to penetrate my mental sky with all of the accompanying anguish that bigotry promotes. In fact, Jim Crow pervaded the entire town. I recall with great despair signs in the windows of restaurants reading, "Negroes, Mexicans, and Indians served in sacks only." There was never a question of what the response of the Hale family would be to such an insulting stipulation. Mom and Dad both agreed that they would not dignify such a policy by catering to it. As a consequence, I never ate in an integrated public restaurant until years later while attending college in Nebraska. The movie theaters, the hotels, and the public swimming pools were off limits for blacks in Topeka.

Until I entered Curtis Junior High School, I had not come face to face with the cold harsh bitterness of *racism*. Even though I was a good student, well-behaved and well-dressed, the racial taunts from my white counterparts were my daily humiliation. There were too few blacks in the school to mount an aggressive response to the overwhelming demeaning climate of irreverent racism. On one occasion, I was chased all the way home by three white hoodlum schoolmates who pursued me for no other reason than the color of my skin. I was running so fast that I ran right past my father's second-hand furniture store. By the time I circled the corner and ran through the alley to the back of the store, he was there waiting to hand me a baseball bat. I will never forget his command, "Beat all of the white hate out of them." As they came charging down the alley, I was ready. But like a dog encountering an angry cat, they quickly put on brakes and began a swift retreat as I chased them out of the alley. They never bothered me after that. I learned an important lesson from that experience. Sometimes, one must confront racism head-on in order to keep it from devouring you. It was my initial episode in moving a menacing mountain with angels watching over me.

Chapter 3

Exploring Adolescence

The power structure in Topeka during my adolescent days was essentially an exclusive club of conservatives. While the city did not harbor many undesirable characters from a criminal point of view, its populace, not surprisingly, was made up of people who, for the most part, were anchored by tradition and a closely knit community life. There was a kind of fundamentalist fanaticism there that gave in grudgingly to any new ideas. There were approximately 60,000 residents within its compact limits, and fewer than 3,000 of them were African-Americans. Topeka, like most of Kansas, was a land of contrasts and extremes. The summers were often uncomfortably hot (I recall that temperatures often reached 100° Fahrenheit and above and remained at that level for sometimes as long as a week or ten days), and the winters were cruelly cold.

By midwestern standards, Topeka was a well-heeled community with its assortment of businesses, hospitals, banks, insurance companies, warehousing facilities, railroad offices, grain mills, and meat packing plants. Its reputation and stable economy were boosted by the State Historical Society Museum, Forbes Air Force Base, its Goodyear plant, the main office of the Atchison, Topeka and Santa Fe Railroad, the internationally famous Menninger Foundation, and the CGF grain elevator, the second largest in the world when it was built.

Unappreciated and unwelcomed by most of the white power brokers, blacks generally were assigned to the back-bending toil of menial jobs. Life for black folks was sure enough *serious business* in the hell-fire existence of everyday life. Only a scattering of black professionals, such as preachers, physicians, lawyers, and a lone mortician, were semi-independent. Local restraints limited black entrepreneurship to a few beauty and barber shops, an occasional bar, one struggling hotel, and another despicable piece of real estate that was palmed off on the black community as a movie house.

The tense and repressive atmosphere of Topeka did not offer many positive outlets for black people. It was no accident that my father, possessing a spirit of personal responsibility and adventure, sought to improve his lot. He had taken part-time jobs as a waiter at the Jayhawk Hotel and at the Topeka Country Club. He had closely observed the sophisticated and resourceful clientele from the local community that frequented these establishments, and he was eager to establish some kind of business that would engage their cultural interests. It was this spirit of ingenious exploration on his part that was consummated in the establishment of Hale's Bookstore that was discussed in an earlier chapter. It was there, under the happy auspices of my father's and mother's influence, that I gained an unusually rich exposure to an atmosphere that would afford me a huge head start in academic and scholarly pursuits. Bacon was right, "Reading maketh a full man." I never fully appreciated the advantages that my parents' bookstore gave me until I was able to contend with the best minds from some of the most influential homes in my day-to-day classroom encounters at Topeka High School. Academic competition flourished at this magnificent center of learning. Although the institution, known for its exquisite Gothic architectural beauty, was by no means a divine center of educational opportunity and democracy, it afforded us the advantage of being exposed to stellar teachers like Dr. Carmie Wolfe, Mr. Lloyd Kistler, Miss Bernice Fuller, Miss Olive Collins, Mr. Don Gleckler, and Miss Ruth Phillips.

While there always was more than a considerable degree of ongoing friction between black and white students at the school, there is some measure of credit that is due certain teachers who went out of their way to be civil and accommodating. Don Gleckler recruited me to sing in the Senior Glee Club, an advanced group where singers were selected on ability rather than class in school. It was a rare opportunity for a sophomore to be selected for this exclusive group. I was honored and excited to be chosen and to participate in the harmonious operetta, Gilbert and Sullivan's *Pirates of Penzance*. There were two other blacks, James Cathey and Fred Holmes, both seniors, among the thirty-five vocalists. We were especially proud to have the opportunity to make appearances in assemblies and at banquets and civic meetings.

I never forgot the very fine commendation which I received from Miss Bernice Fuller, one of my English teachers. She inscribed my yearbook, *The Sunflower*, with these encouraging words: "To a fine boy. Keep your head and you'll go far. You have been very outstanding." Mr. Kistler, my history teacher, always applauded my classroom contributions as well as my written compositions. I always received one of three or four A's, in a class of thirty to thirty-five students, that he handed out at grade card time. Though I was often distressed by the tensions that kept black and white students separate and hostile, I took refuge in waging a relentless effort to demonstrate that blacks had *smarts* that extended beyond athletic powers. I shall never forget the all-school assembly where I was honored as a recipient of the coveted *Honor T* for academic and leadership accomplishments. Nothing could have made my parents more proud.

The curse of racism was as apparent at Topeka High School as anywhere else in the community. The fact of so-called integration was blurred by the fact that there were separate basketball, swimming, wrestling, golf, and tennis teams. The only teams that included a rare black or two were the football and baseball teams. It was no wonder then that, when opposing teams with a substantial number of black players came to play Topeka High, black students from Topeka High cheered for them lustily. This was especially true when we played Wichita East that had a star black quarterback by the name of Linwood Sexton. Nearly half of Wichita's roster was composed of black players. I recall how agitated the white students were in such situations, but the black students, who had little to aspire to at the school and who were relegated to second-class status as a part of institutional policy, could not be blamed, having been isolated, alienated, and excluded from major activities and functions at the school.

Nevertheless, in order to buoy one another, we staked out our territory, which we designated as *Little Harlem*, the center of the main corridor on the second floor. We were a solid wall of blackness—conversing, socializing, signifying, devising, and eyeballing every pretty girl and handsome guy within vision's pathway. Even student government activities were segregated. It was during my junior year that black students of Topeka High had a part in the school's self-government. A Negro Advisory Council was established and a general election was held among the nearly three hundred black students in attendance, and I was elected to serve as a Junior representative. In their first bi-monthly meeting, council members elected me vice-chairman. I was also voted to serve as the council's representative on the larger school-wide Student Council. I, along with other aggressive black students—particularly William Gaines, Aileen Moffett, Virlene Hurst, Dorothy Crawford and George Hayden—were largely responsible for challenging the school's segregated stance, and pressed the issue to the point where, under an amendment to the High School Charter voted by the entire school, a representative was elected by black students to serve as their representative on

Student Council with full voting privileges. I was indeed fortunate to have been selected as the council representative during my junior year, even though there were a number of black seniors who were quite capable of assuming that role. Encouraged by these recent victories on behalf of black students, the stage seemed set for me to use my endowed gifts to clear the paths for further conquests. I was determined, with God's help, to catch a new vision of my ultimate destiny—that was to become a courageous pioneer in helping to move mountains for my oppressed people. I had no doubt that angels were watching over me.

It was also during my junior year in high school that I, as a healthy fifteen year old, had the opportunity to take advantage of a summer job at the Army Supply Depot in Topeka. I worked on the assembly line helping to package airplane parts for the military. A near tragic accident offered me the opportunity very early in life to learn how foolish it is to raise barriers against people merely on the basis of color. As I was performing my task at the assembly line, a man nearby was driving a lift and was carrying crates of airplane superchargers from one part of the warehouse to another section for storage. In the process of lifting one crate carrying a 280-pound supercharger, he miscalculated the positioning of the crate on the two arms of the tongs that were designed to hold the crate in place until it could be transferred to its place of storage. No sooner had the arms of the machine lift brought the carton onto its two arms then the crate slid off the lift and began falling from a height of about twenty-five feet toward where I was standing. My attention was focused on what I was doing, and I was not aware of my imminent peril. As I heard screams around me, a young white boy snatched me off the assembly line in a split second, just as the massive carton of destruction came crashing to the very spot where I had been standing.

As it was, the corner of the crate scraped my back within an inch of my spinal cord. Except for a three-inch superficial scar, I bore no ill effects of that terrifying experience until seven years later when I began to experience back spasms and occasional bouts with sciatica. I am only here today because that young, white, eighteen year old boy placed his own life in jeopardy in order to save mine. The story of how Bill Sapp saved my life ever reminds me that it would be terrible to assume that people are either good or bad, intelligent or unintelligent, or kind or mean based on their racial identity. When all is said and done, one's humaneness lies in the values or moral ideas which he or she holds most precious. My acceptance of this principle foreshadows how I deal with people generally, regardless of race. A new sense of universality was born in me as a result of Bill Sapp's unselfish act of putting his own life at risk while, at the same time, transcending racial considerations. I knew then as I do now that angels were continuing to watch over me.

Even with the social inequalities that loomed large at Topeka High School, there was a creative fanaticism that burned within me. It was an obsession to demonstrate that whites had no monopoly on excellence. There were four of us, the Cathey brothers—James and Eulis—Fred Holmes and myself who formed a quartet, *The Harmony Four*. We rehearsed at my house under the watchful and approving eyes of my mom and dad. James, the baritone, was an excellent singer and arranger, and his brother, Eulis, had a smooth second tenor that could rival Nat King Cole. Holmes was a bottomless base, and I was assigned first tenor. We established a substantial repertoire of spirituals, a few American folk songs like "I've Been Working on the Railroad" and "Down by the Old Mill Stream," and a few moderns (for that day) such as "I'm Going to Buy a Paper Doll That I Can Call My Own," "Moonlight Becomes You," and "Pennies from Heaven." In a few weeks, we had taken the school assemblies by storm. We had gained such a powerful grip on the student body that we were called upon to sing for nearly every special occasion. Soon our singing almost became an all-absorbing preoccupation as demands were made for our services before local civic organizations, churches, banquets, parties and other festive occasions. Once we sang for soldiers at a special USO confab, and we were extended an offer to sing at USO sponsored functions around the country. The offer was a hefty $500 per month, $125 each. That figure represented much more than most black adults were making those days. It was an offer that wide-eyed teenagers were not prepared to refuse. We would begin singing for servicemen year round, just as soon as we completed our school year. While proud of our reputation and accomplishments, our parents had other plans, namely college. They hammered home the importance of a higher education. We, of course, made grudging concessions to our parents' wishes for one simple reason: by and large, children obeyed their parents in those days. Nevertheless, our voices were heard by many hundreds of enthralled listeners as countless opportunities mounted before our high school graduation.

With all of the hoopla and recognition that came from quartet singing, there was one tragic classroom episode that occurred less than six weeks before I was scheduled to graduate. I was literally hanging on by my fingernails after my encounter with Robert Schlicter. Unhappily, the incident occurred in the Senior Glee class during the time when the regular instructor was absent and a substitute teacher, Mr. Rue, was in charge— at least he was supposed to be. During warm-ups for a particular song, someone in the tenor section was off key, and Mr. Rue inquired as to who was the guilty party. Schlicter pointed in my direction, where upon I retorted that it was not me. Regrettably, after the group sang another score, Mr. Rue stopped the glee club and inquired again as to who was off key. Schlicter pointed in my direction once more. I again retorted vehemently. At this point, class members began to razz and ridicule Schlicter with such railing and unbalanced remarks as, "Are you going to let Hale get away with calling you a liar?" In the meanwhile, Mr. Rue made no effort to stop the badgering, either of me by Schlicter or of Schlicter by those taunting him. Not to be outdone, Schlicter turned and shoved me in the stomach and then upbraided me in despicable terms that I will never forget: "Come on Hale, you're a good nigger. Admit you did it."

At that point, the lights went out in my head. All I can remember is that school officials and the nurse were carrying him out on a stretcher, and I was summarily dismissed from school by Mr. W. N. Van Slyck, the principal. I was afraid to tell my parents what had happened, and I attempted to get solace by visiting and conversing with my girlfriend, Evelyn Jackson, at her home that evening. But that momentary inspiration was broken when I received a call from home and was summoned immediately to tell my side of the story. The parents of Schlicter had called my parents, threatening lawsuits and damages because their son was missing several teeth and would probably lose others that appeared too loose to save. I shamelessly recounted what had happened, placing substantial blame on the substitute teacher who had let things get out of hand. Such a situation would have never taken place had Mr. Gleckler been there. Though not a rigid man, he maintained an atmosphere of discipline where foolishness and horsing around were unacceptable. After listening to my story, my parents said that they were convinced that I had been dismissed from school illegitimately and without due process and that they would stand by me. The next morning my father accompanied me to Mr. Van Slyck's office and assured him that he would retain Elisha Scott, a local black attorney who had proven skills in court and who was both respected and feared in many quarters. I was reinstated on the spot, and the episode was never discussed with me or my family after that, either by school officials or by members of Schlicter's family. Once again, it was the interplay of these circumstances involving race, so common in Topeka, that helped me to hone my thinking in terms of addressing the issue of racial inequities for years to come.

There is a value in adolescence that contributes both to growth and happiness. However, young people are often caught between the expectations of their parents on one hand and the pressure of their peers on the other. My parents were Seventh-day Adventist Christians, and as a result, religion held powerful sway in the activities of our lives. As strict fundamentalists, the use of tobacco and alcohol was taboo. Dancing and movie attendance were prohibited. The Sabbath—from sunset Friday to sunset Saturday—was observed with rigidity, and church attendance was mandatory. The Bible was universally read and accepted as the infallible word, supplemented by the writings of Ellen G. White, the denomination's imperious prophetess. The church struggled hard to prepare its youth for what one might call a resistance movement to the social patterns which were common in contemporary American culture.

Our little church on College Avenue was often a beehive of well-organized activities that involved the youth in Bible games that developed a memory for Bible verses, a facility for finding Bible texts with rapidity, for gaining a thorough knowledge of major Bible characters, and for becoming painstakingly familiar with church doctrines.

The rewards of social interaction and acceptance were in constant display at Topeka High School. The after-school dances and the Friday night and Saturday activities were in abundance. The pressures of socialization offered a range of choices that, for the most part, isolated Adventist youth. It was difficult *to be somebody* in one's own right when one chose to exclude oneself from participating in those social situations that contributed to peer support. After all, the criterion for success to most adolescents is acceptance by their peers.

Fortunately, our church was composed of a wise set of parents who helped establish ongoing activities—Saturday evening house parties, picnic outings, church socials, and attendance at recreational and cultural events—for the youth of the church. There were some very promising young people who held membership in the lone Adventist Church: William, Anna and Milton Woodson; Evelyn, Winnie and Wilma Jackson, Marcella Oliver, Marcus Woods, Raphael Smith, Wanda and Laura Jane Foster, William Sidney Crutcher, and myself. As a group, we became crystallized into a self-perpetuating fellowship. We did everything we could to affirm each other, even as our parents made every effort to keep our maturation process from being sidetracked and our personalities from being undermined. Harvey Perry, one of our Sabbath school teachers, was a master amateur historian, who kept us wild-eyed with his detailed rehearsal of the achievements of great African men and women. His wife, Odell Perry, brought out the best of our musical potential, as she gave piano lessons to most of us. It was our church family that helped to forestall many anxieties that we might have had were it not for their efforts in building on our interests as well as our native potential. It was this stalwart underpinning that furnished us with the tools that we needed in order to cope at school, in the community, and in later life.

Chapter 4

A Student at Oakwood College

During my senior year at Topeka High School, I had been awarded a four year academic scholarship to attend Howard University. Howard was considered by many to be the Harvard of black higher education. This recognition came to me at the honors convocation assembly during the spring of my senior year. While I was certainly grateful for having been accorded this honor, I was very much aware that the recognition and the scholarships that were awarded that day were clearly defined by race. I maintained a strong academic and leadership record at Topeka High, placing me in the top ten percent of the eight hundred graduating seniors. It was an experience of disenchantment and disillusionment as I observed several of my classmates, whose academic records were not on par with mine, being offered multiple scholarships (some as many as four or five) to the most prestigious institutions in the country. My academic record, while very strong, was only good enough for school officials to recommend me to a historically black university. Once again the disease of racism had imposed the germ of its influence in my pathway. But that fact alone was more than sufficient to keep me striving.

In the meanwhile, plans were being made for me to attend Howard University. My trunk had been carefully packed and labeled. Elder Calvin E. Mosley, Jr., the young pastor who had earlier baptized my parents into the Seventh-day Adventist Church, heard of my decision to attend Howard University and took upon himself the initiative to visit my parents in an effort to influence them to send me to Oakwood College in Huntsville, Alabama. Because of their deep respect for him, they agreed to send me to Oakwood. Founded in 1896 as the Oakwood Industrial School by the General Conference of Seventh-day Adventists, it developed in successive stages to Oakwood Manual Training School, Oakwood Junior College, and finally was reborn as a senior liberal arts college in 1943. Today it stands as a historically black co-educational institution accredited by the Southern Association of Colleges and Schools and approved by the Seventh-day Adventists Board of Regents. It is also a member of the United Negro College Fund.

But before I launch too quickly into my experiences of being a student at Oakwood College, I must share with you that long and painful pause that I endured in my train ride between Topeka, Kansas, and Huntsville, Alabama. Somewhere in that dark age of segregation, as separate as black and white was in Topeka, it was only a pinprick to the dark wilderness of segregation that I would experience upon entering the deep South. The doubts that assailed my vivid imagination about the horrors of southern life, having been exposed already to the hypnotic headlines of black newspapers like *The Kansas City Call* and *The Pittsburgh Courier*, were not entirely groundless. Even as I sat on the train and looked out the window, as we passed through rural areas of southern Missouri, Arkansas and the lower Ozarks, the obvious distinctions between the two societies—black and white—were depressing. Even white poverty paled by contrast to the unconscionable slums that punctuated the obscenities of black subsistence. The images of despicable looking outhouses, littered front and back yards, half-fed cats and dogs, rickety hats, snotty-nosed children with matted hair, and the haggard faces of forlorn adults were a shocking unveiling of reality for which all of my reading had not prepared me. The Jim Crow coach (for "Blacks only") in which I was traveling was both an obvious symptom and reality of the legal and customary patterns of rigid segregation to which I would be continuously exposed. I found myself shaking my head in dismay when I had to change trains in Memphis—from the Missouri Pacific to the Southern. The foreboding signs that separated blacks and whites in waiting rooms, and at water fountains, hovered like threatening death in the wonderment of my young and impressionable mind. I drew myself almost into a knot as I planted myself into a rear seat for the final leg of the journey in the land of vengeance and unprecedented violence toward black people. I learned early that there was a pervasive and systematic legal and psychological imprisonment that threatened to destroy black people through the dark ways of its own unchristian practices.

As the train came to my final stop in Huntsville, I felt a magic of momentary relief that the long journey had come to an end. Yet, a sense of strange uncertainty engulfed my psyche, not knowing what intangible net of unfamiliar circumstances might eventually encompass me. The train station seemed almost surrounded with an assortment of tobacco-chewing rednecks, hillbillies, poor whites, and a handful of distraught-looking blacks leaning against the far end of the station. A black taxicab driver approached me, "Carry you somewhere?" In response, I gave up my bags and assisted him in putting my footlocker in the trunk of his car.

In short, I was to be introduced to my first view of Alabama's landscape, red with the dust of barren terrain, towering pines, countless fields of cotton, and motionless swamps. We proceeded in a rambling and serpentine way along one dirt country road after another. I learned soon enough of the irrationalities of rural southern life. We traveled along roads that were floundering with the overrepresentation of unpretentious cottages, unpainted stores, and unimaginable poverty. We swung around a creaking wagon bearing bales of cotton and one old black man who swatted his reins over a slow, temperamental mule. The total scene was an ugly promise of the future.

At first bewildered by the contrast between Topeka—a small, clean, relatively picturesque community—and the unexpected gloom through which we had just witnessed on our curious journey to the Oakwood campus—I was wonderfully pleased as the tiny taxi coughed its way through the entrance into Oakwood's campus. My tired eyes were refreshed with the obliging grandeur of those tall and magnificent oaks that dominated the campus. Then there was a mixture of pine, cedar, and magnolia that held me momentarily spellbound. "Well, here's your school," the driver pointed out.

I could see students crisscrossing the campus as I gathered my effects to push toward the weathered buildings in the foreground. "Reckon you could use a little help" was my warm and congenial introduction to the college from Harold Wright of Germantown, Ohio, as he grabbed one of my bags and proceeded to escort me to Henderson City, an off-white wooden building, the edges of which, seared by the years, had mellowed into soft deep browns and tinted to etchings of green moss. As we strolled along and struggled with my world's accumulated gear, I observed the stateliness of the central campus as there was a circular track that wound itself among the trees as the sunlit sky silhouetted the outline of each building that encompassed the ring of natural beauty that hung like a jeweled bracelet around the wonderment of God's natural beauty.

It was high noon, and I had arrived just in time to see and hear Phrozine Anderson ring the old college bell, long rope and all, as a signal for lunchtime.

In January of 1944, I was a sixteen year old freshman when I walked through the Oakwood College gateway to be included among nearly three hundred young women and men who had come to Oakwood. It was *the* place to keep us shielded from the world as young black Seventh-day Adventist collegiums in those days. Oakwood College had been established as a Christian school to prepare black Adventists to live a Christian life in the midst of a world that was generally opposed, in a meaningful way, to orthodox Christian standards. In a way, we were both isolated and insulated from the world. After all, students who were admitted had to make a covenant to abstain from the use of tobacco, alcoholic beverages, and coffee, to refrain from attending movie theaters and dances, and to agree to attend Sabbath and morning and evening worship services on a regular basis. It was this vital and vigorous interdependence in the essence of Christian education that was attractive to parents who wished to have their children sheltered from the vagaries and vices of the world and that prompted parents to send their sons and daughters to Oakwood. And most of us who attended made the best of it because we loved the Lord, we loved our parents, we loved each other, and we had learned to do what we were told. And so we came to Oakwood—"the place where loveliness keeps house," they said. Thank God for all of the natural beauty—the gigantic oaks, the undulating meadows, the winsome woods, the magnificent magnolia trees, and the frolicsome creatures of earth and sky. It was a resplendent wonderland of God's handiwork.

But it also had a rich, rich history. From the time Oakwood first opened its doors to sixteen students on November 16, 1896, it has made remarkable and spectacular success, even while experiencing a variety of setbacks that would have stifled or closed institutions of lesser will and vitality. Then there have always been the giants among the teachers and staff who stood in the trenches and who, for the most part, guided and taught us well, given their limited resources. How could I ever forget the dedicated dynamism of teachers like Mrs. Inez Booth, Professor O.B. Edwards, Elder C.E. Moseley, Jr., Dr. Eva B. Dykes, Mr. Samuel Darby, Mr. H. T. Curtis, Mr. Charles Galley, Mr. R. L. Reynolds, Elder E. E. Rogers and Dr. Natelka Burrell. Then there were the dedicated staff persons: Mrs. Eugenia Cunningham, Dean Charles Gray, Dean Marian Gresham, Mr. N. E. Ashby, Mr. Lewis E. Ford, Dr. S. O. Cherry, Mr. Dennis Crosby, and Mr. Sowells.

But beyond the natural grandeur of outdoor surroundings and the bank of dedicated teachers, there was a mythological legacy of making a fetish out of primitive and ungarnished circumstances and ascribing *loveliness*

36

to it. We slept barracks-style in cold dormitories that were worn with years—that reeked of poor plumbing, even on those rare occasions when lavatories and showers were in synchronized working order. Henderson Hall, the weather beaten, whitewashed men's dormitory where I stayed, seemed to sag and squeak with the faintest of west winds. Because of the school's limited resources, no apologies were really plausible to the disturbing inquiries of students in the cafeteria line when the food ran out day in and day out. It was those days that we call *the good old days*—rationalizing the bewilderment of what was our predicament, like we often do when we attempt to protect our sanity by giving ego-saving designations to negative situations. It was in those early days as a student that I began to pinpoint some disturbing dichotomies and inequities between what was available at Oakwood College in comparison to the conveniences and resources at white Seventh-day Adventist institutions of higher education.

I knew then, if ever given an opportunity, I would join hands with others to help make Oakwood the productive and competitive institution it ought to be within the sisterhood of Seventh-day Adventist institutions.

Dr. Eva B. Dykes, my English teacher, had a *giant* of a reputation, having been one of the three first black women in America to have been awarded the Ph.D. degree, which she earned in 1921 at Radcliffe College, the women's division of Harvard University. Then, too, she had recently resigned from her position as associated professor of English at Howard University, where she had served for many years and had been in the company of such distinguished colleagues as Dr. Ernest E. Just, one of America's most eminent biologists, who was professor of physiology in Howard's medical school; Dr. Ralph Bunche, diplomat, U.N. mediator, and Nobel Peace Prize recipient; Alan Leroy Locke, the first African-American to be a Rhodes scholar; Dr. Charles Harris Wesley, former president of Wilberforce University and later Central State University; and Dr. Mordecai Wyatt Johnson, Howard's internationally renowned president.

These associations of hers were not lost on any of us as we sat and listened raptly to her every word and suggestion. There was no way that we could minimize her right to engage and immerse us in the minimum essentials that she demanded of us as a means of gaining proficiency in the English language. Her homework assignments were so voluminous that on one occasion we conspired to demonstrate our displeasure by marching to class single file across the campus, each one of us carrying our *overtaxed* suitcases with the requirements for her class. Dr. Dykes had such a glowing personality and remarkable sense of humor that, when she spotted our mischief, she joined us in hilarious laughter at the absurdity of our demonstration and proceeded to teach the class and underscore her main points without missing a beat. She knew, like William Arrowsmith, that "the teacher, like the text, is... the mediator between past and present, present and future..., and that the teacher is the student's only evidence outside the text that a great humanity exists." No one could accuse Dr. Dykes of being indifferent to her profession or for lacking concern for her students. It was she who served to galvanize my initial interest of how powerful a tool that teaching could be in the advancement of learning. She was a model of committed integrity who had laid aside the honorifia of her vast repertory of credentials in order to galvanize us into being the best that we could be. She was thorough and unrelenting in the process, and those of us who took her seriously, and who understood greatness as we witnessed it before our very eyes, were not only able to cope in that setting, but also profited in the long run.

But there were also other college experiences that pointedly prepared us for later life. The religious and spiritual life at Oakwood proffered its own singular and unique quintessence. Out religious worship was punctuated with music only as it is experienced in the black church, an experience which Dr. Wyatt T. Talker declares "was born and developed and shaped in a specific social context of suffering and oppression." Oakwood College, as an institution, is unrivaled as the center of African-American socialization in the Seventh-day Adventist Church. The impact of its culture, religiously and musically, surfaces in the church life of black Seventh-day Adventist churches throughout America. The sheer musical force of Friday evening vesper services at the College transformed the mundane activities of the week into the context of a serene musical symphony of spirituals and gospel songs that were charged with messages of inexhaustible faith and hope. It is no secret that the power and impact of the preacher is only as effective as is the musical expression that accompanies his/her preaching. And so it was at Oakwood that the importance and dominance of music was a tradition that was a companion of good preaching, and together they reflected a cohesive and integrative spiritual influence.

In those days, it was also said that any four young men could comprise a quartet. It was not at all uncommon to hear numerous quartets serenading late in the evenings, and particularly during hours after vesper in the dormitory. Among the more visible quartets was one composed of Lee Paschel, Charles Dudley, Lucius Daniels, and Charles Graham. Hardly anyone who attended Oakwood during those days remained untouched by the genius of Dr. Eva B. Dykes who directed choirs from time to time and who, even on occasions, served as piano accompanist for visiting concert artists. The names of Ann Galley and Inez Booth as faculty are legendary musicians, as are numerous students of that era: Howard Hodge and Velma Beaman as pianists, and James Calloway, Arthur Hobby, Horace Jones, as soloists. And, of course, Joseph Powell could sing the bass notes right off the piano.

Confined as it was, it was the social life at Oakwood that challenged us to be creative. The tradition of campus families on campus provided students with an interlocking network of support. The fellows who were roommates on campus always called each other *old lady*. My roommates were Vertis Barnes and Richard Brown, and all three of us were natives of Kansas City, Missouri. It took us a while to get accustomed to the words *old lady*. But, after all, such terminology was a part of the campus culture. Vertis and I were leaning on the windowsill in our room and surveying the campus and the campus coeds as they strolled by. "Old ladies," Richard, pounding his right fist into his left hand, shouted, "we'd better get out of here and begin us a campus family before we find ourselves in the position of having no takers." It did not take us long, while peering through the window, to discover that Oakwood was alive with a bevy of attractive young Christian women, and it took very little coaxing for us to seize the opportunity to meet as many of them as possible before the pickings got slim. Now, to establish a family required some degree of assertiveness. One who was not a ministerial student was somewhat at a disadvantage because Oakwood had a reputation for turning out young preachers who had gained a considerable reputation nationwide as heralds of gospel.

Some parents had sent their daughters to Oakwood with the specific purpose of capturing a young preacher. So ministerial students were in demand. Some of the more visible ministerial prospects were Lee Paschal, Charles Bradford, Joseph Powell, Eugene Carter, Charles Graham, Lucius Daniels, Franklin Hill, and James Dykes. So the competition was keen! We felt quite fortunate to be on campus with such an assortment of bright young ladies among this body of Christian youth. But in those days the regulations were very severe in terms of boy-girl relations: no holding of hands, no crossing of boundary lines that separated the young men from the young women, and only rare parlor visitations in the women's dormitory. Such visits were generally reserved for upper-division students under the scrutinizing eyes of Dean Marian Gresham. In fact, if a couple paused on campus and engaged in conversation that was considered a bit too long, they were subject to the threatening leer of Mother Cunningham or the menacing and demonstrative exclamations of "Move on!" from Nathaniel Ashby or Dean Charles Gray.

Nevertheless, these momentary encounters, disconcerting though they might have been, never daunted our efforts to gain the attention of the young ladies' eyes in the midst of a complicated labyrinth of strictly imposed *thou shall not's*. Soon my campus family was in place—such arrangements were usually discussed and determined in the dining room at mealtime. Then there were the arbiters—friends who would speak a word in your behalf if circumstances made it difficult for you to make your own contacts. However, the peaceful genesis and flow of my campus family was determined by a single incident. One day while walking on campus, a tall and attractive young woman of regal bearing was coming down the walk from the opposite direction. We immediately exchanged smiles, and I introduced myself. "My name is Frank Hale. What is yours?"

"I'm Geraldine Graves," she responded. "I've heard of you. Oh yes, we've anticipated your coming. I am a secretary in President Moran's office, and, of course, we were aware of your joining us this semester. I hope you enjoy it here," she continued.

I was almost immediately mesmerized by her affability, her tone of voice, her deftness in that initial encounter, as well as her well-favored good looks. She was easy on the eyes. It wasn't too long before my campus family was in place. Geraldine and I were the parents; Rita Anderson was our campus mother; our campus sisters were Aileen Spencer, Henrietta Knight, Elizabeth Jones, Helen Beckett, Phyllis Mitchell, and Virginia McClure. Our brothers were Vertis Barnes, Richard Brown, Louis Hackney, and Hollis Knight. Campus families did not exist in a void; as relationships changed, they changed. So, from one year to the next, families expanded, dwindled or were modified to one degree or another. These families provided a happy circle of ever-expanding Christian social contacts that gave meaning to our yearnings for maturity in socially acceptable ways and provided the bedrock of experiences that would eventually enable us to form lasting relationships.

Life in Henderson City was a study in raised and lowered expectations. I was no longer in an exclusive setting where my father and mother could defer to my personal wishes. The fact is, because I am an only child, they made every effort to prepare me for life in such a way that I should not expect or want the be-all and end-all of life to revolve around my desires. They prepared me for the pitfalls of monopolistic self-centeredness. My parents' lifestyles were ones of outreach, sacrificing their own best interests in favor of other people's needs. Their way of life was not lost on me. The dormitory was a community of fellows who shared their wares—toothpaste, soap, food purchased from the campus store, and goodies that came well-packaged from home. And there were times when an article of clothing was borrowed when a fellow's wardrobe got low. My generosity usually faltered when someone wanted to borrow my clothes. Because we all have different standards of hygiene, I found it difficult to engage at that level of interpersonal participation. In fact, I had a serious *shaking* encounter with one young man who unceremoniously borrowed my jacket without my approval. One who has never been to Oakwood might not be aware that the term *shake* or *shaking* refers to wrestling. It was a tradition in long standing when I arrived. It was one of the initial tests applied to newcomers among the males in order to assess their strength, agility, and general athletic prowess. Riley Brown, Louis Hackney and Charles Montgomery had earned reputations as premier shakers on campus. Most of the guys at one time or another participated in such an exercise, usually to cheering and the enthusiastic egging on and urging of a crowd of instigators. It was all in fun when these athletic skirmishes occurred. However, there were times when serious combat was initiated to settle unhappy differences of opinion that had not been mediated through reasoned discourse or prayer.

A. Wellington Clark, Jr., better known as *Wimpy* in the dormitory, served as Dean Gray's proctor. He sometimes earned the ire of the fellows because of his efforts to keep the halls quiet during study period or because of his specific admonition if any one of us got out of line. It is sometimes difficult for students to yield to their peers, no matter how right or correct they might be in their counsel. And Wimpy had plenty to counsel us about: running up and down the halls, engaging in water fights, visiting other rooms after curfew, and throwing the galvanized garbage can down the stairs after the lights went out, to mention a few. Dean Gray was a kind, slow-speaking and slow-moving person who surfaced only in the worst of situations. He could utter the word *boy* with such disdain that you never wanted to do what you had done again to earn his disfavor. I, nevertheless, found him to be a caring and compassionate person once I got to know him.

There are certain personalities whose images stand out in my mind today as clearly as they did when I was on campus. I can see Purnell Lewis (*Mule*, we called him), knocking on our dormitory doors after vesper and standing there holding two unvarnished slices of bread in his hand, with the hungry appeal, "I've got the bread. You got the spread?" He gave more than a blundering hint for some peanut butter, or jelly, or cheese— or whatever we had to place between those empty slices of wishful and hopeful thinking. By the time Purnell had made his rounds, he had built his sandwich into such a healthy bank of commodities that it would have taken a gargantuan appetite to consume it all. Yet Purnell always seemed to have more than a sufficient appetite or craving to demolish the ponderous pile of delectables that were in his grasp.

Another significant episode of dormitory life was when Vertis, Richard, and I decided to display our entrepreneurial skills by opening a store in our dormitory room. The college store, managed by Mother Cunningham, was characterized by its empty shelves and general lack of variety as far as foodstuffs that were appealing to young people. With the possible exception of peanut butter, jelly, bread, and a few canned juices, there was little that could appeal to our varied tastes. One day on my own, I went to downtown Huntsville and canvassed some of the wholesale grocery outlets to see what might be available as products for our new venture. The shelves of the wholesale warehouses were teeming with new discoveries that made my mouth water. The next day Vertis and Richard accompanied me to Halsey's Wholesale, and in short order we purchased a case of Van Camp's vegetarian beans, a case of green peas, jars of peanut butter, salad dressing, paper plates, cups and napkins, punch concentrate, and plastic knives, forks, and spoons. We stopped by a bakery and purchased large loaves of sandwich bread. That evening we opened our store, selling dinner plates with beans, peas, a sandwich, and punch for twenty-five cents. Business was so swift that we made $72 for the first week, but what had begun with flow and without upheaval and perturbation came to a sudden halt. President Moran summoned me to his office on Sunday with this opening inquiry: "What's this I hear you are doing in the dormitory?"

Sensing what he had in mind, but not letting on, I responded, "What do you mean, sir?"

He stood behind his desk and pointed his finger at me before declaring, "You don't have a license to sell food on this campus, and you must close your business immediately!"

What he did not know was that we were a step ahead on that point because we had gone to the appropriate city office and had purchased a certificate of approval before returning to the campus. I reached in my coat pocket and handed it to him. It was obvious that what he had perceived as insolence offended him. Then he thundered, "I'm not going to let you compete with the college store. You're out of business as of now! Do you understand?"

"Yes sir," I answered courteously, sensing that the future has even far greater disappointments for those who try to buck the status quo.

I deeply revere the memory of my introduction to an extended period of manual labor. Since Christian education at Oakwood focused on the student's need for physical, mental, and spiritual development, all students were encouraged to engage in some form of physical or vocational labor. Early on, I was recruited, along with numerous other male students, to assist in the eastward expansion of the administration building (later designated as Moran Hall). A part of our work involved carrying large stones from the Oakwood mountains up high ladders for the masons who would fit them into their appropriate places. *King* (President Moran), as we affectionately called him, led the way up the high ladder time and time again, carrying huge-size stones. His example gave a reality and a vigor to the work of those of us who observed him and, as a consequence, learned a great deal about the dignity and efficacy of hard labor in order to accomplish one's goals. He demonstrated that even as president there was no honest work, within the limits of his time and ability, that he would not undertake. While it was difficult to earn all of one's way during a college year, we had the opportunity to reduce our expenses substantially by working on the farm, by landscaping the campus, by cleaning campus buildings, by gardening, by performing kitchen and dining room duties, by cutting timber in the mountains, by driving the school truck, or by assisting in an assortment of other chores that required daily attention. There were other opportunities for the young women that included typewriting or stenography, flower bedding, sewing, table waiting, dormitory room cleaning, dairy work, lawn care, and kitchen and dining room assignments.

As a freshman, I worked hard for the twelve cents per hour that I earned. I was pleased to assist my parents in covering the costs of my room, board and tuition which amounted to about $500 per academic year. I never questioned whether or not they could afford to give me a college education. Although I was not able to take advantage of the scholarship which was offered me to attend Howard University, I did not lose any sleep over having to work part of my way at *The Oaks*. Even though I am the grandson of a Virginia farmer, I had never in any way experienced farm life before attending Oakwood. During the second semester of my freshman year, I was given a farm assignment working for Mr. Dennis Crosby. One of my duties was to milk four or five cows twice a day—at four o'clock in the morning and at four in the afternoon. I was kicked more than once before I learned the art of milking, and I lost more than one bucket of milk that had been kicked over by a discontented heifer. Those who held dairy jobs were viewed as having favored status in the hierarchy of labor classifications on campus. Those of us who worked in the dairy often were given a quart of milk to carry back to our rooms as a reward for our labors. Given the short supply of food in cafeteria, especially by the time the farm workers were able to get to the dining room, such a bonus of appreciation was a boon to our self-esteem and an obliging accommodation to our appetite.

Mr. Crosby was a patient and wonderful supervisor. He objectively pointed out a student's shortcomings and made positive suggestions for improving them. While I never observed Mr. Crosby in any irksome, angry mood, a story circulated on campus indicating that some years before a mule had kicked him without any provocation on his part. The story goes that the assault so infuriated Mr. Crosby that he balled up his fist and hit the mule as hard as he could on his side, and the mule fell with a thunderous thud to the ground. One needed only to observe the powerful and muscular symmetry of his arms to appreciate the believability of the legend.

Student leadership opportunities were in abundance at Oakwood. Even as a freshman, I looked up to a number of classmen who seemed destined to go far in life. I was particularly impressed with Lee Paschal and James Dykes who held responsible positions in most of the major organizations on campus. Paschal held the post of president in numerous organizations, including the Seminar, the choir, Student Council, Epsilon Sigma, Excelsior, and the Senior Class. His laid-back maturity and reserve placed him in a position of influence and favor to the extent that he was unrivaled in terms of the successive honors that were bestowed upon him during his years at Oakwood. Dykes was a number one scholar of no mean attainment. He possessed marvelous powers of the mind, and he was keen at comprehending circumstances and situations and changing them into opportunities. Facile with a pen, he used this gift to make significant contributions as editor of the *Acorn* and later as editor of the *Spreading Oak*. His presidencies included the International Relations Club and Colporteur Club. I recall, too, that he served as Sabbath school superintendent.

There seemed to have been no monopoly on leadership as each semester unveiled a group of students who were closely bound together by the common bond of Christian fellowship and of altruistic service. Among the more active student leaders were Joseph Powell, Gloria Saddler, Ruth Bracy, Charles Bradford, Franklin Hill, Donald Crowder, Ruth Jordan, Gene Carter, Ruth Mosby, Charles Dudley, Charles Daniels, Turner Battle, III, Samuel Bond, and Cordell Evans.

The young men on campus could not harbor the excitement they experienced when coming in contact with some of the charming young ladies that were in abundance at Oakwood. Each fellow attempted to outdo the other in the assessment of his choice as to who was the most ideal young lady among the garden of campus beauties. While physical attraction was among the assets used to rank the *ideal* young woman, among the other qualities that were rated were such things as personality, speech, appearance, manners, poise, common sense and, above all, character. The ebb and flow of excessive conversation unlocked the lips and tongues of even the most timid among us when the subject of the young ladies was placed on the table. Fellows who had vague and blurred ideas about issues in general suddenly became focused and clear-sighted in this fashionable arena of give and take. What some did not admit, however, was that they had come to Oakwood with the design of securing a helpmate just as intensely as tradition had ascribed to our female counterparts.

When the choice prizes of feminine pulchritude had finally been exhausted, a cosmopolitan array of young women came to the forefront: Vivian Gardner, Jessie Godley, Ruby Cartwright, Esther Mason, Cordell Evans, Ruth Dean, Ruth and Gloria Saddler, Nannie Benson, Phyllis Mitchell, Vivian Moody, Leatrice Jones, Lillie Warnick, Lovey Davis, Marian Blevins, Velma Beeman, Ethel McKenzie, Geraldine Graves, Henrietta Knight, Ruth Mosby, Virginia McClure, Helen Beckett, Lucille Hackney, Ruth and Margaret Daniels, Grace Kilby, Clara and Evelyn Hamilton, Marjorie Peterson, Frances Hudson, Gwendolyn Jordan, and Eunice and Oletha McQuerry.

Two rather humorous incidents stand out in my mind, and I get a good wholesome laugh every time I review them. Mr. Ashby, the school registrar at that time, was a very short man, perhaps measuring at the most five feet tall. He always seemed obsessed, in the authoritarian manner, to impose his staff rank on the students. It was a bit comical to observe him striding at least three of four paces ahead of his towering spouse when they traversed the campus. Each day, Professor Ashby could be seen standing at military attention to observe the behavior of each student in the halls as classes changed. He made no bones about keeping the noise level and frivolity at a minimum. One day Louis Hackney, a muscular and well-proportioned young man about six feet in height, was hurrying down the hall to one his classes when Professor Ashby bellowed in his characteristic military manner, "Louise Hackney, stop the running and report here!" The professor, with a scour on his face, rebuked Louis with these words: "Hackney, you'll never get as high as I am in the world unless you learn how to follow directions."

Humiliated and embarrassed in front of his peers, Hackney retorted, "Mr. Ashby, you'll never get as high as I am in this world unless you get on a stepladder."

The hallway exploded with uncontrollable laughter as Mr. Ashby, clearly outdone, was last seen summarily escorting Louis into his office. That scene was almost worth my entire stay at Oakwood.

There was another episode that would qualify for inclusion in Ripley's *Believe It or Not*. Now, every young man at Oakwood knew that visiting a young woman in her dormitory room was off limits. One could not only endanger his stay at Oakwood by violating this policy, it might even sabotage his life-calling, especially if he were a ministerial student. There was one young man, however, who dared to defy the regulation, and on a dare, he launched forth into the unknown. He made a visit to Butler Hall to take a birthday present to his young lady. Appreciating his obliging gesture in behalf of one of their own, the young man was able to gain the cooperation of the monitors at the front desk to serve as lookouts in their complicity to shield him against any faculty or staff person who might interrupt his *noble* enterprise. To the utter dismay and horror of everyone involved, the young man had no sooner been welcomed into the lady's room, when one of the monitors sighted Dean Gresham coming toward the building from Irwin Hall with her flashlight guiding her each step of the way. Panic ensued. The impact of the moment sent everyone scurrying. There was a frantic rush and pounding on the young lady's door. The front entrance provided no way of escape for the imperiled young man. His only road to freedom was through the ladies' rest room and through a beckoning window and screen that left his relatively new suit ripped from stem to stern. A great hush fell over Butler Hall that evening and, for that matter, over the entire occurrence. The gavel of mercy dropped on this episode for the young man and woman sharing with each other in the brinkmanship of this historic miscue; no one was ever brought before the tribunal of the government committee for this serious violation of standards because no one ever said a mumbling word for what could very well have been a full blown campus fiasco.

Those two incidents are among the never-to-be-forgotten feast of things that I experienced while journeying in the land of *The Oaks*.

The year 1944, my first year at Oakwood, was a year of historic significance to African-American Seventh-day Adventists. It was the year that Gunnar Myrdal, the renowned Swedish socialist, had published his penetrating analysis of black-white relations in America in the celebrated work, *An American Dilemma: The Negro Problem and Modern Democracy*. He had made the assumption that racial integration was the only viable option for racial harmony in America. Ironically, 1944 was the year that black regional conferences were formed. It was the formation of these conferences that provided a structure and laboratory for the development of an expanding leadership within the church. On one hand this development might be viewed from a historical perspective as a step backward in view of the later *Brown v. Topeka* decision which nullified the *separate but equal* theory; but on the other hand, the monumental and accelerated growth of the black work since the organization of black conferences is incontrovertible. That development has also had major implications for Oakwood as these conferences have served as vital *feeder stations*, promoting and assisting Oakwood in the recruitment of students. The conferences have also been extremely generous in their allocation of financial resources for the advancement of the institution.

The conferences as initially organized were as follows:

Allegheny Conference—J. H. Wagner, president
Central States Mission—T. M. Rowe, president
Lake Region Conference—J. G. Dasent, president
Northeastern Conference—L. H. Bland, president
South Atlantic Conference—H. D. Singleton, president
South Central Conference—H. R Murphy, president
Southwest Conference—W. W. Fordham, president

After a glorious year and a half at Oakwood, I transferred to another Seventh-day Adventist college, Union College in Lincoln, Nebraska.

Chapter 5

Life at Union College

It has always been amazing how black colleges and universities have done so much, so well, with so little. And Oakwood College was no exception. Our teachers were so loving and so sharing. They were people of inestimable spiritual and intellectual value. Then, too, I had in a relatively short period of time, developed friendships that would last for a lifetime. But one thing was lacking—the College was unaccredited. It lacked the resources—fiscal, human, and material—to make it sufficiently competitive in the sisterhood of historically black colleges and universities at that time. Its reputation, to that point, had been based on its success in training ministers for denominational employment. Most other academic disciplines were undernourished. Dr. Dykes was the sole doctorate in the institution. While there were many positive factors that contributed to the development of student life, appropriate corrective measures were not in place that could strengthen the institution's overall academic program at the time.

Faced with the prospect of pursuing a profession in medicine, dentistry, or higher education, I convinced my parents that I should transfer to Union College. Union had three distinct advantages: it was a Seventh-day Adventist college; it was accredited; and it was much closer to home (about 175 miles from Topeka).

It was in June of 1945 that I enrolled in summer school at Union. The cafeteria lines were bulging with students at the lunch hour. I would not believe my eyes when I noticed Ruth Saddler standing about thirty paces away in the lunch line for the young women. I took aim, quickly headed in her direction, and queried her as to her reason for being there. After all, we had both been students at Oakwood the week before, just prior to the end of the school year. "Union is closer to home and a lot stronger academically, I understand, so my parents and I decided that this was the best place for me," Ruth elaborated. Her home was in St. Louis, Missouri, so I was quick to understand her rationale given my similar assessment.

Legends had mounted about the academic strengths of Union because counted among its stellar black students had been the Lewis brothers of Atchison, Kansas, both of whom became respected physicians; Professors Otis B. Edwards and Ernest Rogers of Oakwood College, George Henderson, Thomasine Longware, and Gaines Partridge, the principal of Shiloh Academy in Chicago. We had not been told, however, about the racism that pervaded the campus. There was a great gap that existed between black and white students on campus. This gap was consciously and systematically encouraged and enforced by the school's top hierarchy. This phenomenon was quickly observed in the college cafeteria where the tradition and practice was to have blacks and whites sit at separate tables. It was observable in dormitory arrangements and in all-white assignments to positions on the school paper and yearbook staffs. It was apparent in the composition of the faculty that included no people of color. It was glaring when Dean Rees would call and question any white girl who paused, if only for a few moments, to have an exchange of conversation with a black male student. The school had a way of shutting us off and shutting us out of those places and positions reserved for *whites only*. The signs weren't there like those in Alabama, but the reality was.

The fertile and creative curiosity of my own faculties sought an antidote to those unethical intrusions on my personal dignity. The expression of music has always provided the umbrella of refuge and catharsis to those social predicaments and circumstances that are a part of the day-to-day individual and collective lives of African-Americans. I called upon three of my black classmates to join me in organizing a quartet composed of Clarence Schmidt, second tenor; John Davis Butler, first tenor; Roy Matthews, bass; and myself, baritone. We called ourselves the Hub of Harmony Quartet. Soon we joined Elder Mote, accompanying him to places where he preached. The journeys took us to remote areas in the state like North Platte, Chadron, Nebraska City, Kearney, and Scottsbluff, before gaining enough experience and confidence to share our doubtful abilities in Omaha and Lincoln.

Those great country Nebraska meals held more than a little attraction for us. But it was those substantially scrumptious Sunday morning breakfasts after a Saturday night program that we eagerly anticipated. Mounds of grits, fried potatoes, vege-whatever, and pancakes immersed in golden butter and maple syrup made the long and laborious trips well worth it all. Since that was out remuneration, for the most part, we ate folks out of house and home without apologies.

It wasn't long before the summer was over, and soon the presence of black students was enlarged. We enjoyed a great fellowship among ourselves, and we struggled to demonstrate that we had the native capacity to compete successfully and academically with our white counterparts. Three teachers stand out as being especially warm and congenial in their efforts to welcome and to involve us to the extent that they could in college activities: Dr. Winton Beaven, Dr. Virgil Logan, and Mr. Wayne Hooper.

I remembered the advice of my mother before I left for college. She admonished, "Remember, you'll have to do twice as well to get half as much." My mother was a native Virginian, and she was reflecting on her observations and experiences over the years in dealing with white folks. It did not take long for me to recognize my experiences mirrored her racial reflections in many ways. I came to love and respect my association with some of the brightest black young people with whom it has been my experience to know over the years. There were the Bookhardt brothers— John Frank and Leroy; their sister, Lois; John David Butler; John Washington; Sylvia Chandler; Jimmy Valentine; Gloria Mackson; Charles Seard; Ruth Saddler; Milton Woodson; LeCount Butler; Herbert Alexander; Clarence Schmidt; Gaines Partridge; and Vertis Barnes. There was also a cadre of black students from the West Indies who kept white teachers and students goggle-eyed with their astute and scholarly achievements. Sidney Beaumont, Oscar Harriot, Roy Matthews, Joyce Arneau, Henry Wiseman, and Oliver Phillips helped to set an academic pace that aroused in each of us a sense of racial pride, notwithstanding the distractions that were always evident.

There were a number of very able teachers and scholars that adorned Union College in those days. I was particularly impressed with Dr. Frank Marsh, my biology teacher; Dr. Guy Jorgensen in chemistry; Dr. Lowell Welch who taught me Bible Survey; Dr. Leslie Hardinge in Sermon Preparation and Delivery; Dr. Robert Wood, in Physics; and Elder Young in Greek. I majored in speech with minors in chemistry, biology and religion. While I made top grades in biology, physiology, speech, English, and world religions, nothing satisfied me more than earning the top grade in Greek and a ninety-seven percent overall average while making one hundred percent on the final examination.

I was especially elated to have beaten out all of the ministerial students and religion majors in a class of about forty students and where the competition was fierce. While I didn't have the top grade in organic chemistry, I did set the record in the Star Chamber competition, an exercise where students had to identify chemical elements and the catalytic agents that triggered them into chemical compounds. It was nearly thirty years later when I had the good pleasure of seeing Dr. Jorgensen again in Loma Linda, California, that he told me that no one had ever equalled or surpassed my record during his tenure as professor of chemistry at Union. While several of my friends had developed an interest in pursuing medicine, my interests were so varied that I had not come to grips with any determination concerning my choice of profession.

I was never satisfied with just being a good student—that was not enough to gratify my boundless energy and enthusiasm for life. I became heavily involved in extracurricular activities—especially musically, often referred to as *The Hub* in those days.

The Hub of Harmony Male Chorus, organized in 1945, cannot be adequately explained unless one gains some familiarity with the political and ethnic focus of the times.

The year of 1945 seems to have been the year of tragedy and triumph. The formal end of World War II came with dramatic force on September 2, 1945, when official surrender ceremonies were conducted by General MacArthur on the battleship Missouri in Tokyo Bay in response to Japan's unconditional surrender. On the same day Americans at home hysterically celebrated V-J Day—Victory in Japan Day.

Earlier that year, April 2, 1945, the nation had been sobered by President Franklin Delano Roosevelt's untimely and dismaying death, as Harry S. Truman, the bespectacled senator from Missouri assumed the mantle of the presidency. Yet, thirteen days later on April 25, 1945, the United Nations Conference had met in San Francisco, hammered out the United Nations Charter, and that historical document was subsequently approved by the Senate on July 28, 1945.

It was the year that Truman appointed a Civil Rights Commission in response to the agitation of established black organizations such as the Fraternal Council of Negro Churches, the NAACP, and CORE.

Curiously enough, *The Hub*, a group of young African-American men who attended Union College in Lincoln, Nebraska, gained unsuspected stature as musicians on the college campus, even when our obvious physical difference from the dominant group prevented the two races from even eating at the same table in the college cafeteria. Singing together, first as a quartet and then as an ensemble, was an emotionally saving strategy that enabled the group to survive the tension of racial isolation and alienation which was commonplace in the day-to-day lives of the twenty or so black students who were very thinly represented among a campus community of students, staff and faculty.

It was during the summer of that year—1945 again—that Clarence Schmidt, John Davis Butler, Roy Matthews and myself began singing together as a quartet. We spent evenings and weekends sharing our past with each other and enjoying ourselves musically as an alternative to boredom and exclusion. With no more than twenty African-Americans enrolled, and motivated by the need to have spiritual and emotional support, we organized a male chorus of approximately twelve members and made plans to enter the Amateur Hour Contest in January of 1946. The original group was composed of Vertis M. Barnes, Jr., John Davis Butler, Joseph LeCount Butler, Andrew Donnelly, Frank W. Hale, Jr., Arthur Hobby, Roy Matthews, Gaines Partridge, and Jimmie Valentine.

In less than three weeks, the Hub had organized, developed a repertoire, rehearsed, and molded ourselves into a relatively well-oiled choral group, singing *down home spirituals* as our dominant trademark. And so it was that on January 11, 1946, the Hub climaxed the Amateur Hour Program with spectacular success. Winning the chorus group prize and the grand prize, the Hub was the overwhelming favorite of the eight hundred cheering and applauding students who greeted us with unbridled and impassioned approval at the conclusion of our renditions.

We had borrowed a musical chapter from the famous Wings Over Jordan Chorale Ensemble, a black gospel group from Cleveland, Ohio, that sang on a national radio broadcast every Sunday morning under the direction of Reverend Glenn T. Settle. This superb singing group interspersed narration between selections to introduce the audience to the selections which were to follow. Our theme song, "City of Light," had been composed by Walter Kisack years before when he was a student at Oakwood College. Andrew Donnelly (Topeka, Kansas) with the velvet texture of his baritone voice, provided the narration that was to become a significant transitional fixture which led us across the momentary crevasse at the conclusion of one selection while, at the same time, enlivening our senses and voices to the numbers which followed.

Arthur Lee Hobby (Kansas City, Kansas) possessed an incredible tenor voice that captured the audience with its pathos. He was able to turn a simple phrase with such warmth and energy that the audience experienced intermittent chills of joy and sadness, depending upon whether he was leading out in the exuberant spiritual, "In His Care," or the more somber selection, "I'm Tramping." In the years that followed, the membership in the Hub of Harmony continued to grow as new black students enrolled at Union College. Among the new faces that joined the group was Milton Woodson, the first tenor from Topeka, Kansas. Woodson was unrivaled at his position once he became a member of the Hub. The range and timbre of his voice was such that he had sufficient intensity to carry the first tenor section all by himself. The Bookhardt brothers, John Frank and Leroy, brought their musical gifts from their native Florida. John was an impressive second tenor whose rich and colorful voice provided the mainstay in the section over a number of years. Leroy was the foundation and pillar of the bass section. His rock-like adherence to musical fundamentals gave us a superb guarantee in his range. Over time, he was buttressed by the solid bass performances of John E. Washington from Independence, Kansas, and Bertrand Nunley of San Antonio, Texas. In earlier days, Vertis M. Barnes, Jr., of Kansas City, Missouri, and Roy Matthews of Kingston, Jamaica, and William Woodson (brother of Milton) had been the glue that held the bass section together. LeCount (Joe) Butler of Washington, D.C., and Welcome Bryant of Omaha, Nebraska, along with Donnelly, owned the baritone section. They negotiated the requirements of that range with extraordinary texture and precision.

Herbert Alexander and Jimmie Valentine, of Kansas City, John D. Butler of Washington, D.C., and Gaines R. Partridge of Omaha, Nebraska, were among our *swing* voices who occasionally alternated between the second tenor and baritone sections as the need required. Their versatility was an important ingredient that kept us going when another member was absent due to some unforeseen circumstances. Welcome Bryant of Omaha and Charles Seard of Greenville, Mississippi, gave strong support to the well-established baritone section.

As director of the group, I found myself in a pinch hitting role, supplementing any section that I felt needed bolstering at any given time. That excluded that bass section, of course, as my tenor voice had not the slightest inclination to pursue that depth. Not possessing the native vocal ability of some of my associates, I spent a good deal of time developing our repertoire and arranging for our appearances throughout the city, the state, and surrounding states.

There were two very important faculty supporters who were instrumental in our becoming more daring in our desires to share our musical talents beyond the Union College campus. Dr. Winton Beaven, a speech professor at the college, was in great demand as a speaker at local organizations. On numerous occasions, he invited us to sing before civic organizations, such as the Kiwanis and Lions, where he had been invited to speak. We not only reveled in the fact of his confidence in us, but we often enjoyed a free lunch as a bonus. On other occasions, we were given a small honorarium for our services.

Wayne Hooper, an arranger and composer for the Kings Heralds Quartet, was a member of the music faculty at Union College for a period of time. Because of our travels off campus, he was assigned to our group as a kind of sponsor-chaperone. His congenial personality and musical genius were of significant advantage to us. He melted right into our rehearsal sessions and concert tours. Because he was such a Christian gentleman, we never felt *captive* to his role as our assigned sponsor.

Our musical opportunities and journeys carried us to Kansas, Missouri, North and South Dakota, Oklahoma, Texas, Iowa, and Minnesota. We were in great demand to appear in S.D.A. churches throughout the State of Nebraska, making appearances in Omaha, Scottsbluff, North Platte, Chadron, Kearney, and numerous other cities. The Lincoln community was also open and welcoming. Governor Val Peterson had us to perform at the lighting of the Christmas tree. Dr. Gerald Kennedy, pastor of St. Paul's Methodist Church, invited us to sing before his two thousand member congregation on several occasions. Clyde Malone, executive director of the Urban League, called on us at various times to assist in his programs. The Christmas season gave us an opportunity to gain some consistent financial remuneration as we were invited to sing at Christmas parties promoted by business and professional organizations. Our resourcefulness carried us up and down Sheridan Boulevard, going from door to door and singing carols during the holiday season. It was not uncommon for us to receive generous donations as the Christmas spirit seemed to have engulfed all those with whom we came in contact. On one occasion, we went to a home where a party was in progress and the host, upon hearing us, searched his pockets and gave us a ten dollar bill. His gesture was contagious, and before we left that home we had garnered over two hundred dollars. These blessings were vitally important in helping us to maintain ourselves in meeting our day-to-day expenses. Most of us had work assignments at the college during the week, and on weekends some of us had jobs off campus, caring for lawns, washing cars, doing odd jobs at local businesses, or shoveling snow during the winter season at nearby homes.

The winters in Nebraska were ravishing ones—always close to zero or below, and even some members of the faculty and administration had ice water flowing through their veins. It was a super cold campus, at least in those days, for black students.

One day as I sat alone in the dining room at a table that could seat four, I felt that I could suffer the personal humiliation and indignities of that institution no longer when I was asked by the directing hostess to move to another table so that four white girls could sit at the table where I had been assigned. Black and white students were always directed to separate tables as they came out of the cafeteria line. Such a practice was denigrating enough on the face of it, but it was doubly humiliating for me to be asked to move from a table to which I had been assigned because another group of whites preferred that table to another that was not to their liking. Because I refused to move and began eating my meal, the cafeteria manager was informed. When she came and insisted that I move to another table, I held my ground. In a few minutes in response to their call, the president of the college, Dr. Cossentine, summoned me to his office. The United States was more than three years into the Second World War, a war that our government had promised would "make the world safe for democracy." Surely there was enough room in that world for a Christian college campus, I told myself, for black students to be able to sit down in a dining room, to be comfortable, and not to be subjected to the racism and ridicule brought on by policies and practices that were obviously at variance with all that the church stated that it stood for.

And so upon completing my lunch, I proceeded to President Cossentine's office. Why was it, he asked, that I did not comply with the institution's policies? Why was it, I asked, that blacks were treated differently than whites at a Christian college? President Cossentine was unsympathetic and dogmatic. He reminded me that rules were rules. In deference to his position, I attempted to be modest in my demeanor, but I stayed on the point. I inquired, "Since we have so many rules—against the use of alcohol, tobacco, profanity, attendance at movies, etc.—why isn't there a rule against racial prejudice, discrimination, and racial practices that are inhumane?" He began to tell me that two-thirds of the students at Union College were from the Southwestern Union Conference, comprising Oklahoma and Texas, and that the college had to be concerned about the feelings of those students from southern states. Whereupon I responded, "Oh, I see; it's a matter of dollars and cents. You are afraid of losing those southern students if you accord equal opportunity and justice to black students."

He sat stunned for a moment, and then answered, "Hale, you have twenty-four hours to make up your mind whether or not you're going to abide by the rules of this institution."

Quick as a flash, I responded, "I don't need that long, Mr. President; I will never again yield to the kind of human indignities to which black young people have been subjected at this institution." I left his office, knowing that the dean of men would have my bags packed and ready for the next bus to Topeka, Kansas. But that ultimatum was never effectuated, and within the next few weeks, at the beginning of the second semester, the policy was rescinded.

Our spiritual life was undergirded by our participation in our Sabbath activities in downtown Lincoln. Joining other black students from Union

College, we initially worshiped in the home of Sister Virginia Haskell. She, along with the Crosby and Johnny Napue families, was the nucleus of the S.D.A. black fellowship. We enjoyed the opportunity to study together and to engage in the delicious food that had been prepared for each Sabbath. Soon we outgrew the Haskell home and arranged to have our Sabbath services at the local Urban League in order to accommodate the nearly two dozen students who were in attendance. This weekly experience became a laboratory for our development as future leaders in the church as we held various positions in our small edifice. In those days, opportunities for us to be included and nurtured at the College View Church on the Union College campus were rare. We never even considered taking a back seat approach by attending services where our potential and participation were not welcomed. We made it a point and an obsession to develop ourselves spiritually and personally to the best of our ability. So every Sabbath we joined together in fellowship and worship at our downtown location, and the Lord greatly blessed our efforts.

Allon Chapel and its development were aided immeasurably by a number of very able and supporting young African-American ladies who were outstanding students at Union. These included Mary Bell, Lois Bookhardt, Melvine E. Butler, Sylvia Chandler, Vernice Jones, Ruth Saddler, Anita Smith, Gloria Mackson, Marcheta Valentine, and Josephine Ford. Mrs. Marguerite Thomas, the mother of Bertrand Nunley, played a significant role at every stage of Allon Chapel's growth as a mentor and spiritual advisor.

All of us were indebted to Oscar Harriot of Kingston, Jamaica, a seasoned veteran, who placed his profound and infinite knowledge of the Bible and of life continually at our disposal. As a Sabbath school teacher he kept us enraptured with the rich content of his presentations as well as his command of the King's English. We affectionately referred to him as *Mr. Churchill* or *Prime Minister* in acknowledgement of his singular impact on us.

That fellowship included numerous other students of African descent who were enrolled at Union College. They represented a variety of countries and islands from South America and Caribbean settings. These students joined hands with us in our worship and in our day-to-day assertions to push upward and outward, penetrating, to the best of our ability, whatever remained veiled from us. We grew together, reciprocally influencing each other in an ascending cause of calculated togetherness.

Among our brothers and sisters from outside our shores who were loyal and constant in our voyages of spiritual, academic, and social discoveries were Joyce Arneau, Sidney Beaumont, Sadie Benjamin, Ignacio Carillo, Samuel Gooden, Oscar Harriot, Gloria James, Roy Matthews, Oliver Phillips, John Ryan, Andrew Sainten, and Henry Wiseman.

A number of non-Adventists began to attend our services, and as a consequence, we urged Elder Fletcher Bryant, pastor of the Omaha S.D.A. Church, to come and conduct an evangelistic crusade and revival in Lincoln. His meetings were productive, and our little church continued to grow to the point where our membership grew to about thirty-five.

Meanwhile, by late 1947, the Hub began making plans for a city-wide concert. Over the years, we had been singing at churches, civic and social organizations, and for a variety of special events. Nearly all of our appearances were for gratis, except for an occasional free meal or a small donation. We seldom charged anyone for anything—we just loved to sing! So, we began to lay out plans for a program that would assist us in our own scholarship endeavors and provide funding to purchase a church facility.

There was a Church of the Brethren on the corner of 22nd and "Q" that was for sale. Mr. Showalter, owner of a local roofing company across the street from the church, was instrumental in arousing our interest in its availability. When he took me through the church, which was right around the corner from where I was living, I became excited and invited two or three other Hub members to go with me to take a second look. Milton Woodson and Joseph LeCount Butler became as excited as I had been. The church had a capacity for about 250 people. It had a lovely lower level, equipped with classrooms, a fellowship hall, and kitchen fully equipped with cooking utensils and dinnerware. Next door was a three bedroom parsonage. The total cost was $9000.

The Hub accepted this opportunity as a challenge! Our mission was clear. In a spirit of Christian competition, we began to mobilize our efforts to prepare for a spring concert to be given at the University of Nebraska Coliseum. The result is history. On April 18, 1948, we sang before five thousand wonderfully supportive patrons in that great auditorium. It was a historical moment. God had once again intervened and made a way out of no way. We had no agent, no public relations team, and no promotional experience. As a group, we simply turned it over to God and gave it our best shot by selling our tickets to individuals and to businesses as we went door-to-door for months in advance. God richly rewarded our efforts. Out of our proceeds, we gave the Central States Conference $3000 as a down payment on the church we had located. We gave Union College $500 to establish a Hub of Harmony Musical Scholarship Fund. We shared the remainder among ourselves to meet the continuing financial stresses of being in school.

Elder Frank Bland, president of the Central States Conference, and his staff facilitated the transaction that gave us a new church after we had provided one-third of the cost. The good news is that that church, Allon Chapel, became our base of spiritual and developmental support during our sojourn in Lincoln.

While the Hub was established during an era where blacks and whites were escorted to separate tables in the cafeteria at Union, we were, nevertheless, challenged by an excellent academic program at the college that kept us focused in our studies. While we were not indifferent to the racist indiscretions that confronted us at the time, we had neither the time nor the energy to get bogged down in full scale confrontations that might have taken us off course. So, our activities of protest were somewhat restrained within some bounds of purpose. We did not meet the issue head on except for the cafeteria situation which was resolved in early 1946, but rather had to circumvent the problems by involving ourselves, once again, with the black church in Lincoln.

Beyond such considerations, we, individually and as a group, performed exceedingly well academically at the college. Many times our names were listed among the top ten when grades were posted after test results in individual classes. The record speaks for itself. The career profile of Hub members will stand shoulder to shoulder with our counterparts who were in school with us at the time.

Union College has done a great service by reestablishing a Hub of Harmony Endowment Scholarship Fund. We are also pleased that we were invited to be part of Union's Centennial Celebration in 1990. We are especially pleased to know that Raymond Davis has formed Hub of Harmony II, and they are a great group. As I listened to them recently at Allon Chapel, my yearnings were rooted in nostalgia. I knew that it would only be a matter of time before Hub I and Hub II would join forces. Regeneration is the basic force that changes people and gives us opportunities to share in the ongoing potential that God has put within all of us. That's why we participated in the Centennial Celebration at Union College.

The roll call of Hub of Harmony alumni includes Dr. Herbert Alexander, Ph.D., professor of Life Sciences (retired); Mr. Vertis M. Barnes, Jr., M.A., parent counselor and director of community relations, San Diego (California) Unified School District (retired); Dr. John Frank Bookhardt, M.D., private practice, Omaha, Nebraska; Dr. A. Leroy Bookhardt, M.D., fellow of the American College of Surgeons, Orlando, Florida; Dr. John Davis Butler, Ph.D., professor emeritus of Foreign Languages, University of the District of Columbia; Elder Joseph LeCount

Butler, Sr., M.A., pastor, chaplain, counselor (retired); Mr. Raymond Davis, remodeling contractor; Mr. Otis B. Edwards, Jr, M.S., Air Force Logistics, project manager, Presidential Aircraft (retired); Dr. Frank W. Hale, Jr., Ph.D., vice provost and professor emeritus, The Ohio State University; Mr. Wayne Hooper, M.A., Kings Heralds Quartet and Trust Department (retired); Mr. Bertrand Nunley, B.A., supervising case worker, State of Illinois (retired); Dr. Gaines R. Partridge, Ed.D., dean of student affairs, associate dean of admissions, dean of men, Loma Linda University (retired); Dr. Clarence Schmidt, Ph.D., psychoanalyst/psychotherapy, New York, private practice; Dr. Charles Seard, M.D., private practice, Los Angeles; Dr. Jimmie R. Valentine, M.D., private practice, San Diego, California; Dr. Harold Washington, D.D.S., California Youth Authority, Camarillo California; Dr. John Washington, M.D., diplomat, National Board of Medical Examiners, Los Angeles, California; Mr. Milton J. Woodson, B.A., B.S., chief physical therapist, Veterans Administration Medical Center (retired); Mr. William D. Woodson, M.A., special education teacher, Menniger Foundation, Topeka, Kansas (retired).

But life for me was not all music with the Hub in those days. In the midst of all of the musical attraction and excitement, I began to feel the tug at my heart as I began to spend more time with Ruth Saddler, who I had begun dating as early as September of 1945. From the very moment that I had first met her as as student at Oakwood College, I respected her. She was an original, and from the moment I laid eyes on her, I knew it. There was delicacy in her manner and a subdued brightness in her spirit that captured my attention. She had been the special friend of Lucius Daniels while at Oakwood, just as I had enjoyed the companionship of Vivian Moody. But now that she was in Lincoln, Nebraska, attending Union College, she unconsciously managed to torture my patience and exhaust my nerves as I saw in her those same qualities which she possessed at Oakwood. She managed to preserve them so easily and so unpretentiously that I became more and more riveted to the splendor of her remarkable feminine dignity. She was a beautiful girl, well-calved and well-sculptured as well. The days, weeks, and months fermented our relationship to the point that, just prior to the Thanksgiving break in 1946, I asked her to marry me as we promenaded just outside the downtown Nebraska State Capitol building. Time seemed an eternity—for minutes seemed like hours before there was an exchange of words. Always mysterious, self-contained and feather-soft in her movements, she finally responded noddingly, "You'll have to ask my parents." I was proud as a peacock, because I had earned her acquiescence. Even though I had double duty—to convince both my parents and hers—that night I lay on my dormitory bed half-bathed with the shades of moonlight that shadowed my beckoning walls, half-glowing in the cheerful rehearsal of all that had transpired, half-edged with sleep, and half-faltering with the anxieties of what could scuttle our best laid plans. Time squared itself with us when on December 26, 1946, I gained the approval of her parents for her hand, as they shared in the consent which my parents had accorded a few days earlier. We were married on June 16, 1947, with ten dollars I had borrowed from my dad to purchase a license. Six months earlier I had begun to save all of my sparse forty cents and hour earnings so that I could purchase my lovely bride-to-be an engagement watch. I prided myself that I could now place that gold-plated, seventeen-jeweled Benrus embraceable watch on her arm. It represented over one hundred and sixty hours of sweat in washing, waxing and buffing cars at the Hompes Hudson Motor Company, but it was absolutely worth it! I loved that girl and every captivating moment that I spent with her.

Now that I had assumed the responsibilities of a married man, leisure was no longer an option. I felt the need to be more self-reliant and independent than ever before. My father had always insisted that I be resourceful and ambitious. As a full-time student, life was complicated enough, but now I felt the need to demonstrate to the lovely woman whom I had married and to her parents and mine that I was prepared to fulfill all of the requirements of matrimony. Sure of our decision, and certain of myself and God's blessings for us, I carried an air of unequivocal self-content.

Faced with more than a scattering of family needs, I returned to Lincoln during the summer to remove my only belongings from South Hall, the men's dormitory, to seek comfortable lodging for my wife and me, and to pursue job possibilities to keep us in school. I was grounded in the kind of positive thinking that never allowed me to question the difficulty of trying to juggle so many crucial things at the same time. I had developed the capacity to do more than one thing at a time rather well. While at Union, I always had several odd jobs which I undertook after attending morning classes. Still I always wanted spending money in my pockets. I had managed a succession of afternoon jobs that included packaging elbows and tees at a plumbing wholesale supply house, sweeping up hair and mopping the floor at a beauty shop, cleaning the floor and emptying, washing, and polishing brass cuspidors at the Chicago, Burlington and Quincey (CB&Q) railroad station, and cleaning and servicing the entire building of the Lincoln Urban League, under the supervision of Mr. Clyde Malone. All of these assignments I preformed every afternoon and evening before retiring to the dormitory at about ten o'clock to undertake at least two to three hours of diligent study. In the meantime, I met in rehearsal practices with the Hub, and served as pianist for the Mount Zion Baptist Church Choir every Sunday morning. It was not surprising that I made four B's and three C's one semester and three A's, two B's and a C the following semester. I never attempted to lighten my class load, although I was working on the average thirty-five to forty-five hours per week. I knew what I had to do. The white students were a typical mix—they ranged from bright to dull. But every black student was good—or we wouldn't have been there in the first place. So I had a grand honor to uphold—for myself, for my family, and for my race.

As I began to pack my dormitory belongings, I recounted the fun times that I had experienced while on campus and the excursions that I had taken in the slick 1929 Nash that I had purchased during the school year. It was a $75 wonder, with a body of green, trimmed in black, with staring wheels of glaring red spokes and glistening silver rims, and it was well known on the road between Union and downtown Lincoln. Loaded with students, it had explored every corner of the city, carried us to Allon Chapel on Sabbath, liberated us on Saturday nights to attend socials sponsored by church members in the city, and had gallantly trudged the distance between Lincoln and Topeka on occasional weekends and holidays. Memories lived on as I reflected on those all-night Saturday night rook parties in the Castle (the upper tower of South Hall), the tasty interlude at Chat and Nibble (the little restaurant hangout across the street), and the annual Spring Picnic at which all students participated on the front lawn of the campus. It was there that I had managed to garner a third place ribbon and second place ribbon in the 100-yard dash in successive years. Then there was the year when I took first place in the *Clock Tower* subscription contest by selling more subscriptions by mail to my friends and relatives than any other student. I was rewarded with a lovely portable phonograph and a pair of bronze bookends. Meanwhile, too, in 1946, I had taken second place in the all-school Temperance Oratorical Contest. The young man, Arthur Hauck, who took first place, was magnificent. He expressed his thoughts with solid logic and with a wonderful flow of fluent and liquid diction that captured the attention and applause of the audience and the judges, as well as the six other oratorical finalists. I recalled with delight some of the delightful students that I had come to admire and appreciate: Ellsworth Reily with his fortune of good looks and leadership potential; Mike Lowen, that six foot seven inch hunk of bubbling personality and buoyant athletic ability; Fred Metz, a budding dental student with a strength of character and purpose; Edward Hon, an exacting student of limitless ability; Frank

Akamini, a solid scholar who advanced our knowledge of Hawaiian cooking with his superlative culinary skills; Eugene Sample who had a vision of accurate reporting long before he became editor of *Our Little Friend*; and the Bogdanovich (later Stevens) brothers and their sister— all of whom seemed so blessed with a wealth of good manners and Christian graces.

Even though I was now married and my new wife was staying with my parents over the summer until I could find a place of residence for us, I was determined not to lose my vision for completing my education. God was certainly on our side. I had been working at the Hompes Hudson Motor Company when Mr. Neal Hompes, knowing of my desire for a place to stay, questioned me at the end of the day one Wednesday afternoon. "Frank," he inquired, "how would you and your wife like to stay in an apartment that we have in our home in exchange for doing certain domestic assignments?" I had no doubt in my mind that God had sent one of his angels on a particular assignment to address our needs. Of course, I could not rest until I had made arrangements for Ruth to come to Lincoln so that we could discuss the proposition with Neal's sister, who had the full jurisdiction of managing the home on a day-to-day basis. The date was set when we could all come together to discuss the matter. The family was seeking a couple who would be responsible for cooking, light housekeeping and yard work. Ruth was so graceful and impressive in her manner, as well as in her knowledge of food preparation, that little time was lost in offering us the job. Ruth would perform house duties full time, and I would, as time permitted, perform certain custodial chores, while not withdrawing from my activities as a full time student. We could not have been happier as we shared our blessings with our parents. Our quarters were cozy. We knelt down and thanked the Lord for our two room (bedroom and sitting room) romantic space in that lofty home, patterned after a luxurious Swiss chalet in Lincoln's most affluent neighborhood, right off Sheridan Boulevard. Our economic fears, while not altogether dissipated, were somewhat relieved because, in addition to our accommodations, all of our meals were provided, and we received a monthly stipend of one hundred dollars. Angels, indeed, were watching over us.

Good sense challenged and forced me to take advantage of every economic opportunity. As a consequence, I enrolled at the University of Nebraska during the middle of my junior year. Because I did not receive credit for nearly twenty hours of courses in religion that I had taken at Oakwood and Union, it took me an additional semester and summer to gain status as a full-fledged junior.

Chapter 6

The Academic Countdown
at the University of Nebraska

I had just turned twenty years of age a few months before I was married, and I had not yet settled in my mind my career direction. However, I was constantly motivated by the admiration and inspiration of my mother and the terrific example of my father, who was a man of great genius and remarkable talent. Both of my parents were primarily self-taught individuals who focused on superiority as their goal and excellence as their norm. I don't ever remember my parents doing anything in a half-hearted, slipshod manner. They gave every aspect of their lives their best shot, and God rewarded them with the excellence and the treasured appreciation which they so richly deserved. So, from what I had inherited and seen from them, I was determined to complete the final stretch of my undergraduate education with the personal stamp of my own manhood. I was also especially blessed to have a beautiful young wife who was willing to temporarily sacrifice her education so that I could complete mine.

Dr. Leroy T. Laase was chairman of the Speech Department at the University of Nebraska, and he took me under his wing at the recommendation of Dr. Winton Beaven who had been my academic advisor at Union College. Dr. Laase was an intense professor of matter-of-fact, no nonsense qualities. He immediately directed my attention to great classical leaders of philosophical thought, introducing me to the rhetorical greatness of Aristotle, Socrates, Plato, Cicero, and Quintilian. He laid the groundwork for my understanding the principles of rhetorical criticism in biography and in speech composition. I learned early that rhetorical criticism is a complex undertaking, but it offers an inviting and exciting challenge to the serious student of public address. I had gained immeasurable respect for the oratory of President Franklin Delano Roosevelt and Prime Minister Winston Churchill, so I was more than a little enthusiastic to have the opportunity to become knowledgeable about the forces that shaped a speaker's thinking, the circumstances that prompted a particular speech, and the conditions that modified or determined the outcome of a speaker's presentation. Consequently, my undergraduate experience at the University of Nebraska was greatly enriched as I sat under the tutelage of such fine teachers as Laase, Paul Olson, Bruce Kendall, and Maxine Trauernicht. In addition to taking the communication courses, I took a heavy dose of English and American literature, political science, history and psychology. But it was my courses in communication analysis, public address, debate, and logic that provided me the skills that I needed to develop for leadership. I learned early that the *sine qua non* for communication is authenticity. There is absolutely no substitute for the truth.

Meanwhile, I was coming to grips with the truth of my own economic reality. Ruth and I figured out quickly that, although we were in a position to save a few dollars each month, they were so few that it was going to be impossible for me to finish school unless I undertook some additional sideline opportunities. Fortunately, my duties at the Hompes estate were largely reassigned to the evening when I would help with kitchen duties and serving dinner.

On the strength of my father's promotional experience, I undertook the arduous task of promoting the Southernaires in concert at the St. Paul's Methodist Church. The Southernaires was a quartet that performed every Sunday morning on the ABC radio network out of New York City. They were a household fixture in many African-American homes. My father was a promoter and public relations expert par excellence. Although he had never had any training in communication, he had the kind of personality that had a profound impact wherever he went and with whomever he made contact. He always had a clear vision of what he wanted to do and how he wanted to do it. He also had a magnetic way of developing a team of enthusiastic people who would join him in any enterprise he undertook. Such was the case in Topeka when he single-handedly spearheaded two major concerts, one featuring the Southernaires and the other featuring the noted baritone, Paul Robeson. In both instances, the concerts were a complete sellout at the downtown Municipal Auditorium to a standing room crowd of more than four thousand patrons.

Dad was a super salesman. He could sell a ticket to a tree stump. He had a brilliant understanding of human nature. Above all, he demonstrated the kind of enthusiasm that would motivate others to listen to his ideas and to accept them. His effectiveness, however, transcended style. It was not only *how* he communicated that made him effective, it was also the substance of what he said that generated a positive response from others.

So an integral part of me to assume such a daring promotional undertaking as promoting the Southernaires in concert had its roots in both observing and in helping my father during my teenage years in high school. After arranging for the quartet to come to Lincoln for the sum of $2000 and expenses, I spent so many of my daylight hours, when I wasn't in school, going from door to door, to one business after another, selling advertisements, selling tickets, and procuring substantial donations as *special gifts sponsors*. I was determined to have all costs associated with the event well-covered and in hand weeks prior to the concert so that I could realize the reward of a significant profit even before the concert began. Most great successes are the reward of persistence, and I had worked my poor feet to the calloused bone. I was literally limping as a result of the formidable task which I had undertaken when the moment of truth became a powerful reality. The truth was that there were fifteen hundred people in attendance at the spirit-filled program and that I had earned $1200 after expenses to apply to my schooling, with enough left over to pay down on a much needed temperamental jalopy. The entire experience was maturing; it taught me the importance of the power of patience and continuous energy in accomplishing one's goals. It also taught me the value of initiative, and how one must learn self-reliance—the quality of being responsible for attending to one's own affairs.

Meanwhile, after having spent more than six months in domestic work with a live-in arrangement, vexations began to occur that were extremely trying to both Ruth and me. Expectations from our domestic employer began to mount, as the lady of the house began demanding more and more. With a growing degree of morbid sensitivity, Mrs. Hompes began demanding that Ruth be responsible for the family laundry, for washing windows inside and out, and for doing major household duties in addition to preparing three meals a day. She would fly off the handle for the slightest of reasons. Her mouth and face were always twisted into a reflection of her unpleasant disposition. Wanting to cover every inch of this enormous home on a daily basis, she guarded Ruth's every move, always insisting that she did not move fast enough. Even today, I feel uncomfortable with that assertion, because Ruth has always been a spontaneous, self-propelled dynamo of activity since the first day I met her. There are few people that can keep pace with her activities when she is in good health. I knew, in short order, that it would be foolish and shortsighted for me to allow that situation to continue to compromise my wife's dignity and health. The only things really good in that situation were our living quarters and the sumptuous meals we enjoyed, which we would not have been able to afford otherwise, at least during that early point in our marriage.

God opened the door for us to get a room and to stay with a lovely family, Maurice and Marie Copeland and their daughter, Marlene, who lived at 2137 "R", less than a mile from the university. They were a precious couple. Mr. Copeland was a waiter at the country club, and Mrs. Copeland catered parties and dinners for some of the most affluent families in Lincoln. They made the whole run of the house available to us, so we were always comfortable and feeling very much at home. The money was still sparse, our first child was on the way, and I still was pursuing my studies with fervor. I absolutely had no intention of being a pauper for the rest of my life. I became aware that people will go out of their way to assist and support you if you are determined to make something out of yourself. Aunt Marie, as we affectionately called Mrs. Copeland, was full of surprises. Knowing our situation, she was forever providing sumptuous meals for us. After each catering activity, she would bring loads of sandwiches and an assortment of delicacies and desserts to share with us as well as her family. She also became deeply attracted to and interested in our student colleagues and church friends. On Saturday nights when we would engage in a variety of games, she would join us and would fix an extravagant array of sloppy-joe sandwiches with a large accompaniment of potato salad, potato chips, cookies and punch. When Ruthie, our beautiful firstborn baby girl, climbed into our lives, Aunt Marie and Uncle Cope loved her as if she were their very own, purchasing clothes and toys for everyday ordinary situations and on special occasions. Nothing could have given us greater confidence and support during our sojourn in Lincoln than the tender loving care that was heaped upon us in that household. All night, all day, angels were watching over us.

In another sense, those were troublesome days. The world of my own responsibility as a husband and father continued to whirl about me. The dread of mounting debts, of facing demanding school requirements and a contagion of doubts that, at times, had me on the brink of wavering in terms of whether I should remain in school, kept my psychological back to the wall. I maintained just enough energy to realize that any decision short of sticking it out would prove fatal to my progress and, no doubt, ultimately to my success. It was at such times that I had to call upon the promises of God, the inspiration of my parents, and the love of my wife to sustain me. So I kept on stepping. So many times I had been at the point of dropping out of school and taking a full-time job so that I could properly care for my family. The weight of this consideration became especially heavy after Ruthie had contracted pneumonia for the second time before she was eighteen months old. I suspected that it had something to do with the fact that we were in a bedroom where the cold frigid air of the Nebraska winters could be felt and had twice taken its toll. We were unable to escape the immobilizing effects of the frosty fury that entered from the outside along the edges of the loosely-fitted windowsills in our bedroom. Even though we had attempted to stuff every opening, crack and crevice with newspapers and assorted remnants of clothing, the chill still withstood the presence of two aging floor heaters that supplemented what heat we received from the basement furnace. Nevertheless, true to our educational goals and like the legendary band, we played on.

It wasn't long after our firstborn child, Ruth, came into the world that we found it necessary to explore other residential opportunities. As wonderful as had been our experiences in living with the Copelands, we felt that the close quarters of three persons living in one small bedroom was more than a little forbidding.

My early doubts were soon settled as the wings of Providence once again opened doors for us. Initially, it seemed absolutely inconceivable that our prayers would be answered so soon. My mood of foreboding, wondering whether or not we would be able to locate a suitable location in a short period of time, was dispelled with certainty when a marvelous octogenarian widow, hearing of our plight, invited us to stay with her in her lovely three bedroom cottage.

Mother Spann, as she was affectionately called, was more than a little anxious to have our small family move in with her. As limited as were our means, we were not at all worried about the future. We had quite a good store of faith and resolve as God, in every way possible, continued to bless us. He never gave us time to endure hardship long enough where it became even possible for us to question His leadership.

No extra work was too menial for me. I cut lawns in the summer, raked leaves in the fall, shoveled snow in the winter, and washed windows in the spring. I seized every opportunity available to advance my ambitions. I was determined that nothing would cripple my career ambitions, and the first step of my collegiate career goals was realized when I was awarded the bachelor of arts (B.A.) degree at the university on January 25, 1950. That accomplishment did something to firm up my constitutional character and resolution.

Now I was ready to take on the impelling pursuit of graduate study. There has never been any secular learning in my soul more intense than the desire to develop my mind by exposing myself to choice reading, able teachers and knowledgeable people who have achieved remarkable success in their respective fields of endeavor. Having used every ounce of muscle, stamina, and strength in my being in order to earn my first college degree, I was prepared to transfer all of the experiences and skills which I had gained while pursuing my undergraduate work to the discipline that was required to pursue and complete graduate study. Necessity is not only the mother of invention, it is the priceless stimulus which prods, shoves, and propels us, even beyond the props of our natural abilities. The urgency of a situation gives us wings to scale the heights seldom considered and rarely achieved. Circumstances notwithstanding, I knew that, with God's direction, I could be the master of my fate and the captain of my soul.

Right away, I began thinking of ways of earning money while still in school without having to actually be on the job during the day when I needed to be taking classes, studying in the library, and doing the necessary research for a master's thesis. One day, as I was driving down Sheridan Boulevard, an idea suddenly captivated me. I noticed that the construction of a house that I had just passed was nearly completed. The windows were still dirty and smudged with putty. I turned my car around, drove back to the house, and inquired about how I could contact the builder. It so happened that Mr. Anderson, the president of the Anderson Construction Company, was on the premises. He was the owner of the house being completed as well as other houses that were under construction in the vicinity. I approached him, telling him that I had a corps of student workers who would like to clean the windows of his homes during the final stages of their completion. Aware that we were students and aspiring to prepare ourselves for greater endeavors in life, he appeared interested and impressed. I courted his business by promising superior work through painstaking detail and the commitment to a finished product that would eclipse any work that he had done in that area before. In addition, my prices were favorable, charging four dollars for twelve paned French windows and three dollars for two paned hemispheric windows. Both fees were one dollar less than the going rate. He accepted my offer and assigned me the house where we were standing.

I immediately contacted four of my friends, LeCount Butler, Bertrand Nunley, Milton Woodson, and Bernard Edwards, and offered them ninety cents an hour to work on the assignment. They immediately seized the opportunity, since the going rate for that kind of work in town was from forty to sixty cents and hour. I went to the local discount store and purchased four buckets, four squeegees, four sponges, four bottles of Windex, and four razor blade holders—one item apiece for each of my new employees. My brain was working overtime. I was thinking that if only I could get enough work to keep these guys occupied all afternoon every day, then I would be able to spend most of the day in class and at the library researching my thesis topic. So right away we returned to the site of work. The very first hour was spent in a training program, showing the fellows how to use the razor blade holder to clear the putty from around the edges of the windowsills. I was convinced that they would be able to do the overall job in an expeditious fashion with each pair of them working as a team—one cleaning one side of the window from inside the house and the other working on the other side of the same window outside of the house. Such a coordinated effort was designed to insure efficiency and some degree of speed that would reward us with new opportunities in our upstart commercial enterprise.

This new experience had so dazzled my imagination that I could hardly wait for Mr. Anderson's response after we had completed our first assignment. Mr. Anderson was not only delighted with our work, he immediately gave me the addresses of six other houses that he wanted us to clean. With the world of work that needed to be done to prepare the homes to be placed on the market and ready for sale, our ingenuity cleared the path for us to meet Mr. Anderson's needs as well as our own. I was able to spend all day on campus pursuing my studies, and I would then meet Mr. Anderson at his office about five o'clock in the afternoon in time for us to visit the sites for which we had contracted to observe their progress. It was also during these late afternoon appointments that he made additional assignments. Halfway through one of our on-site visits he said, "Hale, I am so pleased with your work that I am going to recommend you and your team to other building contractors." Industry and efficiency make ordinary situations extraordinary. My buddies and I had stemmed the tide of our economic condition. Progressively, our finances enabled us to meet the countless impossible situations that heretofore had to remain on hold until some miracle came along to rescue us from our trifling existence. God, already knowing our needs and desires, had once again cleared our paths in order for us to experience some degree of civility. What I also learned in the process is that you've got to get off of your imagination and get out and sell yourself if you ever want to accomplish anything worthwhile in life. Business opportunities mounted, and through our earnest, persistent, and hardworking endeavors, we were able to meet the challenges of each day with unlimited good fortune and success.

In the meanwhile, all of us were able to keep abreast of requirements. This fact was an indispensible equivalent to our economic survival.

The school year sped along, but not before I had the opportunity to gain a sense of direction relative to my thesis topic. I had always been enamored with the life and speaking of Frederick Douglass, the famous, one-time slave and abolitionist who had commanded the attention of huge audiences throughout America and overseas. Daily, I trudged through heavy snows during the winter months to capture all that was in the library on my subject. I even shiver now when I think of the winter winds whistling though the open campus and penetrating every layer of clothing on my body. The Nebraska winters were unlike any that I have ever experienced anywhere. They were vicious and unsympathetically bone-chilling. Even the thought of it reminds me of the winter when I was living in South Hall at Union College. One winter night, the winds were blowing with such ferocity that the curtains in our room were swaying as if the windows were open. I felt so refrigerated that I got up to check the thermometer that was just outside the front door on the dormitory porch. It registered 42° below zero, and that was in a time before the wind chill factor was being recorded—but it must have been nearly 100° below zero. I recall putting on a pair of trousers, a sweater, and a pair of socks before returning to bed. All schools remained open. That kind of weather was a way of life, and no one conceded to its brutal assaults—everyday affairs went on as usual. Even as my spirit was rooted in the challenge of pursuing my education to the fullest, my struggles in the classroom, in trying to make a living for my family, and in fighting the raw wintry elements of Nebraska's weather conditions were real.

As dedicated college students, we were so constituted that we were aware that the quality which we put into every aspect of our lives would, both in the short and long run, affect our schooling and our careers. Whatever our hands found to do, as the Scripture had admonished, we did with our might. Each of us approached our work in such a way that the experience became mutually infectious. During that year, it was the cooperative, shoulder-to-shoulder teamwork of my student colleagues who were members of the Hub of Harmony that made it possible for me to pursue and complete the requirements of the master's degree. Without their support, I would have been unable to anchor and fortify myself for the difficulties and battles that confronted me in graduate school. I thank God for the struggles which confronted me during this period. They were sufficient to stimulate my inner strength and bring out a reserve of potential that needed to be challenged. One cannot afford the luxury of floundering when one's back is up against the wall. At those moments in time, it's do or die. We either take the force of the storm and let it lift us higher, as it does the eagle, or we cave into those encounters that can strip us of our pride, our ambition, and ultimately our careers.

For all my money problems and need for sufficient study time, I still found time to engage in some volunteer efforts to challenge the Jim Crow patterns that were evident everywhere in Lincoln. Segregation was rampant. Almost no restaurants served blacks, and local hotels were off limits as well. Blacks who needed a haircut were forced to confine themselves to that rigidly separated neighborhood where blacks resided and where Felix Polk had his barbershop in the back of his house. The deprivations routinely imposed upon blacks almost everywhere were no less apparent in Lincoln, Nebraska, than they had been in Alabama. While there were chilling reminders of the dichotomy between America's words and America's deeds on the subject of democracy, there were faint flickers of hope that engaged my attention as one who wanted to join others in making a difference in promoting my racial equality. It was during my undergraduate years that I had begun to gain considerable respect for black leaders like Walter White, Asa Philip Randolph, Mary McLeod Bethune, Ralph Bunche, and Lester Granger. They seemed to have always been in the forefront, challenging the status quo and somehow being propelled to take on those issues that were pertinent to the masses of black people. The issues that were dominant at the time were white primaries, separate school facilities, poll tax legislation, anti-lynching legislation, and employment practices.

Because of the initiatives of A. Philip Randolph, who founded the Brotherhood of Sleeping Car Porters, President Franklin Delano Roosevelt had issued Executive Order No. 8802 that established the wartime Fair Employment Committee. The order was issued in response to Randolph's threat and crusade to conduct a national March-on-Washington to protest unfair employment practices. President Roosevelt had short-circuited the impact that the protest might have had; however, the march was cancelled. Randolph, not satisfied with the status of oppressed black Americans, began to shake the foundations of the Washington governmental establishment by agitating for integration in the armed services. In fact, he announced plans to lead a drive of civil disobedience against the draft. He had face-to-face encounters with President Truman, who ultimately issued two executive orders on July 26, 1948, one creating an FEPC board to eliminate racial discrimination in federal employment, and the other to establish a President's Committee on Equal Treatment and Opportunity.

Earlier on October 23, 1947, the NAACP had filed a petition to the United Nations and had filed "An Appeal to the World" to intervene in

America's domestic affairs in order to address the issue of racial segregation, racial discrimination, and the general oppression of black Americans.

Thus, the period that was to initiate the decade of the 1950s offered some degree of optimism relative to the issue of race. There was at least some evidence that things were beginning to change in a positive direction for the African-American community. Race relations committees began to sprout into existence across the land. The separate-but-equal doctrine of segregation was being challenged by Thurgood Marshall and the staff of the NAACP Legal and Educational Fund. Black and white people began to organize committees, councils and commissions to combat racism in various quarters. Pamphlets, periodicals, and books on race relations were being published in abundance. None had a greater impact than the monumental work of the Swedish sociologist Gunnar Myrdal. The comprehensive report on the Negro in American society was entitled *An American Dilemma: The Negro Problem in American Society.* This celebrated, encyclopedic study forced America to take a hard look, to do some soul-searching, and to undertake some programs and strategies to address society's major problems.

It was because of this climate that I was determined to become a participant in an arena that would bring America face-to-face with the reality that it could not deny. I became active in SAC (The Student Action Council) at the University of Nebraska. It was composed of a group of dedicated student leaders on campus, not the least of whom was Ruth Sorenson, the aspiring sister of Theodore Sorenson. Theodore later served as special counsel to President Kennedy. In later years, I met another brilliant brother of the same Nebraska family, Philip, who was a professor in the law school during my tenure at The Ohio State University. The University of Nebraska was a wonderful place to go to school. This is not an extravagant statement, when I remember what an effect classroom and student union discussions had on my growth and understanding of contemporary issues. The members in SAC were a precocious bunch. Beyond classroom commitments, many of them had nothing but time on their hands. They read everything they could—*The New York Times, Harpers, The Atlantic Monthly, Foreign Affairs,* etc. While some time was spent in the frivolous, frothy and trivial things that are typical of college students, the acquisition of knowledge seemed paramount.

It was a great discovery when it became apparent to me that most of the black students with whom I was acquainted did not have the luxury of unlimited time to engage in such multiplied opportunities for reading and for the dialectic exchanges that such reading prompted. Black students were too busy trying to survive as they fanned out into the community after classes, pursuing a variety of part-time jobs just to keep the wolf away, as the old folks used to say. My unique connection with Anderson Construction Company had liberated me to have the time to do my thesis research and to participate in some of the activities of SAC. A handful of us decided that it was time to integrate some of the local restaurants, but the walls of tradition were not about to fall simply because we had decided to arrive on the scene. The Mayfair Grill became our first test case. Our strategy was a simple one—eight of us, four whites and four blacks, entered the Grill together and sat down in two separate booths. In a fraction of a moment, scowls creased the faces of white patrons as well as the white waitresses who were begrudging of any activity that dared to tamper with their well-established system of racial apartheid. Time stood still, bodies—black and white—appeared motionlessly frozen, and the road ahead looked endless.

We conversed in subdues tones, posturing nonchalantly, even as we felt ourselves penetrated by the multiple stares of onlookers. Time seemed like eternity as we buried ourselves behind the printed menus that had been well-placed on the tables prior to our arrival. We had shared many good thoughts and ideas about what to do and how to behave in such situations, but each of us now suffered the humiliation and intimidation of a system that gave no hint of change. Although people who had entered after us were being served, no one gave us the slightest attention until the seating had reached its capacity. Then some shallow-brained waitress finally came to inform us that they would not be able to serve us. It was at that point of humiliation and embarrassment that I demanded to speak with the manager. Suddenly, and with authoritarian gusto, he rushed to our area and declared, "We don't serve black people here."

Gathering my best upbringing and speaking in my best English, I countered, "Sir, we are a group of cultured and well-informed students at the university, and we know that we are as civil and as well-bred as any of your other patrons here. We are good citizens, and we don't intend to leave, but if you force us to, we will return with hundreds more, day after day, until you accept us, or until we close the place down."

To our astonishment, he capitulated. "Well, okay then; we'll serve you, but don't give us any trouble."

It was a momentous victory, but then we had misgivings about eating the food of an adversary. What was also so disturbing on that occasion was the fact there were inaudible supporters, even nodding their heads in assent as I confronted the manager. It alerted me to the reality of the multitude of silent people who, too, are imprisoned by a system that forces us at times into unexpected situations of cowardice. The walls of racism that so envelop this nation would tumble overnight if the people who have a sense of justice and fair play would only stand up and be counted.

Over the period of a year, we managed to be instrumental in tearing down racial walls at numerous establishments, including the Cornhusker Hotel, among others.

But the great desideratum in my life at that time was to complete the requirements of that master's degree. My specific focus was to get as much information on the life, speaking and writing of Frederick Douglass as I possibly could. He had become my hero because he emerged as the first great leader among African-Americans in the United States. The famous historian, Carter G. Woodson, eulogized him in this eloquent tribute: "He was not merely a Negro, asking for the rights of freemen, but the developed emancipated slave going through the country as the embodiment of what the slave was and what he might become." Brilliant and eloquent, Douglass—a former slave—became the father of the Black Protest and Freedom Movement in America. It was this reality that challenged me to undertake and complete my thesis on "A Critical Analysis of the Speaking of Frederick Douglass."

The final paragraph in the conclusion of the thesis indicates why I have often considered him my model.

> We cannot think of slavery without him. We cannot think of the abolitionist movement without him. We cannot think of the Emancipation Proclamation without him. We cannot think of great Negro leaders without him. We cannot think of America without him.

Having completed all of the requirements of course work and my thesis, I was awarded the master of arts degree at the University of Nebraska on the twenty-seventh day of July, 1951. But with the life and forthright experiences of Frederick Douglass so indelibly impressed upon my mind, I was more determined than ever before to use the gifts that God had given me to go about the business of joining others in moving the many mountains that had hindered the progress of my people. My academic successes to this point were a compelling account that angels were watching over me.

Chapter 7

My First Teaching Position

―――――▷◅◦▻◁―――――

Graduating from college was like unveiling a glossy directive for the future. Deep down in my soul, there was a cherished yearning to challenge the system of white domination that had not produced its own guarantees of a democratic and free society for my people. Things were relatively calm on the racial front, at least as far as exhibitions of vociferous demonstrations and protests were concerned. Yet the bold and articulate images of Asa Philip Randolph, Paul Robeson, and Thurgood Marshall saturated my desire to confront the frustrating elements that seemed to impale the black community at every turn.

While there was increasing evidence of piecemeal gains in some unprecedented areas of employment, in voting patterns in the South, and in black college enrollment, overall progress was miniscule, particularly among the masses of black people. It was obvious that the system had orchestrated an effective public relations coup, making it appear that the gains made by middle-class blacks solved the bristling tension of those held hostage by the seething and overcrowded conditions of the major metropolitan ghettos.

The day-to-day conditions of race—problems of health, poverty, unemployment, housing, crime, producing despair and doom—dampen one's spirits over time. It is at such times that there is the temptation and the mental mechanism of survival to engage in fruitless fantasy, the kind of extravagant daydreaming that serves as a tranquilizing antidote to all of the torturing torments of a racist society. When people get tired of *fighting the man* full time, they tend to salvage their self-esteem through evasion, escape, and by magnifying small advances. It becomes a strategy of unsophisticated preventive maintenance against social corrosion and insanity. It is no wonder that James Baldwin insisted "that any Negro who is born in this country... runs the risk of becoming schizophrenic."

Those factors called my attention to the fact that knowledge needed to be a primary focus in the culture of African-Americans. Self-interest tempted me to attack my own state of limited means by searching for the quickest and most substantial way of taking advantage of my advanced level of training. There was the tug of matching my talents and my training to the highest bidder. My allurement toward the latter goal was whetted almost immediately following the graduation ceremonies. As I walked briskly and confidently toward the University of Nebraska bookstore to return the master's gown that I had rented, a shiny, long, black impressive limousine pulled up to the curb and stopped. A well-dressed gentleman in the front seat passenger's side initiated the conversation by saying, "Congratulations Frank. How would you like to have a job making $5000 a week?"

As he cast a stealthy and roguish look in my direction, I instantaneously froze, saying to myself, "Something's got to be wrong with such an outrageously exorbitant offer to one whose experience at best was only minimal and marginal."

"What are you going to be doing?" he asked, as his eyes penetrated searchingly for my response. "Come on and ride with us. We have heard of your stellar accomplishment in promotion and public relations. We'll guarantee you a fortune in short order!"

There was something about his wily and mischievous manner that gave me the courage to be categorically decisive with my unexpected visitors. "Thank you for your offer, sir, but I will be pursuing my career in the field of higher education." Even though I had already made my decision to cast my lot with Oakwood College prior to that encounter, there was something about that experience that reminded me that real wealth cannot be measured in possessions alone. As I listened to the inner voice within me, it confirmed my earlier verdict and resolution to serve as a teacher for the advancement of my people. That moment lives in my mind as though it were yesterday. It was the kind of unsuspected experience which, no doubt, is a symptom of the kind of day-to-day allurements that our youth fall prey to at the behest of unprincipled and unscrupulous charlatans. But for the grace of God, through the instant warning of my inner conscience, I might very well have been another statistic among those who surrender and become so easily discomposed in their lust for fame and fortune. It is not always so easy for black youth who are locked into the senseless caverns and jungles of bewildering chaos—struggling with the tensions of crime, poverty, and general discontent in their neighborhoods—to resist the sullen and crafty intrigues of those who offer them an immediate antidote and relief to the profound pain and vicious darkness that enshrouds every waking and sleeping moment of their lives.

The year 1951 was another included in the early 1950s in which the paranoia of anti-communism was kept alive by the tauntings and ravings of Senator Joseph McCarthy who hunted for Communists under every rock imaginable. There was such a wave of hysteria that the government was able to get mass support for its hasty program of military spending, military production, all predicated on an all-out policy of rearmament. Because the country was on an aggressive flurry of military expansionism, support for civil rights and initiatives in behalf of African-Americans came to a virtual standstill.

Earlier in the year, April 3, 1951 to be exact, I had received an offer to connect with Oakwood College from Elder Frank L. Peterson, the institution's distinguished president. It read:

Dear Mr. Hale:

… The local Board of the College met Sunday, April 1, and among the many progressive actions taken was the one inviting you to con-nect with the college as assistant professor of English and speech. Your salary was set at $42.50 per week.

Mr. Hale we hope you will see your way clear to join our staff and help us build a greater Oakwood…

It should not be difficult to imagine my cautionary bent to accepting the call to Oakwood, especially after receiving a second letter from President Peterson on April 22, 1951, which read:

Dear Mr. Hale:

Upon my return from Washington I found your letter. Housing at Oakwood has been one of our great problems, and we are hoping this problem will be lessened when we can secure funds to build homes for teachers.

Professor Banks will be on a leave of absence for the coming year at the University of Southern California. You may have his apartment which is in the Omega House. It has three rooms and a bath. One room is extra large.

As a rule our teachers have provided their own furnishings, but we have furnished a few at their request. The rent for unfurnished varies from $18.00 to $20.00 a month. The water bill is $1.00 a month. Heat is $3.50 a month and our light at the college is now on the city system, and light bills are paid in Huntsville according to the amount used. The same as in other cities...

Although I had been offered a similar position at Lincoln University in Jefferson City, Missouri, for approximately $500 a month by Dr. Cecil Blue, chairman of the English Department, my doubts were quickly set aside as the tug of my earlier experiences at *The Oaks* charged my commitment and my consent to my accepting the call for the lean sum of $170 per month. Every moment was filled with anticipation after that and helped to confirm my dedication to the historic profession of teaching which for so long had been a rewarding tradition on the Banks side of my family genealogy.

That year at Oakwood lives on in my mind as a benchmark to all that has transpired in the vital and vigorous interlocking experiences that have added richness to my life. In August, 1951, my family (my wife Ruth, and her namesake, Ruthie, two years and eleven months, and myself) set foot on the red clay soil of Alabama, anxious to absorb some of nature's great truths, the magnitude of southern culture, and the indescribable beauty of the Oakwood campus that added to the character and fiber of an institution that put Christian education and a Christian atmosphere above everything.

Huntsville, Alabama, where the college is located, is well-situated in the northeastern corner of Alabama. Often referred to as Rocket City, U.S.A., it is the home of the Redstone Arsenal, the rocket and guided-missile center of the United States Army. It was there that Werner Von Braun and other scientists developed the nation's first large guided missiles during the 1950s and designed the rockets that carried U.S. astronauts to the moon in the 1960s. The city was Alabama's first state capitol in 1819 and 1820.

I had certain advantages at the start. I was a member of the Seventh-day Adventist Church, the religious denomination which had created and sustained the college from its inception in 1896. Additionally, I was acquainted with its rich history. As a teenager, I had become absorbed in reading a very challenging document entitled "Our Duty to the Colored People" (later designated the *Southern Work*) which was written by Ellen G. White, a very significant leader and prophetess within the Seventh-day Adventist Church. Her positive influence on matters of race relations was not lost on her son, James Edson White, who constructed and christened a houseboat, *The Morning Star*, and set it to sail from Allegan, Michigan, and ultimately to Vicksburg, Mississippi, where it docked in January of 1895.

It was through the influence of White and his mother which provided the enlightenment and urgency that activated the 1895 session of the General Conference held in Battle Creek, Michigan, to decide that an industrial school for black youth should be established in the South. As a consequence of this action, a committee of G.A. Irwin, director of the Southern District of the General Conference; O.A. Olsen, president of the General Conference; and H. Lindsay, a former treasurer of the General Conference was formed.

Soon their efforts bore fruit as they discovered the 360 acre Beasily estate, approximately five miles northwest of town. The committee made its report to the General Conference, giving, in unabridged detail, a description of the land, the buildings, and prospects for expansion. Irwin and Olsen returned to Huntsville after receiving the approval of the leaders in Washington and purchased the property for $6500. Dispersed throughout the acreage were sixty-five lofty oak trees; thus, the school was designated Oakwood Industrial School. The school opened its doors to sixteen students on November 16, 1896. Eight years later on June 24, 1904, Mrs. White cautioned and encouraged the leaders, "Never, never part with an acre of this land. It is to educate hundreds."

I had been at Oakwood seven years earlier as a freshman student and personally knew members of the Board, the faculty, and the general composition of the student body. I had been schooled in the details of problems—academic, financial, and disciplinary—by such trusted colleagues as Elder C. E. Moseley, Dr. O. B. Edwards, Dr. Eva B. Dykes, Dr. Gaines Partridge, and Mr. Lewis Ford.

But it was my own sense of history that undergirded my new beginning. My creative energies were enhanced by the adherence to those promptings that were underscored by Mrs. White in "Our Duty to the Colored People" when she admonished, "We should educate colored men to be missionaries among their own people. We should recognize talent where it exists among that people, and those who have ability should be placed where they may receive an education." However young and experienced I was at the time, the long look back propelled me to look forward with hope and confidence.

In those days Oakwood was a very small college. There were not enough students—at least enough on Plan I (all cash) to provide the institution with the caliber of teachers and the equipment required to maintain a quality program. Even though the country was on what appeared to be a permanent war economy, there were still huge pockets of poverty. The distribution of wealth still plagued those families which were at the lower fifth of the income ladder which included a disproportionate number of black families. The lowest fifth of the families received five percent of all the income; the highest fifth received forty-five percent of all the income. 1.6 percent of the adult population owned more than eighty percent of the corporate stock and nearly ninety percent of the corporate bonds. It was an aggressive foreign policy that undercut opportunities for the poor on the home front. And as a small college, Oakwood recruitment prospects were dimmed by the fact that most black families felt the severe pinch of economic reality.

While there was a corps of teachers—dedicated, gifted, productive, and cooperative—Elder Frank Loris Peterson, the president of the college, was the central figure who was responsible and effective in sharpening the identity and image of the college from a national and international perspective. A distinguished gentleman of regal bearing, Peterson was greatly revered by teachers, students, and parents alike. Having taught at Oakwood during the period from 1917 to 1926, he possessed a thorough knowledge of the school's history and its mission. A man of voluminous knowledge and talent, he exhibited an air of unaffected superiority that gave those around him a sense of confidence in his competency as the chief administrator of the institution. Stately and articulate, his lectures in chapel were literary gems, and his sermons on Sabbath unraveled the mysteries of the Word with marvelous magnificence and with indescribable linguistic beauty. As students, we sat mesmerized to the miracles of coloring with which he punctuated his every thought and word.

There were other giants in the land who had an all- absorbing influence on the pages of my life at that time. I felt the imperious exactness of Dr. Otis B. Edwards who exhibited little or no softness or flabbiness in his approach to classroom assignments. Dr. Eva B. Dykes challenged students to seize every opportunity, reminding them that four things come not back: the spoken word, the sped arrow, the past life, and the neglected opportunity. Elder C. E. Moseley reminded us all that education which does not ennoble, elevate and refine is a curse instead of a blessing. Thus students who matriculated at Oakwood at that time could plunge into the swing of things, knowing that they had a faculty and administrators that they could count on to insulate them, at least to some extent, from the pressures that are brought to bear on youth at secular institutions of learning. What a wonderful contrast and opportunity that was afforded us to attend a Christian college.

As an institution under the auspices of the Seventh-day Adventist Church, Oakwood stood as a beacon of religious conservatism. The literal interpretation of the Bible was the *modus operandi*. A government committee was in place to enforce all of the decrees of the church and the college. The theory of creationism was undisputed in terms of the origin of man. Strict dietary regulations were held sacrosanct. Dress codes were rigidly adhered to, and the sexes were mandated to keep their distance from each other in matters of physical contact. In short, traditions had been carefully preserved so as not to corrupt cherished principles or to alienate church leadership and those constituencies that never cease to monitor the activities of the college under the watchful eyes of their ubiquitous observations. In sum, conservatism did not surrender at any point without a struggle.

Things had not changed too much from the time that I had been a student at the college. Moran Hall, the stone citadel, named in honor of Elder J. L. Moran, who was Oakwood's first president (1932-1945), still stood in noble grandeur as the major classroom building on campus. Recognizing the singular achievements of several other African-American Adventists, the college board had already designated the women's residence hall as Eugenia I. Cunningham Hall; the men's residence as Frank L. Peterson Hall; the science building as Harry E. Ford Hall; the library as William H. Green Hall; and the demonstration school as Anna Knight Elementary School. Old Mansion, the historic landmark where Andrew Jackson had once attended social gatherings before the Oakwood property was purchased, still—though weather-beaten—had withstood the rigors of every year since the founding of the college. East Hall, originally an orphanage, had served multiple purposes including an infirmary, classrooms, counseling center, offices, and as a place of residence for Dr. Eva B. Dykes. Its extended porches offered promenading opportunities to observe the beauty of the campus profuse with the elegance of splendid trees, some more than one hundred years old, and the generous fragrance of the blossoming honeysuckle and the flowering lilac shrubs and bushes.

It was quite evident to me that some of the teachers did not remain long at their posts, as a considerable number, who were in the faculty when I was a student, were no longer on the staff. When one begins looking for reasons for the relatively high attrition rate among the faculty and staff, it was not too difficult to discover that some of it had to do with the reality of sheer survival. The standard of living, even as modest as it was compared to today's standard, was not the norm at the college. Dedicated as most of those teachers were to the mission of the institution, some simply did not earn sufficient means to grapple with the necessities of day-to-day upkeep. I became painfully aware of the struggle after my first year at the college, having depleted the $3000 in savings that I had preserved prior to my arrival. I had certainly been resourceful, almost to a fault, and had conserved funds by joining J. T. Stafford on periodic hikes to the mountain on a mule wagon that we had borrowed from the farm to cut fallen timber, load the wagon, and drop the pile of wood between our two houses for winter fuel. We scraped the bark from sassafras trees to use in flavoring hot tea throughout the year. Additionally, we took full advantage of the reduced prices that were available to us when we purchased milk from the college dairy or obtained fruit and vegetable products from the farm. Lawrence Jacobs, the farm and dairy manager, was always an accommodating spirit and gave ungrudging service to any who visited the farm or dairy.

There was a nucleus of faculty and staff who appeared to form the backbone of the institution. Elder C. E. Moseley, Jr., was unrivaled as a teacher and preacher of truth. As a solid Christian scholar and department head, he was indeed a role model of righteousness who was responsible for shaping and placing his stamp on scores and scores of ministers. Elder Otis B. Edwards was a rock of integrity and comprehensive knowledge in the field of history. He brought a sense of consistency and persistence to his profession that earned him the respect of both his peers and his students.

Dr. Natelka Burrell was a professor of education, and she molded the character and shaped the destiny of those students who had determined that the field of teaching would be their lot. Without any of the base airs that are derived from a gilded heritage, she possessed a refinement and dignity that bespoke her inner integrity. As a consequence, she won universal respect, admiration and affection.

Though not the picture of professional refinement, Professor Robert Reynolds was known for his matter-of-fact direct style in teaching and in conversation. He was always able to capture the attention of his biology students with his humorous and satirical comments about life. There appeared to be no stress sufficient to dim his self-tutored outlook on life. Students gave him high marks for his method of teaching, that was direct, colorful, clear, and occasionally sprinkled with a few choice obscenities. He brought a surprising degree of free speech to the campus that appeared to go unchallenged.

Dr. Gaines Partridge was the spokesman through which most of the extracurricular activities of college were channeled. He did much to raise artistic standards on campus. An appreciative student body responded to the pathos of his dramatic skits, flourished by the colorful paintings that he designed for his backdrops. Many in the campus community were especially receptive to the lure of the floodlights that Partridge introduced as a new mechanical device that brought realism to the stage productions that were so masterfully performed by students. Partridge also maintained a rather enigmatic presence among the young men because of his highly visible role as dean of men. His firm and towering presence represented grief for those whose lifestyle was sufficiently imperfect and irksome as to provoke his ire. All in all, he saw to it that the lighter side of life was not neglected even in such a provincial and conservative setting as a Christian college known for its singularly austere standards.

Aside from the limited number of diversions to which the Oakwood family was accustomed, none offered more social enjoyment than the *Oakwood March*. This activity brought the student body alive at some impromptu moment after a series of table games, musical chairs and the kind of ongoing social chatter that was a part of a typical Saturday night social gathering. The Oakwood March could very well have been labeled the *Oakwood Strut* as it was full of extraordinarily vigorous and fanciful variations. It was the one time in the evening when the fellows, trained to be gallant, rushed to capture the young lady of their choice before crowding the floor to the tune of "Steal Miss Liza, Little Liza Jane." Most of the young ladies, precociously well-mannered, blushed with approval and excitement when they were fortunate enough to be on the arm of the beau of their choice. The marching was so full of variations: some marchers were tame, moving sedately and measuring each step; others introduced their latest innovations with combinations that were a vigorous mixture of whirling, gyrating, and jigging. There were times when it was necessary to tap certain couples on the shoulder, suggesting that they assume a more orthodox pattern in their movements. The faculty, recognizing that there were few outlets for the students on such occasions, were far more indulgent than the language that was expressed in the student handbook concerning appropriate behavior during such social activities.

There were only a few opportunities for recreation at Oakwood during those days. I can think of no first-class physical facilities that would accommodate swimming, basketball, bowling, shuffleboard, tennis, track or even baseball. A few students had become enthusiastic when arrangements were made for them to rent skates so that they could skate on the cement basement floor or Moran Hall. It was a complicated exercise to be able to maneuver around the assortment of steel poles that kept the first floor from crashing into our subterranean play space. It was a noble communion that the students enjoyed in that cave of contentment every Sunday because, at other times during the week, the walls silhouetted the figures of students as they crammed into the makeshift classroom space. The creaking of the floorboards overhead helped us to identify the symphony of dragging feet, swift strides, and syncopated shuffles that were rambling, strolling and promenading in the halls above.

Young enough myself at age twenty-four, I joined vicariously in the thrill of their congested arena of activity. I felt, too, given the limited economic resources of the college at that time, that there was no intent on the part of the administration to provide additional space for the students to enjoy their skating activity. I felt within me a gnawing uneasiness and helplessness concerning the situation, about which I could do nothing at the time. After all, I was the new kid on the block, and I was hired to teach, not to make waves. In the meanwhile, though, I scarcely suppressed my complicity with those wonderful youth and their need and right to share in some of the marvelous diversions that should be accompaniments of youth, I seriously committed myself to the tasks to which I had been assigned. That charge included teaching two sections of freshman composition, college grammar, and introduction to public speaking.

To begin with, I felt an uncompromising commitment and loyalty to the profession of teaching. The image of Luvada Lockhart, my fourth grade teacher, was indelible. Already I agreed with William Arrowsmith, who insisted that teachers possess the human skills which gives them the power to humanize others. But his uncompromising punch line stated that, "If that power is not felt, nothing of educational value can occur." I felt keenly that among the most despicable and odious tragedies in life is for a so-called teacher to dim or crash the radiant hunger that a student has for believing, becoming and belonging.

Earlier, I had flirted with the possibilities of my becoming a physician, a lawyer, or a preacher. In fact, while debating my options as a college student, I carried minors in chemistry, biology, religion, English, and music. My parents' bookstore had provided me with the ammunition of intellectual excitement to the degree that, for an extended period, I was very tentative about my career choice. My ambivalence was due primarily to the reality that I enjoyed the subject matter of most academic disciplines.

Then, there was a family tradition of teaching across the range of elementary, secondary and higher education institutions. Four of my aunts, Georgette Banks, Ida Banks, Gladys Banks and Isy Banks, had all been elementary school teachers in Virginia. Six of my first cousins were also teachers. Dr. Elfleda Tate holds the Ed.D. degree in higher education from the University of Southern California; her twin sister, Dr. Marian Patterson also has a Ph.D. in higher education with a concentration in mathematics from the University of Southern California. Four of my cousins, registered nurses, taught school at different times during their careers. They are sisters: Susie Green Brown, Georgette Green Thompson, Edwina Green Jackson, and Evelyn Green.

With such a rich family tradition, I felt limited only by my failure to accept what was both conspicuous in my genes and in my zeal to contribute to the advancement of black young people.

It was also overwhelmingly clear to me that Christian education was the route that I should take at the time. I felt, too, that it was unalterably treacherous to focus solely on reading, 'riting and 'rithmetic to the exclusion of religion, respect and responsibility, as was the case in public education. So my decision to go into the teaching profession was based on spiritual, family and racial perspectives that, while not altogether in concrete, were at least beginning to congeal. I had absolutely no inclination of what time would bring in terms of my own identity, personal or professional.

That first year was both joyous and overwhelming as I was obsessed with the opportunities and possibilities that my freshman year in the profession afforded me. I experienced some anxieties that were too piercing to conquer right away. The reality of my youthful years began to sink in as I compared my inescapable immaturity to some of the Korean veterans who initially clung to some degree of skepticism because of my inexperience. I refused to be boxed in by my youth, but instead attempted to make it unmistakably clear that I was prepared for the challenge. Thus, I pledged all of my inner spiritual and educational resources to serve as a bridge between my students and myself. I came to regard my work as a ministry within itself as I observed light in the eyes of those who were focused on taking advantage of every morsel of truth that I could confer.

Life is an intersection of spiritual and secular tracks. Christian education concentrates on the all-important aspect of character training. It makes spirituality the center of the universe so that it is not overshadowed by the worlds of prestige, power, materialism, and success. These aspects of human existence are not corrupt within themselves when God is the nucleus of our lives, but at best, they are only fragmentary when He is not our priority. My new position made it extremely important for me to recognize and accept God as my co-pilot.

Every day offered me a new thrill in the classroom. Even at moments when I felt a sense of unreadiness or panic, I had the remarkable advantage of having Dr. Eva B. Dykes, the chairperson of the Department of English, as my mentor. It was not necessary for me to search the pages of black history for a role model to quicken my vaulting desire to be the best teacher that I could be; Dr. Dykes was a revered institution all by herself. Intensely passionate about learning and teaching, I captured her spirit and never hesitated to seek her advice and counsel on those matters about which I only had a superficial knowledge. My performance as an instructor and as one of her faithful assistants endeared me to her. She depended heavily upon me to spend long hours into the night, grading themes which she had required her students to write in class. I found myself spending extended hours that often left me wilted and out of joint upon completing assignments which she had required of me. It was not uncommon for us to grade papers from 6:00 P.M. (after supper) until 10:00 or 11:00 in the evening. After the first two or three months of this routine, I had to humorously remind the good doctor that I was not married to the English Department and that I needed to spend most of my evenings at home. Fortunately, she did not offer the slightest challenge to my civil protest.

Oakwood was a center for training prospective black ministers for the Seventh-day Adventist Church. In a short time, my wife and I developed some warm relationships among a few choice friends, a number of whom were ministerial students. James Melancon, Herman Vanderberg, Eunice Vanderberg, Mervyn Warren, and Calvin Rock were especially close to us. All five spent considerable time in attacking what was set before them at the dinner table with some degree of frequency. We could conceive of no greater joy than to have them as members of our extended family. So often when it was necessary for me to attend out of town meetings, Melancon, Warren, and Vanderberg voluntarily checked on my wife and Ruthie, my three year old daughter. They did errands, brought logs into the house during the winter for our wood-burning stove, and did periodic checks to be sure that my family was comfortable and secure. Calvin Rock served as my reader, grading papers after I had supplied him with the answers. Occasionally, we invited him and Clara Peterson (his fiance) to dinner, of course, only with approval of Clara's father, President Peterson. If my recollection is clear, Calvin proposed to Clara in our living room during one Sunday evening.

The academic and disciplinary demands on the students were heroic, so much so that a number of those who were there at the time assumed positions of leadership and influence in later years. Included among them were the following: William Allegne, Charles Campbell, James Edgecombe, William Scales, Lemuel Seely, Robert Sloan, David Taylor, Antoinette Bailey, Eloise Daye, Herbert Doggette, Eunice Jones, Ted Jones, Benjamin Reaves, Joseph Rhyne, Simon Johnson, Lona Nell Lea, Doris Mickle, James Washington, Donald Blake, Lyle Follette, Helen George, James Hammond, Douglas Tate, Vivian Watson, Jesse Wagner, and Milton Young.

Of course it was a very dedicated and committed administration and faculty that superbly contributed to the development and future advancement of the college. Most of them brought a high degree of conscientiousness and devotion of duty to their responsibilities. They quickly reaffirmed my faith in the value and integrity of Christian education. President Peterson had a loyal corps of administrators: Otis B. Edwards, dean of the college; Adell Warren, business manager; Roberta C. Edwards, registrar; Ruth E. Mosby, dean of women; Robert L. Woodfork, dean of men; Ruth N. Stafford, director of health services; J.G. Towery, librarian; and James Meredith, accountant.

A number of capable thinkers and teachers adorned the college faculty; however, few, with the notable exception of Dr. Dykes, enjoyed a national reputation. The cut-and-dried tradition of Oakwood being the primary province for religion majors and ministerial students alone forced the institution to face the challenge of an increasingly industrialized society. This, of course, brought demands for specialized training in business and in the sciences. While academic major requirements still remained prescriptive, the elective system was gaining in popularity on campus, and students were permitted to choose more courses in cafeteria fashion.

Peterson's administration was packed with an array of solid hardworking teachers and staff persons: John Beale, Clarence Richards*, Ernest Rogers, and Robert Woodfork in Religion; Otis Edwards* and Murray Harvey in History; Robert Reynolds* and John Bookhardt in Biology; Charles Galley* and Celeste Frazier in Business; Emerson Cooper* in Science and Mathematics; Eva B. Dykes*, Henrietta Emmanuel, Ruth E. Mosby, and Frank W. Hales, Jr., in English; Natelka Burrell*, Katrina Nesbitt, Gaines R. Partridge*, Violin Plummer, Ruth N. Stafford, and Violet Wiles in Education; Thomasine Longware* in Home Economics; Inez Booth, Hugh Creary and Samuel C. Jackson* in Music; and Carpel Desvarieux and Flora Ossario in Foreign Languages.

The professional and industrial staff included Wilma Minisee, secretary to the business manager; Katie Walker, assistant to the accountant; Festus Valentine, manager of the college store; Marile Emerson, director of the laundry; Ralph Davis, manager of the broom industry; Joseph C. Emerson, maintenance manager; Dennis Crosby, supervisor of the farm and dairy; George Harris, superintendent of grounds; Chessie Harris, college matron; and Genevive Richards and Eugenia Cunningham, post office mistresses.

(*) Indicates department heads.

The Oakwood Academy (secondary school) also had its share of competent and dedicated teachers. Its capable principal, Joseph Stafford, was buttressed by John Beale in Bible, Cordell Evans in Mathematics and English, and Marcheta Valentine in Spanish and Home Economics.

Good music has always been a dominant force on the Oakwood campus. Year after year the college was blessed with a new infusion of rich artistic talent to match her rich tradition of artistry. Inez Booth had been a fixture in the Music Department dating back to the late 1930s. She was a mainstay as a teacher and as an instrumentalist on the organ during chapel and Sabbath services. Samuel Jackson brought a no-nonsense exacting temperament to his position as Director of the College Choir. Students knew better than to be inattentive and frivolous during his rehearsals or performances; yet when it was time to relax, no one could be more engaging and jovial.

Lush with musical talent, the college was teeming with gifted musicians. Instrumentalists Ann Battle, Allen Breach, Ted Jones and Gracye Howard were always enhancing to the soloists or groups that they accompanied from time to time. They also elevated the musical taste of the environment with their own individual presentations. There were vocalists like William Scales and Pearl Harvey who were stimulating as their voices reflected the inspirational spirit of the campus. The College Choir, the All-Girls Chorus, and the Oratorio Society poured most of their creative efforts into church services during the Divine Hour on Sabbath. The Oratorio Society blazed brilliantly during the Christmas holidays in its historic and customary presentation of Handel's *Messiah* which began with the candlelight procession, *Adeste Fidelis,* and concluded with the majestic and awe-inspiring "Hallelujah Chorus" under the direction of Samuel C. Jackson. Featured soloists were Majorie Vincent and Hugh Creary.

The musical reputation of the campus also flourished under the blossoming influence of the Oakwood College Male Chorus. It was during the spring of 1952 that President Peterson asked me to accompany the group on a tour of the Far West. Combining a pleasing robust style with personal charm, with rhythmic and nostalgic songs, and with stately masculine dignity under the direction of Samuel Jackson, they were immensely popular, both at home and on the concert circuit. I will never forget how steadily we worked our way across the country in three cars, taking the southern route, to make concert appearances in Memphis, New Orleans, Phoenix, Albuquerque, San Diego, Los Angeles, Bakersfield, Stockton, Fresno, San Francisco, Sacramento, Denver, Topeka, Kansas City, and St. Louis, before coming to a providentially profitable halt after a six-week absolutely exhausting but stimulating experience.

The more than seven thousand mile journey taught us more than enough about tolerance. The press of tight masculine bodies crammed against each other stretched one's patience after a while. To cut the boredom, in between stops, there was persistent singing and rousing harmony in order for the fellows to maintain their sanity. It took more than a little doing when folks were huddled together in one another's territory—and at times not sufficiently deodorized to bear the pungency of what had become a corporate predicament. At such times, all of the harmony in the world sounded flat and could not conquer the frustration and fatigue. Time goes unaccounted for between long stretches in seemingly endless journeys.

We, nevertheless, always looked forward to our next assignment—usually on the evening after we had traveled most of the day. Thank God, Pop Willis, one of the veteran senior students, assisted me in monitoring the activities of the group. There were those non-timid souls among us who relished independence and challenge to a fault. Milton, with his booming voice, was a nourisher of dialectic, as gardeners are of plants, growing them from nothing but by the heat of controversy and watering them daily with blood. He loved to debate just for the fun of it. Had my will been less daunted, I might well have been ready grist for his unyielding adventurism.

Then there was Jesse who possessed soft-boiled hazel eyes of unusual power. He could disquiet a young lady at a glance and take the manhood away from a man for whom he had disdain. He could woo with his tongue as his words were sufficient to befuddle the girls, unsettling them into blushing pleasure and shock. Fierce in refutation, he was quick and elaborate in argumentation. Yet, when he wanted to be, he was smilingly smooth, to the extent that he was able to mesmerize most anyone into accepting his point of view when he put his mind to it. His fresh and charming personality predictably would carry him far. I enjoyed the spirit of these two fellows in particular because they never allowed custom to hide the wonders of their inquisitiveness.

We were welcomed with exuberant enthusiasm everywhere we went. The church members handled our ravishing appetites with shocking ease. Usually we arrived at the sponsoring church where a sumptuous meal had been prepared for us several hours before the concert. We soon discovered that it was still a man's world as the ladies, young and old, waited on us hand and foot. Our plates were scarcely emptied before we were offered great quantities of delicious food which we lost little time in consuming.

Dr. and Mrs. John Richard Ford were a perfect host and hostess when we arrived in San Diego, California. As a path-breaking thoracic surgeon, Dr. Ford had established an extensive practice, along with his hand-picked team of physicians, at his beautiful and expensive clinic on Imperial Highway. The Fords' magnificent home rested on one of the highest points in the city overlooking the San Diego harbor. It was indeed a well-chosen earthly paradise. Their fanciful food and hospitality were so sumptuous that we managed to ignore time. The rush was on to refresh ourselves, change clothes, and go to the church for the evening program. When the true moment came to perform, the men recognized and savored it and were ready. The net effect of all the concerts that were given was to recruit students for the following school year by happily promoting the college wherever and whenever possible.

It was still a time when many black Americans tended to judge institutions on the basis of brick and mortar. Some of us knew that there were yet unrealized horizons to be discovered in the classrooms and laboratories of Oakwood. We were still in competition with some of our prestigious institutions like Walla Walla College, Pacific Union College, La Sierra College and Columbia Union College. Nevertheless, we knew that our faculty and our students were vested with the essentials of brain, heart, and soul sufficient to meet the needs of those young people who were seeking to invest in a college that would prepare them for this life and the life to come. We were on the march to liberate those doubters among our people who had become prisoners of their suspicions concerning Oakwood. Our young men conducted themselves in such a superb manner that our application pool increased in an impressive way with each city we visited. A new spirit of warmth and friendliness was created as we talked and fellowshipped with pastors, parents and prospective students. An atmosphere of cautious optimism began to pervade our psyche with each successful appearance.

It was also quite evident that people were beginning to take the mission and contributions of the college quite seriously as they gave heavily and made substantial monetary commitments during the intermission when I had the responsibility of making a fundraising appeal. It was a fantastic spectacle of sacrificial giving as people poured money into the offering plates, some unflinchingly writing checks for $100, $250, and $500 with unrestrained fervor, each giving as God had both blessed and impressed them.

Our prospects never looked rosier than when we were invited to share in the encouragement that came from people like Brother Verrett. Professor Jackson and I were invited to have dinner with him and his family in Oxnard. The Verretts were the parents of Shirley Verrett, who was already being nationally recognized, heralded, and well-launched on her career as an opera singer. She appeared to be cruising uphill toward the main entrance of the Metropolitan Opera House. Brother Verrett was a chocolate-colored hulk of a man. I could tell from his expressive personality and appearance that he knew how to engage life by combining the maximum of his own resourcefulness with the maximum of opportunity. In the secular realm, he held substantial real estate holdings, and in the religious realm, he was faithfully dutiful as a local elder in his church.

When we arrived in Oakland, California, we were initially greeted and welcomed by Henrietta Knight Perry. She and her husband, Wiley, took us to the church in preparation for our evening musical. Henrietta had been one of my campus sisters when I was a student at Oakwood. Her legacy was a rich one, as she was a part of that extended lineage that was rooted in the heritage and influence of Miss Anna Knight, one of the earliest missionaries to India. There was always more than a little curiosity that flavored the discussions which centered around the Knights. There was the novelty of their very fair complexion which offered not the slightest hint of blackness. All of them—Sister Knight, Henrietta, Roscoe, and Hollis—had dark, wavy hair, high cheek bones and aquiline features. Their physical appearance was a reminder of the intolerable indiscretions of slavery. It was rumored that their relatives straddled both sides of the family fence. On one side, there was a big family of sons and daughters who were all white. There was another side of the family that had complexions ranging from white to an olive or sun-bronzed healthy look on whom the physical realities made it perfectly clear that nighttime integration was a fact of life even in Mississippi during those early days. The white side of the family was said to include some very distinguished state officials that included a former governor, as well as local officials. It was interesting, too, that both sides of the family exhibited a breadth of tolerance for each other that was not commonly practiced between whites and blacks generally.

One afternoon while we were in Oakland, out of a clear sky, Henrietta suggested, "Frank, I want you to meet a very interesting man in our congregation. His name is Brother Ridgeway, and he has traveled extensively, collecting artifacts from around the world." I was pleased to accept the invitation which turned out to be a fruitful opportunity. P. W. Ridgeway was a man of cosmopolitan interests. He had traveled around the world twelve times and was already making plans for other excursions. His real estate holdings had propelled both his resources and his interests. Short and somewhat bent, he nevertheless had the manners of a gentleman of quality. Ready to share the accumulated knowledge gained from his many travels, I found him to be a man of fascinating and unquestionable charm. It was an eye-opening and stunning experience to visit his home—a rechristened museum, as it were—filled with hundreds, no doubt thousands, of artifacts from every corner of the globe. We literally stood knee-deep in artistic objects—figurines of wood, clay and rare stone, statuettes with multiple sets of features, masks of every description, warriors in exotic headdresses and quilted armor, and cleverly carved woods that depicted the history of ancient peoples.

I recount with pride and pathos how generously he responded when I suggested to him that someday he should consider sharing his collection with Oakwood, where students, who had never had the opportunity to travel outside of the country, could experience the power, riches, and elegance of his collection. "I will be happy to share the excitement of my many travels with the Oakwood family at the appropriate time," he told me. "God, our Lord, is evident in the lives and artistry of men everywhere," he added in praise.

"Thank you so very much, Brother Ridgeway. I'll keep in touch. What you have here is a cultural heritage that must be conserved and preserved in all of their authenticity. You will have made a contribution to all of us and also to generations yet unborn," I responded.

One of the special delights that I experienced during my tenure as President of Oakwood College was when Mr. Ridgeway shipped a major part of his collection as a gift to the college. Those glorious artifacts had finally met their destiny nearly fifteen years after Brother Ridgeway and I had first discussed the arrangement. His collection will command the respect of students, faculty and staff for decades to come.

While singing and recruiting in Oakland, it was my special pleasure to speak at the church where Elder Harold Lindsay served as pastor. It was evident that he was well-loved and respected, as he gave himself unreservedly to young and old alike without losing anything of his dignity or authority.

Of all the cities we visited in California, San Francisco was, perhaps, the most interesting and attractive. It is very striking because of its magnificent setting, situated on and around more than forty hills. Its captivating appearance reminds one of a giant magnificent amphitheater, as its various residential neighborhoods punctuate the interlacing slopes which rise above the city. We all enjoyed the opportunity to visit those magnificent landmarks that accent the city's rich history—the Civic Center, Market Street, Chinatown, Telegraph Hill, the cable cars, Golden Gate Bridge, Fisherman's Wharf, Alcatraz, and the sparkling blue waters of the Pacific Ocean to the west and San Francisco Bay to the east. Our trip provided rich returns for us, not only because of the spectacular sights which we enjoyed but also because we reaped a high harvest of interest and success among the parents and prospective students which we canvassed. We were especially pleased to gain the wholehearted support of Elder J. E. Cox, Sr., of the Market Street Seventh-day Adventist Church. It was obvious that his years of faithful service to the denomination had made his life an epic of vision, courage, and perseverance.

Despite all of the strain of nightly concerts, we looked forward with great anticipation to the wonders of the unforeseen days ahead. The wheels of our three-car caravan kept humming toward our daily destinations, and the fellows kept singing in our conquest of time, distance, and boredom before arriving at our next appointment. The western lands of America are often barren and limitless. Highways seem to stretch into oblivion and tend to encourage drivers to risk breakneck speeds that would be appallingly dangerous on most other highways. I simply mention this aside to document one of the many influences that contributed to the thrilling saga of our musical tour.

The West, with its raw uninhibited spaces, reminded me of one of Gertrude Stein's famous quotes, "In the United States, there is more space where nobody is than where anybody is." Yet, we fought the elements and the thrill of pursuit to get to Salt Lake City, Utah, the headquarters of the Church of Jesus Christ of Latter-Day Saints. Although we were scheduled to give a concert at the local Seventh-day Adventist church where Elder McCloud was pastor, we were intensely interested in visiting the six-spined Mormon temple and the world-famous Mormon Tabernacle that featured a 375-member choir during its weekly radio broadcasts. Significantly, it was not difficult to become awed by the enormity of these great edifices. They are splendid monuments to an unyielding attachment to the past and an unbounded faith in the future. I left there subdued by the unprecedented impact that freedom of religion has left on America. It should not be taken for granted.

The amazing multiplication of miles continued as we traversed through Colorado, Kansas, Missouri, Kentucky and Tennessee, before returning to Oakwood. One cherishes the memories of such a lavish set of experiences. The campus community was skeptically wondering about our six week experiment in recruitment. Not one to be pushed about, I prepared a detailed report and account of our experiences and shared it with President Peterson, who, in turn, invited me to share the same in chapel, capitalizing on the good results that we had achieved in terms of student applications and the substantial funds which we had received. As outspoken champions of Christian education, the men had been very effective in stimulating broad interest in the college. Their mission had been to swell enrollment during the following year and improve campus morale. The Male Chorus became prime movers in the promotion of Oakwood College. Their role affirmed the fact that students are, perhaps, the most effective and vitalizing force in the recruitment of other students.

After my initial success as a good-will ambassador for the college and the near completion of my first year as a teaching professional, I began to look to the future with fresh and vibrant expectation.

At the time, Dr. Dykes was the only faculty member on the staff who held the coveted doctoral degree. While Oakwood was beginning to attain some respectability, its place in the family of historically black colleges and universities was not among the elite. My belief was taking firm root that an institution of higher learning should be broad-based in its academic offerings and that its faculty should possess the highest degrees attainable. The religious zeal of the denominational fathers had established the institution, but its academic standing was wobbly, as it was not able to furnish the spread of educational opportunities that many eager youth would have sought had they been available.

While I craved for more learning, the pursuit of the Ph.D. degree was beyond the purse of a novice teacher who was earning only $42.50 a week. Even the thought of such a pursuit was utterly implausible until I began to dust off certain possibilities that had begun to erupt in my fertile desire to become a champion of my people.

It was during this time, too, that I was especially touched by the fact that students who attended Oakwood had very few social outlets. They were literally starved recreationally. I became dedicated to the *revolutionary* principle that all religion and education without social development was dehumanizing. Determined and intense, I was sufficiently convinced of my point of view to the extent that I approached President Peterson with a two-pronged proposal. I urged him to consider a plan which I had in mind to raise funds for a magnificent new physical education building where students could skate, play basketball and volleyball, and could enjoy a number of intramural recreational activities. I volunteered to lead out in such a project, if he would consider appointing me as Director of Public Relations alongside my regular teaching duties during the following year. I pledged myself to give the full force of my commitment to this project in addition to my other duties without any additional compensation. I did appeal to President Peterson for an opportunity to pursue the doctorate at college expense at the end of the academic year 1952–53, if I kept my end of the bargain.

President Peterson was amazingly receptive. He recognized the importance of placing the physical, mental and spiritual aspects of Christian education on equitable grounds. He read the future of the institution with strikingly effective and penetrating vision. He was aware of the harmful excesses which could easily occur among youth and which could undermine the mission of the institution, if the social and recreational needs of the students were overlooked. He, too, was cognizant of the need to begin a program of advanced education for faculty members, so that the college would not be confined to the limitations of denominational requirements only. It was extremely important for the institution to measure up to the academic standards of accrediting bodies. While not in any way infringing on its singularly divine mission, Peterson had a way of circumventing certain traditions without losing sight of the purpose for which the institution was founded.

As a consequence, he approved my offer without the slightest reluctance. It was his decision at that moment that turned two keys: the key to Oakwood's broad-mindedness in matters of social and recreational opportunities for its youth and the key to my future as a professional in higher education. I can never forget the pervasive influence that Frank Loris Peterson has had on my life.

So, in June of 1952, I was appointed Director of Public Relations, along with my other assignment as instructor of speech and English. My two full-time jobs had me teaching classes all morning, assuming public relations responsibilities all afternoon, and grading papers far into the evening. It was during that year that my overwhelming load of obligations enlarged my prospects for the future and ultimately propelled my career into inestimable regions of opportunity.

I accepted my new appointment with a sense of relief and inspiration. While I was not totally aware of what I was getting into, I was heartened by the fact that I could depend upon the goodwill of the students and faculty in this new undertaking. Oakwood College had never before made a public appeal, but I was convinced that the time was ripe to approach the citizenry of Huntsville and Madison County, Alabama, for their support in the erection of a recreational facility at Oakwood.

The only two institutions of higher education in the area at that time were Oakwood College and Alabama A&M College—both black institutions. In each case, their faculty and student body poured multiplied thousands of dollars of patronage into the business communities of the area. Good will for Oakwood ran incredibly high in the community because of its specialized emphasis on Christian standards and Christian behavior. At any rate the case for the college as a character builder was consistently reinforced as students from the college rarely were guilty of even the slightest misdemeanor or encounter in the community. There were also numerous services that the college offered the town. Its dairy and farm provided milk and produce; its print shop supplied businesses with stationery, invoices, and other materials; and its broom factory furnished stock for various business enterprises as well as for local households. These reasons, along with others, were merged into our justification for beginning a powerful public relations campaign in behalf of our project.

As there had been no precedent for such an effort, it was impossible to contemplate what our most energetic efforts might yield financially. Thorough preparations were made. The student body was organized into committees. An intense excitement prevailed on campus as students and faculty entered heartily into the spirit of the campaign. Student leaders were elected to organize committees on publicity, solicitations, volunteers, public relations, special gifts, campaign brochures, program and float decorations. I chaired a general steering committee that set the goals and policies of the campaign and which assured the responsibility for the success of the program.

The steering committee was recruited well in advance of the campaign. Motivation of the committee members came quite spontaneously because the committee was composed of those persons who chaired the other campaign committees. I knew that their involvement was needed if our campaign was to be successful. The campaign enthusiasm was fed by the wholesale involvement of the student body.

A magazine slick, high quality brochure was printed that highlighted the history and academic offerings of the college. It also pictured students in a variety of settings: classrooms, offices, the library, in dormitory rooms, at study, in chapel, in worship services, in social activities, and in work assignments. It also featured some of the profiles of distinguished alumni. The brochure offered the reader an opportunity to contribute and to help meet the cost of erecting a new recreational facility. It also included the pictures of a community advisory committee which supported the campaign. The advisory committee was a big league panel of local black and white notables that included Mayor Searcy; Roy Stone, chairman of the County Board of Commissions; Carl Woodall, chairman of the Retail Merchants Association; Henry Rhett, furniture store owner; P. S. Dunnavant, clothier; Milton Cummings, cotton wholesaler and broker; Judge Elbert H. Parsons; and Mr. Lawrence Hundley, funeral director and mortician.

November 18, 1952, was a most memorable day in the history of Oakwood College. Prior to the *Brown* decision of 1954, Huntsville captured a special moment in black-white cooperation. A parade, including fifteen floats, created a procession of pageantry that will go down in history as a singular model of biracial cooperation and harmony that both races indicated had not ever occurred before. Alternating units of automobiles, floats, bands, cadet formations, and cheerleaders paraded through the center of downtown Huntsville, ending in front of the courthouse at the city square. A black high school band from Council High School, a white band from West Huntsville High School, and the Alabama A&M College band joined the celebration in lock-step rhythm and harmony. It was a testimony to the vigor and relevance of brotherhood when it holds itself to the unsparing standards of Christian and democratic principles. Mr. Cummings and Mr. Rhett made personal contributions of $1000 each that day. President Peterson keynoted the occasion with a stirring appeal for community support. The college choir filled the airways with brilliant renditions under the direction of Samuel C. Jackson, and I congratulated the community for its dedication to the advancement of education and urged them to place their contributions in the buckets which were in the hands of the young ladies that we had positioned on every corner in the business district.

This bold venture represented an important key to the future development of warm and amicable relations between the college and the community. Through the generous support of the community, more than $25,000 was raised that day. With the help of the South Central Conference of Seventh-day Adventists, the completion of the college gymnasium and recreational center became a reality. A solid seven-inch maplewood floor was installed that would accommodate skating along with such traditional activities as basketball, volleyball, shuffleboard, and table tennis. A large university can make a lot of noise with thousands of cheering spectators in a football stadium, but it seldom can equal or secure the spirit and united support and fervor that is generated on a small college campus where the contagion of togetherness is unparalleled.

Once that prime project was completed, I embraced my desire to pursue the doctorate with merciless abandonment. I lost no time in applying to The Ohio State University where I could pursue the course of study for meeting the requirements for the Ph.D. degree in Communication, Political Science and Educational Administration. Ohio State had a strong faculty in those areas, and my parents were living in Springfield, Ohio, about forty miles from the campus in Columbus, Ohio. I had high academic marks from my record at the University of Nebraska, and I was approved for admission into the doctoral program at Ohio State only a few weeks after I first applied. It was a timely opportunity and another wake-up call to remind me that angels were watching over me.

Chapter 8

Bucking the Odds in Buckeye Country

———◦◦◦◦———

It was in early June of 1953, baffled by my new opportunity to pursue the terminal degree and by my unfamiliarity with what seemed to me a major metropolitan city, I began to search for temporary housing near the university. I was forced to take this approach during the summer with the hope that by the end of the summer I would be able to find suitable housing so that my family could join me at the beginning of autumn quarter. Suffice it to say, open housing was not a readily available commodity for blacks at that time. I was forced to seek information about what might be available for blacks through the grapevine, that underground mechanism for transmitting and receiving information which is so common in the black community. The doors of segregation and discrimination that obstructed the free passage of people of color in every area of public life were very well in place in Columbus. While I made no concession to the spirit of the times, I was well aware that my immediate mission was to prepare myself in such a way so that at the appropriate time I would be better equipped to wrestle against the principalities and powers of racism.

The opportunity for housing came when I was introduced to Mrs. Seward who owned a rooming house at 63 East Eleventh Avenue, which was only about three blocks from The Ohio State University campus. Mrs. Seward was a very resourceful person. She had furnished her upstairs bedrooms and her basement, as well, with double-decker beds so that each of her rooms would accommodate three or four students. She was primarily interested in housing male graduate students, charging each the sum of $6.25 per week, as I recall. Her place was quite clean and was furnished with the necessary items for study and rest. Each room included chairs, student desks, lamps, and ample closet space for our limited wardrobes. Most of us functioned at subsistence levels, and clothes were not a priority item on our agendas. It was at Mrs. Seward's residence that we developed friendships which would last a lifetime. Such was my fortune after meeting Samuel DuBois Cook, who was in serious pursuit of the Ph.D. in political science.

We both applied ourselves with uncommon zeal in preparing for our life work and chosen professions. Both of us were dedicated to giving our services to black institutions of higher education, and each of us had aspirations for opportunities that would place us in the vanguard of high-level administration posts where we could give effective guidance to our black youth. Sam and I shared a library carrel, one using it in the morning and the other in the afternoon, until such time that each of us could have our own individual carrel. I developed a very high regard for Sam during this period, as both of us sought excellence to the extent that we made our home in the library, laboring day and night in order to fulfill our mission. In defiance of how we were so often labeled as black people, we dismissed the trivialities that might have absorbed us in order to meet the challenges of the classroom and of research with freshness and with vigor each day. We imposed a regimen upon ourselves that would not allow us the luxury of complacency. Over the years, Sam and I, along with our families, have enjoyed a cherished friendship. Sam has earned a well-deserved reputation as a scholar and as president of Dillard University.

For my part, I was at the library when the doors opened at 8:00 A.M., and when I was not attending class, I contented myself with a rather one-sided focus on study that laid the groundwork for my well-directed application in the future. To secure the confidence of the faculty in the Department of Speech was my conscious priority. After all, the summer of 1953 was my first quarter at Ohio State, and I wanted it to be a stellar one. You can imagine my exhilaration upon receiving a 4.0, having obtained an A in each of the four courses in which I was enrolled during that summer. The die was cast. I was thoroughly convinced of my ability to complete the requirements for the Ph.D. degree and, in addition to the faculty members who had taught me, the word of my successes had encompassed every corner of the department. As I walked through the corridors of Derby Hall, the headquarters of the Speech Department, I was constantly approached by faculty members who had not taught me with salutes of "Congratulations, I heard you had an excellent quarter," and the like. The feeling was both invigorating and, at the same time, a bit ominous because I knew that this young black man was under the departmental microscope.

Nevertheless, I took the plaudits in stride, thanking God for his direction and his providence in my behalf.

I went to work in search of housing for my family so that I could bring them to Columbus. My daughter, Ruthie, was five years of age, and my son, Frank III, was about to have his first birthday. Good fortune and God's blessings made it possible for us to claim residence in the new Clifton Park Apartments on the east side of Columbus. We were exuberant over the fact that we could move into a three bedroom apartment, never before occupied, for the moderate sum of $250 per month. My finances wore thin even though I received my monthly check from Oakwood. Thus, I immediately plunged into the race of seeking some additional financial resources before school began autumn quarter. Fortunately, the toil of my summer scholarly efforts paid off. I was offered a $1500 assistantship in the Department of Speech, and I secured a part-time position selling life insurance three afternoons each week for the Supreme Liberty Life Insurance Company. Mr. William Savoy, the local manager, was a fine Christian gentleman who gave me the flexibility of scheduling that allowed me to sell insurance as my time frame would permit.

At the start of autumn quarter, I found it necessary to budget my time religiously to meet the demands of study, of teaching, of grading papers, of selling insurance, and of spending some limited time with my family. Professor W. Hayes Yeager, the chairman of the Department of Speech, gave me a contract that spelled out my teaching responsibilities, and he assigned me to teach the Public Speaking class and to use as the textbook the one which he had authored, *Effective Speaking for Every Occasion*, published by Prentice-Hall, Inc.

I had certain advantages at the start. I had had an extensive preparation in speech communication at Union College and at the University of Nebraska, and I had passed through the boilerplate stages of teaching speech for two years at Oakwood College after completing the master's degree. Ever since the day when Dr. Winton Beaven encouraged me to go into the field of speech, I had it on my mind to become as effective as he was as a teacher and as a public speaker. Up until that time, I was without any intelligent guidance concerning the best steps to take in making real professional preparation for what I thought would be my field of service and satisfaction—college and university teaching. As my first teacher of speech, Beaven had made a profound impression on my young mind when I sat in his classes during my sophomore and junior years at Union College. He, as a communicator, was the embodiment of what he taught—intelligent, articulate, and caring. Now that I was under the spell of a compelling life career in the field of communication, I looked back with gratitude on the serious impact that Dr. Beaven at Union College and Dr. Laase at the University of Nebraska had already had on my career up to that point.

It was at this point that I had a definite plan worked out in my mind for my future. I wanted first to complete my education, develop my skills as a teacher and attain the rank of full professor, become an efficient administrator as a stepping stone to becoming a college president, experience overseas travel, take cover in the sanctuary of seclusion to author meaningful books and publications, and give generously of my experiences in designing and creating programs that would aid in the development and advancement of black youth.

Compared to Oakwood's campus with approximately four hundred students, Ohio State, with it nearly thirty thousand students, was a monstrous, excitement-charged swarm of humanity that might have frozen the incentives of one less determined to conquer the odds. I did not suffer the usual fate of newcomers into the graduate programs—anonymity. That I was one of a sprinkling of blacks on campus helped me to stand out. This was particularly true in the Speech Department. Fortunately, I was blessed with having been assigned as an advisee to Professor Earl Wiley. As a specialist on Lincoln, he was very familiar with the issues surrounding the moonlight and magnolia traditions of the slave system, its dark shadow, and the disruptive influence of abolitionism. He was made to order for my understandable interest in dealing with the troublesome issues on race.

His strong sense of history more than compensated for his lack of height. He was a scholarly gentleman who had published widely, and he exhibited a quiet restlessness that would not countenance routine. Always hungering with youthful fervor for excitement and great causes, I was charmed by the warmth, compassion, and cherubic expression of this grandfatherly professor whose outlook was always so innocent, so uplifting, and so unbounding. He was always there for me—guiding, counseling, correcting, reproving, and ever-encouraging my advancement. Those soft blue eyes always welcomed me with a smile that radiated support and optimism. Never once did he brandish the leverage of his power or position to make a point. What a wonderful thing it would be if all advisors were sufficiently secure within themselves that they would not find it necessary to stoop to the excesses of berating and denigrating their advisees in order to inflate their own withered egos.

In the course of my doctoral study at Ohio State, I enjoyed a very fine relationship with the departmental faculty members with but one exception. I had been taken seriously by teachers from the start because I took my classwork seriously. Professors Franklin Knower, Wallace Fotheringham, Paul Carmack, John Black, and Ruth Becky Irwin were deep-rooted and experienced scholars who had already established their imprint on the national scene. Inevitably, their influence made a not-to-be-missed impact on my fiercely idealistic outlook. Professor Louis Nemzer of the Department of Political Science was my minor advisor. His classes formed the basis of my interest in international relations, international organizations, and international law. His approach to teaching was always delightfully penetrating and decidedly human. I was not at all surprised that Dr. Nemzer was in the early vanguard of those white professors who fought for eliminating those practices at the university that had tragically scarred its reputation in the area of race relations.

My seemingly benign beginning was laden with potential pitfalls all along the way. The bruising reality of competition made it necessary for me to stay on my scholarly toes. There were about ten other doctoral students who were enrolled in the Speech Department at that time. At least half of them were models of dedication, superior intellect, and an unending reservoir of energy. I learned early that I could not afford to let up in terms of seriously applying myself to my studies. I knew better not to look back or to become complacent, as I had assessed the requirements of academic survival with unalloyed objectivity. I owe a debt of gratitude and appreciation to those creative and colorful student peers whose consistent focus helped to keep me on track, even at times when I felt frail and fragmented beyond measure. There was a common alliance among us as we studied together, compared classroom notes, shared bibliographies, and encouraged each other to go to unconscionable extremes in order to succeed.

Among the most generous of my student colleagues were Keith Brooks, Dwight Freshley, Sheila Goff, Robert Goyer, John Rickey, Jaime Williams, and Raymond Yeager. They were a great bunch!

The academic year 1953–54 was a most rewarding one for me. My classroom successes as a student and as a graduate teaching associate kept me under the spell of a compelling life-career objective. My blessings were the result of a combination of factors, not the least of which was the support that I received from my family. The pervasive influence of my lovely wife was irresistible as she encouraged and supported me at every turn. Not once did she ever erect any barriers of doubt or dismay relative to the regimen and routine which kept me confined and telescoped to academics. I successfully completed my first year's residence, passed reading examinations in Spanish and French, and finally the written general comprehensive examinations before being admitted into candidacy.

Inevitably, I found myself drawing zest from my first year of academic successes. Beyond the realm of academics, I was developing some warm relationships with some of my neighbors who shared tenant status with me at Clifton Park Apartments. These were John and Jean Bowen. John was an aspiring young law student who later would become a significant factor in the Republican Party of Ohio. It was John who first introduced me to the hazards of swimming by shoving me into the apartment's outdoor swimming pool. Somehow I was able to get out, even though I had never been in a swimming pool before. Thinking that at age twenty-seven I should have known how to swim, he considered his act a friendly joke and became desperately apologetic when he learned otherwise.

History has a way of repeating itself. Mary Claytor and her husband lived on the same floor. Little did I realize that nearly forty years later I would be a proud member of the committee that approved her Ph.D. dissertation. Mary became supervisor of guidance services (K-12) in the Columbus, Ohio, Public Schools. As an active and resourceful volunteer for the United Negro College Fund, she was the recipient of the organization's most prestigious award, the Frederick Douglass Patterson Award in 1993. Marceo Hill lived across the street from us. While holding a significant position in state government, he was also involved with the American Tennis Association. It was his singular leadership that produced numerous champions among black Americans. He was responsible for Central State College having the top tennis team among all of the state colleges and universities in Ohio during the 1950s and 1960s. As mentor and coach, he was unrivaled during those years. A number of national tennis tournaments were held under his sponsorship at Central State, attracting such stellar athletes as Arthur Ashe and Althea Gibson, both Wimbledon champions.

The montage of my varied activities was not without a religious center. As an active member the Seventh-day Adventist Church, I was conspicuously engaged in the services that were held at the Ephesus Seventh-day Adventist Church on Cleveland and Spring Streets. The church itself was something of a historical monument, having been purchased in 1921 from Shiloh Baptist Church for $25,000. In recalling my two-year participation in the church during my student days at Ohio State, I felt warmly welcomed by members of the congregation that included such strong families as the DeShays, the Berriens, the Pattersons, the Neals, the Bradleys, the Millers, the Watkins, the Townes, and the Rhynes. Elders J. Milton Thomas and Jacob J. Justass served successively from 1951 to 1954, and from 1954 to 1957. The congregation was well-endowed with a number of striving youth who were later to make their individual marks in their professions: Samuel DeShay, Richard Neal, and Joseph Rhyne, Jr., became prominent physicians; William DeShay, a veteran minister; John Pitts, a hospital administrator; and Emma DeShay, a registered nurse. The church, like most black Adventist churches, stood firmly on the Scriptures as the inspired word of God; yet it was distressingly slow to raise its voice against the social and economic abuses that stared it in the face from sunup to sundown. On the other hand, it gave a tender and compassionate touch to its own members. Our family was treated with incredible love and warmth throughout our temporary sojourn.

Mine was a hectic pace as I began the 1954–1955 academic year. I did not permit myself to be overawed by the schedule that I had set in an effort to intensely investigate the life and speaking of Salmon Portland Chase, so that I could digest and capsulate it into a respectable dissertation. I was forced to act decisively because of all that I had to do. My investigation carried me to the Ohio Historical Society for one month, the Pennsylvania Historical Society for one month, and the Manuscripts Division of the Library of Congress for six weeks. With studied care, I prepared an extensive outline which I followed religiously. I offered myself no deference in terms of leisure and gave myself no quarter in terms of wasting time. I made no effort to call my close relatives while in Washington, D.C., lest I would have to turn down their invitation to lunch or dinner or some other social courtesy.

What I lacked in professional experience, I made up for with unrelenting and determined drive. Another unquestionable asset that was always at my disposal was the marvelous motivation that I always received from my parents. When I needed a good emotional boost, I could always make a telephone call to them, or when I was in Columbus, I could get into my car and go racing the forty-five miles to Springfield, Ohio, to savor their love and loyalty which was immutable.

I spent the spring and summer of 1954 reading as much as I could about Chase. I had come upon his name quite by accident in searching for information about the emergence of the abolitionist movement in Ohio. It was then that I discovered how he had made such a powerful and profound impact on the anti-slavery movement within the state and throughout the nation, even to the point of overshadowing certain more visible distinguished national spokesmen. I was pleased to discover that there were volumes of naked materials available in the Ohio Historical Society concerning his tireless and decisive contribution in helping to stir public opinion on the issues of anti-slavery and abolition. I relished the opportunity of having this gold mine of information at my fingertips. After all, the Ohio Historical Society was located on the Ohio State University campus on the corner of Fifteenth and High Streets. It was a godsend!

It was my obsession to come to know Salmon Chase, as tradition would say, like the back of my hand. I had to become thoroughly acquainted with this white man who had embraced the cause of black people and to determine whether his motivation was spiritual or political. As black people, we have learned to be cautious and skeptical of white persons who espouse our causes. Too often we have been betrayed, so we find it necessary to confront our would-be friends. History has placed them in the predicament of having to earn our trust over and over again—one of the unfortunate casualties of man's inhumanity to man.

Quite naturally, the curse of slavery could never be eradicated unless it was attacked and challenged by those who were in positions of influence and authority. This was no easy task in view of the substantial economic gains that came to those who benefitted from the system. Then, too, notwithstanding the agonies and harshness of the system, there were many who continued to rationalize their untoward behavior toward slaves by idealizing their bondsmen as a happy lot of singing, dancing, banjo-strumming laborers.

Salmon Portland Chase, although born in New Hampshire, spent considerable time in Ohio after joining his uncle Philander Chase, the Episcopal Bishop of Ohio at Worthington, in 1820. Bishop Chase was one of the original founders of Kenyon College. After graduating from Dartmouth College and completing his law degree in Washington, D.C., Salmon Chase returned to Ohio and was admitted to the Ohio Bar in 1830. Active as a lecturer for the Cincinnati Lyceum, his career began a meteoric rise that culminated in his election as senator in 1849.

But even before Chase finished law school, he demonstrated his sincere interest in having slavery abolished by obtaining signatures and drew up a petition to Congress in an effort to have slavery and slave trade abolished in the nation's capitol. This incident, in 1827, was Chase's first public act that identified him with the anti-slavery movement. Chase was so powerful in his attacks against slavery that he was recognized as the leader of the Ohio *anti-slavery men* from 1837 to 1849. His own words underscored his position on slavery, as recorded in Albert B. Hart's biography on Chase:

> ... I heard with disgust and horror that mob violence was directed against the Anti-Slavery Press Anti-Slavery men of Cincinnati in 1836... From this time on... I became a decided opponent of slavery and the Slave Power.

Meanwhile, all shades of opinion existed in the North regarding slavery. Many were indifferent and played it politically safe by refusing to take sides. On the other hand, Chase took up the anti-slavery cause as a moral imperative. In fact, he changed parties from time to time, supporting the one which he thought demonstrated the greatest effort toward the elimination of slavery. Because abolitionists were unpopular in many parts of the North and the northern bankers were in bed with the South due to economic ties, Chase had far too much to overcome to stymie the influence and coalition strategies of men like Henry Clay and Daniel Webster.

Nevertheless, Chase was astute enough to combine the efforts of Whigs, Free Soilers and anti-slavery Democrats, and as result, he was nominated governor of Ohio in 1855. It was the merging of those political elements that gave birth to the Republican Party in Ohio. Chase's chief activities, during his four years as governor of Ohio, were devoted to the anti-slavery cause. Chase's effectiveness as an anti-slavery spokesman is reflected in the gratitude which the black people expressed toward him in 1845, by presenting him a silver punch bowl on which was inscribed, "To the Attorney General of the Fugitive Slave." When he became governor of Ohio, he used it as an official punch bowl for lemonade and, subsequently, an heirloom, because of its association with his anti-slavery career.

In my research, that culminated in my dissertation entitled *A Rhetorical Exegesis of the Life and Speeches of Salmon Portland Chase*, I gained tremendous respect for a man who refused to equivocate in the face of strong hostility. His logic, though often overshadowed by the emotionalism of the issue, undermined the empty-headed arguments of those who jeopardized such fundamental American rights as freedom of speech, freedom of the press, freedom of inquiry, freedom of travel, freedom of education—nearly all of our priceless freedoms. Chase, like very few, exposed the tragically scarred body and soul of America.

With the dissertation and the final examination on it approved, I was awarded the Ph.D. degree in Speech and Political Science on June 10, 1955. I will never forget the fanfare of that magnificent occasion with all of its pomp and circumstance. There were 1907 graduates in all, but only sixty-seven of us were being awarded the Ph.D. I noted that there was only one other black person in the Ph.D. line-up besides myself, a gentleman by the name of Thomas Thackery Williams who completed the requirements for his degree in Agricultural Economics and Rural Sociology. The Spring Commencement is always held outdoors in Ohio Stadium, the same arena where the football gladiators clash on Saturday afternoons during the autumn. The graduates, divided by college, sat in the curve of the horseshoe as their families and assortment of friends and acquaintances watched and cheered from the sides.

For most people, the excitement generated by hundreds of exhilarated, and sometimes intoxicated, graduates in black robes accentuate the occasion. However, my two-year old son, Frank III, already an early fan of television comics during those days, responded with unpredictable glee at the precise moment when I was being hooded with the flashing mantle of Scarlet and Gray, yelling at the top of his voice, "Daddy's Superman!!" In the section where my wife sat holding him, a wave of laughter rippled into a crescendo as my son's response had triggered the significance that the occasion had for the graduates and the supporters who had come to applaud them. The die was cast, expectations already high, even from the youngest member of my family. If I hadn't already accepted the challenges which the future offered, I was alerted then that I was expected to step *into* life and harness it; step *up* in life by reaching my full potential; step *over* the obstacles in life that may come my way; and step *out* of the allurement to conformity and be my own person, staking my claim on what is right and what is reasonable. Yet I knew that none of this would ever be possible without angels watching over me.

Chapter 9

The Second Time Around at Oakwood

Earlier, on May 16, 1954, I had received a communication from President Peterson, advising me that it was his last official epistle as the chief officer of Oakwood. The College Board had elected Elder Garland J. Millet to succeed him as Oakwood's third president. President Peterson's missive was sent to me just one day before the famous Supreme Court decision of *Brown v. Topeka.* I found myself a bit frustrated because Peterson had been a very strong supporter from the day that I had stepped foot on Oakwood soil. In fact, he unabashedly proclaimed during one chapel hour before I left to begin my doctoral work at Ohio State, "When Frank Hale gets his Ph.D. at Ohio State, I'll have mine." His character was so magnanimous that he accepted our attainments vicariously as his own. What a man and what a Christian gentleman! He was more than a benefactor; he was a true friend.

Something happened to me with the epoched Supreme Court decision that outlawed segregation in public education. I felt more than connected to the human drama that had unfolded from the very community of which I had been a part as a student from grades five through twelve in Topeka, Kansas. I would recall some of the earlier strategies that Topeka blacks had undertaken to buck the entrenched system of segregated education that comprised the dignity and progress of both children and adults. Growing sentiment to seek positive change had unified blacks to the extent that called meetings were held in houses and in churches to discuss the strategies for dismantling the segregated Jim Crow status of Topeka. I recall my parents taking me to a Sunday afternoon forum at St. John's AME Church where several hundred blacks had gathered to discuss such issues as the whites-only restaurants, movie houses, and the segregated school system. Reverend Burwell, the pastor of St. John's, was one of those few enlightened ministers who made his edifice available to those who were interested in challenging the status quo. The urgency that black people had felt in the desire for fair treatment had now been codified into a landmark court decision. It came about as a result of their dedication, determination, and unyielding struggle in spite of bitter opposition.

Their victory was not lost on me. To succeed, we need to persevere, and our passion for success must be large enough to match our goals. With God's help, I had made a conquest in pursuit of the doctorate and had accomplished my goal. The journey back to Oakwood—515 miles—was a long one. There was a certain degree of uncertainty that haunted me. While advanced education makes a man think a little more of himself, I did not know what to anticipate in terms of what my relationship would be with the new college president, Elder Millet. While I had considerable satisfaction in knowing that I had made every attempt to expand the boundaries of my mind, I wanted to be assured that my preparation was not for naught. No one other than Dr. Dykes held a doctorate at the college, so I became the second faculty member to hold the Ph.D., and the first to have earned the degree while a member of the faculty. Later that summer, in August of 1955, Dr. O. B. Edwards was awarded the Ph.D. degree in history from the University of Nebraska.

The education and exposure which I had received at The Ohio State University had saturated me with a greater grasp of contemporary issues. Being more liberally educated, I was gaining a sense of self-confidence and inner satisfaction which the assurance of knowledge bestows. My immersion into the sciences, literature, history, music, art, and political issues had helped to arouse my ambitions. My engagements of discussion with some of the great faculty and student minds on campus embraced my scope of knowledge immeasurably. I regarded my education with a sacred trust, and I had absolutely no intention of hoarding it. It was my intention to take advantage of every chance possible to do something that would motivate both students and my colleagues to be the best that they could be.

One of my first projects was that of developing a speech minor, designing a speech classroom in the lower level of Moran Hall, and organizing a speech choir. As the school year began, I had many evidences from President Millet that my programmatic efforts would be supported. I had the satisfaction of supervising the renovation of the ground floor at Moran Hall where the new speech classroom was designed, where a speech laboratory was constructed with a one-way vision mirror, and where office space was assigned me. The attractive atmosphere of this new space allocation helped to contribute to growing and flourishing interest in the field of speech communication. My classes were always filled to capacity, and some of the most talented students elected to enroll on their own. Fortunately, I felt that I commanded the respect of the students as fully as any faculty member. I developed a rich rapport with a number of the young men who were in my classes, a number of whom have played very important and significant roles in the growth and advancement of the Seventh-day Adventist Church and in secular institutions as well. I well remember the animation which was generated by some of my ambitious students. Among them were Benjamin Reaves, Willie Lewis, Herman Vanderberg, William Scales, James McLean, James Edgecombe, Dorrence Henderson, William Alleyne, Herbert Doggette, Charleste McNorton, Antoinette Bailey, Simon Johnson, Doris Mickle, David Taylor, Milton Young, Erycina Rahming, and Eunice Jones.

It was during these years that my appetite for classroom teaching was enhanced because of the ardor and enthusiasm of the students. They were a tonic and irresistible because of their contagious zeal for knowledge. They always appeared ready to respond to the challenges that I set before them. It is not uncommon to observe a high degree of self-consciousness among some black students. Many are discouraged from asserting themselves because they are afraid to confront the world that has placed so many obstacles in their way. In such an environment, some have taken the road of least resistance through timidity, reticence, and by shrinking from any activity that would expose their vulnerabilities. I have always attempted to have them capitalize on their strengths and to disregard the kind of morbid self-consciousness that would paralyze their potential. It is incontrovertibly true that we must love ourselves before we can find ourselves. Nothing could be more rewarding than encouraging and empowering students to secure the ground under their feet by affirming the strength of their will by anchoring it with the will of God. It is in this realm of social responsibility that the true teacher reigns supreme.

Having spent two full years in the highly charged intellectual environment of The Ohio State University, I felt compelled to counterbalance any suggestion that there was at Oakwood an atmosphere which was anti-intellectual. It was always assumed by some people, Adventist and non-Adventist, that a heavy emphasis on Christian education would somehow diminish the academic growth of any educational institution. I was aware, too, that in some ways faculty may very well have contributed to such a perception. What reputation did the institution have in terms of its research in political, social, scientific, and business areas? What impact had it made in the aesthetic worlds of art and music? What was its image nationally on academic matters? I sometimes found it disturbing that religion as it was taught and practiced seemed quarantined from life. While there was a preoccupation with religious traditions—morning and evening worships, chapel services, Friday night vespers, religious workshops, religious emphasis weeks, and a whole complement of devotional experiences, there did not appear to be an analogous emphasis on academic matters. I have always been impressed with the multidimensional Christ who "increased in wisdom and stature, and in favor with God and man" (Luke 2:52).

It was certainly spiritually refreshing to share in the vigor and vitality of those religious traditions that permeated every warp and woof of the campus. Evangelistic outreach efforts were in abundance. Consistent applause was available to those who exhibited high level abilities in their preaching at Friday evening seminars or at the sessions conducted by the Evangeleers. The dormitories overflowed with harmonies from an assortment of quartets which competed for recognition at Sabbath afternoon MV (Missionary Volunteer) programs or at Saturday evening *amateur hour*-like musical events.

There was no observable clue that the institution had declared a religious war against the disciplines of science, history, psychology, politics, art, music, and mathematics; however, these areas of knowledge seemed almost totally responsible for taking care of themselves. There was no sturdy platform that offered students the opportunity to engage in the kind of dialectic that would reveal the genius of their minds. While I could not speak for every teacher, I'm not sure that students generally were encouraged to think hypothetically or to suspend their commitments while engaging in their best thoughts. I recall a few instances where students' questions were squelched with fierce spontaneity if they dared invade the sacred territory on issues relative to divorce, Darwinism, immortality, democracy, God, homosexuality—any of the questions that might come to a fertile mind seeking truth. To suggest that somehow inquiring, exploration, the play of the mind, or the ventilation of all of the possible ramifications of an idea is dangerous or wrong, is both backward and anti-intellectual. Knowledge and wisdom should by no means be predigested or prepackaged commodities. Truth and discovery are individual activities. While we cannot dismiss lightly the discoveries of others, each of us grows the extent to which we are absorbed in our own acquisition of knowledge. Life is so burdensome and complex that we must be very careful that we do not impose upon God, insisting that he allow us to flee from the burdens that would augment our own maturity.

114

If Christianity is to be meaningful, it must shape its mission around those issues and experiences that confront people in their daily lives. It must be willing to struggle and sacrifice along with its devotees. Christian education, if it is to be liberal education, must be diverse in its interest, while being *distinctive*.

The Montgomery, Alabama, struggle which began on December 1, 1955, when Mrs. Rosa Parks said "No" to the bus driver who demanded that she give up her seat and let a white man have it, opened the door for me to involve some of our Oakwood students in one of the contemporary issues of the day. I was eager to make the point that Christian education is revolutionary, that true Christianity is not neutral on matters of freedom and human dignity. So after several hundred blacks had been sent to jail for their participation in a boycott to protest the segregation on city buses, I arranged to take two carloads of students to the boycott trial. It was this protest movement that became the launching pad that led to Martin Luther King's national and international prominence. That protest extended beyond the issue of transportation to include a vast world of issues that were a part of the bewildering history of black people in America.

That excursion to Montgomery enabled our young people, many of whom were from the North, to become confronted with the tradition and psychology of the South on the basis of firsthand experience. It also allowed them to seriously weigh their choices. They were placed in the position of asking certain questions of themselves: *What is my responsibility as a Christian witness concerning such matters? Is it possible for me to be neutral in the face of injustice? How can I be liberated from the chains of convention? Is it Christian to put the security of good favor above the helplessness of one who is in need?*

It is my aim to help students to confront themselves with the naked realities of everyday problems. I thought it a terrible mistake to somehow divorce religion (especially Christianity) from those immoral practices that so often are supported by the muscular trappings and resources of government. The students were well pleased with the opportunity that had been afforded them, and they discovered something profound and persuasive in the experience that they could use for years to come.

Among the most engaging and delightful persons that I have known and learned to respect through the years, Chessie Harris stands out as a luminary of spectacular service and Christian commitment. When I returned to Oakwood College in June of 1955, after earning the doctorate at Ohio State, she and her husband, George, had already opened their home in Huntsville, Alabama, in 1954 to children who were orphaned, mistreated, abandoned, or lacking in those amenities that should be available to all children regardless of their race, gender or class. Mrs. Harris is a woman of vision who possesses the unquenchable vitality to match her dream of establishing a little heaven on earth for foster children.

Always committed to eliminating and reducing the anguish of hunger, misery, and despair among children who were neglected or who were victims of unconscionable pain and poverty, Chessie's compassion became the driving force that led to the establishment of the Harris Home for children, which became incorporated in 1957 and licensed by the State of Alabama in 1960. The rest is a magnificent history of what a dream can become if one has the intestinal faith and fortitude to follow her dream.

The Harris Home has served well over a thousand children, adding a sweet taste of *somebodiness* to each of them who saw, in Chessie and George Harris, wonderfully warm parents who had surrendered their lives and their resources in order to make life more meaningful for them.

I was not surprised at all when she was invited to the White House as a recipient of the 1989 President's Volunteer Action Award. Earlier, in 1987, *Women's Day* magazine honored her as one of the five unsung heroines of America for that year. Governor Guy Hunt of Alabama later proclaimed July 6, 1989, as *Chessie Harris Day* for her dedicated service on behalf of children and youth.

The Harris establishment, now numbering fourteen buildings, remains as a monument, a testament, and a ringing endorsement of the beauty of unselfish Christian service.

Having had only two years of teaching before attending Ohio State, my professional experience had merely scratched the surface. Now I was ready to dig in, beyond all superficiality, and fulfill my role and responsibility as a thoroughbred professional. I was totally committed to helping students to develop attitudes that would free them to escape those conditions that would enslave them. We place far too much emphasis on the purpose of education as an economic concept. As a consequence of promoting economic advantages at all costs, we have made individuals expendable. We promote profits above people. It is no wonder, then, that the gun lobbyists intensify their efforts when gun control legislation is introduced; that the earth's resources are being used up for personal gain; that health and welfare of people are held hostage with little regard by the profiteers of the alcohol, tobacco, and drug industries; that the mineral riches of third world countries are raped to satisfy the affluent ethos of wealthier nations; and that the production of pollutants and the perilous armaments of war are generated to gratify the privateers of capitalism in the defense industries.

I believe the role of the educator is to inform and warn students of the social callousness which the powerful exhibit and which enables them to take advantage of the powerless. We also have some responsibility in guiding students into those curricular areas (scientific and technical) that will prepare them to compete *heads up* during the twenty-first century. We may be serving the ideological and economic interests of others when as black students and black faculty we are only concentrated on the fields of humanities, education and the social sciences, but we certainly are not reflecting a conscious effort to augment our own interests. We obscure an important opportunity for ourselves and for our students when we permit them to flounder—unmarketable, untrained, unsuited and unsought. I felt impelled to unleash my best energies. I have known of teachers whose commitment was purely rhetorical, but teaching is a matter of how much one is really willing to invest. Historically black colleges have demonstrated an unparalleled opportunity and ability to affect the status and success of black students and black faculty. I was always optimistic about the ultimate outcome of our students at Oakwood because there were some superb teachers there who would have been a great blessing to any institution that would have had the good fortune of having them on their faculty. In addition to veteran teachers like Professors Dykes, Burrell, Edwards, Moseley, Booth, Stafford, and Emmanuel, there was a younger crop that was sophisticated, generous, and among the best-equipped teachers in terms of both their curriculum and co-curricular activities. Cooper, Rogers, Partridge, Longware, the Alexanders, Mosby, Jackson, Gentry, and Lewis were included in this corp. Among the staff, the services of Warren, Meredith, Crosby, the Emersons, the Harris's and Mrs. Edwards were pre-eminently satisfactory. Obviously any discussion about providing excellent opportunities for students to learn and to take advantage of their potential unleashes powerful and deeply held feelings about the dedicated and committed teachers that taught them.

Once again, black colleges have been on the leading edge of the effort to extend opportunities for higher education to African-American youth. By virtue of their southern geographic base, they have been able to provide a mission and a regional orientation distinct from most other institutions of higher education. These institutions have circumvented the system that has tended to stratify higher education along class and racial lines. They have been open to serve all students without regard to race, color, class, or creed. After a long and satisfying period of growth, they have fulfilled the promise of their mission as their students have graduated, have been admitted to and have graduated from the most prestigious graduate and professional schools, and have gone on to establish significant career profiles throughout the nation and the world. The genius of black institutions of higher education is that they have admitted students of varying academic, economic and cultural backgrounds and have transformed them in such ways that the greater number of black professionals in the country are products of these institutions. America has much that it can learn from these institutions if it is gracious enough to admit that it can.

My teaching load consisted of teaching two courses in Freshman Composition, Speech for the Classroom Teacher, Public Speaking, and English Literature. There are gross misgivings about the teaching profession, as certain cynics have suggested that the profession is not a demanding one. A faculty member's time is consumed with numerous activities such as curriculum development, syllabus preparation, course instruction, preparation of instructional materials, advising students, research, professional affiliations and service, committee assignments, and community service. If faculty members do their work right, their work within the classroom represents only a small fraction of their responsibilities. Then, too, the high expectations of their constituencies: administrators, colleagues, parents of the students, alumni, and the students themselves provide further insight into the demands placed upon the faculty. The teacher who is effective must continually strive. There is no closure on excellence.

Recognizing that the only thing which can save a small college is a faculty of high character and repute, the administration planned to add five new Ph.D. degree recipients during the 1955–1956 academic year. Dr. Otis B. Edwards, dean of the college, chairman of the History Department, and an Oakwood teacher beginning in 1926, completed his doctorate at the University of Nebraska in August of 1955. Professor Natelka Burrell, chairman of the Department of Education, was expected to receive her Ph.D. in educational psychology from Teachers College, Columbia University, in 1956. Miss Cordell Evans was in the final stages of her doctorate in mathematics at the University of Pittsburgh. The college was in the process of recruiting Dr. William A. Osborne to teach in the field of business administration and economics. I looked forward with great pleasure to the privilege of working with these new doctorates, as well as with those faculty who joined with us in leading our students toward spiritual and intellectual freedom.

My wife and I were saddened when Professor Samuel Jackson accepted a position as a member of the music faculty at Tennessee State A&I University in Nashville. Professor Jackson and his wife Sarah, along with their son, Craig, had been our next door neighbors from the time we first connected with Oakwood in 1951. Sam, although prone to exasperated moments of fierce demands as a choir director outside of the classroom situation, was always brimming with humor. Sarah was always warm, radiant, and quick with a natural smile. Ruthie, my daughter, and Craig were the same age, and both of them required all of the energy of the parents, as they had energy to spare.

In the meanwhile, we also bid farewell to Mr. Myles Martin who served on the faculty of the English Department while serving as literary advisor to the *Spreading Oak* and directing public relations activities. He authored a booklet entitled "The Program in English Cooperation at Oakwood College," which outlined the extent to which faculty and departments throughout the campus joined with the Department of English in requiring certain standards which were considered minimum essentials for English proficiency. Martin left the college to pursue the doctorate.

Among the new faculty faces that graced the campus that year were Lucille Herron in music, Irene Meredith in mathematics, Gaines Partridge in education and art, Katie Shorter as cashier, Jannith Lewis as librarian, and Phillip Giddings in secondary education. Several students of high academic distinction began to emerge as future leaders. *Spreading Oak* editor Benjamin Reaves was scheduled to enroll at the Seventh-day Adventist Seminary in the fall of 1956. Jimmie Brown was scheduled to work in a tent effort with Elder Charles Dudley in the summer before being taken on as a worker by the Southwest Region Conference in the fall. Erycina Rahming, graduating with high distinction as an English major, would be teaching church school in West Palm Beach, Florida. Eunice Jones was awarded the position of medical secretary and accountant in the medical center of Dr. John Richard Ford in San Diego, California.

As the year 1955 unfolded, other headliners had their day: Oakwood enrollment spiraled to 405, a forty-four percent increase over the previous year; plans for the Oakwood gym were finalized so that groundbreaking was slated for January of 1956; the student body swarmed into Huntsville and surrounding areas in an In-gathering Kick-off Field Day and garnered $2300; the new six-pillared men's dormitory named in honor of Frank Loris Peterson opened; Elder C. T. Richards became the new pastor of the Oakwood College Church; a $1000 scholarship was established in honor of Mother Eugenia I. Cunningham and Elder Louis B. Reynolds, editor of *Message* magazine; Elder J. H. Laurence, veteran pastor and evangelist, conducted an inspirational and impressive Week of Prayer; and Oakwood hosted the fifteenth Annual Conference of Alabama Colleges with C. G. Gomillion of Tuskeegee Institute presiding as chairman.

It was the year that James Gaston Towery accepted a position as reference librarian at Simpson College in Iowa after serving a three-year stint at Oakwood. It was early during that year in preparation for his departure that Mr. Towery began to rid the library of countless papers and periodicals which he apparently considered obsolete. One day, out of curiosity, I began to rummage through some of the piles of materials that had been placed just outside of the library. I was shocked to discover a small booklet entitled *The Southern Work* near the top of the pile. Through the years, I had craved ownership of this rich gem which I was then holding as an utterly implausible catch and keepsake in my trembling hands. For years I had heard its contents discussed by veterans within the church, but I had never been fortunate enough to see one, let alone to own a copy. Ellen G. White had taken a stand on the race question in that golden volume. Her crusade for understanding and justice, so direct and incredibly clear, did much to balance or at least overshadow all the forms of misinterpretation that were being assigned to her based on her statements in volume nine of *Testimonies*.

There were two very poignant statements that I hailed with enthusiasm as my eyes became glued to my newly-found, prized possession. Mrs. White knew that she was challenging prevailing opinion when she said:

> I know that which I now speak will bring me into conflict. This I do not covet... but I do not mean to live a coward, or die a coward, leaving my work undone. I must follow in my Master's footsteps. It has become fashionable to look down upon the poor, and upon the colored race in particular. But Jesus, the Master, was poor, and He sympathized with the poor, the discarded, the oppressed, and declares that every insult shown to them is as if shown to himself. (*Southern Work*, p. 4)

Moreover, Mrs. White declared, in convincing language, the equality of all races:

> The black man's name is written in the book of life beside the white man's. All are one in Christ. Birth, station, nationality, or color cannot elevate or degrade men. The character makes the man. If a red man, a Chinaman, or an African gives his heart to God, in obedience and faith, Jesus loves him none the less for his color. (*Southern Work*, p. 8)

White rendered a terrible indictment against those who contributed to the waywardness of blacks, and she insisted that special efforts should be made to upgrade their position. She put her concern quite pointedly in these words:

120

Are we not under even greater obligation to labor for the colored people than for those who have been more highly favored? Who is it that held these people in servitude? Who kept them in ignorance, and pursued a course to debase and brutalize them, forcing them to disregard the law of marriage, breaking up the family relation, tearing wife from husband, and husband from wife? If the race is degraded, if they are repulsive in habits and manners, who made them so? Is there not much due them from white people? After so great a wrong has been done them, should not an earnest effort be made to life them up? (*Southern Work*, pp. 11–12)

It was undeniably disconcerting to me that *The Southern Work* had been out of print for many years. I felt that it was a blot of organizational inaction that the membership of the Seventh-day Adventist Church worldwide, but particularly in North America, had not been exposed to this immensely important document. Its broad distribution would have helped the efforts of those level-headed persons within the denomination who sought to initiate certain reforms that would have expanded opportunities for blacks in every area of church life.

The power of that little book left such an inescapable impression upon me that I knew that at a later date it would become a powerful sword in the arsenal of those who had serious intentions about helping to move the denomination toward a more representative and inclusive body of believers. I experienced a sense of relief, knowing that ultimately Mrs. White's admonition could not go unheeded. I knew that at the appropriate time God would use his servant to help arouse the moral conscience of church leaders and church members when the church could no longer afford to dodge this troublesome issue of race.

It was on February 13, 1956, that the groundbreaking ceremonies were held for the gymnasium, a new college store, a bakery, and a post office building. President Millet called on me as director of public relations to officiate at the ceremony and to give the opening address. It was the president's way of asking me to cash in on the gymnasium campaign which I had initiated during the 1952–53 academic year. Two members of the executive committee of that earlier campaign were present as special guests, Milton K. Cummings and Mayor R. B. Searcy of Huntsville. Professor Gaines Partridge, dean of men, offered the opening prayer, and Dr. Otis B. Edwards, dean of the college, directed the singing of the school song, which he had composed, "To Thee Our Dear Oakwood."

The lighter side of life was not by any means neglected by the Oakwood family. Varied diversions offered the students ongoing opportunities to display their God-given talents. James McLean, a senior ministerial student, won first place in the Annual Temperance Oratorical Contest. James Parker, a sophomore and a student in my beginning speech class, won second prize, and Robert Taylor, a freshman, was third. Mervyn Warren, James Morris, and Oscar Daniels gained honorable mention recognition. Professor Thomasine Longware, sponsor of the Oakwood chapter of the American Temperance Society, was responsible for doing an excellent job in arranging the program for the evening as a crowd of nearly four hundred were attracted to this spellbinding forum of competition.

It was during that year that the Oakwood Chapel Hour emerged as the voice of Oakwood over radio station WFUN every Sunday morning at 10:00 A.M. It was a devotional program under the sponsorship of Elder C. T. Richards and myself. The cast featured some outstanding student talent that included Stanley Gellineau, tenor soloist; children's storyteller, Marie Kibble; the Chapeliers Trio (Claudia Dent, Vivian Steele, and Donna Matthews); the Collegiate Quartet (E. Wayne Shepperd, William Scales, Edward Maddox, and James Edgecombe); and narrators James McLean and Kenneth Lester. More than fifty thousand Huntsville and North Alabama residents heard the program each week. The Collegiate Quartet, later designated the Cathedral Quartet, appeared in New York on the nationally famous *Strike It Rich* television show and won $500 for the choir robe project for the Oakwood College Choir.

The United Student Movement annual banquet exhibited student artistry like no other event on campus. Professor Partridge, a gifted artist as well as a consummate teacher, was usually in thick of things when gala affairs were planned. His sense of color, design and pageantry added a high quality of expertise to such occasions. Nowhere was this more evident than in the banquet's theme, "Slow Boat to China," a sea-attractive vessel, built by the students themselves, under Partridge's direction. The cruiser was decorated as the deck of a ship to carry students and the faculty, who were in attendance, on a formal banquet cruise. As the guests were being served, the vessel anchored at imaginary ports for entertainment. At Honolulu, Vivian Steele and Elbert Shepperd entertained with a Hawaiian duet; at Port Yokohama, pianist Edward Daniels rendered a selection; a woodwind ensemble from Alabama A&M College provided music in Manila; Ted Jones and James Edgecombe entertained the guests with a trumpet duet at Singapore; and Vivian Cervantes, former model and star on the television show, *Surfside Six*, concluded the program with a vocal solo, "Go Mena Nasai," as the ship dropped anchor in China. Such an excellent program was augmented by the cooperative efforts of the USM officers: Robert Williams, president; Charles Joseph, social vice president; Robert Sloan, religious vice president; Ruby Thompson, secretary; Sybil Logan, treasurer;

Walton Whaley, editor of *Spreading Oak*; Joe Avery, editor of *Acorn*; Edythe Sumpter, parliamentarian; Gerald Wells, sergeant-at-arms; and Walter Grant, assistant treasurer.

It was also during the year of 1956 that an excitement swept across the campus when two famous artists decided to enroll at Oakwood as students. Joyce Bryant, world famous singer, began making a new name for herself as an ambassador of sacred music. Even until this day, I have never heard anyone sing "His Eye Is on the Sparrow" with the richness, intensity, the range, or the spiritual passion that were the hallmarks of Miss Bryant's special gift. Vivian Cervantes, a model-actress, brought a striking sense of poise and presence to the campus. Their decision to attend Oakwood had been announced in the media before their arrival, and Mylar Martin and I were invited to Washington, D.C., when the official word of their decision attracted widespread coverage by national newspapers. At the time, the publicity seemed like a golden opportunity for Oakwood to capture a recruitment initiative that would help the institution garner more students. In hindsight, their coming to campus was no doubt overplayed to the point where it might have been difficult for them to settle into the routine schedule of being normal students. Their feet were never quite able to hit the ground, as constant demands were made of their time for appearances, both on and off the campus. This public relations event was unexplored territory for the college, which appeared inviting at the time but, in retrospect, should have been handled much more deliberately and cautiously. I accept more than minimal blame for that imperfect rendezvous with the publicity hounds.

Nevertheless, it was a time that the college gave a lusty welcome to another celebrated twosome, Princess Alice Siwundla and her husband, Hulme, who enrolled as students at Oakwood. They had made a spectacular flight from their home in Nyasaland, South Africa, and had appeared on the *This Is Your Life* television program in Los Angeles. Sponsored by Mrs. Josephine Cunningham Edwards, a missionary author from the Solusi Mission in South Africa, Princess Alice and her family were awarded $2000 for her education, $1000 for groceries, $500 for spending money, a Bell and Howell movie projector, and watches. They, too, like Bryant and Cervantes, took the campus by storm, and calls for their testimonies flourished as they visited and lectured at churches, schools, and civic organizations throughout the country. Life for them became a frenzied scramble between the requirements of school and the demands of those who hungered to learn of their exploits in their homeland.

The Seventh Annual Intercollegiate Workshop was held at Oakwood College December 5–8, 1956, and representatives from Atlantic Union

College, Emmanuel Missionary College, Madison College, Southern Missionary College, Union College, and Washington Missionary College joined the Oakwood College delegates. Guest speakers for the occasion were Dr. Floyd Rittenhouse, president of the Emmanuel Missionary College; Elder Calvin Moseley, then an associate secretary of the General Conference; and Dr. Richard Hammill, secretary of the General Conference Department of Education. Dr. O. B. Edwards welcomed the delegates to the opening session where I gave the keynote address at the request of President Garland Millet.

On December 6, 1956, I received a letter from Elder H. T. Elliott, associate secretary of the General Conference of Seventh-day Adventists, inviting me to serve as a faculty member in the School of Graduate Studies in the East (later designated Potomac University) in Takoma Park, Maryland, for the 1957 summer session, June 17 to August 28. Later, Dr. E. D. Dick, president of the Seventh-day Adventist Theological Seminary, underscored the invitation. After discussing the matter with my family, we decided to accept the invitation and were extremely pleased when Elder and Mrs. Frank Peterson extended us the opportunity to stay in their home, as they would be away for the summer. I was given assignments to teach Sermon Preparation and Delivery and Voice and Diction. It was a challenging opportunity, and I was aware that my every move was being scrutinized.

I must admit I had a great summer. The fellowship and collegiality I experienced were unusually warm, and I imbibed a great deal of white Adventist culture in my visits to the General Conference headquarters, the Columbia Union headquarters, Columbia Union College, Takoma Park Seventh-day Adventist Church, and Sligo Seventh-day Adventist Church. Of course I was very much at home when visiting DuPont Park, The First Church, and Ephesus.

Our children had a *ball* in walking and touring the thoroughfares of the nation's capital. History became alive for them in their visits to Arlington National Cemetery, the U. S. Capitol, the Bureau of Engraving and Printing, Smithsonian Institution, United States Supreme Court, Washington Monument, Lincoln Memorial, Ford's Theater, Jefferson Memorial, National Gallery of Art, and the Pentagon. At the time, Ruthie was nine years old and Frank was five years of age. It was a wonderful experience for all of us, caught, as it were, in the forbidding network of governmental monuments, rivalries, bureaucracies, and the pressing congestion of bustling bodies every hour of every day. Because there were so many places to go and so much to do, we were able to reduce the complexity of the city into a routine of capturing new experiences every day that we were there. It was a phenomenon of world wonders—magnificent churches, cherry blossoms along the Potomac, the merging of Occidental and Oriental cultures, those bearing extravagant credentials and others seemingly threadbare—but all creating a mosaic of both profuse and primitive pageantry. The experience of having spent the summer in Washington, D.C., complemented our lives in ways unimaginable. The sprightly way in which black men and women walked tall and with contemptuous strength left mental souvenirs on the shelves of my mind that I will never forget. It was a brief but profitable adventure before we returned to Oakwood.

Before the 1956–1957 academic year came to an end, the ministerial students had the privilege of sitting under the tutelage of Dr. Owen A. Troy of the Pacific Union Conference and Elder Louis B. Reynolds, editor of *Message* magazine, during a colloquy which they directed February 22–24, 1956. Both Troy and Reynolds were professor-like models of scholarship in their presentations, which were subject-centered, as they underscored the theme of the sessions: "Confronting the Changing World with a Changeless Christ." The sessions were conducted with a forum format so that the students were free to contribute with questions and comments.

Oakwood was a fertile ground for the enrichment that students could receive by taking advantage of the variety of lecturers who visited the campus throughout the year. Elder J. F. Street, pastor of the Berean Seventh-day Adventist Church in Atlanta was the Spring Week of Prayer speaker, and his theme was "Practical Christianity." Principal E. I. Watson of Pine Forge Institute in Pennsylvania addressed the business students during the year. Elder E. C. Ward, Southern Union evangelist, gave a stirring sermon on "Decisions for Eternity" as the Sabbath speaker for the College Days weekend. Elder E. E. Cleveland revealed his thorough knowledge of the Scriptures and his dynamic enthusiasm as he conducted his annual workshop for ministerial students. Dr. Leroy Froom challenged all of our thinking with his brilliant lectures on "Verities of Advent Faith." Dr. Reuben G. Manalaysay, president of the Philippine Union College, addressed the campus community during a Friday evening sunset vespers. There is little doubt that the spiritual and intellectual life of the campus was elevated by those experienced and knowledgeable persons who shared their refreshing perspectives on various topics with us.

It was at the beginning of the 1956–1957 academic year that Elder Jesse R. Wagner, Oakwood alumnus of 1952, was appointed pastor of the Oakwood College Church as well as district leader for Huntsville, Florence, and Gasden, Alabama. He and his family were introduced to the Oakwood church members on Sabbath, September 21, 1957, by

Elder W. W. Fordham, president of the South Central Conference of Seventh-day Adventists. Elder C. T. Richards, head of the Division of Religion, was appointed to serve as the assistant pastor.

The new school year was barely underway before the campus community was battered with the devastating effects of the Asian flu that accounted for 180 reported cases throughout the campus. As a precautionary measure to reduce the spread of this infectious illness, classes were cancelled October 9–13, 1957. The mini epidemic was short-lived as Dr. S. W. Hereford, the college physician, and Mrs. Ruth Stafford, the director of Health Services, along with Miss Agnes Harris, R.N., and several pre-nursing students combined their efforts with immediate and competent care to treat those who were stricken. The benefits of their services extended beyond the victims as the morale of co-workers, acquaintances, friends, and observers was boosted because of their humanitarian efforts.

After the iron grip of the Asian flu had been broken, the college experienced a power-packed Week of Prayer as Elder Calvin B. Rock, who then was pastor of the Miami (Florida) Seventh-day Adventist Church, seized the passionate yearnings of our hearts by presenting a series of seven sermons on the theme "Open Thou Mine Eyes." His style revealed thorough preparation, burning eloquence, and irresistible zeal. The week was a tremendous start and stimulus for the year ahead.

President Millet was never hesitant in giving me assignments that challenged my human relations and administrative skills. Never shrinking from an encounter, I often found myself swimming in uncharted waters, moved primarily by a stern sense of duty. Fortunately, I was fitted by temperament, training, energy, and ambition to take on the unknown. However, in the process, with God's help I was generally conspicuously successful in whatever my hands found to do. In anticipation of the General Conference Session in Cleveland, Ohio, in the spring of 1958, Millet had made Thomasine Longware and me co-chairpersons of the Oakwood College Alumni banquet which was to be held at that time. So the Hale-Longware team, with the strong support of Ruth N. Stafford, who was president of the National Oakwood College Alumni Association, bestirred itself energetically to plan and negotiate every detail of the banquet program so that there would be no doubt that this major event would be first-rate. We effectively achieved our ends by involving members of local chapters in Chicago; New York City; Los Angeles; Detroit; Washington, D.C.; Atlanta; Nashville; Wilmington, North Carolina; Pine Forge, Pennsylvania; Pittsburgh; Columbus, Ohio; Oberlin, Ohio; Philadelphia; St. Louis; New Orleans; Jacksonville, Florida; Oklahoma City; Omaha, Nebraska; Indianapolis; Kansas City, Missouri; Baltimore;

Cincinnati; Dayton, Ohio; Kansas City, Kansas; Memphis; Dallas; Phoenix; Ecorse, Michigan; Topeka, Kansas; Charleston, South Carolina; Huntsville, Alabama; and, of course, Oakwood College.

The Golden Oak Banquet, held at the Hotel Statler in Cleveland, Ohio, on June 28, 1958, was a historic monument to be recorded in the documented annals of Oakwood College. An incredible spirit of festive fervor enveloped the occasion as six hundred alumni, patrons, and friends of the college gathered for the grand celebration of this Oakwood spectacular. The evening was crowned with one sparkling success after another as outstanding artists shared their talents with us: Alleyne Dumas Lee, eminent soprano soloist with the Chicago Symphony Orchestra; Arnold Dean, Oakwood student organist; James Calloway, Chicago tenor; Joseph Wilkens, Detroit baritone; Lyle Follette, Jr., Nashville violinist; Harriet Golson, Oakwood alto soloist; Viola Boyer, Columbus soprano; and Lucille Anderson-Herron, Oakwood instrumentalist.

In the realm of refinement, the setting was superb. Deeply piled carpeting graced the staircase that led into the luxurious banquet room. Beautiful, round tables were elegantly set to suit the royal occasion. It was a spectacular gathering of the sons and daughters of Oakwood College. There were the men and women who had graced the sacred halls of their alma mater, Oakwood College, and were coming out as an expression of their support then and for years to come. The audience was permeated with dignitaries, Adventists and non-Adventists. Most of the regional conference presidents were there, along with Elders F. L. Peterson, C. E. Moseley, Jr., W. S. Lee, and L. S. Follette. Thirty local chapter presidents joined the occasion, some of whom spiced the program with glowing reports of their chapters' activities.

President Garland Millet aroused the guests into a jubilant mood as he unfolded his plans for a $100,000 development program. He also took the opportunity to recognize the individual contributions of the Espie Carters of Oberlin, Ohio, Dr. Turner of Chicago, Elder Louis B. Reynolds, the editor of *Message*, and Mrs. Eugenia (Mother) Cunningham.

Mr. Milton K. Cummings, president of Brown Engineering Company of Huntsville, Alabama, was one of the guest speakers. Cummings had been a solid and consistent benefactor to Oakwood for many years. Dr. C. Leroy Hacker, a Wilberforce University professor, gilded the event with a dynamically challenging oration, stressing the ever-increasing worldwide opportunities for service. Trophies were presented to the Atlanta and Pittsburgh chapters for their winning efforts in the organ fund drive. Special citations were also presented to Mr. and Mrs. Espie Carter for underwriting the cost for the furnishings of the new student lounge.

All in all, it was a fantastically wonderful evening, and I enjoyed myself immensely as master of ceremonies throughout this star-studded, triumphant evening.

Earlier in the school year, I had joined Dr. Eva B. Dykes, Mr. Gaines Partridge, Elder Phillip Giddings, Mr. Sam Pierre-Louis, Miss Henrietta Emmanuel and Miss Ruth E. Mosby in planning and directing Humanities Week. Dr. C. Leroy Hacker, a professor at Wilberforce University and a retired colonel in the U. S. Army, had the student body standing in uproarious acclamation at the conclusion of one of the most inspirational speeches that I had ever heard given at Oakwood or, for that matter, anywhere. His subject was "The Persistent and Inherent Accompaniment of Life."

The world-famous Don Cossack Chorus from Czechoslovakia was a feature lyceum attraction. Elder H. M. S. Richards and the King's Herald Quartet were our guests for vesper services on November 27, 1957. Elder James V. Scully, associate secretary of the Temperance Department of the General Conference was a chapel speaker during the year, and Elder Norman Simons, secretary-treasurer of the South Atlantic Conference of Seventh-day Adventists, concluded Humanities Week with a stimulating message on Sabbath.

Before the end of the year, God had blessed the college in a number of areas: the Oakwood Scientific Society was organized; the College Health Service Center moved into new remodeled quarters in the east end of the administration building; the *Spreading Oak* subscription campaign got off to a flying start, as President Millet had appointed me as commander-in-chief; a new dairy barn was being constructed; Dr. Columbus Ricks joined the faculty as professor of Natural Sciences; Mr. John C. Pitts joined the staff as an assistant to Mr. James E. Meredith in the Accounting Department; and Professor Emerson Cooper was awarded a Danforth Foundation Scholarship to complete the requirements for the doctorate in chemistry at Michigan State University.

The year 1958 was packed with one major activity after another. Even before the magnificent Golden Oak Banquet, President Millet had commissioned me to direct a student promotion and alumni tour to the following cities: Memphis, Tennessee; New Orleans, Louisiana; Baton Rouge, Louisiana; Phoenix, Arizona; San Diego, California; and Paradise Valley, California. We then moved northward up the coast of California and gave concerts in Bakersfield, Fresno, Stockton, Oakland, San Francisco, and Sacramento. And it was in Sacramento where I came down with a serious lower back problem (sciatica) that immobilized me to the point where I was not able to continue the tour, which included Seattle, and Professor Partridge joined the group in Colorado. The tour of good will and promotion was responsible for adding alumni chapters in Memphis, Baton Rouge, Dallas, and Phoenix. The student artists on the trips were vocal soloists Harriet Golson, Dorothy Dorsett, and Stanley Gellineau; orators Walter Fordham, Onnie Jackson, and Garland Millet, Jr.; and organist Arnold Dean. It was another heavily involved year for me. I sensed that President Millet was trying to expose me to the Adventist constituency in preparation for some special assignment.

Six new additions were added to the Oakwood family that year. Dr. Z. H. Coberly joined the Division of Education. Dr. David Kissinger connected with the Division of Natural Sciences and Mathematics. Mr. Robert Stidham was employed as college chef. Levy Baker was appointed college accountant. Miss Geneva Mosby became acting administrative secretary, replacing Mrs. Thelma Dean who took leave for advanced study. Mr. Albert Groves was appointed manager of the college store.

The Oakwood expansion program continued to advance as fourteen new apartments for married students were under construction with Mr. H. L. Wright as the contractor-in-charge. A beautiful new duplex building for teachers was near completion on Faculty Hill, as renovations were underway in Peterson, Cunningham and Henderson residence halls.

Dr. Dykes was in the process of making plans for a six-week summer excursion of Europe with her sister, Mrs. Anita Simms, touring England, France, Italy, Germany, and the World's Fair at Brussels, Belgium.

It was a banner alumni year. Mr. and Mrs. R. Skipworth of San Francisco, California, donated a set of deluxe bound Britannica encyclopedias, a world atlas, and two dictionaries to the Oakwood library. We had met the Skipworths on our student promotional tour when visiting and performing in the City of the Golden Gate.

Earlier in the year, President Millet had been awarded a $2500 fellowship by the Southern Education Foundation to study for a doctoral degree at George Peabody College for Teachers in Nashville, Tennessee. During the absence of the president, who returned to the campus each week for office duties Friday through Sunday, the Board of Trustees appointed me as assistant to the president. My assignment became effective January 1, 1958. While I was personally gratified to have the opportunity of getting my feet wet in this senior administrative area, it was difficult to make decisions and perform tasks Monday through Thursday, only to be second guessed on numerous occasions when the president returned to perform his duties on the weekend. The Board had placed me in a stand-in position, but I sometimes felt that my presence created more trouble than it cured. I observed with some solicitude the impact that this awkward approach had on faculty members as well. The difficulties which I encountered were not due to any untoward action on President Millet's part, but were inherent in the situation itself. The arrangement was a concession to something other than common sense. The predicament to which I had knowingly accepted and subjected myself, nevertheless, provided me with invaluable experiences which would be most profitable to me in my administrative growth for years to come.

The challenge offered me the opportunity to refocus my thinking concerning the character and objective of higher education. I seriously began to reexamine the functions of instruction, scholarship and research, and public service. I revisited the distinction between public institutions of higher education and the role of a church-related college like Oakwood. I began to have visions of how to make our philosophically and morally-based tenets palatable to youth, who often reject the commitments of their seniors as out of date, impractical, ill-conceived, irksome, or intolerable. I hungered for strategies that would help us to motivate the unmotivated for study. In addition, I looked forward to the day when it was generally accepted that teaching cannot be adequately evaluated until its essence, in relation to learning outcomes, is deliberated.

At that time, there was a corp of younger teachers who seemed to be always active in those creative activities in which students were involved. It was quite common for some of us to get together on Saturday evenings for a little social breather in one of our homes. It was a refreshing energizer after a week of intensive challenges. Such a break enabled us to compare notes, to make suggestions for future explorations, and to reinforce our support of each other in meeting our day-to-day goals and assignments. There was a natural kinship that existed among those of us who had come from the Midwest. Gaines and Velma Partridge, Herman and Arthelia Alexander, Jannith Lewis, Thomasine Longware, and my wife and I spent many pleasant Saturday nights eating popcorn and enjoying a variety of delicacies while having free and open discussions concerning Oakwood's present and future. Our sense of loyalty was quickened in the process as we entered heartily into the spirit of whatever was on our minds.

The whole campus was saddened just before the new year opened when a wind-driven fire burned Omega House, the home of twelve Oakwood families, to the ground. Fortunately, there were no human casualties, though the occupants lost most of their personal belongings. As to be expected, several conferences, churches, businesses, and individuals aided in providing assistance to the families which were affected.

Little Richard, a famed rock'n roll star, enrolled at Oakwood to pursue studies to become a minister during the second semester. He had been baptized at the Wadsworth Seventh-day Adventist Church in Los Angeles just months before. Still a bit shell shocked because of the media frenzy that had enveloped the enrollments of Joyce Bryant and Vivian Cervantes, the college made great pains to react to his admission with a steadying deliberation that would not contribute to any sense of sensationalism.

Ironically enough, six days after the United Student Movement had highlighted its annual banquet with a sparkling gala with the theme of "Winter Wonderland" in an exquisite setting of snow-capped mountains, frosty pines, and glittering snowflakes on February 9, the campus community woke up on February 15 under a six to seven inch blanket of snow which was a very rare surprise in the Huntsville area. It was the largest snowfall that the county had experienced in nearly twelve years. This masterful exhibition of God's handiwork was hailed as a triumph of nature, particularly by students from foreign countries and from the Caribbean Islands, many of whom had never seen snow before. Students, with their cameras, captured the picturesque wonderland with photos of glistening icicles hanging from trees and roof lines, frothy layers of snow caressing gigantic tree trunks, and serpentine forms of ice embracing the branches of trees as they moved downward under the weight of the night's extravagant invasion.

I found it very gratifying to join with Professor Gaines R. Partridge and ten Oakwood students in touring five Ohio cities under the auspices of the National Alumni Association. God richly blessed our efforts, as we were able to establish alumni chapters in Columbus, Springfield, Dayton, Cleveland, and Oberlin. The student participants were soloists Dorothy Dorsett and Stanley Gellineau; Arnold Dean, organist; Walter Fordham, Onnie Jackson and James Parker who gave temperance orations; and Leonard Mullins and Lewis Williams, who displayed their artwork.

As the college enrollment began to grow during this period with students hailing from the major metropolitan centers of the country, intramural sports, particularly men's basketball, began to play a significant part. The spirit of competition was no more evident than at the end of the regular basketball season when a tournament was held to determine the Intramural Championship. Each night there was a jam-packed gymnasium as the various teams put on a high-spirited performance for the crowd and particularly for their partisan fans. The Final Four of that year were the Proclaimers, the Phantoms, the Vikings and the Netburners. A few of the players consistently stood out because of their stellar performances: Vernal Murray, George Morgan, Willie Lewis, Ellis "Terp" Young, Charles Bridges, Billy Hill, Henry Barbour, Onnie Jackson, Bob Dent, and Donnie Hayes. It was the Proclaimers who won the championship with a cliffhanger 66 to 65 victory over the Netburners. A large university can attract more people and make more noise, but it is doubtful that it can secure the unified backing of the entire student body as is so evident at a small college.

There were a number of factors which contributed to my professional growth at the time: a determined effort on my part to prepare well-structured presentations for my classroom discourses; a conscious recognition of the need to understand my role in dealing with various constituencies— students, faculty colleagues, parents, fellow administrators, alumni, and board members; a calculated focus to communicate to these constituencies in unambiguous ways; and developing viable professional relationships with personnel at institutions (private and public) outside of the sisterhood of Adventist colleges.

In the meanwhile, my schedule of presentations at state and national meetings began to mount. It was a satisfying feeling to be invited to speak at several institutions within the state, such as Talladega College, Stillman College, Alabama A&M College, Miles College, Daniel Payne College, and Alabama State University. As a consequence, my ability to speak as a voice for black higher education had begun to gain some appreciable currency among my peers within the sisterhood of Alabama's black colleges and universities. Fortunately, too, I received more than my share of opportunities at Oakwood as well.

One of my great challenges was when I was requested by President Millet to speak at the opening convocation of the college on September 14, 1958. My address was entitled "Get Understanding," and the student body responded very enthusiastically to my presentation. In my conclusion, I challenged them emphatically in these words: "Oakwood is your school. Be proud of it. Take care of it. Do not permit anyone to mar, disgrace, or belittle your college. Remember your college is you… Study hard, work hard, pray much and your assets at the end of the year will give an unsullied reputation, a commanding personality, a marvelous sense of tact, a beautiful infusion of enthusiasm, a challenged intellect, a genuine Christian experience. It is because of this potential that I challenge you—that with all of your getting, get understanding."

The march of the civil rights movement was painfully slow. The winds of conservatism, at times, appeared to shipwreck the gains that were anticipated after the *Brown* decision. President Eisenhower, though firm in his belief that Supreme Court decisions ought to be enforced, was very weak in his support of civil rights legislation. The Civil Rights Act of 1957 passed only after the section was dropped that would have given the Attorney General power to bring school desegregation cases. Instead, a jury trial amendment favorable to southerners made the passage of the Act possible. The southerners were fully aware that southern juries were always white, and such juries were not likely to cast unanimous votes for conviction in civil rights cases. One month after the Civil Rights Act was passed, Eisenhower was forced to come face to face with the desegregation crisis of Central High School in Little Rock. When Governor Orval Faubus ordered the state National Guard to bar the black students, which a federal court had ordered admitted into Central High, Eisenhower's hand was forced. Reluctantly he ordered the 101st Airborne in to enforce the desegregation order.

I followed all of these civil rights happenings with great interest because I had drawn the inescapable conclusion that the white establishments of power in this country never shared their power advantages voluntarily, but only in response to intense opposition. For me this was painfully paradoxical when viewed from the deluge of rhetoric that was preoccupied with promoting America as a country "with freedom and justice for all." Events such as had occurred in Little Rock only forced me to relive those exhibitions of intransigence that I had observed all throughout my life and which, far too often, gave an unflattering portrait of black and white relations as they really were/are. I found it personally painful, even in my early thirties, though my skin should have been thickened by then, because of the punctuated confrontations that I had experienced on my own.

I am reminded of the time I went to the Business Equipment Company in downtown Huntsville to purchase some supplies. The college had been a steady and substantial customer with this company for many years. One of the salesmen was waiting on certain white customers who had entered the store ahead of me. As he waited on them, he addressed each one as *Mister*, using the traditional and appropriate handle before each person's last name. When my turn came, he simply addressed me as *Frank*. Blood rushed to my head as I lost all sense of proportion. Vindictively rabid, I turned aside, ignoring him, and went directly to speak to Mr. Monroe, the store's owner. I had intense aggravated energy to spare when I confronted Mr. Monroe. "Well," I said, "I'm more than a little disturbed and I need your help."

"How may I help you?" he inquired. Obviously sensing my irritation, he said, "Have a seat," as he pointed to one across the room before taking his seat behind his desk.

"I have come to register a complaint, Mr. Monroe. For years our college has done business with your organization, and we have spent tens of thousands of dollars, and I wonder why that, when white people come through your doors, they are addressed as *Mister* or *Miss*, and when black people come in they are called by their first names, or as *boy*, *gal*, or some designation rather than their last names. I felt particularly affronted when your salesman addressed me as *Frank*. I've been in this store enough times, and you have sent supplies to me with invoices that include my full name. I'm not so flippant or arrogant that I expect people to call me either *Professor* or *Doctor*, even though I have earned both titles. But I certainly expect people to accord me the title and respect that they would give any white person who walks in off the street who has neither the background nor the credentials which I possess."

With his face flushed to crimson, and the force of his voice practically gone, he said, "I know you're right, Dr. Hale, and that won't happen again."

I only want to make the point that the struggle is endless, and while I neither seek nor possess special magic, it was another instance where I felt, at the moment needed, a kind of new birth, and that I was born to move mountains.

The necessity of involving myself in so many things—in teaching, in administration, in writing, and in off-campus activities—required me to have dependable secretarial assistance. I was especially blessed to have three superb student assistants: Eunice Vanderberg, Helen Williams, and Carol Moore. So many times their work carried them beyond the arrangement of their prescribed time schedules; yet, I could always depend on them as they approached their duties with first-class professionalism and efficiency.

One morning during the month of March in 1959, I received a long distance telephone call from Dr. Charles H. Wesley, the president of Central State College in Wilberforce, Ohio, inviting me to join Central State in September of 1959 as chairman of the Department of English and professor of English and Speech. He was outspokenly complimentary of my leadership and administrative skills, and he assured me that I was the person for the position. While the move offered me an opportunity for leadership and programmatic development that I had never had, I winced at the thought of leaving the institution that I loved so dearly; yet I was aware that I needed "more seasoning," as my dear friend Bernice Reynolds was accustomed to saying. Despite the fact that I had almost been totally sheltered in an Adventist environment, except for my two-year stint at Ohio State, I was generally a stranger to public higher education.

Chapter 10

The Central State College Experience

It was on August 24, 1959, that I tendered my resignation to the Oakwood College Board and to President Millet. In the meanwhile, I had had several conversations and one face to face visit and interview with Dr. Wesley before accepting his offer. And so it was that I officially connected with Central State College in Wilberforce, Ohio, on September 1, 1959.

The arrangement was a comfortable one for me for several reasons. For some time I had been considering engaging with a larger institution in an administrative capacity, one where opportunities for professional growth in research and in publishing were more promising. Then, too, the fact that my parents were living in Springfield, Ohio, only eighteen miles north of Wilberforce, made it an attractive offer as well. It also helped to be the recipient of a contract that helped to make financial responsibilities less burdensome.

I felt, too, that I had left Oakwood in very good standing. My actual performances as instructor, as department head, as director of public relations, and as assistant to the president had given the officers, faculty and student body a satisfactory impression of my academic standing and my leadership potential as well. At the time our family moved to Wilberforce, Ohio, many members of the faculty were living in well-appointed homes within commuting distance of the college campus. Their financial income had allowed some of them to purchase homes of considerable worth and which were located in an impressive area of development rather close to the campus. It was a community of black professionals that rivaled any residential neighborhood in the nearby city of Xenia. Unfortunately, my income at Oakwood College had not allowed me the luxury of having any substantial savings. I was not prepared, even remotely, to purchase anything comparable to what my new peers possessed. By contrast, the administration offered us housing in a barracks-like facility directly across the street from the college's power plant. We had little choice in the matter but to pray that God would soon deliver us from a dwelling that was inadequate in terms of space, that caught the full blast of heat coming from the power plant, so much so that we suffered the unbearable intensity of 90° temperatures in our apartment that lacked thermostatic controls during the winters. Initially, our dreams for our own new home in the future seemed insignificant, vague and indefinite.

Because the rental fee was extremely low, we were determined to save in such way that we would not remain hostage to the daily inconveniences that faced us in such a setting. Ruthie and Frank III were eleven years of age and seven years of age, respectively. Their childish innocence enabled them to enjoy our restricted confines notwithstanding. They were full of contagious enthusiasm as they knocked on the walls that connected ours with the apartment of the Fort family who lived next door. I still relish the memories of how they exhibited boundless creativity and enthusiasm as they engaged in conversations, in a variety of games, and unabashed laughter and energy while not seeing each other, yet defying the walls that separated them. There was a powerful lesson that even adults can sometimes learn in observing the behavior of children. My sweetheart, Ruth, like the children, was always high on adjustment and adapted without the slightest degree of difficulty.

I found the educational climate in some corners at Central State very inspiring. I took steps to meet with members of my department staff as soon as possible. They included Elizabeth Frazier, Essie Payne, Sammye Walker, Evylon Crawford, Lucille Foster, Norman Berry, Gertrude Engel, and Val Faggette. My first meeting with this group was an absolute tragedy. My memory fails to recall any other single instance in my whole professional career that was so full of frustration.

The whole department, each member, seemed vividly struggling with for what was to them my intrusion. As a perfectly new outsider, I had come and had taken a shortcut to the chairmanship of the department. I was never clear on whether any of them sought the position or not. The fact was that no one from inside the group, already there, had been offered the position. Furthermore, the man who had been chairman had left unceremoniously, separating from his family as well as the institution, and I inherited his spouse as a faculty member, along with other problematic

136

conditions that had burdened three or four other department heads during a seven-year period prior to my arrival.

At that initial faculty meeting, one faculty member literally turned her chair around, presenting her back to me. Some with passive expressions of indifference, others with grimacing countenances of cynicism or hostility, and just about all of them, after looking at my youthful thirty-two year old face, seemed to be saying to themselves—if not almost audibly—*Boy, what do you know about anything!* It seemed to me that most of them were in their forties or older.

The ice soon broke beginning with the second meeting. I had gone out of my way to mend whatever fences, which I had not been personally responsible for breaking, after having been psychologically roughed up during my initial meeting with the staff. It had become clear to me that my new departmental colleagues had responded to me in a cold and indifferent manner because they had been influenced by a powerful set of unfortunate circumstances. It was difficult for them to have any real sense of optimism since there had been a rapid turnover in departmental leadership in the years prior to my coming.

As a consequence, I began to reach out to each member of the department individually. I took infinite pains to cultivate their respect for me, as well as for the vision which I had for the department. I felt the power of God multiplied many times as I called upon Him for guidance and support in my new setting. I prayed for the grace to be broad, generous, sympathetic and magnanimous in a situation which I had found cold and unfriendly at first. Then God began to do His thing. As I began to have private conferences with individual members of my staff, availing myself of their historical concerns and needs, something of singular value began to emerge. It was not a new discovery for me, but I learned again that, the more you reach out to others, the more you will get back in return. The New Testament injunctive was so apparent: "Freely ye have received, freely give." God had been so generous to me over the years, reaching out to me, and I was duty-bound to share in an understanding and compassionate way the great torrents of blessings that had been showered on me. As I reached out to cultivate positive relationships, I began to discover new islands of untapped power within myself that God wanted to develop and hone for his use. He opened my eyes to the need of not just viewing people in terms of their external behavior, but to learn to look upon each individual as possessing some unique treasure, something that can enrich your life, if you are willing to take the time to discover it. It would have been a terrible mistake for me to have missed the rich opportunities that I gained from the very wholesome interactions that I had with some very fine colleagues with whom I worked during my seven-year tenure at Central State College.

Mrs. Essie K. Payne, for example, had a reputation as an excellent, no nonsense teacher who manifested a determination to get the very best that she could out of her students. Thorough, polished, and always well-prepared, she taught her classes in such a way that they were never a bore or unprofitable. The students who sat under her tutelage tended to perform at a higher level on English proficiency tests than their counterparts from other classes.

The job of an English teacher can be a tortuous one. The freshman composition course is a monumental challenge for even the most experienced teachers. Teachers must spend hours pouring over unsightly and ungrammatical compositions from the hands of many students who have wasted their time in high school and who throw away many opportunities to develop even minimum skills in writing and speaking. It takes celestial genius and fortitude to deal with the adversity of untapestried compositions on a daily basis. Given the mounting volumes of compositions that English teachers must require, if students are to get the practice that they need in order to be proficient, it is no wonder that some of them burn out because of the harassing impact of their classroom battlefields. The unvarnished fact is that too often they are expected to transform the writing habits of a student in the time period of one or two quarters from what has amounted to a tragedy of inadequate academic preparation in the twelve years that have preceded the student's entering college. The beautiful irony is that, in so many instances, teachers and students have rebuffed the odds through commitment and intensive effort. As a consequence, many students have become shining lights of success with the aid of good teachers who helped them to snatch away the gloom and obscurity of their earlier limitations.

I had been attracted to Central State in the first place in large part due to the larger than life image of its president, Dr. Charles H. Wesley. Wesley was a renaissance man of multiple dimensions who was full of life, fire, and a strong will. He possessed a rich academic background, having earned the B.A. at Fisk University in 1911, the M.A. at Yale University in 1913, and the Ph.D. at Harvard University in 1925. He had served as a presiding elder of the African Methodist Episcopal Church and as president of Wilberforce University from 1942 to 1947 before assuming the presidency of Central State College. He was the author of twenty books and editor of the ten volume *International Library on Negro Life and History*. Additionally, he had been president of Alpha Phi Alpha and held numerous honorary degrees. To whatever men, black or white, one might want to compare to him, he took a back seat to no one. I found him to be a man of superior substance, symmetrical in overall development, and sensible. Regal and toned with a copper-bronzed handsomeness that enhanced his chiseled profile, he had to be aware of his own good looks and personal magnetism. He saw to it that the faculty always knew where he stood on issues of importance. Complementing his superior intellect was his remarkable skill as an orator. It was a great natural gift. Dr. Wesley was the embodiment of a man who was well-educated all over.

But in those days, Central State's reputation was not solely secure in the recognition of its esteemed president. It stood tall in the stature of its outstanding faculty. The campus was ripe with highly regarded legends whose notable credentials and dedication to the development of their students highlighted their powerful commitment and influence. Dr. Lenora Carrington Lane was a fresh, vigorous, and seasoned scholar who, even in her senior years, continued to command respect as a dynamic professor of psychology. There were other courageous and outspoken scholars, such as Dr. Carleton Lee in philosophy and religion; Dr. Paul McStallworth, Ms. Wilhelmina Robinson and Dr. Prince Wilson in history; Dr. David Hazel in political science; Mr. James Henry in geography; Dr. Oscar Woolfolk in chemistry; Dr. Clara Henderson in education; Dr. Ames Chapman in social studies; Dr. Richard Kidd in business administration; Dr. DeField Holmes in biology; Dr. Clara Howe in English; Dr. Stanley Kirton in music; Dr. Vivian Lewis in health, physical education and recreation; and Dr. Thomas Craft in biology.

There were also certain members of the non-academic staff that understood the dynamics of what was required to promote excellence in the academy. Among these were Mollie Dunlap, head librarian; Henry Johns, supervisor of buildings and grounds, who later became business manager; Francis Hawkins, registrar; and Walter Sellers, director of alumni affairs.

The future was promising at Central State as it possessed strong academic leadership. President Wesley constantly challenged the faculty and student body to high scholastic achievements. As the critical and imposing figure on campus because of his position, his powerful intellect, and his penetrating and almost clairvoyant vision, he was able to challenge the campus community to higher possibilities with marvelous effectiveness.

During my seven year stint at Central State (1959–1966), I made up my mind to take advantage of every opportunity possible to become an effective administrator. Thus, I learned to burn the midnight oil, keeping abreast of what was going on in the overall field of higher education. I spent more time preparing for administrative duties than I did for classroom and instructional activities. One should not need as much preparation for the latter activities, if he/she has learned anything at all from earlier years of teaching. This is not to say that one ought to be a slave to worn and frayed notes of the past. However, most creative professionals have mastered some principles of teaching that will enable them to enliven their lesson plans with some degree of effusiveness and spontaneity.

The problems of administration are epic in their implications. They include designing strategies to improve instruction, providing on-the-job training for personnel, creating opportunities for learning what students think and feel, taking appropriate action to solve the problem of racial disharmony, exerting appropriate influence upon the academic program through the control of funds, sharing decision-making power with faculty and staff, and requiring accountability of teachers by establishing performance objectives that can be measured according to those objectives.

So it wasn't too long after I arrived at Central State College that I found myself immersed in programmatic and personnel matters that required a greater deal of my time than I had originally anticipated. Fortunately, I had some excellent colleagues who I depended upon to assist in carrying the heavy load that is expected of a department that contributes its services to the entire institute. All students were required to take freshman composition. As a result, the weight of this responsibility fell upon the shoulders of the English faculty. They dug in and gave so much of their time to assigning themes and grading and returning them in a timely manner. I had some excellent colleagues to undertake and manage this heavy load. This responsibility was rendered by such able teachers as Mr. Norman Berry, Mrs. Evylon Crawford, Mrs. Maxine Crump, Dr. Gertrude Engel, Mrs. Lillian Foster, Mrs. Elizabeth Frazier, Mrs. Essie Payne, Mrs. Ruth Hazel, Mrs. Ophelia Holmes, Dr. Clara Howe, Mr. T. L. Hsu, Mrs. Ruby Kirton, Mr. Robert Kohn, Dr. Norman V. McCullough, Dr. Deckard Ritter, Dr. Haziel McDaniel-Teabeau, and Mrs. Sammye Walker. I, of course, joined them in teaching my fair share of the introductory courses in English. This group of teachers represents the number of teachers who were on the English faculty during my last year (1965–1966) at Central State.

When I first joined the college in 1959, there were only nine English teachers and eight English majors. I began to shift the emphasis in the departmental agenda almost immediately in order to promote student interests in departmental offerings, with the hope that more students would decide to major in English. Up until that time, the senior and veteran teachers in the department had very limited responsibilities in teaching sections of freshman composition. Their major focus had been teaching almost solely in their areas of graduate concentration, specializing for the most part in period and masterpiece courses. With only a handful of students in any of these courses, the teachers in these areas carried very minimal student teaching loads. After all, there were only eight English majors who were required to take them.

I challenged my English faculty to the hilt. I made the point that our freshman students should be exposed to our very best and seasoned teachers in their introduction to freshman composition. I was spurred with the notion that some students, once being exposed to the institution's most capable and heroic teachers, would decide to become English majors themselves. My intuition turned out to be true. I organized the freshman composition sections in such a way that each teacher taught at least two sections, with some of the youthful teachers teaching three or four sections. Even with this yeoman responsibility, the more experienced teachers were still able to teach in their areas of specialty. I was overcome with delight when, after two years, the number of English majors had increased to 122. It was a tribute to the efficient and excellent teaching and mentoring of our English faculty. In response, it was necessary for me to add new faculty members to our department.

At the end of my second year, I was able to convince my departmental personnel that we should establish an English clinic to be held two evenings a week where students with particular writing weaknesses could go to receive additional help from instructors. The students would be referred to the clinic by instructors at the college who recognized their need for assistance. The program, entitled "English Cooperation," was patterned after a program which Mylas Martin had designed and in which I had been a participant at Oakwood College. We succeeded in getting faculty members from every discipline to participate by referring to the English clinic students who had been under their tutelage.

As I gained the confidence of my departmental faculty and the campus community as a whole, I moved aggressively to begin new projects. Our department began to sponsor an annual Good Communications Week during the first week of November of each year. The programs were varied, featuring eminent and prominent scholars, poets, authors, and artists. The swell of enthusiasm and support that this initiative generated was responsible for greater campus and community attendance with each succeeding year. English majors were so aroused that they, out of genuine interest, established their own literary organization, SOCIETAS LITERATI.

Attempting to build on our new foundation of growth and enthusiasm, the English faculty submitted a proposal to the Academic Standards Committee with the recommendation that the department be granted permission to offer a master's degree (M.A.) in English. The appropriate bodies on campus and in the State Department of Education approved the proposal. The approval was granted just prior to my having accepted a new position as President of Oakwood College during that same school year.

The black rebellion of the 1950s and 1960s should have been anticipated. After all, the memories of segregation, lynchings, humiliation and historical abuse were etched deeply in the psyche of American blacks. For those who did not have a memory, and who wanted to dismiss the sad stories of their venerated and wise ancestors, they had no choice but to come face to face with the daily realities of mean-spirited racism.

Even during my very early years when I was eight or nine years of age, I gloried in the victorious feats of heavyweight pugilist Joe Louis. I recall how black adults and black youth gathered around the radio, glued to the announcer's description of every punch that was landed. We cheered and rooted vociferously with tribal pride as he vanquished foe after foe. We hollered ourselves hoarse and kicked up our heels most lustily when he disposed of white opponents. This was particularly true when he dispatched Max Louis Schmeling, who had earlier defeated Joe but, in the return match, was knocked senseless in the early minutes of the first round. From our ethnic perspective, what had been concealed anger up until that event was now the fuel for pay back time. It was also prophetic. In the 1960s Don Lee wrote a poem, "The Primitive," in which he declared, "…they brought us here—to drive us mad" (like them).

It was during this period that the United States was on the verge of facing an all-out battle against one of its most protracted and fundamental problems—racism in American society. My administrative challenges at Central State had prepared me, in part, to exercise some of the leadership skills that I had acquired to take some initiative toward the removal of racial barriers so pervasive in our society.

My first year at Central State had exposed me to the apprehensions which a new administrator, essentially coming in from the outside, has to face. It had been particularly difficult for me to adjust to newness as it related to programs, course offerings, instructional procedures, administrative policies, and the challenge of responding to the impact of an open admissions policy that brought students to campus with widely varying academic and cultural backgrounds and, as a consequence, widely varying needs.

As I have gotten older, I have become more cynical about America's noble intentions regarding racial justice. African-Americans, as well as other people of color, are fed a daily diet of racial discrimination and racial inequities in which the victims pay a heavy price and with considerable pain. It is always refreshing to recognize the extent to which black citizens have moved forward, upward, and have made progress, and that that progress has always come under the pressure and initiation of black people themselves. The white population and power structure has remained virtually silent and static on issues of race. Their voice has been minuscule. They generally have responded only when the destruction of their property is at stake or when they are forced to face the humiliating contradictions of what they have professed on one hand and what they have practiced on the other.

It has been my experience to observe that no institution has become immune from the infectious virus of racism—churches, schools, corporations, businesses, courts, industries, and civic and social organizations. All of them have played no small part in perpetuating the accumulated racial inequities of generations. What has personally bothered me most is the role that America's churches have played in contributing to the racism that has pervaded our culture.

This phenomenon became especially clear to me when, about 1959, I began making plans to have my daughter, Ruth (now Ifeoma Kwesi) enrolled in two of our academies, namely Adelphian Academy in Holly, Michigan, and Mt. Vernon Academy in Mt. Vernon, Ohio. Faced with the rigidity of their responses, I became determined to organize an effort against those denominational practices that had been responsible for a system of sustained discrimination and segregation over many years. As individuals, black people were less able to cope with such problems. The elimination of such practices called for God's direction, a united resolve among black Seventh-day Adventists, and a coordinated set of strategies to move us forward. Thus, on February 26, 1961, I invited a group of laypersons to attend an organizational meeting to establish the Laymen's Leadership Conference, for the purpose of advancing the cause of black Seventh-day Adventists within the denomination and to establish working principles so that: "Every non-white Seventh-day Adventist has all the rights, privileges, freedoms, and responsibilities within our church body of his or her white Seventh-day Adventist counterpart." The extended impact of this organization will be discussed in a separate chapter.

Over the next several years, my will and courage to move mountains of prejudice and discrimination profoundly affected my pattern of living. The magnitude of my multiple tasks—academic administration and my decision to meet the issue of race head on within my denomination—

became quite apparent when I was offered the opportunity to study overseas.

It was at the end of my first year at Central State College that I had been the recipient of a post-doctoral fellowship at the University of London. I was fortunate in that I was among the 120 recipients who had been selected from among a pool of over three thousand applicants. The opportunity was offered to forty students from America, forty students from British Commonwealth countries, and forty students from Europe. I could not have hoped for more. It gave me the glorious thrill of a lifetime to study abroad and under the instruction of some of the most preeminent scholars in the field of English literature, English history, and in the fields of English architecture and English music. My excitement was intense as I took advantage of the magnificent experience that I have attempted to recapture in a descriptive essay entitled "A Look into London."*

My experience in London was a fitting interlude at that end of my first year at Central State College. After all, I had been exposed to the quandaries and dilemmas that a new faculty member and administrator had to endure. The task of coping in an unfamiliar environment with limited resources, with an entrenched and despondent staff, with a disproportionate number of inadequately prepared students with marvelous potential, and with procedures that were often slow, cumbersome and uneven, was more than an ordinary challenge—it was a blazing opportunity that I had to shoulder in order to avoid complicity. But I knew that I alone did not have the knowledge to negotiate or to transform any problems, however simple, complex, or institutionalized. My fulminations would not make them go away. Even though my personal behavior and prayer life had not always been up to snuff, I am sure that I stunned God every now and then by asking Him to deliver me out of tight situations. My broken promises to the Almighty notwithstanding, I had come to the irrefutable conclusion that He would come to my defense. And He did! God's bountiful blessing to me during my first year at Central State allowed me to replay that beautiful tape of God's mystery and majesty in my life: "All night, all day, angels watching over me my Lord. All night, all day, angels watching over me." It was this knowledge of Heaven's abiding presence in my life that from time to time reawakened my spiritual energies, even after they had sometimes been displaced as a result of my sometimes having sacrificed precious beliefs and principles which had been the mainstays of my upbringing.

The 1960s were not happy years on many college and university campuses. There was a growing sense of urgency both above and below the

---

* See Appendix E, page 409.

surface at Central State. The exploitative history of the nation had begun to catch up with itself. A strong sense of resistance on the part of American blacks was in the air, especially among college students. They were tired of those national contradictions that both flouted justice and, at the same time, diminished their dignity., The *Brown* decision and the Montgomery Bus Boycott contributed to an exploding energy among students that led to demonstrations, marches, sit-ins, and a variety of protest measures that were designed to facilitate strategies that would bring about the surgical removal of the cancerous growth of segregation and discrimination in America. Sometimes it was difficult for white Americans to understand that what were considered disturbances and violence by them were but the culminating points of a sequence of historical situations in which there had been neglect, economic exploitation, oppression, lynching, emotional manipulation, cultural deprivation, political disenfranchisement, and provocation. America has always been tempted to magnify the *effects* without looking at the *causes* of racial unrest.

The college campus was an exciting and an unnerving place to be in the 1960s. The reverberations of the *Brown v. Board of Education* decision, the Greensboro student sit-ins, and the successful Montgomery resistance which catapulted Dr. Martin Luther King into international prominence had far-reaching effects. Black morale undulated between hope and despair in the competing stresses of dealing with the emboldened joys of long-overdue gains and the shameless ironies of black people having to fight every inch of the way for those rights that white people expected at birth.

Meanwhile, the limitations of teaching and serving as departmental chair were sufficiently heavy so that I was not able to engage in the kind of proactive engagements that my spirit needed to fulfill its potential as a force to counter the injustices, the inequities and the insensitivities heaped upon my people. Day after day, the smoke of the civil rights battle dominated the newspaper headlines with a wide range of stories that beckoned for our attention from troubled areas that lunged out from every corner of the nation. The national climate was tense and explosive as racial problems escalated on the heels of sit-ins, marches, demonstrations, freedom rides, riots, bombings, police brutalities, and as southern prisons were filled with those who defied laws and practices they considered inhumane and unjust.

All of these events provided me with the fertile ground that made my classes in speech a provocative platform for students to do some very serious critical thinking and to explore provocative ways of presenting their views on such topics among the following issues:

- Is non-violence productive in the long run?
- What is the best way to fight racial prejudice, segregation, and discrimination?
- Has the church been in complicity with the traditions of society that have been unjust to black people?
- Will white people ever willingly and equitably share the resources of this nation with black people?

I was happily amazed at the extent to which my students exhibited considerable diverse talents and experience. Their insights made me, as well as their peers, much wiser. I am certain that we all learned a great deal more from student involvement than had I lectured them *ex cathedra*, expecting them to gain more from the exercise simply because it was I who had directed the experience under the authority of my faculty rank, my degrees, my publications, my scholarly reputation, and my lordship over them as classroom teacher. This was simply another milestone in my teaching experience that helped me to understand that the extent to which we are able to admit that, as teachers, we too are learners and have no monopoly on knowledge. To that extent we make learning easier for both our students and ourselves.

This engagement of students with the contemporary racial issues of the day served as a positive antidote that allowed us to keep abreast and explore the forbidding aspects of racial conflicts within the sanctuary of the classroom. During this period students and professors found it hard to stay focused on studies and research while their peers were actively involved in expressions of protest on the front lines of segregated facilities to dramatize their lack of compliance with those traditions that undermined our humanity and personal dignity.

At the time, my parents were actively involved as members of the Tekoa Temple Seventh-day Adventist Church in Springfield, Ohio, only about eighteen miles north of Central State College. The church itself was composed of a solid cross section of members who struggled to maintain a mood of profound optimism even though the membership was not considered large enough to have the services of a full-time pastor. The church, under the strong leadership of local elders like Elder Guy Henry and my father, Elder Frank W. Hale, Sr., through discipline and unity as a body performed remarkably well in meeting the spiritual and temporal needs of the membership. While Elders Henry and Hale carried dominant roles, the leadership also came from other solid church members and officers such as the Neffs, the Giffords, the Singletons, the Whites, the Foxes, the Espys, the Dorams, the Busters, the Cochrans, the Cordells, the Buffingtons, the Leighs, the Stanley Henrys, the Robert Henrys, the Paul Henrys, and the Morris Henrys.

I found it especially refreshing to travel back and forth between Wilberforce and Springfield each weekend to share in the Sabbath services. The fellowship among these very fine Christians augmented my energies to the extent that I was always full of new vision and vigor when I returned to the campus to pursue my assortment of duties at the beginning of each week. The church members, sensing my zeal, kept me involved by electing me to serve as a Sabbath school teacher and as one of the local elders. One of the issues that confronted the church at the time was the status of the church where they were worshiping on Wittenberg Avenue. Its condition was not one that could be viewed as attractive. We had options to renovate, to build or to buy property. Under the leadership of my father, a Jewish synagogue was purchased on the corner of Fountain and Clark. This dedicated group of saints, numbering less than one hundred was able to purchase the church and pay off the mortgage in about three years. The true valor of this wonderful body of parishioners was rewarded as they began to worship in this beautiful new edifice, which accommodated approximately two hundred people with its main floor and balcony arrangements, its lovely pipe organ, its solid walnut pews, its lower auditorium designed for classroom activities, with a spacious kitchen furnished with the appropriate utensils, and with a sacred assortment of beautiful stained-glass windows with artistic and spiritual themes that were consistent with biblical literature. We were all able to enjoy the fruit of our aggregate and consecrated efforts.

On several occasions, Ruth and I invited the entire church family to come and fellowship with us on our 2 1/2 acre plot where we could all enjoy the beauties of nature while actively participating in Bible study, Bible games, testifying, singing, and praying, as we entered heartily into the spirit of Sabbath worship.

The intense excitement of those Sabbath interludes was always embellished with some vigorous and sumptuous meals that we shared as we alternated in our potluck locations from week to week.

It was during this period that a deep process of personal exploration had invaded my psyche. My soul was shaken and tortured by the long, drawn-out wave after wave of racial confrontations that were a part of the daily diet of American life. I recall the day when the bus with the first contingent of Freedom Riders was bombed and burned by white segregationists in Anniston, Alabama. It was on Mother's Day in that same year of 1961 when black and white riders were unmercifully beaten by a white mob in Birmingham. I looked in horror on television as more than two thousand marchers were herded into police paddy wagons and carted off to crowded jails for disturbing the peace. Each day in my mind's eye

America fell lower and lower from its pedestal of "one nation under God, indivisible, with liberty and justice for all." There were limits to which an honest black American could mouth such hypocritical jargon in the face of the plebeian and unchristian defiance that many white Americans exhibited as black Americans underscored their concerns through massive civil disobedience.

In the meanwhile, black militancy was beginning to gain a fast hold among the masses as the preachments of Malcolm X, James Baldwin, Gloria Richardson, Ossie Davis, and others felt that the time had come to take action that would immobilize the nation. Many thought that demonstrations in and of themselves accomplished little and were more cathartic than productive. Some felt that a nationwide work stoppage and halting the transportation centers by delaying them with thousands of demonstrators, paralyzing train stations, airports, bus terminals, and traffic in large metropolitan areas might in the end exert the limited power of an oppressed people to make their cause the nation's number one priority.

The actions of Governor George Wallace at the University of Alabama and Governor Ross Barnett at the University of Mississippi to prevent Vivian Malone and James Meredith from enrolling at major all-white institutions of higher education, that had been supported by the tax dollars of blacks as well as whites, made it apparent to many blacks that there was a void between black and white America that even Christian persuasion would not bridge.

All the while, I was seeking ways in which I could give students at Central State an opportunity to learn and to share in the historical significance of this very important and dramatic moment in their lives. Some of the young people felt that staying in school was simply a waste of time when so much was taking place which would be intrinsically valuable to them if they could only be a small part of the ever-expanding liberation movement. Some of them simply left school with the hope of returning, but not before they had had an opportunity to be involved and experiment with some of the approaches that would serve them and their people in the struggle to transform America on matters of race and race relations.

The tensions of the time served as a springboard from which we could learn that life is not static, nor is time neutral. As a relatively young teacher in my mid-thirties, I had already observed that knowledge is relative and impermanent. Things remain the same, fixed and with inflexible boundaries, only because people fail to explore new and unchartered realms. We tend to limit ourselves by the frozen edicts and policies of those who claim to have power over us. If we are prisoners to the thoughts of others, we learn only what they teach us. Because only God is omniscient, one of the first things that a free spirit learns is to question authority. The essence of learning is seeking. The essence of seeking is discovering. The essence of discovering is knowing for oneself. The person who fails to understand this will always be the hostage to someone else's agenda. This approach to life requires considerable backbone. Those who challenge established order, structure, and tradition will always expose themselves to resentful power brokers and to the incredulously fainthearted who are dedicated to keeping the peace no matter the costs. Nevertheless, the intellectual and spiritual gains are beyond measure for those who are able to recognize and embrace the validity of their own awakening awareness, reasonable desires, and spiritual insights.

By early 1963, racial turmoil had driven American blacks to such lengths that the voices of militancy were gaining momentum among the black masses. Still, the nonviolent middle-class voices of black leadership sought to move in a disciplined and restrained way to capture the nation's attention. Martin Luther King, Jr., had written a most cogent and stirring expression of his philosophy of nonviolence in his "Letter from a Birmingham Jail" on April 16, 1963. By midsummer, the scope and detail of racial unrest was immeasurable. The reverberations and the repercussions of the Birmingham riots had crisscrossed the country, triggering confrontations in the major cities of the North: New York, Chicago, and Philadelphia. A. Philip Randolph convinced black leadership that the March on Washington idea, first promoted in the early 1940s, was an idea whose time had come. Such a major demonstration was designed to bring about a coalition of black and white support that would lead to the passage of comprehensive civil rights legislation.

The intensity of the mass media promotion of this spectacular undertaking prompted me to seek the permission of President Charles Wesley to offer students the opportunity to attend and participate in this great convocation of national unity where major spheres of business, labor, religion, industry, the professions, and from every other imaginable area of daily life were to be gathered. Students and faculty sprang most eagerly and vigorously to the opportunity, so much so that, in short order, we had a caravan of vehicles headed east and ready to converge on the nation's capital. It was all our way of joining our brothers and sisters from around the country who were coming boldly to vent their indignation with the mindless, dehumanizing indignities of those strategies that were designed to crush the initiative, control the spontaneity, and impose senseless regulations on those who sought to gain the full freedoms accorded to most Americans without regard to race or color. My impression of that historic moment is capsuled in an essay which I have entitled, "The Historic March on Washington from a Personal Perspective."*

There are through the world of higher education many opportunities for growth and enrichment, not the least of which is exposure to scholars, artists, and lecturers of great stature. Among the many personages to whom I was exposed during my tenure at Central State College, two impressed me the most. The first was Martin Luther King, Jr., who, though on center stage in world affairs, never lost his sense of mission for his people. Outwardly calm, one could sense the penetrating depth of spiritual commitment as he spoke with no pretense and absolute candor. He was undoubtedly a man of superhuman courage in order to be willing to carry upon his shoulders the enormous burden associated with a leadership that fermented envy and evoked the vilest of emotions among evil detractors and among those committed to destroying him and his influence by any available means.

I, too, remember the day that James Farmer, the founder of CORE (The Council of Racial Equality), visited our campus. He was a guest in our home in Wilberforce. He, along with Martin Luther King, Jr., Roy Wilkins, and Whitney Young, formed the *Big Four* in awakening America to its plight and responsibility during the turbulent decade of the 1960s. He manifested a strength of courage and character, along with a keen sense of strategy, that made him a superb organizer and a commanding presence with which to deal.

James Farmer was an imposing bulk of a man with an incomparable depth of a bass voice that thundered with resonance and conviction with each word. I had seen him on television in his encounters with reporters, and I was always mesmerized with the uniquely extravagant ease with which he responded to some of the most complicated issues which were put to him. My perception was that his mastery of extemporaneous expression in a one-on-one situation even superseded that of King's. After all. Farmer was a voracious reader, and he had either rubbed shoulders with or sat under the tutelage of such great scholars as Carter G. Woodson, Benjamin Mays, E. Franklin Frazier, Alain Locke, Ralph Bunche, Sterling Brown, Charles Wesley, Rayford Logan, and Howard Thurman while enrolled at Howard University.

Suffice it to say, Mr. Farmer electrified the student body by chillingly describing the unrelenting tensions that had gripped the nation as the

* See Appendix C, page 400.

civil rights movement continued to unfold. The hungry crowd sat enthralled as his booming voice rehearsed the daily confrontations that the Freedom Riders encountered on their southern mission. It was clear from his message that the man who stood before us was amazingly committed and courageous in his efforts to demolish racial segregation and discrimination. He was more than a giant. He was already an institution in his own right!

Jon Robertson, a brilliant young African-American concert pianist, performed a program at Central State in 1965 as a part of the annual Artist and Lecture Series. I had recommended Robertson to the appropriate committee because of my knowledge of his musical credentials and expertise and because of our long-standing friendship. I had met Jon a decade earlier in California, and it was at that time that I began to focus on his budding career with great interest and enthusiasm. I was delighted, in fact almost transfixed, when our paths first crossed. There was something very special about this young, utterly sincere, fast-talking, good-natured brother, exhibiting the kind of wholesome self-assurance that sterling gentlemen possess. I observed him as he sat at the exquisitely beautiful Steinway that brought sheer resplendence to the well-appointed great room of his parent's home, Elder and Mrs. R. Hope Robertson. It was obvious that this young man had the heart and soul of a master musician. Superbly trained and a brilliant technician, I saw all of his energies heighten the impact of his nimble fingers as he displayed a masterful exhibition of finesse and facility. Even as he practiced, it was apparent that this fine musician was destined for a remarkable career in the musical world.

It was a thrilling experience for the Central State and Wilberforce communities as they were blessed by the dazzling renditions of this gifted artist. He brought the packed house to its feet with the total abandonment that he exhibited in Beethoven's "Appassionata." His artistry was characterized by concentrated intensity, blazing speed in the fire and flashing flexibility and dexterity of his sure-handed genius. His virtuosity was exemplified with creative variations as he moved up and down the scales, alternating between thundersome crescendos and almost inaudible dimuendos. Before Mr. Robertson left the Central State College campus, he and I agreed that, if ever God gave me the privilege to become the president and chief officer of an institution of higher education, and if I offered him the opportunity to become a member of my faculty in the Department of Music, we would join hands and collaborate in helping to make that institution the best that it could be. How little were we aware that that covenant would not have to linger indefinitely in order to be fulfilled.

151

Early in the spring of 1966, two significant events occurred: The dedication of Central State as a university and the installation of Dr. Harry E. Groves as the university's new president. It was on the occasion of Central State College becoming Central State University that the Board of Trustees invited me to give the Speech of Dedication and Challenge. It was a signal moment in my career as the platform was lined with such notables as Governor Rhodes, Chancellor Millet of the Ohio Board of Regents, Attorney John Bustmente, chairman of the Board of Trustees, newly installed President Groves, and representatives of the faculty and student body. One except from my speech challenged the faculty in these words:

> As a faculty, therefore, we join hands with those wandering scholars, skeptical critics and itinerant professors who have always been familiar symptoms of social change, cultural communication and intellectual upheaval. We accept without reservation the challenge which the new birth of this institution of higher education affords us. We recognize that it is in the passionate devotion to the dignity of the human spirit and that it is in painting an ever-increasing maturity of ideas among the landscape to the young mind that we buttress the mainsprings of a meaningful democracy.

I felt proud that I was having some influence upon the history of the institution, even as it had already had had a vital influence upon me and my career. It was also in the spring of 1966 during the General Conference Session of Seventh-day Adventists in Detroit that it became necessary for the Oakwood College Board to fill the vacancy created in the office of the president. Elder A. V. Pinkney, who was serving as president, accepted the invitation to serve as associate secretary in the Temperance Department of the World Headquarters. I received a telephone call from Elder Frank L. Bland, vice president of the General Conference, to come to Detroit immediately as the College Board was inviting me to become president of Oakwood College. I well remember how grateful I was for the honor which the board had bestowed upon me by simply extending the offer. It was gratifying because with it came the accumulated feelings of all that I had experienced at Oakwood, first as a student, and then as a teacher. Yet, the offer brought with it an overwhelming sense of responsibility. I knew of the sacrifices that so many had made in earlier days, and the reputation the college had established through those sacrifices. I, too, was aware that it was a troublesome time on black college campuses as young blacks were demanding more of a say in college governance. The black revolt of the 1960s was a part of the daily accountings in the national press. The impact of student sit-ins, demonstrations, protest marches and an assortment of other exhibitions of unconcealed resentment had already begun to weave its way into the consciousness of students at Oakwood; many of them had been powerfully affected by the everyday presence of humiliation brought on by the climate of segregation and discrimination which had persisted throughout their lives. And some of them had the urge to become engaged in activities that would contribute to positive changes, desiring to join many of their peers at other institutions in demanding racial justice.

Thus, it was with some misgivings that I made the trip to Detroit to confer with the Oakwood College Board. I met with and was warmly received by the board. I had had eight years of comparatively pleasing work at the college (1951–1959), and I knew to some extent what I might be getting into. While I had been blessed with a considerable amount of goodwill among teachers and students during my tenure of service at the institution, I was less sure of what the climate would be like in working with the board.

Once the discussions began, I felt quite comfortable. Without any seriously worked out plan of action for my assuming the presidency, the board members seemed anxious to have my thoughts concerning the administration of the college. I was excited, but I was careful to maintain self-control and self-discipline in responding to their many questions. I could tell from their inquiries that the college, though not fundamentally demoralized, was more or less in a neutral zone and needed to be energized. This fact alone helped me to crystallize some things that I had already considered in my judgment of the situation.

I knew from previous experience as a departmental chair that I could never be satisfied with simply an adaptive, passive or reactive role as an administrator. I had always thought of administrative leadership as being idealistic, programmatic, qualitative, charismatic, and of being able to transform ideas into significant actions. There was one thing in my mind that I was clear on, and that was that I was not interested in presiding over and maintaining the status quo. Oakwood's potential was too infinite and boundless to settle for anything short of creative organizational changes.

Apparently, the board was accepting of my visions for the future which included adding new faculty and staff members, establishing an Office of Student Affairs, doubling the operating and capital expansion budgets, approving a five to ten year capital expansion plan, and diversifying the board by adding laypersons to it. More important for me, however, was that I was the person who would have the primary leadership for running the institution. As a lay-professional and not being a member of the clergy, I wanted assurances that, although the board would be concerned with large policy issues, the president would be chief of operations. I was not unaware of what I felt historically had been the inordinate influence of the board chairman in wielding power and influence by virtue of his position with the world church body. If I were to become the first president of the college not a member of the clergy, I never doubted how complicated my role would be in view of a hierarchy, both in and outside of the board, that was riveted with clergy at all levels. Thus, I was not prepared to abdicate the role of the president as the chief executive officer of the institution to a chairman whose role I considered largely a symbolic one.

Fortunately, the board listened and was open to my concerns to the extent that they agreed to grant my various requests, and most of them seemed to be pleased with the fact that I was a highly self-directed individual, possessing a wide range of interests. Consequently, I accepted their offer and was prepared to assume my duties as president of Oakwood College on June 1, 1966.

My own hopes for an enlarged and challenging future were somewhat subdued by the reality that I had enjoyed my seven years of teaching and serving as department head at Central State. I had also established and conducted a Staff Presentations course for junior (those having the rank of warrant, first and second lieutenant, and captain) air force officers at Wright-Patterson Air Force Base, just outside of Dayton, Ohio. Over the period between January 11, 1965, through May 18, 1966, I had conducted a series of thirteen classes for personnel of the Aeronautical Systems Division. This consultancy provided me invaluable experience in working with mature persons outside of the traditional classroom and furnished me with supplementary income which, combined with my college salary, placed me in an income bracket that was significantly above that of my faculty colleagues at Central State. It was a rich experience that had proved profitable in a number of ways, and there was a slight hint of irresolution that momentarily gnawed at me in the process of coming to a decision before I had determined with certainty what I would do.

I remembered the excitement and zeal which our family enjoyed when attending the Central State University Marauders basketball games. Because of our Sabbath observance, we never attended any of the football games, all of which were held on Saturdays. However, the basketball games were usually during the week or on Saturday nights. Ruth and I and the children could hardly wait for each basketball season to begin because the school had established a super basketball record of 109 wins and only 28 losses over a five-year period from the 1961–62 season through the 1965–66 season. In fact, it was during the 1964–65 basketball season when the team went 30–0 and were crowned national champions at the National Association of Intercollegiate Athletics (N.A.I.A.) tournament in Kansas City, Missouri. I knew and taught a number of the players, including Ken Wilburn, Ed Bryant, Todd Day, and Don Rather. Suffice it to say, it was at first difficult for me to abandon the intense excitement of that gloriously victorious basketball fever; but soon my sense of loyalty was quickened for Oakwood College once again, for it was there that I had first begun my undergraduate education, and it was there that I had first begun my teaching career.

Before turning my attention to my initiation into the life of Oakwood as its fifth president, I must linger to unfold those events that led to my involvement with the Laymen's Leadership Conference. My association with this group ran parallel with my tenure at Central State College. The torrid racial outbursts of the 1960s in the secular community also met with a series of unpredictable and unprecedented events in the spiritual realm. And the Seventh-day Adventist Church, of which I have been a member since boyhood, did not go unscathed.

Chapter 11

The Laymen's Leadership
Conference (LLC)

The vision of the need for an organization to combat racial prejudice, racial segregation, and racial discrimination within the Seventh-day Adventist Church came dramatically into my consciousness as a result of a tragic confrontation which I had with the dean of girls at Adelphian Academy in Holly, Michigan, on Sabbath afternoon, April 30, 1960. I had been sent as a representative of Central State College to attend a conference for human rights in the North which was being held at the University of Michigan at Ann Arbor, April 28–May 2. The work of the conference focused on problems of housing, education and employment. The conference faculty included such notables as Morton J. Sobel of the Anti-Defamation League of B'nai B'rith; James Farmer, program director of the NAACP; Frances Levinson, director of the National Committee Against Discrimination in Housing; Frances R. Cousins, research director of the Michigan Fair Employment Practices Committee; James McCain, field secretary of CORE; and Richard Plaut, president of the National Scholarship Service and Fund for Negro Students.

The discussions were powerfully instructive. Throughout the conference, the interplay of economic and social factors, the lack of a fully developed body of anti-discrimination legislation, prejudice, and institutional interests in perpetuating discrimination were examined in the areas of housing, education, and employment discrimination. Each panel addressed facts on the extent of the problem, the history and current sources of the problem, and the different avenues of approach to solutions. Hundreds of persons were gathered, exhibiting an outflow of intense and enthusiastic participation for the pure joy of wanting to make a positive difference on matters of race in our society.

I did not attend the Saturday sessions, but instead attended the small Adventist church in Ann Arbor. Up until that time, I had never visited any of our denominational schools other than Oakwood College. Buoyed by the proceedings of the conference which I had attended during the previous two days, I decided to visit Adelphian Academy on Sabbath afternoon. Anticipating that my daughter, Ruth, would be ready to attend one of our academies within a year or two, I ventured on campus to gain some idea relative to the physical plant, campus layout, dormitory conditions, as well as student and staff attitudes. Aware that the offices would be closed on Sabbath, I had someone direct me to the girls' dormitory so that I might speak to the dean. I spoke with a student receptionist and told her of my desire to speak with the dean.

Within moments a middle-aged lady approached from her apartment quarters. A semi-scowl was on her face as she looked into mine. Attempting to set a conciliatory tone, I admired the beauty of the campus and its physical plant after giving her my name. Her short, abrupt manner was my signal to unburden my inquiry with dispatch. I indicated to her that I had a daughter who would soon be of academy age and that I was interested in viewing and getting information about the academy. She hastily informed me that there were only three Negroes enrolled on the campus among nearly three hundred students. She then told me that she had never had more than three Negro girls in her dormitory at one time. I then asked her if that was the quota or limit on black students, to which she replied in the affirmative. She then made mention that a certain doctor had a child enrolled in the academy and that Elder Louis Reynolds had enrolled his two daughters there. About this time, my throat was parched and my blood pressure was running high. My only response was a dramatic pause and a sigh of disgust, whereupon she inquired of my location and the nature of my work. I advised her of my primary mission in the area at the time, that of participating in a national conference on race relations at the University of Michigan. Then I indicated my title and position as a department chairman in one of Ohio's state colleges. In a sudden shift of attitude, she gathered her best Christian bearing, forced a smile, and then said, "Oh, doctor, perhaps you can pick up an application from the principal who lives... ," and she pointed in the direction of his domain, but the die was already cast. Once again, I had felt the biting sting of galvanized racism and ruthlessness.

I refused to become disillusioned because of her final gesture of personal flattery. What she had indicated in essence was that the academy

158

had a rigid quota on the number of black students who would be allowed to attend the institution and that even those had to come from among families with professional status. I am certain that no such limitations were placed on white students, the bulk of whom I discovered were quite average in ability and socioeconomic status at the Adventist institution where I attended. This experience was compounded by the fact that I later discovered that a number of the white academies were following similar procedures. The bodies of far too many black youth and adults fill the Adventist highways of racism because of the wretched experiences that had befallen them at the hands of so-called Christians. Many had been turned away from white Adventist schools, white Adventist churches, and white Adventist hospitals. While the denomination was quick to champion dress reform, health reform, temperance reform, and Sabbath reform, it dragged its feet unmercifully on those matters of social reform that promoted racial understanding and equality of opportunity.

Perhaps, even more disconcerting was the fact that far too few black leaders had taken a strong position to eradicate the problem of racism. There were notable exceptions, of course, but there were many who were caught in the uncomfortable predicament of taking a strong stand against denominational injustices and, as a consequence, jeopardized their positions as well as their advancement within the organization. Nevertheless, anyone wishing to identify and index a catalog of those who were relentless and dignified in both the pursuit and perseverance in seeking advancement for black people had only to examine the crusading records of certain giants who had taken the painful journey to make a difference. Dr. Owen A. Troy, a model of enlightened vision and scholarship and our most highly lettered minister at the time, was a gadfly, a pioneer, and he was the first black to hold a Union position (as secretary of the Sabbath School Department in the Pacific Union) in North America. Elder H. J. Wagner was a refreshing, stinging man of courage who was seasoned and visionary enough to command the respect of his peers who also served as regional conference presidents. It always seemed that he was the point man among an auspicious circle that included men like H. D. Singleton, H. W. Kibble, N. D. Simons, W. A. Thompson, A. V. Pinkney, L. B. Reynolds, F. L. Bland, D. B. Simons, R. T. Hudson, J. L. Moran, E. W. Dunbar, E. E. Cleveland, C. E. Moseley, F. Jones, E. P. Dorsey, W. M. Starks, J. Justiss, P. Cantrell, L. H. Davis, W. L. Cheatham, and W. S. Lee. Wagner was able to move with ease between black and white leadership; yet, he was outspoken and advanced the struggle, but he did not do it by eating humble pie. His leadership was dynamic because of his administrative and human relations skills and because he was not consumed by

159

trivialities, the allurement of favor among his white counterparts, or strategies that were out of date or self-serving. Each of the men in that circle, in one way or another, performed a highly valuable service to the denomination.

Yet, even a cursory examination of the state of race relations within the Seventh-day Adventist Church would reveal gross injustices and demonstrate a monolithic unreadiness by the church fathers to make any monumental efforts to erase those excessive practices that for so long had made unnecessary and unchristian distinctions between its black and white congregations.

As a child, I had been disturbed by that attitude of many of our white and black brethren on the subject of race. Whites acted as if racial segregation and discrimination were a way of life and that blacks should be contented with their lot. Many blacks seemed to accept their subordinate position as God's will in some instances, while others assumed that the walls of segregation and discrimination would eventually fall on their own. Some relied on the quotation that "the walls would, in fact, fall when men's hearts are changed." They viewed the issue on the basis of inevitability, as if men's hearts would be changed without external promptings. Of course, the denomination, took a more proactive stance when dealing with dietary, health, temperance and Sabbath issues. These issues, too, required that people have a change of heart if they were to become good Seventh-day Adventist Christians. The difference is that we emphasized our stand on these issues loud and clear. In fact, they are among the reforms that we have not left to chance or individual determination. We had exerted strong initiatives to underscore the denomination's point of view and policies in these areas. However, it was beginning to appear that the denomination was engaged in a conspiracy of silence, and it was not difficult to see the effect of that silence in promoting the ill consequences of racism and reducing the opportunities for change and progress. While there had been some discussion at some levels within the church, and even some very positive efforts by certain regional brethren, the impact was minimal in terms of the work in the North American Division. Deserving of kudos for their courage, commitment and creative efforts were men like Elder W. S. Lee, secretary of the Regional Department of the Pacific Union, who had conducted interracial workshops in large conferences throughout the Union. No one could ever doubt the commitment of such stalwarts as E. E. Cleveland, G. E. Peters, and W. W. Fordham, particularly when it came to addressing issues related to the race question, but I don't know how to soften the fact that there was a lack of individual initiative on the part

160

of many of our regional leaders and laypersons when it came to organizing and unifying the constituency of black laypersons and black leaders to establish a national conscience and to create a national strategy for the achievement of racial equality within the church.

I personally prayed and agonized about what measures were to be taken to challenge the status quo. Most black Seventh-day Adventists, like blacks throughout the nation, had a vision of what they would have liked in terms of equal opportunities within the denomination. The problem was that of translating the vision into reality.

It was on January 7, 1961, when I was invited to be the guest speaker at an annual alumni banquet sponsored by the Chicago Oakwood Alumni Association, that I attempted to burst the mythical bubble, that is, that we (black people) should not concern ourselves (the whites and some blacks told us) with the color problem, lest we lose our way. I had come to believe that this concept was a shoddy umbrella that oppressors had held over our heads for too many years. It had served to shield them of the many indecencies which they have perpetuated upon us, while at the same time we have been the ones to suffer from the downpour of their stormy injustices.

Believing that some constructive efforts should be made for relieving the racial inequities which existed within the denomination, I recommended the following to the hundreds of Lake Region Conference banquet guests: (1) An organization should be established on a network basis that will tie the black laymen together all over the field to combat injustices wherever they are discovered and, more positively, to create situations where fellowship can be practiced between blacks and whites. (2) Such an organization should be concerned first with obvious inconsistencies within local areas by encouraging integration in such areas as local church schools and vacation Bible schools. (3) The organization should also concern itself with certain key targets in the national framework, such as the Voice of Prophecy, the Review and Herald Publishing Association, General Conference Headquarters, and our medical and educational institutions. Our concern here, I asserted, should be to insist and to agitate for equal employment opportunities and for our young people to be admitted into our educational institutions inasmuch as our hard earned dollars are helping to support these institutions.

The response to my speech was overwhelmingly positive, even though there were a few who thought that my remarks were too censorious of our black leadership. While my comments were not mean-spirited or intended to upbraid individuals, I felt compelled to be a square shooter and a tough advocate without having to kowtow to tradition or authority for the sake of peace. Even a blind man could see where that approach had led us.

Later on in the month, I contacted a number of laypersons and professionals and informed them of what I was thinking, and I invited them to attend a meeting which I was convening at the Neighborhood House in Columbus, Ohio, on February 26, 1961. Located as I was in Wilberforce, Ohio, I pulled together a number of persons from Ohio as a nucleus for future expansion. The group included Mrs. Estelle Barnett and Mrs. Viola Boyer of Columbus; Mr. and Mrs. Wilbur Latson and Mrs. Anne Valles of Springfield; Mr. and Mrs. Burrell Scott of Oberlin; Mrs. Mae Justiss of Cincinnati; Mr. Mylas Martin of Cleveland; and Dr. Frank W. Hale, Jr. of Wilberforce. After the opening prayer, I began the discussion with these words: "People without a voice and without an organization have a hard time preserving their other God-given rights." I focused the attention of the group on a three-page outline which I had prepared entitled "Why Not Now?"* The introductory statement defined the problems: "The present climate of Negro-white relations among Seventh-day Adventists affects the denomination's program and image adversely and is contrary to principles of Christian doctrine and conduct." The outline was distributed among those present, and a full discussion followed with a detailed elaboration of *problems*, *causes*, and *solutions* in the area of race relations. It was noted that, in the *problem* area, our educational and employment policies and practices were discriminatory and that our policy of racial segregation within our churches characterized us as insincere in our testimony and application of Christianity. In underlining the *causes* of our problems, I pinpointed four specific reasons: (1) We have failed to follow through on the writings of Mrs. E. G. White as underscored in *The Southern Work*; (2) We have failed to develop any sound or consistent communication forum between Negroes and whites that would tend to harmonize the actions of the whole; (3) We have bypassed opportunities to establish race relations institutes for the purpose of discovering the grievances which seem responsible for our disunity; and (4) We have sacrificed the principle of love upon the altars of *bread and butter*, fearing that we might lose some prejudiced dollars from among certain ultra-conservative elements within our denomination. The group then proceeded to discuss and ultimately set down proposed solutions as listed below:

> As a denomination, we need to adopt a positive stand on social and race reform as we have on Sabbath reform, temperance reform, health reform, dress reform, etc.

* See Appendix D, page 406.

We need to discontinue *closed* admissions policies that deny admission to Negro students and to discontinue the quota system as practiced in numerous of our educational institutions.

We need to open the doors of our institutions and our doors of employment to all qualified teachers and people of all fields.

We need to welcome and to open the doors of all churches to all visiting persons and to all bona fide Seventh-day Adventists who seek membership irrespective of race or color.

We need to operate interracial youth camps and activities in order to encourage mutual trusts and respect among our young people.

We need to give ear to and promote the teachings of the Bible and Sister White in encouraging Christian principles on matters of race.

We need to foster race relations institutes which will serve as centers of instruction for developing techniques and strategies that will improve race relations among Seventh-day Adventists.

We need to move with all deliberate speed on the solutions herein mentioned.

I then invited each participant to frankly express his/her views concerning the feasibility of organizing a nationwide laymen's movement to combat racial discrimination and racial segregation among Seventh-day Adventists. Each person agreed that the need for such an organization was great. It was further agreed that the group would empower itself to lay the foundation for such an organization; whereupon each person pledged his/her physical, mental, financial, and spiritual resources to the advancement of such a program.

The group paid a special tribute to Mrs. J. Estelle Barnett, the founder of the Christian Benevolent Association, "for the noble and untiring work which she had carried on through the years as a freedom fighter and as a valiant soldier in the struggle for equality of opportunity for Negro Seventh-day Adventists."

Oberlin, Ohio, became the unanimous choice for the national headquarters because of its historical record and positive image in the field of race relations and because it was the home of Bonnie Scott, the board secretary.

Earlier it was agreed that the name of the proposed organization would be the Laymen's Leadership Conference (LLC). Taking a pragmatic outlook on the tasks ahead, the group wanted its membership to include persons who were strong Seventh-day Adventist Christians, who had attained some degree of visibility and respect in their communities, and who were sufficiently secure to withstand any pressures that might be hurled against them. Consequently, the group made a conscious decision not to invite denominational workers to join the organization, lest they would become vulnerable and/or victimized because of any position which they might take which would be contrary to their superiors.

Frank W. Hale, Jr., and Mylas Martin IV were elected co-chairmen; Bonnie W. Scott, executive secretary-treasurer; and Hazel Latson, corresponding secretary. The meeting adjourned at 5:00 P.M., but not before we had united our hands and hearts in prayer for God's blessings and guidance in the work of the LLC.

At our second meeting, held on March 26, 1961, at the same location, we were able to review a draft of a new brochure which Mylas Martin and I had jointly prepared to be widely distributed. It included a fact sheet, noting the history, purpose, policy, programs, scope, the constitution, how to form an LLC chapter, and a substantial bank of quotations from the pen of Sister White entitled, "Mrs. Ellen G. White Speaks in *The Southern Work*." The Board agreed on the substance, style and format of the brochure and commended Hale and Martin for their creative efforts.

It was during this board session that the following persons were added to the board, based on their willingness to participate: Vertis M. Barnes, Jr., San Diego, California; Helen W. Beckett, Dallas, Texas; Michael A. Blanchard, Chicago, Illinois; Bessie Carter, Oberlin, Ohio; F. Douglas Chandler, Detroit, Michigan; Willie A. Dodson, Washington, D.C.; Dr. John Richard Ford, San Diego, California; Myrtle G. Murphy, Washington, D. C.; A. Samuel Rashford, New York, New York; and Helen R. Sugland, Washington, D.C.

In a very short period of time what began as a fledgling initiative by a handful of dedicated laymen mushroomed into an active movement that gained monumental support from laymen throughout the country. There were detractors, however, who viewed our efforts as another unwelcomed attempt to flagrantly disregard church structure and certainly saw us as out of harmony with mainstream ecclesiastical opinion.

We received hearty support from most of those who sent us letters during the earliest stages of our development. A registry of their comments is as follows.

I am solidly behind this project.—*An academy teacher*

… I will cooperate with you 500 percent!—*A prominent musician*

You represent the type of leadership of which I've always dreamed.—*A general contractor*

This is what we need.—*A juvenile probation officer*

I am for you.—*A public school principal*

I feel confident that God is using you at this time to bring about a social reform in this denomination.—*A college professor*

The time is now.—*A newspaper reporter*

It's just what we need.—*A Regional Conference president*

Certainly in this day our church needs to take a firmer stand on many matters which are vital and important to minority members.—*A social worker*

I was very happy to hear of the Movement. It is something that we have long needed. You can depend on my whole-hearted support.—*A licensed real estate and insurance broker*

I am happy to know that you are associated with such a great cause.—*A minister*

It is the prayer of many that LLC will be the catalyst to speed up the growth and development of Christian Brotherhood between the races within our denomination.—*A veteran minister*

We have waited too long for this kind of action, but it's still not too late.—*A church school teacher*

I received the brochure of the Laymen's Leadership Conference. I think the approach is positive and very fine.—*A Union Conference executive*

I give you my whole-hearted support in your endeavors.—*A leading physician and surgeon*

May the Lord continue to spur you on in the direction that you are going and that He will open the eyes of those who have been sleep over the problem for many years.—*A businessman*

Congratulations to you. Mylas and the LLC!—*An overseas missionary*

I am pushing and supporting you with an invisible stick.—*A Regional Conference president*

When the time is ripe, we will join in the grand chorus to support you.—*An African-American youth*

There were those, however, who had grave misgivings concerning the organization. Among the responses that we received in this vein are the following quotes:

The cause of Christ is not served by an exposé of her sins to the world.—*A church school teacher*

I am in violent disagreement with Machiavelli's philosophy that the end justifies the means.—*A leading evangelist*

Do not resort to use the world's methods to effect a reformation in the Church of Jesus Christ.—*A General Conference officer*

Have you set up an organization in conflict with, and in opposition to, the designated channels of administration and lines of communication for Church government in the Seventh-day Adventist denomination?—*A Union Conference president*

From our earliest beginnings as an organization, we were forced to remain vigilant in our examination of racist practices within the denomination. It was not necessary for us to crisscross the country to discover evidence of racial discrimination and segregation. Our phones began to ring and a volume of letters flooded our mailboxes, apprising us the toll of accumulated humiliating and embarrassing racial incidents within the church politic that were well imprinted in the minds of those who contacted us after learning of the existence of LLC. What we heard and read were reports of black students being denied admission to *white only* SDA schools, of blacks being ordered away from white churches that they had chosen to visit or seek membership therein, of observing the church's role as a full partner in the system of racial exclusiveness, of listening to white leaders and pastors who enlarged the biblical story of Noah's curse on Canaan to justify their attitude and treatment of blacks—giving them a shaky reason to believe something they could not explain, and of blacks not being able to work or hold any position of significance in denominational institutions that were being supported, at least to some degree, by their tithes and offerings, and of using the Spirit of Prophecy to endorse and buttress the whole treacherous system of racial injustice.

As an organization established out of bounds, as it were, outside of the boundaries of the mainstream denominational framework, the LLC leadership was aware that it would be assailed by certain critics—white and black—for not playing by the rules. Some voices accused us of being a movement in a *confederacy against God's Church*. However, I learned early in life that if people can define you, they can confine you, and God helping us, we were not going to let anyone get away with that designation of us. *The laymen's movement was not an anti-church movement; it was an anti-discrimination and anti-segregation movement.* Once again, there were those who would distort the issue and the truth by magnifying process instead of principle and effects instead of causes. The Laymen's Leadership Conference was established in the first place because of its profound dissatisfaction with the snail pace of equality of opportunities for black people within the denomination. We not only had misgivings about white leadership, we lamented the fact that too many of those among black leaders, who were supposed to be representing the interests of black people, were irresolute, accommodating, acquiescent, and shilly-shallying on critical issues that made even the discussion of them an absurdity. This certainly does not discount the contributions of a valiant few who with conviction and dedication were clear-cut in their articulate efforts to carry the struggle to the highest levels within the church. We knew of the establishment of the Race Relations Committee in the General Conference at the Fall Conference of 1960, and that, prior to our activities, no word had been mentioned of it, nor had the committee met. Once our organization was formed and the word of our agenda began to spread, certain members of the committee informed us that the white brethren felt the urgency to make a public announcement immediately even though the Race Relations Committee had been inactive, not having met, even once, since its inception nearly six months earlier. While we supported the need for such a committee, we were further convinced that history should have reminded us against any over-reliance on those traditional approaches that have proved futile to our progress and liberation as a people. And so, with the fever of righteous indignation, we kept on pushing ahead.

From the very onset, it was important for the leadership of LLC to come to a clear understanding of roles. On February 21, 1961, I had received a missive from Mylas Martin, who served as co-chair along with me, suggesting that we divide our responsibilities. He suggested that our areas of assignment would be as follows:

> I'd feel a bit more comfortable, please, if you would take the active leadership. Rallying public support, on planning to go here and there, smoothing matters over, making speeches—all—This is not my forte. You do it well. I? I'd rather sit, think, plan and scheme and hurl monkey wrenches at our "enemies." This is my forte. HALE FOR ACTION. MARTIN FOR PLANNING. Why not?

While I knew that task we had taken on would begin a dynamic and living laboratory where our successes would be determined by God's direction and by teamwork, I had no intention of becoming circumscribed as a tool to anyone's singular thinking or direction. I also knew that, when Mylas got something into his head, he was not easy to convince otherwise. I also knew that by the sheer weight and creative activity of my own mind, as well as my enormous drive and purpose, that I of necessity would be significantly wired into both the vision and implementation of our efforts. My position was not one of arrogance or an unwillingness to be a team player. I knew full well, based on my experiences as a department chairman at two different institutions, that it is essential that a leader be able to transform his dreams into significant actions. As a pragmatic idealist and visionary, and as the one who conceived of the need to institute a national organization of laymen in order to carry the dialogue and struggle for equal opportunity to a new national level within the denomination, I was not prepared to confine myself into a box of another's musings so as to be subservient or subordinate to directions which I found incompatible with where I thought we should be heading. I think my instincts were right because the onus of the organization's success was largely on me because of the expansive, widespread campaigning I had done by letter, by telephone, and by speaking in formal and informal settings. While I had no problem in giving others the opportunity to share their vision, and to offer plans and strategies for implementing those plans, I simply found it inconceivable that I would shortchange and deprive myself of having an active role in the core of what I had spent endless amounts of energy and creativity to get off the ground in the first place. Martin had a mind ideally contoured for caustic and vindictive rhetoric as a man of scarcely veiled hostility toward those whites he found to be denigrating in their attitudes and behavior. He had little patience with what he considered *hassling over the obvious*. I felt more comfortable using his provocative skills as a journalist, rather than one whose magisterial impatience might be counterproductive were he to be given the imperative right to be in charge of planning *carte blanche*.

So I continued to plan and set the agenda for LLC meetings, always conferring and consulting with Martin, as well as other board members, relative to plans and proceedings. Among the plans which I offered and the board sustained were the following:

> Creating a national laymen's organization to serve as a catalyst to promote equality or opportunity for black Seventh-day Adventists within the denomination.

Publishing three thousand copies of *The Southern Work*.

Targeting those institutions (educational, medical, publishing, churches, conferences, etc.) that had policies and practices that were discriminatory.

Planning an itinerary that would enable LLC representatives to carry their message to the major metropolitan regional churches east of the Mississippi River prior to General Conference.

Insisting that LLC representatives be given the opportunity to meet with General Conference and Union representatives at the Autumn Council in Washington, D.C., prior to the 1992 General Conference.

So from the start, while Martin would have preferred a division of labor that would have designated Martin for planning and Hale for action, it was a questionable strategy that was unworkable. The historical moment was such an auspicious one that we—Martin and I—were perpetually involved in thinking, planning, writing and putting our best strategies together in partnership as we exhausted every opportunity we had to deal with the high-handed treatment that had been accorded black Seventh-day Adventists over the years. Mylas Martin was a delightful colleague to have in such a struggle. Sharp in perception and with clarity of thought, he, no doubt, could have commanded a formidable career in law. Possessing a retentive brain, fluid phraseology, and a dogged determination to investigate any detail that would expose even the slightest weakness in the armor of the opposition, he was refreshed by the joy of mind to mind combat over simple as well as provocative issues.

We never really dealt with the issue of who was going to do *what* and *when* after that. Because of his journalistic background, Martin had a way of running press conferences, and because of my background in communication, I had a way of holding and commanding the attention of audiences. Martin, skilled as an indefatigable publicist, moved in and out of the white Adventist hierarchy with some ease, primarily because some were intimated by the potency of what his poison pen as a journalist could do. I had earned a reputation as a scholar of high training, as a defender of the underdog, forceful, pugnacious with a passion when humanitarian issues are placed on the table, and grasping the dynamics of what it takes to win in a struggle of truth over perilous traditions. We were a *terrible* team—young enough to be bold and creative, yet seasoned enough to even command the respect of those who challenged our point of view.

Our initial strength as an organization came from the seasoned members who had agreed to become members of our board. Our standing grew and gained because of the evident sincerity and consistency of our board advocates. Even black members of the church who had for years had many misgivings concerning the denomination's racial policies and practices began to offer us encouragement. Their influence was useful and effective in keeping our new organizational experiment on center stage with the kind of momentum that would bring the church hierarchy to understand that our mission was a most serious one, and that we would not disappear or be dissuaded until there was a satisfactory resolution of our concerns.

Our office was showered with testimonies of frustration over racial incidents that were uncharacteristic of born-again Christians. One member wrote us of an incident which occurred at the Central Huntsville (Alabama) Seventh-day Adventist Church on April 14, 1961. Several Oakwood College students went to the church because the Southern Missionary College Choir was there to perform a concert. When the students arrived, they went in and sat where there were vacant seats. Just before the concert began, it is reported that the pastor, Elder Leggett, got up and said, "Our church is not fully integrated; therefore, we are asking that students from Oakwood College go to the balcony." Humiliated and shocked, the students got up, left the church and returned to Oakwood.

In an encouraging letter sent to us by Paster David Hughes, he stated, "Permit me to take this opportunity to congratulate you and your colleagues for the bold and forthright attack made on the unfortunate racial issues existing in our denomination. I am personally convinced that the Forty-ninth General Conference World Session of SDA's will prove to be the turning point for the long ignored racial issues. I'm sure that it is the prayer of many that the LLC will be the catalyst to speed up the growth and development of Christian Brotherhood between the races within our denomination."

Our files are pregnant with letters from faithful black Seventh-day Adventists who have been confronted with racially embarrassing circumstances and who wanted to share their experiences with LLC, hoping that we could help to remedy an excruciatingly painful experience that has plagued our denomination for years on end. Such testimonies came from such church stalwarts as Mrs. Bonnie Stewart (Oberlin, Ohio), Mrs. Lena Cole (Delaware, Ohio), Mr. and Mrs. J. R. Duckworth (Michigan), Mr. Marion White (Chicago), Mr. Ronald Huggins (Washington, D.C.), Dr. J. Lewis (Huntsville, Alabama), Dr. Elaine Giddings (Berrien Springs, Michigan), Dr. Fred Metz (Denver), Mr. Eugene Garel, Sr. (Detroit),

Mrs. Everyl Gibson (New York), Mr. Robert Taylor (student, Andrews University), Mr. E. J. Specht (Hunstville, Alabama), and Mr. J. Paul Monk (student, Andrews University). They represent only a few of the many who contacted us with their concerns relative to problems which they, members of their family, or church friends had experienced.

By the spring of 1961, we were well aware that the task of overcoming and reversing the accumulated racial inequities of generations of church life and practice and of eliminating the segregated boundaries which accompanied and helped to perpetuate them was a major undertaking. We knew that delay would be suicidal. To eliminate discrimination and segregation within the church called for a comprehensive approach involving a broad range of black members from major metropolitan areas. We knew that our work needed to be carried forward within a framework of Christian and democratic ethos. All we needed was the will and the courage to move beyond appeals based exclusively on persuasion and to alert the powers that be that we were not going to let them escape the responsibilities of their past misdeeds. Our search for solutions adopted persuasion as a strategy rather than coercion. Underpinning our strategy was our hope that the church fathers would have learned something from the reactions of black people who were confronted with stalemates in Montgomery, Greensboro, and other centers of racial unrest throughout the country.

We knew that the shifts of black attitudes towards racial injustice had moved them to a more active stance in their resistance to discriminatory practices. We knew that in order to be really effective that we needed to stir genuine concern among black Seventh-day Adventists. Historically, the issue of race and the discussion thereof had rested almost entirely upon the black clergy. Because legions of black members had struggled with the denomination's approach on racial problems over the years, we had little doubt about our efforts to achieve grassroots support for our actions. We carried our message to a number of major metropolitan churches, including Shiloh in Chicago; City Temple in Detroit; Berean in Baltimore; DuPont Park in Washington, D.C.; and Ephesus in New York City. We generally worked through the offices of the Missionary Volunteer Society or a member who was on our board and who was also a member of the local congregation. There was little doubt that our campaign was appreciated as hundreds attended each of the afternoon sessions we conducted to foster greater acceptance of our goals and the strategies for reaching those goals. We were aware that as a race of people we had to face an all-out battle against racism, one of the most protracted and fundamental domestic problems in American life and culture. While the secular world and even a number of denominations had begun to deal with this intense problem, confrontation was long overdue on the problem of segregation and discrimination within the Seventh-day Adventist Church. The church had already paid a heavy price for the practice of racial segregation and discrimination and their concomitant efforts. Serious defections had taken place as individuals and congregations had departed from the church over the years. Those who left as victims of racism were generally rebuked and chastised as being unfaithful. These denunciations tended to overshadow the unjust, unsalutary, and enormously responsible role that the church had played in their exodus.

Though progress had been painfully slow, we were cheered by the fact that at least a generation of black Americans had moved forward from an almost complete lack of lay direction relative to issues of civil rights, to the point where there was recognition of the serious dangers that continued widespread social and racial inequities would pose to the stability and credibility of the church.

As our efforts began to snowball with increasing support from black SDA's in the pews, certain key figures among the black clergy began to admonish us concerning our mission as well as our methods. They challenged both our judgment and the value of our *modus operandi*. Elder E. Earl Cleveland, then associate secretary of the Ministerial Association of the General Conference, attempted to provide some balance to his chastisement of our efforts by stating that our "aims and objectives are solid and founded on Bible principles" in a letter that he sent to me; however, he went on to state that "I am in violent disagreement with Machiavelli's philosophy that the end justifies the means. And nor can I go along with those who feel that the method must be of the same evil against which it is aimed." Scarcely less troubling was a communication which I received from Elder Frank L. Peterson, also an associate secretary of the General Conference.

Elder Peterson was the most impressive and effective professional preacher and educator that I had known. It was because of him that I had begun my teaching career at Oakwood College, and it was because of him that I had become the first Oakwood faculty member to earn the Ph.D. while at Oakwood. Dr. Eva B. Dykes had come to Oakwood from Howard University with the coveted doctorate already in her possession. It was because of Elder Peterson's motivation and support that I had become the second person to hold the Ph.D. as a member of the faculty. The relationship between Elder Peterson and myself had been long, warm, and mutually supportive. While we were close and our goals for Oakwood meshed, we were miles apart on how to deal with the issue of racism within the Seventh-day Adventist Church.

172

Though generally tempered, gracious, and dignified, Peterson was a hard-crust Adventist organization man. Yet, he was a gentle man and absolutely fair once you saw what he was up to. He had risen far outside of the racist habitat and harbor of his upbringing in southern Florida. Through sheer grit, he had been able to hammer his way up through a system that was rigid and revolting, but which at the same time, added to his front-line experience of dealing with white people. In many ways he had conquered the odds because of the driving purposefulness of his own faith, commitment, and creative energies. Though his avowed aim was to eliminate racial differences, he considered the approach of the LLC as painfully disgraceful and counterproductive.

In a letter dated April 27, 1961, he literally took me to the woodshed: "I want you to know that when I heard that a man of your caliber in the church would head up such a movement, I was deeply wounded..." He continued his strong attack on LLC efforts by stating, "To organize against the church because of any wrongs that may be seen in the church is neither a Godly or Godlike act. To seek to nullify the work of the Seventh-day Adventist Church because of racial reasons will produce only chaos... The race to suffer the most damage will be the race that made the disorderly attack. Please, Dr. Hale, do not let it be chalked against you that you would confederate against God's Church because of racial prejudices." Interspersed with Elder Peterson's strong admonitions and warnings were substantial renderings from Scripture and the Spirit of Prophecy. So here was a three-pronged weapon that had more than a little impact in terms of its sincerity, its persuasiveness, and its personal appeal. The letter was a remarkable document for its frankness and forthrightness; it was an appeal from a church father to a church son; and yet after serious study, prayer and deep consideration of its contents, I felt that Elder Peterson had restricted himself to rather narrow and obscure arguments.

There was no need for me to dwell on the matter indefinitely, so I responded to his queries and appeals in good faith on May 3, 1961. I did not seek to debate the issue point by point raised in his letter. I just wanted Elder Peterson to see and sense the limitations of his own conservative strategy which, for the most part, had left the issues of racial justice sputtering, because the establishment took its time on such matters when it was aware that there was no real or concerted effort throughout the black constituency to rock the boat.

I gingerly ventured an answer to his warning, "Do not enter into any confederacy against the Church of God." I argued that "the laymen's movement is not an anti-church movement; it is an anti-segregation and anti-discrimination movement." I continued, "Are all Seventh-day Adventists members to be forever found to hear but one side, and that side being the side of the oppressors? Elder, it is a most unfortunate thing when those who sit in the seats of justice are bound in deciding racial issues, to listen to the most conservative viewpoints... I speak of many of its (the Church's) most eloquent leaders who have shamelessly given the sanction of the Bible and the Spirit of Prophecy to endorse the whole treacherous system."

Elder Peterson compounded my gloom upon reading his letter especially when he warned, "Please do not use your influence to bring the church into disrepute before the world." Unflinchingly I responded by stating that "nothing could be farther from our imagination... The implication suggests that any laymen's movement designed to improve race relations will be met on the threshold by the church and its leaders to do battle against it. I have never entertained the thought of such a struggle. We want to give whole-hearted support to the newly established Race Relations Committee of the General Conference." Space is not sufficient to detail the full exchange of comments in our letters to each other; nevertheless, I attempted to conclude my response on a conciliatory note when I wrote:

> We want to serve as one channel for assisting the General Conference in pinpointing certain areas of sensitivity among us (Adventist blacks). We want to assume that our leaders will appreciate and solicit a "grass roots" reaction from among those who make helpful and constructive suggestions in the area of race relations. If there are leaders who would suppress such actions by challenging the efforts of those who would snatch truth from the dust, how our brethren could conceive of such men as being stalwart representatives of Jesus Christ is a mystery which I leave all of us to penetrate.

While communicating with Elder Peterson as friend to friend, my missive was also something of a rebuttal as a means of reminding him that there was no easy way to deal a hard blow to ingrained racist contentions and practices. I placed the ball of progress squarely in the court of church leaders when I concluded with this poignant comment:

> I maintain that there is no circle in the church that could sustain segregation and discrimination for one moment, if it were not sustained in the circle of leadership. If the General Conference, the Union Conferences, the Local Conferences, the publishing houses, the evangelists, the ministers, the missionaries, and the educational and

medical institutions would all combine their powers to eradicate the smudge of racial segregation and discrimination among us, the whole system would crack and crumble overnight. Such a challenge is for us the living! I have no other plans but to accept that challenge.

During the months of March, April, and May of 1961, Mylas Martin and I proceeded to work diligently in the preparation of a flyer for mass distribution. We sent a mass mailing of the completed flyers to regional constituents with an accompanying letter on June 22, 1961. The same letter and flyer were sent to the General Conference officers, Union Conference officers, Regional Conference officers, and Regional Conference pastors. The letter made a powerful connection between what the Laymen Leadership Conference (LLC) considered as race reform and certain other reforms that the church had no hesitation in promoting as a part of its central tenets. The letter stated in part:

Seventh-day Adventists are champions of numerous reforms in the areas of diet and health, amusements, music, dress, religious liberty, stewardship, and, of course, the Sabbath. We accept at face value the teachings of the Bible and the Spirit of Prophecy to support our position. We do not hesitate or apologize for the stunning effort which these truths, when presented in a straight-forward manner, may have upon the hearers. We adhere to the principal that right-eous standards are uncompromising; therefore, we are resolute and forthright in our presentation of these teachers.

It seems, too, that one of the roles of the church should be to teach the fatherhood of God and the brotherhood of man that cuts across nation and race, culture and class. We either accept God as the Father of all men ("God hath made of one blood all nations of man"—Acts 17:26), or we deny his fatherhood to all men.

Ours was a forceful argument that went beyond anything which had been attempted by any laymen's group on a nationwide basis in the history of the church. It was a bare-bones challenge to the morality of segregation and discrimination as practiced by the denomination. The LLC was making a frontal assault, which was infused with new vigor, on grievances that the church had been cautious in handling. In fact, it would not be unfair to state that historical evidence points to the complicity of the denomination's hierarchy, churches, and church members in the racism that has pervaded American culture.

Not unmindful of some of the savage injustices which many black Adventists had experienced during the first half of the twentieth century,

LLC unashamedly threw down the gauntlet by challenging the church's racial policies and practices in this scathing paragraph of the June 22, 1961, communication:

> For decades we as Negroes have <u>ADJUSTED</u>! We have adjusted to segregated churches. We have adjusted to quota systems in our schools, our colleges, our professional schools. We have adjusted to the philosophy of "White Teachers Only" in most of our institutions of higher learning. We have adjusted to the philosophy and practice of "Menial Tasks Only" for what few Negroes who have served us in certain of our publishing houses, sanitariums, and other centers. We have adjusted and adjusted. Now is the time to readjust. Communication is a two-way street. Too long has the information been funneling down; now is the time for the reaction and information (of those who have been affected by racism) to start bubbling up. This organization (LLC) is dedicated to the abolition of racial segregation and discrimination within the organizational pattern and framework of the Seventh-day Adventist denomination.

As the summer months began to roll by, the members of the executive committee of the LLC were up to their ears in mailing out new brochures, in responding to correspondence and requests for copies of *The Southern Work* which had become a hot item as a compelling statement of Ellen G. White's sensitivity on racial matters. There were some blacks who were distressed by the militant language of our LLC flyer. On the other hand, there were clergy who openly—at least when speaking to us—supported our endeavors. Martin reported that while on the Lake Region Campgrounds during August of 1961, he encountered Elder Clinton Warren and gave him a flyer. Martin indicated that Elder Warren handed the flyer back to him, stating, "I've already got one. And I think its marvelous." He smiled. "You folks are to be commended for your soundness of approach. I'm behind you one hundred percent."

Martin cited another example of ministerial support in an August 24, 1961, memo that he sent to me on his stationery from *The Cleveland Press*. He mentioned that as he was running across the Lake Region campgrounds, a voice called out, "Brother Martin, come here a minute… I want to chat with you." It was President-elect Elder Charles Bradford. He himself was rushing to get into work clothing to help take down the tents, but he insisted that Martin come to his cabin while he switched into overalls. "I got your Laymen's Leadership pamphlet," he said. "It came in the mail. I've read it word for word and line by line…" Martin indicated that he mumbled an apology for its seeming harshness in some spots. "Man, it's not too harsh," Bradford insisted. "It's just what we need... " He told Martin that, in line with his presidency, he had come into a seat on the new General Conference Race Relations Committee which was slated to meet that fall. Bradford, according to Martin, indicated that he wanted to convey to LLC his personal intention of backing the organization to the hilt.

What Martin found ironic was that Douglas Chandler felt that the LLC flyer was too militant in tone and not spiritual enough. It was an obvious contrast to the all-out, whole-hearted, unqualified approval that had been offered by Elders Warren and Bradford.

A momentum throughout the country began to build for the initiatives that LLC had taken; LLC board members were understandably cheered as our message spread from coast to coast. We continued to meet in some of the major regional churches in order to gain support for our cause by promoting the validity of our challenge. On October 21, 1961, the LLC board conducted a rally at the Shiloh Seventh-day Adventist Church in Chicago. Mr. Michael Blanchard, a board member, had made arrangements for LLC to make a progress report to area black members affiliated with the Seventh-day Adventist Church. Hundreds gathered for the afternoon meeting, and it was obvious from the very beginning that those in attendance were strongly behind the all-out assault that LLC had taken on segregation and discrimination within the church. There was unanimity among them against any flimsy, anemic or weak-kneed approach to the issues that were before us.

When those who were gathered there became aware that LLC representatives had been invited to meet with General Conference and Union officials that coming Monday, they took up an offering to purchase airplane tickets for Mylas Martin, Burrell Scott, and myself. Among the local persons attending the meeting and showing enthusiasm for our efforts were Werner Lightner, James Calloway, Marion White, Pat Burns, Samuel Bond, Michael Blanchard, and Howard McHenry. There was no doubt that black Seventh-day Adventists were fed up with the humiliation which they had borne over the years. The days of waiting for those who sat in the citadels of power to determine what was best for black people was over. Our dissent was controlled, analytical, intelligent, and filled with data and resources to document our case. We made no bones about our desire to meet with Elder Figuhr and to gain certain commitments from him prior to the World Conference scheduled for August of 1962.

The LLC board convened on Sunday morning of October 22, 1961, at the home of Mr. and Mrs. Michael Blanchard in Chicago. It was at that time that I read two telegrams from Elder L. E. Lenheim, president of the

Columbia Union Conference. One telegram was dated October 18, 1961, and it read:

> General Conference advises you have interview with Columbia Union representatives and North American officers just as soon as some of the individuals return to City. I shall contact them and endeavor to arrange an appointment. Will advise you later as to time and place.

The second telegram from Elder Lenheim, dated October 20, 1961, nailed down our appointment as follows:

> Sunday schedule completely filled. Suggest appointment Monday night, October 23 at 7:00 in Union Office.

Contemplating what effect the meeting might have on race relations within the church in the future, the board officially voted to send Frank W. Hale, Jr., Mylas Martin IV, and Burrell Scott as representatives of LLC to the meeting which would be held the next evening at the Columbia Union Conference office in Takoma Park, Maryland. In a gush of hastily determined actions, the board voted that each Board member would recruit at least ten persons by telephone from their respective areas of the country and ask each person contacted to send Elder Figuhr a telegram, before our meeting the next day, to register their support in behalf of LLC.

So as not to become disconnected from our philosophy and our mission, the board voted to strongly present the following recommendations to the General Conference officers and the North American officers for their consideration:

1. That the General Conference make a public statement and the earliest possible opportunity that will encourage all Seventh-day Adventists to take a new and positive look at the concept of love, brotherhood, and racial understanding;
2. That all pastors of our nation be urged to make explicit in their sermons the mind of Christ and the Spirit of Prophecy on the problems of race;
3. That we will provide our pastors every support with speakers, materials, and organizational help, to assist them in the reinforcement of a positive approach to race relations;
4. That as an end to material harmony and understanding between the races, we will organize Race Relations Councils and Institutes in every Union in North America;
5. That all Seventh-day Adventist institutions have an obligation to remove racial barriers in employment;

6. That we condemn the existence of segregation and discrimination in medical education, hospital and nursing training programs, patient admittance, and care within hospitals, hospital staff appointments, and hospital personnel policies;
7. That we discontinue the quota system in our educational institutions;
8. That we establish the principle of open membership in our churches, and declare any attempt to insulate a church or church-related institution against racial change as unchristian.
9. That a new treatise be prepared and published, reinterpreting our position on race relations in light of the twentieth century, the Bible, The Spirit of Prophecy, and most specifically, *The Southern Work*. It was also suggested that a new book be compiled and published from the writings of Ellen G. White, entitled *Counsels on Race Relations*.

Before the meeting was adjourned, those present had no difficulty in acknowledging how remarkable the Lord had been in giving impetus to the movement in such a short period of time. We challenged each other to hold fast the profession of our faith through the help of the Holy Spirit before repeating the Mizpah. Board members in attendance were Michael Blanchard, Bessie Carter, Frederick Chandler, Frank W. Hale, Jr., Hazel Latson, Wilbur Latson, Myrtle Murphy, Bonnie Scott, and Burrell Scott.

While it was by no means certain that our presence at the meeting on the next day with Union and General Conference officers would be sufficient to give the denominational leaders a reason to take a strong and historic stand in behalf of equality of opportunity, we nevertheless felt that God was using our organization (LLC) to share with our denominational leaders the depth of frustration and bewilderment that black Seventh-day Adventists felt about the gap of opportunities between themselves and their white counterparts within the church.

It was a time of broiling racial tensions throughout the country, and up until that moment in history, the denomination shrank from pursuing any straightforward position in promoting integration. As a consequence, many black Adventists felt abandoned by policies and practices which let human dynamics operate by themselves. And it was in that setting and environment that six General Conference and Union men and one Regional Conference president met with six Laymen Leadership Council (LLC) personnel in a precedent-shattering conference held in the Columbia Union Conference office on Monday, October 23, 1961, at 7:00 P.M.

Present for the General Conference were Elder W. B. Ochs, vice president; Elder W. P. Bradley and F. L. Peterson, associate secretaries; Elder L. E. Lenheim, president, Columbia Union; Elder T. R. Gardner, Columbia Union secretary-treasurer; Elder Neal Wilson, religious liberty secretary, Columbia Union; and Elder W. L. Cheatham, president, Allegheny Conference.

LLC spokesmen present were Dr. Frank W. Hale, Jr., Mr. Mylas Martin, Mr. Burrell Scott, Mrs. Bonnie Scott, Mrs. Willie Dodson, and Mrs. John Richard Ford.

There is no written record of how broadly pleased LLC representatives were at having the opportunity to underscore our concerns which had been rather widely circulated even prior to that time. The historical evidence of those denominational deficiencies that relegated black Adventists into the position of being second-class Adventists was preponderant. From the LLC perspective, we were simply there to contemplate and recommend remedies. We were quite encouraged.

"A lot of people in the General Conference are awaiting the outcome of this discussion tonight," said Elder Lenheim during the four-hour discussion. He must also have known that thousands of LLC supporters were also awaiting the outcome of the meeting. According to Elder Lenheim, on the day prior to the meeting, October 22, Elder Reuben R. Figuhr, president of the General Conference, had come to his office and talked with him "for an hour about the LLC." He requested that an exact report of the meeting be given him.

During the intensive session, I was struck by the contradictory nature and role of those LLC representatives who sat around the table. There was a conservative thread among us that really believed that the black-white situation in the church would change. While we believed in the American dream, we wanted to believe that, no matter how tragically flawed the system was within the church on issues of race, conscientious Christians would seek and institute change. We truly believed in the doctrines and teachings of the Seventh-day Adventist Church. We were not rebels. We simply wanted black Adventists to share in the blessings and opportunities that white Adventists enjoyed by virtue of their racial status. This meeting with the Adventist hierarchy gave us an opportunity to put the establishment on notice that we rejected the conventional school of thinking that the Jim Crow caste system within the church would somehow dissipate on its own over time. It was a rationalized approach to the problem that we simply found unacceptable.

Martin was uneasy and almost unforgiving in his manner from the beginning. He had already informed me before the meeting, "We're just wasting our time. Those men are not going to turn their backs on their white supporters. They aren't going to do anything anyhow." No one would have ever accused Martin of being profoundly naive. After all, his confidence in the church fathers had been eroded by decades of unbearable political and economic pressures that had produced a very unbalanced social order within the church that was both unsettling and unfair to black parishioners. Mylas had really intimated that he might not even attend the meeting. With careful and delicate sincerity and flattery, I insisted that his help was needed. By touching his commitment and loyalty to the cause to the quick, he capitulated and came.

The LLC representatives were candid. We put the devastating facts on the table. We could tell from the comments that were made from the other side of the table that behind the scenes there had been a flurry of activity. It was as if the General Conference and Union brethren were aware that momentum was gaining rapidly for something to be done to address the racial inequities within the church immediately. We sensed, too, that they wanted to capture the platform and the initiatives before the leadership and direction of questions on race were channeled into other hands. I could sense that their mood was hectic, anxious and driving. We knew from their probing questions that we were making history. While previously these arguments had been scanty or unconvincing, they invoked a spirit of humanitarianism, racial equalitarianism, and agreement in a curiously accommodating approach that we had not observed before in speaking with any of them individually or in smaller settings prior to that time. They were so accommodating and considerate in a kind of unintentionally patronizing way, I began to feel that they might be rigging the whole situation and taking the initiative, so as to deprive the LLC of the leadership that it had exerted with considerable influence over the past year.

Nevertheless, our presentations were forceful, eloquent, and at times, bare-knuckled, as we had a real zest for stripping the denomination of those racial practices that were degrading and demoralizing to its black constituents in North America.

LLC representatives presented its list of nine recommendations to the General Conference and Union representatives and requested an audience with Elder Figuhr, the General Conference president, calling for his response to the nine recommendations.

Four days later, in a historic move on Friday, October 27, 1961, the Fall Council voted a statement of policy which included the assertions: "The religion of the Bible recognizes no caste or color… God recognizes men as men." For the first time in its two-year history, the leaders of the

Seventh-day Adventist Church had taken a public stand on the matter of racial prejudice and racial bias. The two-page document entitled "Resolution on Racial Matters" was released the same night to UPI, AP, and other news services for publication in newspapers across the country. The Fall Council had adopted it unanimously.

A reproduction of a portion of the release as it came over UPI was as follows:

WASHINGTON, OCT 28 (UPI) The Seventh Day Adventist Church yesterday "strongly reiterated" its conviction that racial segregation is incompatible with the Christian faith. A statement adopted by the Annual Autumn Council of the Denomination, said "No distinction on account of nationality, race, or caste, is recognized by God."

The Church, which claims members in 196 countries, said this truth is "clearly enunciated" in the Bible.

"Any denial of this universal brotherhood of men would eat the heart out of a Christian church," the statement said.

Adventist leaders announced the denomination will "continue to encourage the employment of workers" in Adventist institutions solely on the basis of merit, "without regard to race, color or national origin."

They said efforts will also be made to provide "expanded opportunities for overseas mission service on a non-racial basis." Many U.S. Negro Church workers are already serving in overseas missions, they said.

LLC co-chairmen Frank W. Hale, Jr., and Mylas Martin IV, made a telltale joint statement, expressing their gratitude as result of the decision:

We're extremely grateful to God. This forthright public stand indicates that our leaders intend to correct the evils of SDA segregated schools and quota systems; the hostility of many white SDA congregations to their Negro brethren, and numerous racial ills among us. The resolution is great step forward.

Apparently, Martin changed his opinion about how successful our efforts had been in our October 23 meeting, because later in a letter he sent to Elder Charles D. Brooks dated January 18, 1965, in referring to that meeting he declared, "It was not a fruitful session. Nor were any subsequent efforts of Dr. Hale successful." I was more than a bit stunned when a copy of Martin's letter to Elder Brooks was shared with me several years ago. While I never quite understood why Martin felt it necessary to prop himself up at the expense of another, I always sensed an undertone of rivalry that I simply ignored because I was aware of my own intellectual strength, my disciplined eloquence, and the role that I had engineered in the first place in what had become a fascinating human drama with all of its dimensions in bucking the white power structure of the Seventh-day Adventist Church. The ground-swell for fair treatment by black men, women, and children had finally struck a resonating chord that led inexorably and relentlessly to the General Conference and its decision to put the matter on the table for public scrutiny. If nothing else had been achieved up to that point, we were at least able to detail a panoramic account of what the struggle for human dignity within the denomination had been all about.

Martin was brilliant enough in his own right, though sometimes reckless and rash in his tactics. He possessed an unflinching stand in his unequivocal stance against bigotry. He was quite capable of spraying distractive and diversionary rhetoric with cold-blooded venom at the slightest impulse, sometimes not knowing where to draw the line with his fervor. His skill as a journalist armed him with skills that were sometimes more suited to polemics than to logic. Nevertheless, Martin was an invaluable asset to LLC because of his ready willingness to take on the tumultuous. I turned to him constantly for his advice on various matters, and he was not bashful in supplying it. His strategic usefulness to LLC can never be underestimated.

Following the October 23 meeting and the historic announcement which came four days later, the LLC set out to engage in a significant watch dog activity, starting a Parents' Drive on November 21, 1961, to enroll SDA children and youth into every consciously-segregated Adventist school, from elementary school to college. We urged black Adventists to have their children to apply to local church schools, boarding academies, and SDA institutions of higher education.

In the meanwhile, while we were pleased that the Autumn Council had adopted a strong "Resolution on Racial Matters," our cold-eyed assessment of the situation made us aware that the church was certainly not in the vanguard of promoting racial harmony and understanding. A brief chronology of written pronouncements by other national church bodies underscored the fact that the Seventh-day Adventist Church was in the rearward of those denominations taking a bold and public stand on the side of racial justice. It is no secret that after years of defiance and intractability the church finally came kicking and screaming into the civil rights fold of religious organizations. By late 1961, the Adventist Church had been preceded in its first public statement by the following major church organizations:

WHAT OTHER CHURCHES HAD SAID

AMERICAN UNITARIAN ASSOCIATION
...THEREFORE BE IT RESOLVED: That the American Unitarian Association urges all people of good will to work unremittingly in all phases of local, state, and national life towards... eliminating racial restrictions on membership in churches...

May 28, 1957

AMERICAN BAPTIST CONVENTION
Our Convention has spoken out against segregation and has repeatedly urged church leaders to work as unceasingly for a nonsegregated church as for a integrated society.

We rejoice that integration is progressing in the churches of our American Baptist Convention.

June 22, 1956

...We dedicate ourselves to the following objectives:

THAT membership in each Baptist church shall be open to all people of its community regardless of their race or national origin.

THAT each church shall choose its minister on the basis of character and ability without regard to racial background...

THAT each Baptist organization, school, home, and hospital shall follow practices that are consistent with clear policies of racial non-discrimination...

May 31, 1957

CHURCH OF THE BRETHREN
We reaffirm our belief that discrimination owing to color is out of keeping with the teachings of the New Testament and with the stated position of the Church of the Brethren.

Annual Conference
June 12–17, 1956

DISCIPLES OF CHRIST
WHEREAS other churches, confronted with the same challenge are endeavoring to let the church be the Church—letting it be known that their church is open to any and all people, regardless of

race of ethnic origin... we urge and encourage all ministers and churches of our communion to be willing to bear any cross or persecution or reprisal brought upon them by their fearless witness to the rights of all people, regardless of race or ethnic origin...

International Convention
October 11–16, 1957

EVANGELICAL UNITED BRETHREN
We believe that discrimination in employment based on race is unChristian. Therefore, we urge all Evangelical United Brethren General Departments and Institutions as well as each local church to take immediate steps to end any such discriminatory practices now obtaining...

General Conference
December 8–9, 1956

...We suggest that we take the following specific actions to better human relationships between the races:

1. Promote a Christian ministry in our communities without regard to race. This means welcoming all races in all phases of church life.

2. Appoint ministers of other races as well as white ministers in our churches that are multi-racial in character, as has been done in several of our churches.

General Conference
October 9–17, 1958

LUTHERAN CHURCH—MISSOURI SYNOD
RESOLVED, that since Christians are constrained to do justice and love mercy, we acknowledge our responsibility as a church to provide guidance for our members to work in the capacity of Christian citizens for the elimination of discrimination, wherever it may exist, in community, city, state, nation and world.

June 20–29, 1956

THE METHODIST CHURCH
There must be no place in The Methodist Church for racial discrimination or enforced segregation.

In this spirit, we recommend the following: ...That Methodists in their homes, in their work, in their churches and in their communities actively work to eliminate discrimination on the basis of race, color, or national origin.

General Conference, 1956

UNITED CHURCH OF CHRIST

Congregational Christian Churches

We commend the National Association for the Advancement of Colored People and other organizations that have employed the judicial processes... to define and enlarge the scope of human rights for all our citizens.

General Conference, 1956

PRESBYTERIAN CHURCH, U.S.A.

We call for the launching of 'operation desegregation' in our churches and church-related institutions...

General Assembly, 1956

THE CATHOLIC CHURCH

It is a matter of historical fact that segregation in our country has led to oppressive conditions and the denial of basic human rights for the Negro. This is evident in the fundamental fields of education, job opportunity and housing. Flowing from these areas of neglect and discrimination are... (a) sordid train of evils... "

Statement of the Catholic Bishops of the U.S., 1958

UNION OF AMERICAN HEBREW CONGREGATIONS, 1959

Because of our profound commitment to the equality of all men under God, the Union of American Hebrew Congregations has consistently opposed every form of discrimination.

Out of this conviction, we have supported the decision of the U.S. Supreme Court in the school segregation cases and have pledged to do all within out power to make this decision meaningful in our respective communities. We here rededicate ourselves to achieving an harmonious and peaceful implementation of this decision.

...In this holy task, we pledge our cooperation to all those forward-looking religious, racial, and civic groups who share our concern in realizing the goal of equality which is basic to the democratic heritage and the Judeo-Christian tradition.

45th General Assembly, 1959

Even though LLC was pleased that the church had taken a more aggressive position in its stand on racial harmony, we had been in the fight too long to reduce our efforts. We felt that God's leanings had brought us to this point, and we believed that the full weight of Scripture, the Spirit of Prophecy, and the Holy Spirit's leading would enable us to accomplish our goals. While optimistic, we were hopeful that the church would not be guilty of hedging its bet by refusing to take a strong stand in facilitating and promoting the cause which had been at the heart of its public pronouncement.

Soon after Fall Council, letters and petitions of support began arriving at our Oberlin office. We also enjoyed the advantage of letters from parents who were discouraged because their sons and daughters were being routinely told that their applications were being placed on hold until the institutions had reviewed the applications of students from their local conferences. Quite often, too, black students were referred to Pine Forge Academy as an alternative. For example, if a black student who lived in Columbus, Ohio, applied to Mt. Vernon Academy, approximately fifty miles away, that student could only be considered after students from the Ohio Conference had been reviewed. Black students were, as members of the Allegheny Conference, expected to apply to Pine Forge Academy which was over five hundred miles away. The Conference boundaries were obviously racial as well as geographical. It was an arrangement that was counterproductive to a slowly flowering civil rights movement within the denomination. Both Burrell Scott and myself had experienced such discrimination firsthand as our daughters, Erica Scott and Ruth Hale, had become victims of such an arrangement when they had applied for admission into Mt. Vernon Academy. Both of them had received such communications after Fall Council. My daughter received such a missive from Principal J. R. Shull on December 15, 1961. We received communications from parents who had had similar experiences with Broadview Academy, Indiana Academy, and Cedar Lake Academy.

Zorita Duckworth of Niles, Michigan, had received a communication from Principal Carl W. Jorgensen of Broadview Academy on April 25, 1961, urging her to come to the campus by May 29 for assurance of summer work. Once she arrived on campus on May 30, several tactics were used to discourage her from remaining on campus. She was told such things as, "Since you didn't send a room deposit, I don't know whether the dean will take you now." Additionally, she was told, "We must take care of our own conference first, and we just never have room enough."

After waiting for four hours, Zorita's parents, Mr. and Mrs. J. R. Duckworth, were permitted to leave her at the school with the understanding that no conclusion had been reached whether she could remain more than four weeks. It was on August 23, 1961, that Principal Jorgensen sent a letter to Zorita stating, "We have not written to you because we have been uncertain as to whether we would have an opening." How was it that Principal Jorgensen could invite Zorita to the campus in his communication of April 25 to work for her school expenses for the approaching academic year, and then summarily reverse his decision by being indefinite as to whether there was an opening for her or not in his August 23 communication? It was this kind of duplicity that continued to mount as we received numerous complaints from black Adventists from around the field.

Eudora Mitchell of Delaware, Ohio, had attended the Adventist Church on North Sandusky Street for four years and had been taking her children regularly to Sabbath school. When it was announced that there would be a baptismal service, she advised Elder Yakush of her desire to be baptized. He advised her, "I will come by to see you." The following week, he came by to see her and, after an exchange of greetings, he rebuffed her desire for baptism by saying, "You create a problem because you are colored, and there are separate conferences, and they have agreed that white elders baptize white people and the colored elders baptize the colored people." Mrs. Mitchell, embarrassed and discouraged remained home with her children for two Sabbaths until she was encouraged by another sympathetic member to return to the church anyway. She and her children continued to attend the church until Elder Judson P. Habenicht, a new pastor, came to her house and told her that she and her children should attend the colored church where they were needed. He also advised her that she could not hold an office in his church. When she inquired of him, "Why aren't we welcomed at this church," he responded that, "Integration creates a problem because of interracial marriages as a result of associations between white and colored people."

It was this encounter with one of our *Christian* pastors that resulted in Mrs. Mitchell's not attending the white Adventist church any more. There were scores of similar instances that came to our attention as imposing reminders of just how entrenched racist practices were embedded in the fabric of the Seventh-day Adventist Church. We knew that these occurrences were not just isolated instances or farfetched singular examples of racist behavior. They were, in fact, a part of a towering expression of racial tyranny that had been tolerated over the years. It was a practice that had for far too long found ready soil in the Adventist Church. It was this rising evidence of such moral ambiguity on matters of race by church members that rallied LLC members and supporters to bring relief to black Adventists by challenging those institutions and individuals that were guilty of unmistakable acts of discrimination and segregation.

It was on Sunday, June 24, 1962, at 10:00 A.M. that the National Board of the Laymen's Leadership Council met in the conference room of the Y.M.C.A. at 515 South Center in Springfield, Ohio. The meeting was opened with prayer by one senior board member, Mrs. Estelle Barnett. Everyone knew how important this meeting was to be. After all, the General Conference Session in San Francisco was scarcely a month away. As board members, we were a close-knit family, and some of us had been very close friends over the years, long before the birth of LLC. There was Mrs. J. Estelle Barnett, a stately woman of regal bearing, who had spent a great deal of her own time and money for racial justice. She had discovered the face of racial fanaticism in her direct dealings with the Ku Klux Klan in Zanesville, Ohio, when she challenged the city fathers to improve conditions in the black community. In 1945, she established the Christian Benefit Association, a burial society to meet the needs of black Adventists. Burrell Scott, who during the 1960s had been president of the Western States Youth Federation, was a very successful building contractor in Oberlin, Ohio, where he was a member of the City Planning Commission. Bonnie Scott, Burrell's wife, had served the organization most efficiently from its early beginning as the executive secretary. Bessie Carter had been on a one-woman crusade for years supporting youth in their ambition to pursue higher education goals. She and her husband operated the Washington Hill Convalescent Home of Philadelphia and the Carter Rest Home in Oberlin. The Michael Blanchards of Chicago were well-established in a lucrative large renovating construction company in Chicago. Vertis Barnes, Jr., was the senior counselor at Morse High School in San Diego, California. Anne Valles, the daughter of Elder Coopwood, was a lady who was a strong defender of humanitarian values. She was passionately dedicated to our mission, and she was so well-read that, when she spoke in her soft and sophisticated manner, people listened because of the infinitely rich substance of what she had to say. Wilbur and Hazel Latson were remarkable for their devotion to the work of LLC. They eagerly gave of their time and energies to the organization. Hazel displayed uncommon efficiency in her duties as corresponding secretary. Wilbur, when not involved in LLC projects, served as a mathematician-computer programmer for the Wright-Patterson Air Force Base in Ohio. Dr. John Richard Ford, another member of the board, was a prominent San Diego surgeon who had challenged the American Medical Association to deny affiliation to any county or state society that continued to practice racial discrimination. Myrtle Murphy, A. Samuel Rashford, Helen R. Sugland, Helen Beckett, Viola Boyer, Willie Dodson, and Douglas Chandler were thoroughly self-assured Oakwood College alumni whose influence was expansive from coast to coast.

Although Mylas Martin had taken great pains to secure the permission of the Ellen G. White Estate Trustees to reprint *The Southern Work*, their response to the request was delayed to the point that LLC took the initiative to have the booklet republished at its own expense. The organization was aware that *The Southern Work* had become public domain and was no longer subject to the protection of the United States copyright law. Thus, as the first item on the agenda, it was voted that three thousand copies of *The Southern Work* be printed for distribution at various camp meetings at the cost of $1.00 each. The total cost of the printing of the publication amounted to $675.22.

I then shared with the board an interesting and eye-opening telephone conversation that I had had with a Mr. McCready of the Continental Can Company in Mt. Vernon, Ohio. McCready, in addition to being a supplier of cans for the SDA-owned health food companies, was a Seventh-day Adventist also associated with Mt. Vernon Academy as a board member. He informed me that he was sympathetic to our cause and would help us in any way that he could because he had observed the injustices displayed concerning admitting Negro students into Mt. Vernon Academy. During the meeting, I shared with the board a twenty-seven minute telephone conversation that I had had with Elder Neal Wilson, the religious liberty secretary of the Columbia Union, on Friday, June 22. As an emissary of Elder Figuhr, Elder Wilson indicated that Elder Figuhr was concerned with what the LLC was going to do at the General Conference, whether we were going to demonstrate, picket, have sit-ins, etc. I told Elder Wilson that LLC had not decided or concluded what its tactics would be. Elder Wilson suggested that we have a meeting with the North American and World Council officials. I indicated to him that the meeting should be held early in the week so that progress can be evaluated before the end of the General Conference session. I also insisted that a letter or telegram should be sent to confirm this invitation. It was quite apparent then that there was a tug of war going on. I could tell from Elder Wilson's inquiries that there was something of a black scare among the General Conference brethren. The possibility of LLC being publicly critical about its own church organization was more than a little unnerving to them.

I indicated to the board the extent to which the church hierarchy had gone to neutralize our effectiveness in San Francisco. I brought to their knowledge the fact that I had contacted the Whitcome Hotel in San Francisco for a place to set up LLC headquarters during the General Conference sessions. I was informed that we could have the space, and that confirmation was to be sent mail. Later, I was informed by phone that the General Conference, in the meanwhile, had engaged all of the available space, and as a consequence the hotel backed off of its original commitment to us and then gave me a negative response. Nevertheless, the limits notwithstanding, I proceeded to contact Brother Walter Kisack of the San Francisco area, and requested that he find office space for LLC, preferably at the Jack Tar Hotel, and close to the Cow Palace where the major meetings would be held. Kisack agreed to make the arrangements in exchange for my agreement to speak at an Oakwood Alumni Association meeting which Kisack was also scheduling.

As the board meeting continued, we discussed the need for LLC to be sensitive to the concerns of people of color worldwide. I had received a letter from Dr. Warren Harrison of the West African Union in which he stated that the West African Union wanted to be taken out of the Northern European Division because of the many racial injustices encountered by members of the West African Union. He also pointed out that Newbold College in England would not accept black male students unless they were married. The policy came about as the result of a mixed marriage some years earlier.

Burrell Scott indicated that he had recently talked with Elder Neal Wilson who informed him that men of color from other countries would be interested in LLC activities, and he suggested that we meet with them at General Conference time to inform them of what we are trying to accomplish, not only in North America, but all over the world field.

The following recommendations were voted upon and unanimously accepted:

> That the General Conference officers be informed that the LLC officers accept the invitation of the GC Conference President Elder R. R. Figuhr to meet in San Francisco with him and his group of GC officers to discuss the race problem within the denomination.

> Note: It was pointed out that the invitation to meet with GC officers was subject to a written request from them.

> That LLC requests Elder Figuhr to let LLC officers know the exact day, time, and site of such a meeting by Tuesday, July 10, so that every LLC Board member across the nation may be duly notified and attend.

> That Frank W. Hale, Jr., be empowered to answer the query of the General conference officers regarding our coming activities at the General Conference in the following way:

> *LLC desires to say that we believe in order and decorum and that we approach the coming session and conference in a spirit of prayer.*

That we, the LLC Board members meeting here today, formally and fully commit ourselves to a policy of conservative publicity regarding poor racial situations within the denomination; that in each and every instance such publicity take the form of open petitions to the General Conference.

That Frank W. Hale, Jr., and Bonnie Scott be responsible for the arrangement and ordering of the LLC convention set-up, details, discussion groups, press conferences, television-radio interviews, mass meetings, banquets, etc.

That the entire LLC Board be prepared to endorse LLC pre-statements and that objections be registered only by withholding signatures from controversial statements.

That Mylas Martin IV be responsible for the written copy of the prepared pre-statements and all press releases.

That positively no prepared press releases or printed public statements shall be issued under any circumstances by anyone other than the chairman (Hale) and the executive secretary (Bonnie Scott), or without the signed written approval of both.

Following the board's unanimous support of the recommendations above, a heated discussion ensued on whether or not specific instances of racial discrimination by the denomination should be released to the San Francisco press by LLC before LLC was to meet with General Conference representatives. Mylas Martin moved to release such specifics prior to the meeting, and his motion was seconded by Bessie Carter. It was Martin's contention that this tactic was the only way that General Conference officials would know that we meant business. I challenged that approach immediately because I did not want to short-circuit any opportunity which we might have had to meet with General Conference officials. I was aware of just how sensitive these brethren were. There was the unwritten rule that had always forbidden explicit criticism of top leadership. Policies and practices were always the prerogative of the inner sanctum—who, like Caesar's wife, were beyond suspicion. I thought that we should be as discreet as possible so that no criticism could be made regarding any premature move of the LLC, thereby leaving the door open for negotiations with the brethren. It was my opinion that, should the General Conference not live up to our expectations of having the meeting or of inviting us to a meeting that was unproductive, then at that time we would be free to open up our hearts, our files, and specific instances of racial injustices to the press. Instead of going to the press with our grievances before a meeting with GC representatives, I suggested that we place an announcement in the San Francisco papers, stating that LLC was in town with some background of the organization, listing the office address where LLC representatives could be contacted. This latter statement was generally agreed upon, and Ms. Carter withdrew her second to Martin's motion which died for lack of a second. Martin, however, went on record as being opposed to the decision of the LLC Board not to publish the specifics of racial discrimination before our meeting with GC officials.

When the board concluded this discussion, we then proceeded to discuss our *modus operandi* once we arrived in San Francisco. We determined that we should plan to arrive in the city by Thursday, July 26, in time to establish and set up our headquarters and be available for the public on Friday, July 27. It was apparent to me that we were on the water's edge, and it was now time for us to be prepared to step in and face the challenges head-on.

I had prepared a tentative calendar, agenda, and chronology of events for us to discuss in some detail in anticipation of our arrival in San Francisco. It would have been wonderful if we could have planned to be in the city three or four days prior to the opening of the conference, but there were limits imposed by our limited financial resources as an organization. Nevertheless, I suggested an array of activities that needed to engage us on Friday, July 27. They were as follows:

- Having a strategy conference with LLC Board members.
- Setting up LLC office headquarters.
- Enlisting volunteers for office and field service.
- Informing as many regional persons as possible of the location of LLC headquarters by distributing printed flyers.
- Getting *The Southern Work* from the Railway Express office.
- Distributing information concerning the sale of *The Southern Work*.
- Having a sign made to identify LLC headquarters.
- Contacting Walter Kisack concerning the alumni meeting.
- Preparing newspaper stories for release at the appropriate time.
- Organizing a solid program for a news meeting to be held at the Jack Tar Hotel on Sunday, July 29.

Once the office headquarters were set up, we agreed that those involved with office assignments should perform the following duties:

- Explaining procedures for organizing an LLC chapter.
- Arranging for LLC appointments in other places.
- Distributing LLC literature.

- Getting signatures or pledges from blacks.
- Selling copies of *The Southern Work*.
- Making daily bank deposits.
- Keeping accurate financial records on sales and contributions.
- Informing visitors of LLC activities during the GC sessions.
- Recruiting new members.
- Inviting people to the Sunday afternoon rally in the Jack Tar Hotel ballroom.

Bessie Carter, Wilbur Latson, Bonnie Scott and Frank W. Hale, Jr., were voted trustees for LLC incorporation, and Burrell Scott was voted to be the agent.

Following this action, Mylas Martin IV resigned as co-chairman of LLC for health reasons. The board voted to accept his resignation with regret and with a note of thanks for his untiring efforts in the growth and development of LLC.

It was also noted that the transportation expenses of board members be submitted after their return from General Conference. The meeting was adjourned as board members joined hands and with each member offering a brief petition to God in behalf of our efforts in San Francisco.

At the close of this historic board meeting, I could almost hear my heart booming in my ears. There was so much to do and so little time. I assumed that tensions were mounting on both sides—with General Conference officers and with LLC officers. I had received information from various quarters suggesting that there were those among the denomination's top brass that wanted to sit down with LLC representatives, and that there were others, including certain regional men, who were opposed to any overture which they felt would give credibility to our organization. Nor was there any single unequivocating opinion among black Adventists. It is very difficult for those who have been *carefully taught,* and who have been denied the opportunity of free movement and expression, to organize and mobilize their thoughts and efforts toward any intrusion into the deeply held convictions of those who have been in command of the outward circumstances of their lives. However deep and passionate were the individual convictions among many black Adventists, validated by personal experiences that the relations between white and black Adventists were less than desirable, it was common to discover those who were not strongly committed to any action of resistance to rectify the situation. Their restraint was based on changes which they assumed would be wrought by time, and not by rocking the boat. It had been my observation that those in power often rely and capitalize upon the differing opinions of those victimized as to the desirable scope and pace of the integration process.

In order to ease my lingering anxiety relative to whether or not there was to be, in fact, a meeting between GC and LLC officers, I sent a letter to Elder Neal Wilson, our go-between, on June 29, 1962, indicating that I hoped to have heard from him or Elder Figuhr by that time. In precise terms, I indicated that the LLC Board had had a very productive meeting five days earlier, and that "we are making very definite plans to 'carry the ball' to GC in the area of our discussion last week." I also made it clear that we were prepared to do whatever was necessary and appropriate to pursue our goals in these challenging remarks:

> I have every reason to believe that if the brethren will accept this suggestion in good faith, something can be worked out as a positive means of satisfying the desires and needs of minority members within the denomination. As I mentioned to you in our telephone conversation, we consider ourselves a conservative group; however, there is a point of no return—when deliberate speed has failed—when only appeasement becomes the order of the day, and when those who seek the truth are labeled as ones possessing "hysteria."

> I have every confidence in your sincerity and concern for right, and I strongly appeal to you to make every effort to effect the conference mentioned above.

What part Wilson played will never be known in the negative decision which the GC officers made in deciding not to meet with us once we were to arrive in San Francisco. Elder Wilson communicated that decision to me by telephone on Monday, July 2, 1962. I lost no time in informing the LLC executive officers of that decision. The die was cast. I knew now that it would be necessary to go directly to the press in order for any meaningful dialogue to occur between LLC officers and the president of the General Conference, Elder R. R. Figuhr. His final slap in the face was glaringly unacceptable.

After contacting the LLC officers, I made reservations to fly to San Francisco, leaving the morning of Thursday, July 26. Mylas, Burrell, and Bonnie assured me that they would join me there no later than Thursday evening. Needing to have volunteer assistance immediately available upon our arrival, I contacted two of my former student secretaries who lived in the Bay area, soliciting their help. Both Helen Smith and Carol Moore responded positively and enthusiastically to my invitation. Each of them were brilliant stars as receptionists, typists, and in any other capacity where they were needed.

It didn't take long for us to get the LLC office headquarters in good shape. We had been accorded lovely facilities that provided for adequate secretarial and clerical space, a lounge area to accommodate visitors, a work area for compiling and collating materials, and a conference area where we could have committee sessions and press conferences.

Given the magnitude of what we wanted to accomplish, we decided that the initial challenge to the General Conference officers would not come from the LLC as an organization, but from Bonnie and Burrell Scott as parents whose daughter had been denied admission into Mt. Vernon Academy in Ohio. On his arrival at the Jack Tar Hotel, Mylas Martin immediately went into action. We, he and I, agreed to call a press conference immediately with the Scotts as principals, outlining the nature of their case and that of similar cases with a prior history. It was also divulged at the time that my daughter, Ruth, had received a similar denial on December 18, 1961, from the same institution. School officials indicated that their applications were deferred, rather than denied, until the academy gave preference to members of their conference from Ohio and West Virginia. G. C. Sowler, the school's registrar, in his response advised, "I trust you have given due consideration to the excellent school for your people at Pine Forge, Pennsylvania," which is more than five hundred miles from the Scott and Hale homes. It took no real genius or vision to understand that the boundaries were primarily racial rather than geographical.

It was not difficult for us to anticipate the questions of the media. In his opening address, Elder Figuhr had stated that, "Christ laid the foundation for religion by which Jew and Gentile, black and white, free and bond, are linked together in one common brotherhood recognized as equal in the sight of God." His message in and of itself conceded the validity of what he had anticipated our efforts would be. Citing other cases of racial segregation within the Adventist Church, Scott declared, "Our fathers were willing to take it. But I don't want to take it." Quoting Scott again, July 28, 1962, edition of the *San Francisco Chronicle* wrote, "Some of our ministers believe there's a separate white heaven and a colored heaven." It was at this first press conference that the Laymen's Leadership Conference (LLC) was identified as an organization of Seventh-day Adventist Negro laymen who had come to the World General Conference to make an appeal to church officers to end discrimination which purportedly existed in Adventist churches, medical institutions, publishing houses, and educational institutions.

It was not at all difficult to measure the impact of that opening press conference as daily papers carried major headlines citing LLC contentions.* Typical were these:

* See Appendix A, page 395, and Appendix B, page 397.

196

"Adventists Challenged to End Racial Segregation"
San Francisco Chronicle—July 28, 1962

"Church Academy Hit in Racial Issue"
Oakland Tribune—July 28, 1962

"Adventist Sabbath Rites Draw 25,000 at Parley: Charges of Racial Prejudice Denied"
San Francisco Times—July 29, 1962

"Adventist Head Asks Patience of the Church's Racial Critics"
New York Times—August 1, 1962

"Adventist Head Denies Race Bias"
Oakland Tribune—July 28, 1962

"Lower the Church Bars"
San Francisco Call-Bulletin—July 30, 1962

"Adventist Elect Negro Executive… After Group Demands Full Integration"
The San Francisco Examiner

Newsweek, Time, Jet and other national publications carried similar stories, and LLC headquarters were flooded with telephone calls and telegrams of support.

Unfortunately, the hierarchy designated Elder Frank L. Peterson as the official spokesperson to respond to our challenges. Even more unfortunately, he permitted himself to be used in that capacity to minimize the impact of our efforts by stating that "this great organization and its colored constituents are moving forward and we are working amicably together." Some of his comments even left the impression that blacks were satisfied with their status.

At no time in my professional life had I ever felt more dismayed, because I considered Elder Peterson my father in higher education. After all, it was he who, as president of Oakwood College, lured me to the institution to begin my professional career. He had also provided me the opportunity to take leave of the institution to pursue and complete the doctorate. The feeling of love and respect was mutual between us. Peterson was one man that I had always looked up to as an exemplar of his race because of his priestly bearing, his ready wit, and his deferential charm that made him highly respected among all circles within the church. On the other hand, I was aware that he was an *organization man*, and that his precociously ascendant advancement within the structure of the church was an unmistakable portent of his genius in championing popular and unpopular causes.

Nevertheless, while it was not an auspicious moment for a small band of LLC officers to tackle the church fathers, who had the advantage of stating their case before the nearly twenty thousand members who had gathered in the Cow Palace for their major meeting, LLC called for a rally of its supporters on Sunday, July 24, at 3:00 P.M. at the Jack Tar Hotel. Hotel personnel estimated the standing room crowd to be in excess of one thousand in the hotel's largest ballroom. The ballroom was peppered by a swirl of electric energy, joyous anticipation, and a frenzy of excitement and racial pride, as those gathered there could not overlook the fact that black Adventists were redefining due process beyond any intentions that traditional decision makers either anticipated or could endorse.

Howard B. Weeks, director of public relations for the 49th World Conference, and Shirley Burton of his department were seated on the front row. They made no attempt to hide the fact that they were there to record what the LLC was going to do. Nothing could have pleased Mylas Martin more than this bold step that LLC had taken in having its own meeting and breaching the established calendar that had already been put in place by the church regulatory body. All of us knew that our actions would be considered an unjustified intrusion on the General Conference schedule of activities. It was Martin's earliest intention, even before Elder Figuhr had refused to meet with LLC officers in San Francisco, to use the tactic of exposing the church and force it into meaningful dialogue by using the public, mass communications media. Having given the GC officers an opportunity to meet with us and their having refused our gesture, all LLC officers subsequently agreed to using the leverage of publicity to tell our story.

Brains were no recent arrival in Martin's head; he stood calmly before the crowd demanding equality to the undelivered promises of the General Conference. Smart as a whip and calculatingly focused, his smooth tranquilizing tenor tones arrested the attention of an audience whose very presence testified to their pride and hope for changes and circumstances that had eluded previous generations of black Adventists. He referred to the patterns of prejudice, discrimination, and segregation within the church as "appalling" and demanded that the church "get its house in order" before "all the king's horses and all the king's men would find any such attempt futile" if their lack of assertiveness was too long delayed. Mylas had a clarity of thought and elegance of phraseology, a retentive brain, a doggedness for the jugular, and a determined drive within him that very few could rival. His speech was interspersed with and interrupted by spontaneous applause from the audience. It provided an enormous boost as an opening statement.

Bonnie and Burrell Scott had accomplished wonders by just being bold enough to tell their story at the opening press conference conducted by LLC. It became Bonnie's turn to stand before the assembled crowd, and she seized the moment with grace and courage. She was so systematic in the circumstances that had prompted her decision to unfold the story of her daughter's being denied admission into a white Adventist academy that it appeared that the audience was hanging on every word of her testimony. She made the point that she and her husband were not rebels, as they had been Seventh-day Adventists all of their lives. Her well-balanced presentation concluded with this powerful challenge: "We simply want to be treated fairly."

There was not a person in the crowd who could have anticipated the dramatic impact that Mrs. J. Estelle Barnett was going to have on the packed ballroom. Lightning appeared to dazzle from her eyes and an all-pervading burst of energy flowed from her regal presence as she mesmerized the crowd with her frontal attack on those white people in the denomination "who have been convinced, but haven't gotten within a breath of being converted," she snapped. The seventy-five year old stalwart and former probation officer and social worker from Columbus, Ohio, refused to bow to the allegations made against LLC in a spiritually militant response according to the *San Francisco Call-Bulletin*: "We are not heretics, as has been said, nor a left wing group, but Christians. The time has come when, as Christians, we must stand up like men and women and be counted." Remarkably buoyant and feisty, the veteran silver-haired lady held the assemblage spellbound as she pounded away, making point after point with her high-pitched voice and commandingly intense manner. The throng was on its feet at her conclusion.

The occasion was a living laboratory of how to use teamwork to deal with a structure permeated by racism. It was extreme dissatisfaction with the plight of blacks within the denomination that had driven the LLC to that point and that had ignited an avalanche of support against those who scoffed at our efforts and/or our methods to achieve equality.

The executive officers had asked me to give the keynote address at the rally. It was my assignment to drive home to the denominational leaders that a major policy overhaul was needed to free blacks from the political and social isolation which black Adventists experienced within the church. Consequently, my paper was entitled "Human Values and Denominational Policy: An Open Letter to General Conference Officers and All Seventh-day Adventists." I went to the platform with some degree of trepidation on one hand because I knew that such a forum was unacceptable to the *powers that be* and that our future usefulness was subject to the whims of those who were in control of the levers of influence within the organization. However, I also knew that the scales of justice tilted in our favor because the inherent fallacies of segregation had already been scuttled, at least on the secular front, in *Brown v. Topeka*.

As I looked out across an expectant audience, alive with the hope of unbridled freedom, I offered a silent prayer, and in a moment, I felt light, resilient, and spiritually confident. It was as if I was an educator-turned-minister. I felt no need to pussyfoot, bow, scrape, or to condescend in any manner. Such behavior, without qualification, had never been a part of my demeanor in the first place. So from the very beginning of my presentation, I chided the General Conference officers for pursuing policies that were designed to promote tranquility at the expense of people of color. I asserted that " …pastors, school administrators, medical directors, and a number of other denominational officials have dared to embarrass, to intimidate, and to exclude people of color from their institutions for the sole social purpose of preserving the regional character of our organization and maintaining the peace. The human rights which are being violated and the human damage being done are the incalculable moral costs which are sacrificed in the process." I made it clear that such an approach was both treacherous and cowardly: "We don't know of anyone who is satisfied with gradualism or 'freedom on the installment plan' when their rights are being squashed."

There were those who challenged our proactive stance when dealing with the issue of race. They maintained that the church could not afford to take a partisan position on the political and social issues of the day. They argued that such matters were not compatible with the gospel commission. I retorted that it was clear to me that:

> There are men who would exploit the principles of freedom and justice for their personal and selfish ends, but the fact is that freedom for the Negro within the church could have no great meaning if were not associated with the biblical injunction of the Golden Rule as well as with the social and political life of the community. It must be the church that sets the standard with the community following, not the other way around.

I insisted on making the point that we have permitted the social scientists and political scientists to snatch our religion from us if we say that the concern for racial harmony is their responsibility.

The *San Francisco Chronicle* of July 30, 1962, carried the headlines, "Open Letter on Adventist Racial Bars." In its opening paragraph, staff writer Donovan Bess stated that "The Seventh-day Adventist Church hierarchy was accused of flagrant and extensive discrimination against 50,000 American Negro members of the denomination." The article went on to indicate that "the letter was written by Dr. Frank W. Hale, Jr., Chairman of the English Department of Ohio Central State College. Hale is a prominent Adventist lay leader who last year helped to organize other Adventist Negro laymen into a dissident group formed to demand 'full citizenship' for Negro Adventists."

While acknowledging and praising the church leadership's extraordinary successes in building a vigorous worldwide missions program, and being aggressive in promoting diet, temperance, and dress reforms, I asserted that the church had been less assertive in its approach to racial equality. In fact, I pointed out unflinchingly that "the higher echelons of the church have been guilty of the most flagrant hypocrisy in race relations and a contemptuous indifference to the Golden Role laid down by Jesus."

Responding to and denying statements made by church officials that Negro members were divided on the issues of racial equality, I declared, "We are not divided. We are using this form of public protest because this is our only sounding board. At least we now know that they (the church officers) will respond to us through the press." My statements were made amid vigorous and loud applause to the local newspapers. The *Oakland Tribune* of July 30 covered the occasion by stating that:

> "Total integration of the Seventh-day Adventist Church must happen now," Dr. Frank W. Hale, Jr., leader of a Negro Adventist integration drive declared yesterday because "there aren't two Gods—a white God for the whites and a black God for the blacks." Hale, founder and head of the Laymen's Leadership Conference said, "The day of reckoning has come. The world is now too small, too crowded, too perilous, and too rapidly changing to permit further temporizing with bigotry and discrimination."

The letter urged the General Conference officers to set up a program to:

- Organize race relations institutes.
- Remove racial bars in employment.
- Condemn and discontinue segregation and discrimination in medical education, hospital and nursing training programs, patient admittance and care within hospitals, hospital staff appointments, and hospital personnel policies.
- Discontinue the quota system in educational institutions.
- Establish the principle of open membership in churches, and censure attempts to insulate the church against racial change.

The impact of this mass meeting was immediate and extensive. The media carried headlines from coast to coast. The August 1, 1962, edition of *The New York Times* carried a two-column eight-inch story by Laurence E. Davies, quoting Elder R. R. Figuhr's response to my presentation, as well as my own in response. Nearly one hundred black ministers, led by Elder Charles Bradford, president of the Lake Region Conference of Seventh-day Adventists, met to back an attack on segregation within the Seventh-day Adventist Church. They appeared to want to repudiate any suggestion that blacks enjoyed their segregated status. Bradford declared, "The Negro ministry of this body are not satisfied with any form of segregation." Elder R. B. Hairston of the South Atlantic Conference asserted: "At least ninety percent of the ministers are behind the objectives of this (lay) organization, and believe these men are on the right track." J. L. Reaves, a pastor who served Adventist churches in Virginia and Maryland admitted that "the laymen had to get this integration crusade rolling because we Negro ministers were too afraid."

On the heels of the public appeal and protests of the Laymen's Leadership Conference, the church elected Elder Frank L. Peterson, aged sixty-nine, as one of its four general vice presidents at its business session on the same day as the LLC rally. This was a most interesting development, especially after it was rumored that Peterson had been turned down for the same appointment earlier in the week because of his age. Nevertheless, his election was a small victory, but a mighty precedent to remind us that our efforts had not been futile. The concluding footnote to punctuate our pioneering venture is the fact that we sold more than 2,800 copies of *The Southern Work* in a period of four days. That effort alone shattered the invisibility of this significant document and set the stage for its republication by the General Conference in a few months thereafter.

The ink had hardly gotten dry from the San Francisco headlines and less than sixty days had passed when Elder Raymond F. Cottrell, the associate editor of *The Review and Herald*, wrote an editorial entitled "Rendering to Caesar What Belongs to God," in which Cottrell quoted David Lawrence, the editor of the *U.S. News and World Report*. Choosing to ally himself with Lawrence, Cottrell took issue with those church groups that participated in the historic civil rights March on Washington on August 23, 1963, to influence the passage of civil rights laws. My response to Elder Cottrell's editorial was immediate. While Cottrell attempted to underscore the point of our traditional stand on the separation of church and state, he, on the other hand, ignored the legislative support that we had sought to influence relative to our position on matters of temperance, health reform, and Sunday laws. Just daring to sleep in the same bed with a person noted for his anti-black sentiment was enough to drain the last drop of our credibility among our Christian colleagues.

My response to Elder Cottrell was as follows:

"A Response to an Editorial of October 17, 1963,
in *The Review and Herald*"

Elder Raymond F. Cottrell
Review and Herald Publishing Association
Takoma Park, Washington 12, D.C.

Dear Elder Cottrell:

In an editorial ("Rendering to Caesar What Belongs to God") of October 17, you justify the Seventh-day Adventist position for not supporting the "March on Washington" by citing as support an editorial in the *U.S. News and World Report*.

My brother, I cannot abandon my conscience by not recording my protest against what appears to be a subtle, yet cynical, disregard for the principle of human freedom as it affects the Negro in particular.

For years the American Negro has smarted under a continuous train of almost unprecedented abuse and venomous prejudice at the hands of David Lawrence. More recently, his editorials of June 10, June 17, July 1, August 5, August 19, September 9, September 16 in addition to his comment of September 23 to which you referred—firmly expose all the impertinencies of which Lawrence is capable in order to keep the Negro at "arms length" and beyond the circle of human brotherhood.

How shall we ever convince the world of our sincere concern for human equality, while we openly join hands and ally ourselves with those who make their livelihood by generating and fertilizing the prejudices of men?

You indicate that the church should not "enforce its opinion" in legislative matters. But do not Adventists seek legislative support and influence public opinion for their position in the areas of temperance, Sunday laws, and health reform?

Furthermore, the "March on Washington" was far more than an appeal for favorable legislation in the area of civil rights. It was a symbol of the involvement of men "in all walks of life" who were expressing their discontent over the plight of the dispossessed. It was a uniting of men and organizations—with the church strongly included—who were responding to the incredible patience that the Negro's discipline of non-violence has exhibited.

The redemptive role of the church discovers its challenge in eliminating those barriers which frustrate, thwart, and degrade life. Racial exclusiveness is one of those barriers which has diluted the concept of the Christian ethic because it alienates man from man as well as man from God. If the church is not prepared to bridge this gap, to whom shall we turn for the promulgation of the Great Commandment?

Sincerely yours,
Frank W. Hale, Jr., Ph.D., Chairman
Layman's Leadership Conference

After the March on Washington, a great wave of enthusiasm rippled across black America in the wake of its impact with a glowing sense of expectations as projected in the civil rights anthem, "We Shall Overcome." Those of us who were heavily involved in the activities of the LLC considered that the church's attitude had been lagging behind that of the worlds of sports and politics. Yet, difficult as it was, we had tried to understand the conservative stance that the church had taken. It had believed that pace could not be forced, nor that integration could be imposed by legislation. While the church's position was that there must be a process of education to address the tensions and solve the problems of race, it had been less than assertive and enthusiastic in its efforts to convert the unconverted on racial matters. It appeared to be weak and faltering in making any dramatic changes to promote racial harmony. Its concessions seemed to have come only after the proddings of those who had felt the sting of ugly racial incidents. It was the Civil Rights Act of 1964 that technically and legally liberated black people from much of the bondage that they had experienced during the first half of the twentieth century. Even in the church, segregation and discrimination seemed to have had God's seal of approval up until the dramatic civil rights crusades of the 1960s.

As conflicting opinions among Seventh-day Adventist Churchmen began to surface on how best to solve racial tensions, several black leaders not only began to speak out, some began to pursue their line of discussion with pen and ink. In a crisply worded document, "Seventh-day Adventists and the Social Revolution," Elder W. W. Fordham, president of the Central States Conference, scored a significant point in these words, "...the Negro's bid for freedom in the land of the free must be placed in proper perspective by Seventh-day Adventists." In responding to those who feared the rejoinders of reactionaries if the church were to take a strong position relative to the evils of racism he retorted, "We do not hesitate to speak out against the evils of tobacco, though we make enemies of the powerful tobacco interests. We are raising our voices to the damaging efforts of alcohol, and become the enemy of the liquor interests. We take public issue relative to Sunday laws, and become the enemies of the majority." His paper was presented at a number of regional camp meetings and was read by Elder R. R. Figuhr and Elder W. R. Beach.

It appeared that Elder Figuhr still had not relaxed his rigid position on the race question in early 1964. In the January 2, 1964, edition of *The Review and Herald*, he addressed the topic in "A Letter from Our President." He reverted to the Testimonies Volume 9, 1904–1909 era as a frame of reference. He simply brushed the issue aside by stating that "the subject is too charged with emotionalism" for the church to take a position. It sounded as if the General Conference president was reversing himself and the church's position as so boldly stated in the Fall Council Resolution of 1961. Elder Charles Bradford, disturbed by Figuhr's letter, responded in his poignant and provocative manner:

> We have with great courage and in no uncertain terms handled issues charged with emotionalism, e.g., the Sabbath question and healthful living. From a human standpoint such controversial issues would have made it impossible for the movement to grow and prosper. But God honored the faith of his witnesses. And when we with pen and voice and loving example condemn every practice that smacks of prejudice and racial superiority the world will have a demonstration here and now (not by and by in the Kingdom of Heaven) that the third angel's message breaks down every barrier and creates the new man in Christ who is neither Jew nor Greek, black nor white. It is our power as leaders of the flock to not only look forward to but hasten that day.

J. Paul Monk, a seminary student at Andrews University, wrote me a letter on February 26, 1964, expressing his concern and that of other black students at Andrews University who had listened and suffered under a lecture that had been given on race by a Dr. Leif Kr. Tobiassen of Norway. It was his thesis that it should not be the function of the church to attempt to change the sociological structure in which it finds itself—that the church should take its shape from the environment in which it finds itself. The group of black seminarians were inviting me to come to Andrews to tell the other side of the issue. When Paul Monk approached President Richard Hammill, requesting that I be invited to the campus, Hammill's curt reply came in a letter dated April 7, 1964.

> I am sorry I cannot concur in your suggestion that Dr. Frank Hale be brought to campus to discuss the matter of race relations. I think

the discussion of race relations is a good thing. I would suppose that
if you had one recent discussion of this that it might be a good thing
to let people think about it for a while before adding another right
on to it so soon thereafter.

It was obvious from the tone of Hammill's letter that a single
unequivocating opinion—the one that he espoused—was quite enough.
The issue was too important to him to welcome dissent.

Of course, the subject of race did not disappear on the Andrews
University campus. Bruce Moyer, a seminary student at Andrews
University, proceeded to circulate a questionnaire on June 16, 1964,
dealing with the subject of the "Adventist Pastor and the Civil Rights
Movement."

It was on June 25, 1964, that Robert D. Taylor, Jr., sent me one of the
most encouraging letters that I have ever received from a former pupil
and friend. To begin with, he declared, "I'm now completing my study
here at Andrews University, and while in residence here, I have been
appalled and disturbed by the poor *social* climate which exists on campus,
primarily as a result of the conservative, illogical, obstructionist position
which certain administrative and personnel hold regarding the questions
of human dignity and race relations." He went on to indicate that when
I was not invited to address the student body, a panel discussion on the
topic of integration was substituted and held on May 21, 1964, and was
quite profitable.

While members of the university administration had curbed their
tongues in discussing the problems of race on campus, God intervened in
a spectacular way when on June 13, 1964, Dr. Sakae Kubo gave the eleven
o'clock sermon at Pioneer Memorial Church on the Andrews University
campus. His subject was race relations. Taylor commented, "Much weight
was added to the presentation of this sermon by the fact that it was presented by one who was neither Caucasian nor Negroid; it was given by a
respected seminary professor and New Testament scholar." Taylor was also
encouraged by the fact that the entire service appeared tailored to squarely face the issue. The Scripture reading, the special music ("The Pharisee
and the Publican"), and the closing hymn ("In Christ There is no East nor
West") all indicated planning for a decided effect. Dr. Kubo's sermon was
favorably received, "even from members of the staff and administration."

In ruminating a bit on the state of racism within the church, Taylor
offered this courageous reflection and comment:

I personally appreciate what you have to do relative to the problem
of race relations in the SDA Church, and I hope you will find

encouragement in the fact that others are becoming aware of the problem which the church now faces. It is most unfortunate that the Negro ministry has been reticent about speaking out on this issue; however, some of us who are now entering the work feel somewhat differently about the role we should play in encouraging progress toward true fellowship and brotherhood among all members of our faith. You may consider me a friend of the cause you have fought for, and whatever I may do to help strengthen God's work and bring this denomination closer to a more Bible-centered position on this subject, I am more than willing to do.

Taylor's letter was a remarkable testimony from a young seminarian who was yet to graduate, but who, nevertheless, was prepared to serve faithfully, forthrightly, and with courage once he was fresh out of the seminary.

Throughout the years of 1964 and 1965, several racial incidents occurred that flew in the face of the General Conference's earlier declaration on brotherhood. Elder S. K. Lenhoff, pastor of the Hinsdale (Illinois) SDA Church refused to baptize Cynthia Cathcart who was an employee of the Hinsdale Sanitarian and who had been attending evangelistic meetings conducted by Elders Detamore and Bentenger. They insisted that she attend Shiloh SDA Church, a black congregation which was located thirty miles from her domicile. Ms. Cathcart sorrowfully reported this insulting situation to Samuel Bond and Werner Lightner who relayed the information to my attention in a missive dated November 6, 1964.

On November 7, 1964, Jannith Lewis, the head librarian at Oakwood College, and Irene Meredith, a mathematics professor, went to visit the Central Seventh-day Adventist Church in Huntsville, Alabama. The church is located about five miles from the college campus. They were stopped at the front door by a Mr. Tripple, the head deacon, who admonished them that they could not enter the church. After some urging, the deacon opened the door and the ladies were seated. Elder Roy, the minister who was speaking at the time, interrupted his sermon and stated that the church was not integrated and, based on the Testimonies, Volume 9, he would like for them to leave the church. Dr. Coberly, an elder of the church and a member of the Oakwood faculty was seated on the platform, and he urged the pastor to continue the service. Dr. Korgan, the first elder of the church, and also an Oakwood faculty member, urged the pastor to continue the service. The church was split on the issue as some members approached them personally and asked them to leave. One member chided the pastor, reminding him that the Bible stated we should not judge.

Another member stated that the church should follow the law of the land, and that was integration. The pastor said he had a letter which stated that such a situation was a local matter. He had prayer and dismissed the congregation. Some of the women left the church crying and asked Ms. Lewis and Ms. Meredith to forgive them.

Such embarrassing confrontations only served to underscore the primitive state of race relations within the church. The incalculable negative consequences of any protracted deliberations on the part of the church hierarchy to steer clear of any decision that would collide with the conservative and irresistible forces within the church would signal its abandonment of the Christian principles it has vowed to uphold.

This situation as reported to me by Ms. Lewis was corroborated in a letter which I received from Dr. Korgan on November 25, 1964. He stated, "Needless to say we are deeply disturbed… but I am not going to rest until men in authority meet this situation as Christ taught."

Isolated instances notwithstanding, the church began to take a number of actions that, at least, began to spell out those basic principles that promote racial harmony. The Spring Council (April 13–15 of 1965) focused on the need to implement policies relative to open church membership, removal of barriers to employment, and to equal and equitable treatment in hospitals as patients and as professionals. The Atlantic and Pacific Unions exerted strong leadership in declaring full integration. The boards of Southern Missionary College and Southwestern Union College voted to admit students without regard to race. Several Southern Union academies began to open their doors and the Florida Sanitarium and Hospital was being fully integrated in the nursing staff and in receiving patients. These actions certainly represented a positive beginning, but my common sense instincts alerted me to the reality that what is written on paper is only as good as its implementation. As the resolutions began to pyramid, I discovered a vast repertoire of vague and undefined resolutions that would only be as effective as the good faith aims and efforts of our leaders.

By early 1966, the Columbia Union Conference, had begun to conduct human relations workshops throughout the Columbia Union. The agenda for these meetings generally included discussions on the denomination's public image and public relations, cooperative endeavors, employment in Adventist institutions, consolidated schools, youth activities, evangelism, exchange of pulpits, transfer of members, and other minority groups. Those participating were General, Union, and local conference representatives. Elder Neal C. Wilson, president of the Union, and Elder Charles D. Brooks, field secretary of the Union, played key roles in each of the meetings.

208

One of the workshops was held on Sunday, January 30, 1966. It gave evidence that the denomination was beginning to dig its heels in on an issue that had brought mostly skull-wracking frustration up until that time. I was more than pleased, and I shot off a letter to Elder Neal Wilson on February 3, 1966, with sincere and unmeasured compliments:

> The Human Relations Workshop in Columbus on Sunday gave convincing evidence that our denomination is making constructive efforts toward the betterment of race relations among its members... It was refreshing to be a part of such an experience that was marked with such warmth, sincerity and orderly direction.

I sent a similar communication to Elder W. R. Beach, secretary of the General Conference, who had shared with us his vision of the importance of a "New Creation" in his opening introduction at the workshop.

In the meanwhile, Mylas Martin started bugging me about wanting me to run for Congress from my base in Ohio. He sent me an extensive and spirited rationale for such a campaign on February 2, 1966. As motivated as I was for the economic, social, and political advancement of my people, Martin would have needed a whip and a scourge to have driven me into that horror of horrors with all of its mudslinging, unethical and win-at-any-cost tactics.

As a journalist, Mylas had a grip on the political climate in Cleveland and northern Ohio, and he was a friend of many of the editors of local newspapers. He knew Louis Saltzer, the undisputed king-maker of candidates running for office, and he wanted to introduce me to Tom Boardman, the editor of *The Cleveland Press*. My reaction—flattered, yes. My response—unequivocally no! Mylas, too, had spent time with Robert Kennedy and Orin Lehman, the latter of whom had been campaigning for John Lindsay's old seat in the 17th Congressional District in New York. He had followed them around as they went stumping—pumping hands, slapping backs, and kissing babies as a prelude to either conquest or defeat. I found no way of justifying in my own mind the appropriateness of what I thought bordered on insanity. While Mylas was steadfast in pushing the point and I so much respected his artistic and elite expertise in this realm, I was firm and matter of fact in my decision.

It was about this time that Elder F. D. Nichol, editor of *The Review and Herald*, was preparing to issue a six-part series of articles on the subject of race in one extract from E. G. White and five historical narratives by her grandson, Arthur White. This series of articles originally appeared in *The Review and Herald* beginning in the March 24, 1966, issue and continuing through the April 21, 1966, issue. In harmony with an action of the 1965 Autumn Council, this series of articles was republished as a twelve-page reprint and was widely circulated throughout the World Church.

I remember my feeling of elation and relief when I first read the copy of *The Southern Work* that I had retrieved from the trash pile outside of the old library at Oakwood College. Up until that time, everything that I had ever read and had interpreted for me from Volume 9 of the Testimonies had inflicted pain upon my ego as a black person. I was not immune from the outrageous consequences of slavery. I had always reacted with outrage when all that was said and written appeared to condemn my people for the ruinous state in which many found themselves. Mrs. White made no bones about the deplorable conditions of black people—the immorality, the depravity and the ignorance. But she did not stop there. She placed the blame squarely on the shoulders of those responsible, and she was bold in her castigation of them on pages 11–12 in *The Southern Work.*

> Are we not under even greater obligation to labor for the colored people than for those who have been more highly favored? Who is it that held these people in servitude? Who kept them in ignorance, and pursued a course to debase and brutalize them, forcing them to disregard the law of marriage, breaking up the family relations, tearing wife from husband, and husband from wife? If the race is degraded, if they are repulsive in habits and manners, who made them so? Is not much due to them from the white people? After so great a wrong has been done them, should not an earnest effort be made to lift them up?

Ellen White was solid on two points: Who was responsible for the condition of black people, and what should be done to rectify—"lift them up"—the situation. Degradation was the problem; restitution was the solution.

Elder Nichol's office had sent me preliminary drafts of the series of articles which he planned to publish. On February 25, 1966, I sent a response to my reading of Nichol's original draft. My most pointed reaction to the draft was summed up in the following statement:

> Perhaps the most perplexing part of this series is the question who was responsible for the Negro's sub-human existence and behavior that made him unacceptable to society for so long. One wonders, for instance about the statement, "Great changes have since taken place in the status of colored people. The depiction of degradation, squalor, and ignorance does not represent the conditions as they are today."

> To leave the quotation in this fashion reminds us only of the grim facts of the Negro victim without reference to the mountain of

indignities which created his plight. Such an isolated statement would once again place the incubus out of reach of "resourceful bigots and respectful God-fearing men" onto the backs of the oppressed.

It seems Christian and proper that it be firmly established that the Negro has been spiritually, socially, and culturally impoverished in such a disproportionate ratio, only because he has been brought face to face with conditions which exploited him in a most inhuman way at the hands of those he was expected to emulate.

I received a response to my four or five suggestions from Elder H. D. Singleton, secretary of the Regional Department, who was collaborating with Elder Nichol in the publication of the series. In his letter of March 9, 1966, he stated, "Certain of your suggestions I tried to incorporate in the articles as I could. I would not say that your batting average was 100 percent, but it was quite high, at least 75 percent."

He continued on to say, "You may be interested to know that the White Estate board has voted to recommend the publishing of *The Southern Work* in its entirety, thus making it available to any who wish to have it."

It was on March 29, 1966, that Elder W. R. Beach, secretary of the General Conference, responded to a letter that I had sent him on February 23, 1966, suggesting that a human relations workshop be held at the time of the General Conference session which was to be held in Detroit. He indicated that, "the brethren have agreed to look with favor on having the Regional Department arrange for a General Conference presession meeting with regional workers on June 13, at which time the North American Union president would be given the opportunity to talk about the progress that has been made in the field of human relations in their fields."

He also pointed out the General Conference was making plans to include an insertion "in the *Church Manual* of a proper selection from the Spirit of Prophecy on the human relations stand of the church."

I was beginning to feel deep down in my heart that the denomination was beginning to employ its spiritual ethos, its intelligence and its energy to affect the psyche of the membership in positive ways relative to the role of the Christian on matters of race. I had no illusions about how far we had to go, but I felt secure in the fact that now we had begun to question our position and our condition in terms of human relations. Now that the questions were on the table, we could begin a serious quest for humanhood, as the uncompromising challenge to the imperative which Jesus left us: "By this shall men know that ye are my disciples, if ye have love one for another."

I was now ready for my newest challenge, the monumental challenge of assuming the presidency of Oakwood College.

Chapter 12

As President of Oakwood College

Just as I was facing the challenge of becoming a new college president at the rather tender age of thirty-nine as far as college presidencies go, the nation was also facing a new challenge. The rising tide of race consciousness had swollen to peak proportions with the passage of the Civil Rights Act of 1964, the Voting Rights Act of 1965, and with the insistence of black people that they become an integral part of the *American way of life*. That insistence was both subtle and open even as violence was unleashed by some whites, and as certain forms of segregation and discrimination were being abolished— traditions that had become cornerstones of American life and practice. Oakwood College, located in Huntsville, Alabama, had, due to the unfortunate influence of conservative church leaders, focused its mission primarily on the *by and by* rather than the *here and now*. However, when I arrived on campus to take on my new duties, I became immediately aware that the students of the 1960s were far less subdued in their approach to social and political issues than were the students who I had encountered two decades earlier when I first enrolled at Oakwood.

I could tell from the pulse of this new generation of young people that they were neither inclined nor prepared to acquiesce to the appalling pressures of generations past. They accepted more than a limited sense of responsibility to become free by their own efforts. There was a quality among them which was determined to assert itself to the point of making them despairing of traditional social patterns, of being willing to sacrifice so much for the good of their race as a whole and fortifying their courage in the defense of truth.

It was a time of great challenges. It was a fertile time to put Oakwood's grand objectives to the forefront. It was a time where change could take place without enormous and unimaginable upheavals of conscience. It was a time when the college could be brought to recognize how little conscious control it had had in addressing some of the issues that had been responsible for shackling the spirit and the potential of human beings. It was a time to defy and resist those habits of thought and action which had made us less human. It was a time for new ideas and new methods. It was a time to challenge the absurd and to avoid any complicity with institutionalized mechanisms that exploited people, positive programming, or progress in general. It was a time to redirect rather than to detach oneself from the system. It was a time to capitalize upon the fervent hopes and expectations of students, faculty, staff, alumni, parents, and loyal constituents. And I was happy to assume and to claim, with all of its contingencies, the challenge that such an elaborate mystique had to offer.

In the course of the previous seven years (1959–66), I had become steeped in the secular approach to black higher education. The profile of that rewarding experience gave me a profound academic and administrative awakening that I desperately needed as I was summoned to my new assignment at a meeting of the Oakwood College Board of Trustees on Friday, June 25, 1966, in Detroit, Michigan. I accepted the call which was formally announced at the Oakwood College Alumni banquet at the Tuller Hotel in Detroit by the newly-elected board chairman, Elder Frank L. Bland. I had certain advantages at the start. I was not only a member of the denomination which had created and sustained the college and was well acquainted with its ideals, its traditions, and its habits of thinking, I had been there for a year and a half as a student and for eight years as a faculty member. Nevertheless, I knew that it was important for me to review my theories on all phases of higher education—programs, course offerings, instructional procedures, and administrative policies. After all, I hoped to design plans that would make Oakwood a better and greater institution than she had ever been. As such, there were a number of things in my mind which I thought would move the institution in that direction:

- It was important to clarify some priorities among the many tasks facing the college.
- Oakwood needed to dramatically increase its enrollment.
- The key to a quality institution is the character and scholarship of the faculty. More attention needed to be given to the selection of new faculty and the professional development and advancement of those faculty who were already in residence.

- It was extremely important to promote and enhance the image of the college as an institution that was in touch with the progressive trends in higher education and moved, therefore, to organize its goals around achieving the eminence to which it aspired.
- There must be an insistence on recognizing the significance of teaching, so that it would not be undermined by the *monomania* of those who champion research as the *sine qua non* of the academic community.
- The college of the future must rely upon a wide variety of professional and lay experts in order to solve the multiplicity of problems with which it is confronted on a daily basis. Those problems cannot be solved if the college continues to select its board membership almost exclusively from the ranks of the clergy. The board must become more diversified.
- Students also needed to become more involved in college governance in shaping the future of the institutions.
- Denominational funds needed to be increased to provide for the capital expansion and improvement of the college, so that it would become more competitive with its sister institutions within the denominational higher education cluster.
- The function of the college must reach beyond narrow denominational confines. Its impact and influence must reach into the larger community where the advantage of its training and brain power could be acknowledged and appreciated.
- All of the above would be coincident with the major spiritual focus of the college so that there would be no question concerning the institution's priorities, assumptions, or direction.

It stands to reason that these plans were not as definite or as clear cut at the time as I have outlined them here on paper. They became more apparent as they evolved as a result of corporate (faculty, staff, administration, student, and board) planning. They, nevertheless, provided a platform, no matter how hazily perceived at the time, from which I could at least offer my visions for the future.

Recognizing the fact that character development was central to our mission, I challenged the student body early in the school year with this statement at the opening convocation:

I congratulate you for having selected Oakwood College as the institution of your choice in higher education. You have come in an era of great expectations in the face of historic dilemmas. There is open before you an unparalleled opportunity to build new and firmer foundations under your feet. You stand at the gateway of ecumenism, of a "new morality," of the flowing of modern imagination, and an unprecedented explosion of new knowledge and new technologies.

We are proud that you have recognized the great advantage that Oakwood College has to offer you. I have no apologies to make to anyone that we do things in a big way. We have a set of values that distinguishes us from being just another institution of higher learning. We have a solidarity and a unity of spirit and purpose that have helped us to accomplish many things over the years.

From our strengths have come great actions. We have great visions today, and we can move forward to greater achievements tomorrow.

I challenge you to show the world that Oakwood College makes men and women of boys and girls; that it provides remarkably clear insights for the development of the human spirit; that it attempts to establish religious convictions that are exhibited in outward patterns of behavior; that it encompasses an environment that is a potent force in spiritual, academic, and social development; and that it considers experiences—actual and vicarious—a most important aspect of total development.

You are Oakwood's greatest ambassadors. Let your influence be positive and dramatic, for you are our most important investment.

One of my very first actions was getting board approval to make a substantial increase in personnel so that we could enrich and upgrade the whole enterprise so as to break the bond of what was perceived as mediocrity in some quarters.

In a short time, through providential direction, as well as our hunger for academic and spiritual respectability, we managed to recruit able faculty and staff for the academic year 1966–1967. The selective list included these persons: Edwin Alcantara, Ph.D., professor of Business Administration; Freddie Bargas, M.A., instructor of Spanish; Maxine Brantley, M.A., assistant professor of Education; Stewart Brantley, M.A., superintendent of the physical plant; Charles Bridges, M.A., instructor of English; Joseph Camara, M.A., associate professor of Biology; Carrie Davis, B.A., residence hall dean of women; Gentry Israel, B.A., assistant instructor of English; Alyne Dumas Lee, assistant instructor of Music (Voice); Helen Lindsay, M.A., visiting professor of Education; Timothy McDonald, B.A., principal and instructor, Oakwood Elementary School; Gaines Partridge, Ed.D., dean of students and chair, Division of Education; Lucino Quirante, Ed.D., associate professor of Education; Sheila Smith, B.A., assistant instructor of Secretarial; Ruby Bontemps Troy, B.A., director of admissions; Eunice

216

Vanderberg, B.S., administrative secretary to the president; Clora Young, M.A., instructor of Sociology.

It was a daring pyramid of additions that inevitably helped to alter the tone and function of the college. Sophisticated personnel, organizational energy and administrative intelligence are crucial ingredients to the successful operation of any organization.

I lost little time in adding laypersons to the board of trustees, and these included E. U. Carter, owner of rest homes in Oberlin and Cleveland, Ohio; Dr. John Richard Ford of San Diego, California; Esther Lowe, a veteran public school teacher of Detroit, Michigan; and A. S. Rashford, a loyal alumni leader and supporter of New York City. Oakwood was now beginning to recognize, to appreciate, and to use the diversity of human skills, and I was pleased that I could play a small part in the realization of that innovation. It was a very small risk to take when faced with the challenge and the need for invigorated vision and leadership.

Without the slightest hint that I would become president of Oakwood College, I had submitted an article to the *Oakwood Alumnarian* in April of 1966. The topic, "The Way Ahead," had been suggested by the editorial staff of the periodical, and it was published in the August 1966 issue as a guest editorial. The following example is an excerpt from the editorial:

> It may be pointed out that such a theme as "The Way Ahead," however glowingly and enthusiastically it may be envisioned, is wholly futile unless it brings into focus what an institution does with, to, and for its students.
>
> It must select its particular functions, determine the direction of its resources, limit its activities, frankly and publicly declare its intentions, and adhere to them in practice. If its objectives are clearly understood, an institution will carve out for itself a unique place among the whole group of higher education institutions.
>
> The role of Oakwood College in maintaining educational and religious balance under the adverse conditions of pioneer life, and in nurturing its growth in recent decades is a story of the triumph of a virile religious faith. It is this spirit that must be preserved if its "moral and spiritual" character is not to be attenuated by a variety of compromises that would render opaque its objectives.

Unknowingly, I had, in a sort of serendipitous projection, chartered a course that I would need to follow in the days ahead in my new position as president of Oakwood College.

It didn't take long, because of the nature of my new assignment, for me to become extremely active as the official ambassador of the college. The relationship with the Regional Conferences is a very key aspect to Oakwood's growth and development. One of the immediate effects of their support is student enrollment. The flow of students into the college is determined, in great measure, by the extent to which the institution is promoted and marketed in the territories from which they have come.

Early during my first year as president, I had the opportunity to serve as a lecturer and as a consultant at workers' meetings for the Lake Region Conference, the South Central Conference, and the South Atlantic Conference.

As an advocate of sound college–community relations, I also addressed such local Huntsville groups as the Exchange Club, the Association of Huntsville Area Contractors, and served as the luncheon speaker for the advisory board of the United Negro College Fund.

During my first year, I thought that it was important and advisable that I challenge the student body on the subject of values. I felt then, as I do now, that it is well for us who are charged with administrative responsibilities to lift ourselves occasionally above the details of management and paper shuffling and consider the broad principles which the founders and benefactors of the college, our own sense of what is right and primary, and the reasonable demands that good sense imposes upon us.

As a consequence, very early in the school year, I sent a short article, "From the Desk of the President," to the *Spreading Oak* staff to be published in its December 1966 issue. I wanted to make an intense point on the importance of values without straining the point. Always believing that the ideal is something to work towards, I focused on the need for the college to retain its spiritual moorings:

> Oakwood College is you—each of you. Therefore, Oakwood College is the type of institution that you represent it to be. Thus, what our institution is, by and large, is what others see of it through us. What an all–powerful influence we have in determining what our college is and what it shall become.
>
> Since our college is what we are, the phrase, "set of values," looms as an important factor in establishing what we are. A person's set of values reflects his character and personality by revealing the things he considers important. A student who is motivated by a philosophy of Christian education can ill afford to meet the situations of life by "doing what comes naturally." His performance is determined by a higher order, by a Christian set of values and by ethical guidelines.

To assist the student to develop a highly refined system of values, the College has set lofty objectives in three areas—religious conviction (religion is the core of our curricula), environment (religious services—chapel, dormitory worship services, vespers, Sabbath services, Weeks of Prayer, etc.), and experience (Christian and denominational standards—foods, dress, music, recreation and social conduct).

Ours is a great student body. We are witnessing a fine school spirit and a responsible capacity to adapt to college standards and ideals. Obviously, we are peculiarly equipped by reason of our religious and denominational heritage to set high Christian values and standards for ourselves. Our own unifying sense of purpose and direction, to advance the cause of Christ, our college, and ourselves individually, leaves us with little choice.

Early in the school year, I requested that Elder R. H. Pierson, the newly elected president of the General Conference of Seventh-day Adventists, visit the campus and address our college community. He graciously and generously accepted and was the guest speaker for an All–College Convocation on October 10, 1966. Following his inspirational message, the Oakwood College Board of Trustees convened an all–day session. Elder Pierson brought a diverse set of credentials that made him particularly attractive to a diverse student body and faculty. He had served as a missionary for twenty–five years in Asia, the Caribbean and Africa. We wanted to believe that he could not possibly be lukewarm on such a contemporary issue as the "Fatherhood of God and the Brotherhood of Man." We knew, however, that it would take some time before we would be able to determine how he would exercise his influence on such matters. But, we were willing to wait.

It was at the October 10 meeting of the Oakwood College Board of Trustees that the board took an unprecedented step in accepting and endorsing a five-year plan for future expansion. It was a significant departure from considering one building project at a time. The major multi-year expansion program included a college center designed to house a food service center, an administrative wing, recreational facilities, student association offices, the college bookstore, a faculty lounge, a music room, a reading room, and a executive dining room. Other approved projects included a men's residence hall, a classroom building, a women's residence hall, a library, and remodeling the cafeteria area of Cunningham Hall. The time had come for Oakwood to begin to think in long-range terms and also the correlative obligation to arm the institution with a strong academic base.

It was also during the 1966–1967 academic year that Oakwood experienced its initial participation in *Who's Who Among Students in American Universities and Colleges*. We were cheered as thirteen of our students qualified for this honor. Those so recognized for this distinction were as follows: Phillip Carey, Donna Craig, Lela Gooding, Julia Howard, Halstead Howell, Bernard Johnston, Seth Lubega, Naomi McKenzie, Oliver McKinney, Llewelyn Swan, Lawrence Thongs, James White III, and Meretle Wilson.

It was a fortunate experience each day as I observed young women and young men move about the campus full of ambition and hope, and full of expectancy as they seized the opportunities available to them for personal growth and advancement. Walter Pearson, the president of the United Student Movement, was a young man divinely endowed and superbly equipped with talents that would carry him far. One could predict his future fortune because of his eagerness, his sense of purpose, his ability to articulate his goals, and because of his dynamic personality that was always bubbling over with a spirit of enthusiasm. There were others, too, who knew how to shoulder responsibility and how to exercise their influence in positive and creative ways. It was no surprise that when class officers were chosen for the 1966–1967 school year David Reid was elected president of the senior class; Phillip Carey, president of the junior class; Kay Bryson, president of the sophomore class; and James Warren, president of the freshman class. Other student headliners, whose contributions and activities kept them in the forefront of Oakwood day-to-day life were campus stars like Thomas McNealy, Helvius Thompson, Wilma Mitchell, Gabriel Hunt, Henry Holt, Herman Davis, Rose Mapp, Carmen Fuentes, Theodore Watkins, Rosa Taylor, Ivan Warden, LaJean Martin, Joyce Cordell, Victor Wallen, Thermatus McKenzie, William Frazier, and Ruth Hale.

The dynamic influence of Elder E. E. Cleveland radiated out from the Department of Religion and Theology among ministerial students and Bible workers throughout the year. But at no time was his influence as apparent as it was when he conducted his annual evangelistic workshops at the college. The workshops were designed to give a practical touch to evangelism for the upper division theology majors. But when Cleveland, considered by many as the dean of evangelistic competence, arrived on campus, students, regardless of their areas of academic concentration, crowded in to taste of his fund of knowledge, evangelistic expertise, and spirit–filled teaching and preaching. During the first week of February in 1967, Elder Cleveland's workshop focused on his tent efforts in Trinidad, West Indies, where 812 souls were baptized.

The academic year 1966–1967 was studded with firsts. It was a year that saw the college install for the first time a president who was not a member of the clergy. It was the year that the Oakwood Board voted a multi-year expansion program. It was the year that the college established an office of the dean of students. It was the year that Oakwood College was approved for *Who's Who Among Students in American Universities and Colleges.* It was the year when the president of the General Conference spoke to the student body. It was the year that Oakwood had its first official presidential inauguration on April 10, 1967.

It was a marvelous celebration of pageantry that exposed Oakwood, its lovely campus and rich traditions to towering educators, professionals and business persons who had, up until that time, only limited knowledge of the institution. Their contact with the college gave a powerful boost to our struggle for recognition outside of our own denominational structures as representatives were present from the American Association of School Administrators, the United Negro College Fund, the Speech Association of America, the Association for the Study of Negro Life and History, General Electric, Northrup Space Laboratories, U.S. Army Missile Command, Space Incorporated, Brown Engineering Company, as well as delegates from numerous universities and colleges.

Dr. Charles H. Wesley, a Harvard Ph.D., director of the Association for the Study of Negro Life and History, and former president of Central State University (Ohio), was the keynote speaker. "Smallness and intimacy are among the best assets of a small college," said Dr. Wesley. He urged President Hale to keep the individual in mind and not to succumb to the race of "education by numbers." The inaugural activities were attended by representatives from thirty-five different colleges and universities or learned societies from across the United States.

In my response, I indicated my goals for Oakwood in this vigorous passage:

> We accept the challenge to prepare our youth for that unending quest by the mind and spirit for truth. The great acceleration of knowledge during our century has laid the foundation for a new order as we witness great economic, political and social changes within our society. In addition, these changes have been accompanied by a profound revolution of contradictions. On the one hand, we have yielded to a new sense of responsibility as exhibited in our great international and domestic assistance programs to the under privileged; while on the other hand through misdirection and frustration we have led ourselves into measures of equivocation relative to war, racial discord and the new morality.

Earlier in the year the board had voted to designate the new women's dormitory as Bessie Carter Hall. Mrs. Carter, a former dietitian at Oakwood—along with her husband Espie Carter—provided generous scholarship support for needy students, on occasion financing the education of six or seven students at a time. The college was taking the opportunity to express its appreciation for the many contributions which the Carters had made to the institution over the years.

All in all, my first year as a college president was a whirl of back-to-back, never-ending, interminable assortment of activities, and I was thoroughly convinced that my magnificent adventure had just begun.

As my mission and own unselfish nature prompted me to give ungrudging service to the college and its constituents, I had to make certain that the legitimate needs and demands of my family were not overlooked. My beloved wife, while engaged in her own profession as an elementary school teacher in one of Huntsville's public schools, still kept pace with her role as the first lady of the campus. With both of us matched against such formidable professional demands, we discovered early that we needed to plan private times for ourselves and for our children and to escape without apologies from the heightened hierarchies of workaday, lock-step living.

When we arrived at Oakwood in June of 1966, my oldest daughter, Ruth, was seventeen, Frank III was thirteen, and Sherilyn was four. To their misfortune, they were always in the spotlight as the *president's kids*. To their advantage, as members of the college community, they became inseparably wedded to the ideal of unlimited human potential and progress. Though still quite young, and not yet convinced on all matters of maturity, they still gained a glimpse of those who possessed invincible optimism and who recognized that there were unexplored vistas that stretched invitingly into the future. We felt confident that such a fertile environment would inevitably have a positive and rich impact.

Educational advantages aside, it was necessary for us to take time out as a family in order to boost and enhance our own bonds of wholeness and balance. The enormous challenge of parenting made us aware that we could not shift our role as parents to other sources. The demands at times seemed overwhelming, considering all with which were involved, yet we recognized that our children, like all children, needed to be assisted in incorporating the view that they were made and loved by God, who had a very special purpose for each of them in bringing them into the world. So we took time out from our merciless schedule to go to the park, to have cook–outs, to visit friends, to travel the countryside, to go shopping, to seek out used book stores and antique shops, to plan Saturday evening fun with a few friends, to take weekend trips to Ohio to visit parents and grandparents, and to engage in an assortment of uncomplicated activities that allowed us some free time from the frenzied pace of our daily dominated schedules.

A most significant aspect for the 1967–1968 academic year was the self-study of Oakwood's program to fulfill requirements of the Southern Association of Colleges and Schools in which the college held membership. The study included a searching look at each of the institution's academic units, as well as the programs which supported them.

Equally or more important, and of greater monetary concern, was a program launched by the United Negro College Fund (UNCF) in cooperation with the Academy for Educational Development. The college was required to present to these bodies a complete inventory of its program for the past seven years, along with a projection of its anticipated progress for the next ten years. It was clear that the UNCF needed to demonstrate to the foundations that were supporting it that they were getting the most out of every dollar that was funded. The implications were quite obvious. For institutions to expect continuing support, they would have to deliver student graduates who would be able to compete in the open marketplace. Those institutions who could not so deliver would "receive damnation," according to Dr. Stephen Wright, who at the time was executive director of the United Negro College Fund.

Spectacular indeed was the growth and professional advancement of the faculty. An institution of higher education gains stature and distinction to a great extent by having highly trained and competent personnel. Faculty of high scholarly and teaching ability are, beyond a doubt, the most important component in helping an institution to achieve maximum credibility relative to the intellectual life of the campus. I was pleased that we were able to add eleven new faces to our faculty and staff for the academic year 1967–1968: Frankie Clay, M.S. instructor of English; Harry Dobbins, superintendent, college dairy; Boyce Dulan, B.S., assistant instructor of Mathematics and Science; Kathleen Hall, M.S., assistant professor of Mathematics; Beverly McDonald, B.S., Elementary Critic teacher; Norwida Marshall, M.A., dean of women; Lloyd Mulraine, M.A., instructor of English; David Richardson, M.S., instructor of Chemistry and Physics; Jon Robertson, M.S., assistant professor of Music; Rosa Taylor, B.A., assistant instructor of Secretarial Science; Claude Thomas, Jr., B. S., dean of men; and Mervyn Warren, Ph.D., assistant professor of Religion.

Two members of the faculty, Dr. E. E. Rogers and Dr. Leo Moreno, completed the requirements for the doctorate during the year. Dr. Rogers completed the doctoral requirements in Homiletics and Speech at Michigan State University, and Dr. Moreno completed his requirements for the degree in Education at Indiana University.

Thus, conditions were becoming increasingly favorable for building up the faculty, even as several of our faculty were on leave to engage in advanced education. Those taking advantage of leave opportunities were the following: Charles Galley, Business, University of Pittsburgh; Clarence Nembhard, Biology, Howard University; Esther Osborne, English, Howard University; and Talbert O. Shaw, Religious Ethics, University of Chicago.

The 1967–1968 academic year was a curious mixture of triumphs and tragedies. Each school year began with a candlelight ceremony of induction that officially initiated and installed the new freshmen into the meaning, the mission, and the objectives of the college. This evening occasion had the mark of extraordinary importance because the president was expected to give the welcoming address, faculty dignitaries were expected to be present, upper classmen were assigned special roles, and the freshmen were carrying candles which were to be lit by upper classmen whose candles had, in turn, been lit by faculty, whose candles had been lit by senior administrators, whose candles had been lit by the president. It was a spectacular and awe-inspiring and brilliant introduction to each school year.

Unfortunately, however, destiny duped us in a cruel way the very evening that the candlelight service was scheduled. As I was returning from town in preparation for the evening's activities, a car pulled out of a Kentucky Fried Chicken establishment and rammed fiercely into my automobile. Sensing the inevitable impact, I grimacingly pressed my upper teeth against my lower lip, and the full crushing force of the crash totaled my 1965 Mercedes Benz and sent my teeth like scissors through my bottom lip, leaving it to hang limply on the slightest thread of skin, which required 105 stitches to mend. Fortunately, Professor Marvin Anderson was in the vehicle with me and was able to accompany me to Hunstville Hospital where plastic surgeons performed excellent and enormously tedious surgery in order to save my lip. It was a dangerously close call, but once again in my life, angels were watching over me.

Shortly after I had arrived at Oakwood, I sought the acquaintance of people of prominence in the affairs of the city and county. I also knew that Oakwood had a story to tell in terms of the quality programs which it had to offer. Therefore, it was important for us to learn how to cooperate intelligently, consistently, and effectively with representatives of the press. Our assertiveness paid off as the institution began to receive broad local, regional, national and denominational coverage. Local newspapers began to carry stories on Oakwood on the average of once a week. One outstanding story pointed to Oakwood's history in a Sunday edition with half-page, lavender headlines. The caption was "City's Oakwood College Flourishes." Another edition (*The Huntsville Times*, January 15, 1967) carried a quarter page feature on Dr. Eva B. Dykes. Its caption was "Leading Negro Teacher Says 45 Years on Job Not Enough." And still another issue featured the West Coast recital tour of the college choir. On March 17, 1967, the *Southern Tidings* carried a five-page article on Oakwood, highlighting its history, its objectives, and its future plans, and with a biographical narrative of its president.

A striking example of Oakwood's new opportunity and advantage to capture national exposure occurred when I was one of twelve Seventh-day Adventist educators who was invited to meet with President Lyndon B. Johnson at the White House on the National Day of Prayer, October 18, 1967. The group was led by Dr. Charles Hirsch, secretary of the General Conference Department of Education.

President Johnson was a broad-shouldered man with a chiseled handsomeness that exuded an easy-going graciousness which gave me the impression that he was well-intentioned but strong-willed. I, of course, was already favorably disposed toward him because of his assertiveness and strong efforts in the passage of the 1964 Civil Rights Act. His sense of caring and doing something to alleviate the plight of black and poor people had earned him my appreciation and respect.

Even as we continued to make positive inroads within the media, there were problems that still remained to be solved on campus. I sought to address a number of these problems through working committees of the faculty. The Committee on Spiritual and Cultural Standards undertook a series of research projects and related them to specific problems affecting the college community. Among the problems studied in the light of the appropriate counsels of the Bible and the Gift of Prophecy were the following: the problem of motivation; reverence and decorum; music workshops; student attitudes toward standards and authority; the divine purpose for individual talents; familiarity between sexes; qualifications for student admission; and the importance of self-control.

The Committee on Education presented a symposium on "The Aims of Christian Education." The Committee on Effective Teaching held a symposium on "Criteria for the Effective Teacher." The Deans Council was helpful in establishing policy for the residence halls and in assisting in creating a stable spiritual and social climate on campus. The Academic Standards Committee introduced a new procedure whereby all students on academic probation had to periodically check with their teachers and their advisors to determine their academic progress. The instructor and advisor then had to turn in written evidence of the student's progress into the office of the academic dean. The new procedure was designed to keep the student abreast of his progress so that he would know what he needed to do to maintain an acceptable scholastic record.

As with all colleges, enrollment was a precious commodity at Oakwood. In 1965, the college enrollment was 433. In 1966, it was 570; and in the 1967–1968 academic year, 640 were matriculated in September. Over the same period, the senior classes spiraled from 39 to 63 to 84. We were cautiously optimistic that we would be able to attract as many as 1000 to 1200 students between 1970 and 1971 if we had the available residence hall space.

Almost, as if by magic, the reputation of the Department of Music changed when Jon Robertson, a celebrated concert pianist, was appointed its chairman. Robertson had studied and performed in the United States and Europe. He had appeared with the Glendale (California) Symphony Orchestra at age nine, playing Haydn's *D Major Concerto*. By age eleven, he had begun to tour the Caribbean and South America. Prior to coming to Oakwood, he had attended the Juilliard School of Music and had won the school's highest scholarship award for five consecutive years. The campus thrilled with a new sense of excitement as he made an immediate impact on the Huntsville musical community, showcasing his talent and that of Oakwood's choral groups and student soloists. Robertson enriched an enduring musical heritage that had already been set in motion by members of the musical faculty like Inez Booth, Johnnie Mae Pierre-Louis, Anne Galley, Samuel Jackson, Alyne Dumas Lee, and Hugh Creary.

The rising tide of musical consciousness was punctuated by the fact that the college had added two performing professionals (Lee and Robertson) to its music faculty within a two-year period. They not only added to the cultural enhancement of the campus, their presence attracted talented students who elbowed for admission into the college just so that they could study under these talented giants. I was especially pleased that my earlier conversation two years before with Robertson, at Central State College, had paid off.

No sooner had things begun to glow in the classical musical realm than Satan made it his business to see that we would begin losing ground by retreating to the lighthearted and lightheaded nonsense of the uninhibited musical world. This became quite apparent at a freshman talent program that became a frenzied exhibition of raw entertainment only three hours after the conclusion of the Week of Prayer. Saturday night, November 11, 1967, was a dark, dark, night at Oakwood College.

Faculty and staff members who attended the function struggled to find answers to a charged atmosphere that spectacularly and shockingly reflected a total disregard for established denominational and school guidelines. Because I had not been in attendance at the function, I had to rely upon the information which I received from respectable sources who were more than a little piqued by what had taken place. It seemed that the occasion had lent itself to debunking the old-time social and conventional tradition of the college and mirrored the restlessness and uncertainty of the times. In short, the champions of fundamentalism were losing ground to the modernists.

It was my understanding that the talent show in Moran Hall suddenly and dramatically took on the shape of a night club, a ballroom and a burlesque show. The jive talk, the imitations of street speech, the hepster's swagger, the pop music with its emphasis on the release of the sensual, the off-color banter, the tasteless jokes—all combined to explode in our faces with traumatic impact to indicate that social behavior at Oakwood College had taken a dangerous swing toward irresponsible expression. The hooting, cheering, whistling, the stomping of feet, and wild applause bellowed approval. The audience muscled its way past the moral code of the institution in unchained approval. In short, it was a response to a campus society that had lost its consensus on appropriate standards of conduct, language, and manners. Perhaps, it was most aptly put by the colleague who remorsefully stated, "I stand accused." He was speaking for all of us—*we* stood accused!

On Sunday morning, November 12, I called a special meeting of the faculty and staff to address the problem. I went to the point immediately:

> As your president, let me assure you that I am a traditionalist in matters of the soul. We simply cannot negotiate moral principles. The new permissiveness has already left its impact of decadence in our society… The urge and press for total liberalization in all matters has opened a Pandora's box with a bewildering assortment of acceptances with the emotional chant and accompaniment of "anything goes."
>
> Now where do we go from here? The force of our concerns are deep. Our general premises are already established by denominational guidelines. The specifics of dress, music, and social behavior are fairly outlined in the student handbook. What then is the problem?

The problem is largely one of implementation, and that responsibility belongs to all of us—students, faculty, staff, and administration.

On Tuesday, November 14, 1967, I called a special college convocation, with the approval and support of the administration, faculty, and staff, to challenge the entire campus community. We knew, as had been demonstrated, diversions contemptuous of Oakwood's standards, beckoned to our students. The fun and frolic of worldly pleasures had overrun the campus over the weekend, and the moment required a legitimate stage and a legitimate message in order to short-circuit the lures of the Evil One.

Challenging the campus community, I seized the spirit of leadership with these words:

> The Saturday night fiasco was not a spontaneous revolution. It brought to a climax a situation that has been evolving on this campus, I understand, for a number of years.
>
> Pop music didn't just suddenly become a problem. It began seeping, then creeping, long before it began to lurch and lunge at us. At banquets, at other talent programs, on the hi-fi sets in the sequestered nooks of dormitory rooms, and all too often at skating sessions, the spiral began its downward spin that has now left us all in a blur. All of this has happened right under our direct observation "as we passed by on the other side."
>
> The lack of restraint has expressed itself in the physical contact of couples meeting in the shadowed corners of unsupervised buildings, and promoting the annual Bonfire Blanket Carnival as we legitimized these practices "by passing by on the other side." In much the same way, the abbreviated dresses, mini-skirts and all have been "sanctioned by our silence."
>
> Today, therefore, we have come to declare war. We must declare war, not against people, but against practices. It will be a war against sin. We must—all of us—students, faculty, staff, and administrators—stiffen our backs against compromise. Tawdry exhibitionism is unacceptable on Oakwood's campus. Improper behavior must not be welcomed or accepted anytime or anywhere. As a family, we must work hand in hand.
>
> Therefore,
>
> 1. We are urging each person on this campus to become sensitive to the importance of dress.

2. We are urging each teacher to refuse to admit any student into his classroom who is improperly clad.

3. We are urging every student, faculty, and staff member to speak to any person whose hands appear wayward in his contact with the opposite sex.

4. We are urging the dean of students and the Deans' Council to establish guidelines immediately for proper skating patterns, so as to eliminate the current musical practices now being followed.

5. We are urging the Departments of Religion and Education, along with the Deans' Council, to formulate plans for conducting a meaningful faculty session on social and cultural standards at Oakwood College.

6. We are urging the academic dean, with the assistance of the Deans' Council, to develop an orientation program or course with a comprehensive syllabus on the philosophy and practices of Oakwood College for all entering freshmen.

7. We are urging the Social Activities Committee, with its faculty-student representatives, to establish some meaningful guidelines relative to program content in the secular situation.

8. We are urging the Religious Interests Committee and the Music Committee of the college to combine their efforts to establish meaningful guidelines relative to program content in the sacred situation.

9. Finally, we are urging all to apply the "doctrine of good sense" as we attempt to determine what is right and proper for our Center of Christian Education. Let each of us begin with ourselves. We must lean completely upon Divine Guidance if we would reverse the spiral of permissiveness on our campus. Whether we are successful or not will be determined as much by our love as our firmness. We must salvage each in the process.

Praying that God will give us the glue to stick together and the guts to push forward in faith.

If you want to take a stand against compromise—

If you want to declare war against sin—

If you want to join hands as students, faculty, staff, and administration—

Join me in the spirit of that great poet, James Weldon Johnson, when he said—

"...Lest our feet stray from the places,
Our God, where we met Thee,
Lest our hearts drunk with the wine
Of the world, we forget Thee;
Shadowed beneath They hand,
May we forever stand,
True to our God, true to our native land."

It was a challenge to the community to not abandon those values that had made Oakwood unique. A hushed, respectful response did not offer a clue to what might or might not happen in the future.

Wondrous indeed were the numerous opportunities that we made available to students to come into contact with eminent leaders and professionals. Many of our students had been insulated and isolated from broad cultural experiences because of their socioeconomic backgrounds. Recognizing that many of the students had not been able to escape the blight of their limited financial resources prior to coming to college, one of my determined initiatives from the onset of my administration was to off-set their severe cultural handicaps by promoting and sustaining a wider range of cultural experiences and diversions on campus. A number of head-liners had their day. Dr. C. Warren Becker, professor of Music at Andrews University, appeared in an organ recital on January 8, 1968. McHenry Boatwright, celebrated bass-baritone, overwhelmed the audience with a superior performance on January 13, 1968. In the meantime, I had been the speaker for Senior Presentation at Columbia Union College in Takoma Park, Maryland. Elder Dunbar Henri had already conducted the Fall Week of Prayer. Oakwood sponsored its first Education Emphasis Weekend (January 25–27, 1968) as Dr. T. S. Geraty of the General Conference and Elder Jerome Becker of the Southern Union served as speakers and consultants. Dr. Leonora Carrington Lane, a noted psychologist and consultant, attracted enthusiastic audiences during her three days on the campus. Dr. Herman H. Long, president of Talladega College, was the keynote speaker for Negro History Week on February 5, 1968.

A group of eminent black professionals representing vice president Hubert Humphrey's *Plans for Progress* program visited Oakwood College during the year and spent a full day on campus. They met students throughout the day to present information about companies which were equal opportunity employers and how students could prepare for prospective careers in business and industry. The companies sending representatives were Michigan Consolidated Gas Company, Union Carbide Corporation, Bank of America, U.S. Steel, New York Life Insurance Company, Boeing Company, Mumec Nuclear Material Engineering Company, and American Airlines. This team of black professionals was a smashing success among both male and female students.

It was also during the first two years of my administration that I developed a profound interest in promoting private philanthropy as a means of supplementing the resources of the college and as a means of getting private donors to buy into establishing scholarships as a valuable investment toward the advancement of our young people. While our initial contacts produced meager results, they led to our receiving a number of financial gifts from sources that had not contributed to the institution before. During this period we received contributions from the following sources: The Endeavor Foundation, $10,000; Harris Pine Mills, $25,000; Dr. and Mrs. John Richard Ford, $8000; Dr. T. R. M. Howard, $2000; Mr. and Mrs. Frank W. Hale, Sr., $1000; Mrs. Edna L. Williamson, $1000; Dr. George Harding, $500; Mr. and Mrs. Amos Skipworth, $500; Mr. J. Fife Symington, eight shares of Pittsburgh Plate Glass Company stock and four shares of duPont Company common stock; Ford Foundation (Consortium), $15,000; Ford Foundation $6000 in travel grants; Catherine Hughes Waddell, $500; and the Baldwin Piano Company, $750 in the donation of a piano.

The year 1968 was a significant year in the history of Oakwood College as it sponsored its first off-campus Alumni Homecoming Event, March 5–7, 1968, at the Carriage Inn. Nearly two hundred alumni, friends, and guests were in attendance. Mr. A. S. Rashford, president of the New York City chapter, was named Alumnus of the Year, and Mr. and Mrs. English Glenn Simons of Wisconsin, who had contributed seven children to the college, were selected as Parents of the Year. Nearly $6000 was presented to the college toward a swimming pool, and another $5000 was presented for scholarships.

The place where *loveliness keeps house* continued to be a marvelously popular tourist attraction throughout the year as the lure of its many assets attracted those who were curious, as well as those who were committed to its progressive programs and outlook.

Perhaps the crowning act of the 1967–1968 school year was when the groundbreaking ceremony was held for the new million dollar college center on November 6, 1967. The audience included students, faculty, staff, alumni, and board members. Program participants were Elder O. A. Blake, under-treasurer of the General Conference; Joe Davis, administrative assistant to the Mayor of Huntsville; Dr. J. Larson, dean of academic affairs; Dr. O. B. Edwards, chairman of the Department of History; Mr. William Niles, president of the United Student Movement; and Dr. Frank W. Hale, Jr., president.

Attempting to escape the hodgepodge approaches of the past, I insisted that the college select a certified architect to design the new college center. Although I had to challenge my board chairman's idea that securing a competent architect was a waste of money, the board membership, almost to a person, recognized that there was a need for the institution to raise its aesthetic and artistic standards. Though Elder Frank Bland had been a bit quarrelsome about the need for Oakwood to employ an architect, he subsequently capitulated to the general consensus of the group. Up until that time, Mr. Wren and the business manager had volunteered their best thoughts in determining the motif as well as the location of campus buildings. Of course, their recommendations could not escape board approval. The high quality expertise of the Atlanta based firm, Alexander, Rothschild, and Joyce, provided the college with a most durable and attractive facility. The architectural firm had designed the Atlanta Braves' baseball stadium and had done superior work at Georgia Tech University. A select committee had the opportunity to visit these facilities before arriving at a decision. Thomas Joyce was the local architect in Huntsville, representing the firm's office, and he was a marvelous person with whom to work.

In order to keep abreast of the times, as well as my work, it was imperative that my office have a competent secretarial staff. Eunice Vanderberg was a rapid-fire typist who was very efficient. It was not necessary to apply the whip and the spur to make her productive. She was a self-styled machine of sorts who was able to perform tasks almost as rapidly as I had assigned them. Equally effective and efficient was Rose Mapp, my part-time student secretary. She was more of a student receptionist who knew how to meet and greet the public with her genuine warmth and gracious office diplomacy. Vanderberg and Mapp were a masterful team, often working into the late hours of the night to complete reports for special meetings of the faculty and of the board as well as manuscripts of speeches which I had to deliver on an ongoing basis. I have often wondered how far my career might have gone without the secretaries that it has been my privilege to have had working with me over the years.

The musical talent at Oakwood played a tremendous role in brightening the artistic firmament of the campus. The Concert Choir and the College Male Chorus were traditional features. Several young ladies' groups captivated the campus from time to time. These included The Excelsiors (Equille Green, Joyce Ellison, and Joyce Lawhorne), The Debonairs (Rachel Tramel,

Carmen Fuentes, and Linda Willis), The Tempos (Cheryl Galley, Andrea Bradford, and Ruth Hale), and The Philomels (Joyce Lewis, Patience Barnes, Rosa Gaskins, and Julia Howard). Notable among the young men's singing groups were The Sons of Music (Allan Johnston, Elverton Mapp, Alfred Hampton, and Leroy Hampton), and the Ethereals (Irwin Dulan, Byron Dulan, Robert Gilbert and James Sampson). Oakwood, through the years, has remained inseparably wedded to good music.

The full impact of Dr. Martin Luther King's assassination on April 4, 1968, was at once apparent on the Oakwood College campus. Scores of students stood motionless in clusters—weeping, sobbing and attempting to console one another—as radio and television carried the tragic stories of his murder at the hands of a half-crazed, fanatic rifleman. King's dramatic death helped to erase——at least temporarily—the tensions that existed between him and radical black militants who had not bought into his turn-the-other-cheek ethic. It was impossible to escape the full impact of his life and of the grinding war that he had waged against racial injustice in America. King was gunned down at the very peak of his fame. Not even the doubtful or the cynical dared challenge his authority as a leader. So the depth of sorrow on the campus was natural, as it was everywhere, especially among those black Americans for whom he had given his last full measure of devotion, his own life in the fiery furnace of racial bigotry and hatred.

Over one thousand students, faculty and staff gathered in Ashby Auditorium on April 15, 1968, to pay tribute in a memorial service to Dr. King. On the occasion, I challenged the audience to demonstrate restraint in these words:

> A national sense of emotion has gripped our hearts. It is a time, however, when great discipline is needed in the midst of the most inhuman provocation. If the good for which Dr. King has given his life is to triumph, then we must seize the constructive initiative. We must learn to live with chronic crisis with Christ at the center. We must strive to preserve our freedoms without strangling them to death with unchristian means; yet we must guard against those ideologies and practices that would directly infringe upon our liberty.

I then issued a formal proclamation declaring an indefinite state of mourning for the Oakwood College community and further stated that the American flag located at the bell tower in the center of the campus would be flown at half-mast for a period of thirty days. It was significant that most of the student body and the faculty were wearing black apparel. The tragic murder of King left no doubt that the nation has a long way to go if it was to overcome the nightmare of bigotry and to fulfill its stated destiny as leader of the free world. The shameful cancer of racial hatred had so absorbed certain elements within the society that grave dangers of racial conflict hovered like dark heavy clouds over the atmosphere. As the news of King's assassination penetrated the airways through radio and television, defiant and angry blacks, venting their frustrations, ran haywire through business communities, smashing windows, overturning cars and trucks, hurling Molotov cocktail bombs, and setting fires that burned city blocks of real estate to the ground. Major cities like Detroit, Los Angeles, Philadelphia, and Washington, D.C., were vast infernos even as scores and scores of innocent people lost their lives as a result of reckless and willful gunplay on the part of incensed civilians and undisciplined policemen.

Seventeen new faculty and staff members were added to various departments during the 1968–1969 academic year. The new personnel were as follows: Carl Anderson, Ph.D., acting head and associate professor of History; Nigel Barham, M.Th., M.A., instructor of History; Marsha Chambers, B.A., visiting instructor of Home Economics; Alfonzo Green, B.S., M.B.A., instructor of Business Administration; Michael Harris, M.M., instructor of German and Music; Malita Herbert, M.A., assistant professor of Biology; Charles Hogan, Ph.D., acting chairman and associate professor of Education; Dorothy Hudson, dean of women (Carter Hall); Elizabeth Lindsey, M.S., instructor of English; Roy E. Malcolm, M.A., registrar; Shirley Minisee, B. A., director of food services; Jennifer Rouche, M.A., instructor of Biology; Joe Wheeler, M.A., acting head and associate professor of English; Pattie Mailler, assistant to the dean of women (Cunningham Hall); Thaddeus Privett, cashier; Lillian Johnson, secretary to the director of admissions; and Pearl Mulraine, secretary to the dean of students.

One of the ongoing revolutionary features of Oakwood has been its consistency in setting forth the principle of learning by doing. Through its auxiliary units and services, it has fostered the concept that the workbench is as essential as the blackboard. This focus was designed with an emphasis on creating socially useful adults through the process of educating students for life and for eternity. Thus, students were afforded excellent opportunities to gain valuable experiences by working in the dairy under the supervision of Mr. Harry Dobbins, in the bakery with Mr. Preston Calhoun, in the college store with Mr. Harry Swinton, in the college cafeteria with Mr. Lake and Mr. Miller, on the grounds with Mr. James Holloway, and on the farm with Mr. Lawrence Jacobs.

The election of officers for the United Student Movement was always a stimulating and highly competitive drama as candidates for office designed artistic posters, erected eye and ear catching slogans, and polished their platform speeches with impeccable rhetoric and stylistic flourishes with unabashed abandonment. At such times, the campus became a friendly battlefield of entrenched rivalries as candidates attempted to hammer home the strengths of their individual platforms, hoping to gain the endorsement of as many who would listen. Some were so bold and passionate in advocating their positions that it was apparent that they evidenced superb powers of leadership that would carry them far beyond the campaign that they were involved in at the college. Their unflinching zeal was a clear indication that some of them were destined to accomplish great things because of their political acumen.

The newly-installed officers of the United Student Movement for the 1968–69 school year were as follows: Pierre Hunt, president; Bernell Mapp, general vice president; T. Michael Brown, religious vice president; William Gibson, social vice president; Loraine Bowie, cultural vice president; Lawrence Stewart, athletic vice president; Irene Bowie, *Acorn* editor; Sharon Mitchell, *Spreading Oak* editor; Leroy Hampton, treasurer; LaJean Martin, secretary; Carolyn Ward, assistant secretary; Norton Webb, parliamentarian; and Samuel Bognton, sergeant-at-arms.

It was during the same year that Barry Black became Oakwood's first student missionary, serving in Peru.

The magnificent college center was ready for occupancy at the beginning of winter quarter. The center was composed of three major units: student activities, food services, and administrative offices. The student activities area included a multi-game room, a ping-pong room, a snack area, a student bookstore and offices for the United Student Movement, student publications, and the Missionary Volunteer Society.

On the upper level, the administrative wing accommodated the offices for the president, dean of academic affairs, dean of student affairs, business manager, director of student finances, director of admissions, accountant, and an alumni and public relations office.

The 450-seat cafeteria included private student and faculty dining rooms, as well as the "Acornette," and the president's dining room adjacent to the faculty lounge.

The building was completely air-conditioned with 25,200 assignable square feet of area. Materials used in the center were reinforced concrete and precast concrete for reasons of economy and maintenance. The exterior carried a patterned Mediterranean motif. The entire structure, situated with the mountains to the east and the historical campus to the west, was equipped with glare-reducing gray glass. Exterior ornamental iron railings were used to border the promenade which completely surrounds the building on the balcony level.

Alexander, Rothschild, and Joyce were the architectural firm. Gresham, Williams and Johnson were the building contractors. Ivan Allen received the contract for the furnishings. Paul Demazo completely designed the kitchen and food service areas, and the kitchen equipment was furnished by Goodwin Restaurant Supply, Incorporated.

The center was a first-class, twentieth century quality addition to Oakwood's campus. It was a phenomenon because it was the first facility in Oakwood's history that had been designed by a certified architectural firm. It was dedicated on March 16, 1969 as the W. J. Blake Memorial Center.

As president, I served as master of ceremonies for the occasion. Our guests included the Honorable Joe Davis, mayor of Huntsville; Elder Frank L. Bland, chairman of the board; and Elder W. D. Bradley of the General Conference. Elder Bradley was the speaker for the occasion. A tour of the new building followed the dedication program, and at that time, two large, colorful murals depicting the history and the progress of the college were unveiled.

Early in the planning for the college center, I had mused over the possibility of chronicling and portraying Oakwood's history in some distinctive way. The need to display, in some unique way, Oakwood's brilliant history for generations to come was uppermost in my mind. Undeterred by the complexity of such a project, I contacted and commissioned two Redstone Arsenal technical artists, Hugh Miller and Don Davis, to paint two murals. One mural covered the period from 1896 to 1936, and the second mural covered the period from 1936 to 1969. The artists put in more than five hundred hours on the paintings, and they indicated that the research covering the seventy-three year history of the institution, up until that time, was the hardest part. Working hand-in-hand with me, they spent long hours delving into Oakwood archives to find out what scenes and personalities to include. The project was made possible through the generous financial support of Dr. and Mrs. John Richard Ford. Dr. Ford was the director of the Ford Medical Center in San Diego, California. The Ford Science Hall was named after the benefactor's father. The original paintings in the college cafeteria were also gifts from the Fords.

The 1968–1969 school year was blessed with a litany of firsts for the college. The Department of English, under the able direction of Mr. Joe Wheeler, opened and dedicated its 2500 paperback Heritage Room Library.

On February 7, 1969, Oakwood College received national recognition as the first place winner of the national competition among the thirty-six member colleges and universities of the UNCF in raising the most funds per capita (based on student enrollment) in the annual campaign of the organization. Brenda Spraggins was crowned Miss UNCF at the 23rd Annual Conference of the United Negro College Fund in New Orleans. Her rendition of Verdi's "Pace Pace" was greeted by the audience with enthusiastic rounds of applause that accelerated to a standing applause in giving bold approval to the golden voice of the young artist. She was accompanied by her voice coach, Alyne Dumas Lee, who had achieved international recognition in her own right as a soloist with the Chicago Symphony.

The 1968–1969 academic year was a year in which a church building campaign got underway. The concept of a religious education center was introduced, so that the General Conference could be called upon to make grants beyond the normal commitment that it would make for a church edifice solely. Plans were made that would incorporate a sanctuary, as well as classrooms, offices and laboratory facilities for the Department of Religion.

As building chairman, I solicited the cooperation and support of Elder R. E. Tottress, the pastor of the Oakwood Church, to get the project underway. The firm, Alexander, Rothschild, and Joyce drew up the initial plans, and before long, with the help of the church membership, we raised the initial sum of $25,000 to get the project moving.

It was during the same school year that the board, on February 12, 1969, approved a proposal for a new men's dormitory. The facility plan, designed by Don Kirkman, a Seattle, Washington, architect, included the suite concept in which eight young men would share four bedrooms, bath facilities, and a living room—lounge area in each unit. The residence was later completed and designated as O. B. Edwards Hall in honor of Dr. Otis Bernard Edwards who had served the institution as professor of History, chairman of the History Department, and dean of academic affairs. Dr. Edwards was also the composer of Oakwood's *alma mater*, "To Thee Our Dear Oakwood."

True to his word, Mr. P. W. Ridgeway of Oakland, California, shared a significant portion of his artifacts with the college. He sent the college an impressive collection of valuables that he had garnered in his travels worldwide. Included among the treasures were objects, paintings, sculptures, drawings, and crafts from Europe, Africa, the Orient, and the Caribbean countries. Estimates of his contributions have run as high as $500,000.

Dr. Lewis J. Larsen, academic dean, announced his resignation in the spring of 1969 in order to accept the position of academic dean at Southwestern Union College. As a tough administrator, Larsen developed strict policies to improve academic standards. During his tenure, the overall grades of students improved, as well as the number of students who made the Dean's List and Honor Roll. Dr. Emerson A. Cooper, chairman of the Division of Natural Sciences and Mathematics and head of the Department of Chemistry was appointed to succeed Dr. Larson as dean of academic affairs.

During this same period, Dr. Mervyn Warren, who had recently completed the requirements for the Ph.D. in speech at Michigan State University, was appointed chairman of the Department of Religion and professor of Religion and Speech. He succeeded Elder Clarence T. Richards who had served ably as departmental chairman up until that time.

1969 was a mournful year in the sense that Oakwood lost three of its beloved students in tragic accidents. Elizabeth and Timothy Beale and Donald Robinson were precious jewels in God's treasury of youth that will be long remembered for the buoyancy of spirit that each gave to the campus.

All of us were especially proud when two of our students, Raymond Winbush and Raymond Blackburn, were selected to study at Yale and Harvard Universities during the summer. Winbush served under the Yale Intensive Summer Studies Program, and Blackburn was included in the Harvard Medical Career Program. Both were selected because of their strong academic potential in demonstrating capabilities to do graduate work.

The Honors Convocation provided a foretaste of the kind of leadership that Oakwood alumni would demonstrate in the future. Among those receiving high recognition were the following:

Freshmen: Isaiah Ash, Theresa Bailey, Richard Brown, Jr, Eulus Dennis, Joyce Eubanks, Tommy Ray Graves, Jacqueline Henry, Lois Hill, Alvin Jackson, Jorge Kuzmicic, James Lamar, John Lavendar, William Linticum, Grace Edrene Malcolm, Richard Maddox, Charles Miller, Brenda Pearsall, Annie Richardson, Pamela Rowell, Gladstone Simmons, Linda Warren.

Sophomores: Melvin Davis, Brenda Goodman, James Hawkins, Yvonne Hodge, Diane Moore, Joseph Warren, Joann Williams.

Juniors: Boyce Berkel, Joyce Cordell, Margery Lawrence, LaJean Martin, Amos Okrah, Annette Rankins, Earl Roberts, Frederica Weeks.

Seniors: Kay Bryson, Wilma Foster, Marcia Freeman, Pearlie Breer, Carvason Griffith, Ruth Hall, Lydia Mays, Thermutus McKenzie, Barbara Ann Patrick, Edith Sloan, Joann Walker.

Quite a number of these students went on to complete graduate and professional degrees establishing significant career profiles in a variety of fields.

The problems of a small private denominational college differ greatly from those of large institutions. In the development of healthy social communal comradeship, intramural athletics played a significant role. Basketball retained supremacy as the sport which involved the largest percentage of male participants and as the sport which attracted the largest crowds with the most enthusiastic responses. There were eight regular teams, divided four each between two divisions, the Lunar Division and the Apollo Division. The Lunar Division was composed of four teams: Brothers, Oppressors, Bulldogs, and I.B.C. The Apollo division was made up of the four other teams: Smirnoffs, Dominators, Crusaders, and Chaperones. The tournament champions were the Smirnoffs, and their leading players were Captain Lawrence Stewart (21 p.g.), Sonny Williams (18.3 p.g.), Edward Taylor (28.6 p.g.), and Donald Robinson (16.3 p.g.). When time permitted I took the time to look in on some of the most action-packed basketball games that I had ever seen. Several individual competitors come to me as I rehearse in my mind's eye some of the flashy acrobatic displays of basketball wizardry that it was my pleasure to witness. Some of the other key players who made quite an impression on me were Sam Boynton, Ernest "Terp" Young, Will Battles, Tony Meyers, Herman Wright, Richard Brown, William Byrd, Alfred Fenison, and Tony Howard. Some of the best games took place between the Oakwood College All-Stars and the Columbus, Ohio, All-Stars coached by Eugene Miller and highlighted by the stellar shooting of Charles Colbert. The Columbus team, seasoned with veteran church players, was able to surprise and conquer the Oakwood team on at least two occasions over a five-year period. The game of softball provided a spring sports attraction that also included participation by student athletes. With an influx of students from Bermuda, the Caribbean, and Africa, interest in soccer began to grow with the establishment of the Southampton Bombers and Los Santos.

One of the most celebrated athletes at Oakwood during those days was Walter Horton, a six-foot, 240-pound specimen of sheer iron strength. A serious ministerial student from Sacramento, California, Horton had become seriously interested in body-building at age sixteen.

During one chapel period, we invited him to demonstrate his prowess before the student body. In a fantastic display of muscular precision, he demonstrated military presses, squats, chin-ups, bicep curls, tricep extensions, and bench presses. The applause ran wild as he ran through his series of exhibitions with grace, balance, control, and amazing strength. It was no wonder that he bore such titles as Mr. Alabama, Mr. Mid-Southern, Mr. Western America, Mr. Northern California, Mr. California, Mr. Pacific Coast, Mr. Washington (state), and Mr. Iron Man. What a man!

A large university can make more noise, but it is doubtful if it can catch and secure the kind of spirit that is so important to the vitality of a small college where each student can feel the impulse and the excitement of what might be considered trivial on a major college or university campus.

As with all colleges the residence hall has been a prominent feature in the life of Oakwood College. The new men's dormitory was beginning to take shape as it was our plan to have it ready for occupancy by September of 1969. The erection of this new facility was one of our major promotional and public relations strategies as we targeted young black males for enrollment for the 1969–1970 school year.

During the past year, I had used all of my available energies to advance the college, and I was ready for an extended vacation which my family undertook beginning June 17, 1969. Our seven thousand mile journey took us to St. Louis, Oklahoma City, Albuquerque, the Grand Canyon, Los Angeles, San Diego, the central California camp meetings, San Francisco, Oakland, Yosemite National Park, Nevada, Yellowstone National Park, Idaho, Wyoming, Denver, Topeka, Indianapolis, Louisville and back to Huntsville. It was a glorious tour adventure in sightseeing, enjoying the beauties of this great country, and renewing old friendships and establishing new ones. The rich blessings of Heaven had renewed my vitality, and I was ready to get back into the saddle of the presidency on July 15, 1969.

If one were to be asked what were the factors that made an Oakwoodite different from a student or an alumnus of other colleges, while it may be difficult to determine or analyze all of the specifics, there are certain factors which exert their combined influences in making Oakwood students unique. It has something to do with the fact that most of the students are Seventh-day Adventists. It has something to do with the fact that many of them came from good stable homes. It has something to do with college traditions which they knew about before they came. It has something to do with the spiritual atmosphere of the campus which promotes high moral standards. It has something to do with the fact that the campus is free from the cliques and social distinctions which Greek societies tend to promote. It has something to do with the mutual respect that exists between faculty and students and the kind of mutual interaction that takes place as a result thereof. It has something to do with the responsibilities that students assume once they are admitted into the college. It has something to do with the expectations that the college community has of students after they are admitted into the institution.

During the middle of the summer of 1969, I was invited to serve as a speaker-consultant at the Wawona Youth Camp in northern California. I spent two weeks there promoting and recruiting for the college from July 28–August 10. After I left the camp, I continued recruiting for the College in Sacramento, Stockton, San Francisco, Oakland, and Los Angeles. I enjoyed the warmth and hospitality of some very beautiful Christian people including Mr. and Mrs. Harvey Mackey of Santa Barbara, California; Mrs. Gloria Hemphill of Mountain View, California; Elder and Mrs. C. J. Williams of Stockton, California; Elder and Mrs. William Galbreth of San Bruno, California; Elder and Mrs. R. Hope Robertson of Los Angeles, California; Dr. John Washington of Los Angeles, California; Pastor Robert Taylor of Perris, California; Mrs. Dorothy Newson of Sacramento, California; and Elder and Mrs. G. Nathaniel Banks of Gardenia, California.

The new men's dormitory (later designated as O. B. Edwards Hall) was opened on October 12, 1969. Several new faculty members were added to the roster at the beginning of the year including Dr. Donald Blake in Natural Sciences, Mr. Charles Smith in Behavioral Science, Mr. David Grandison in Natural Science, Ms. Marjorie Felder in English, Mr. Lloyd Wilson as dean of Peterson Hall, and Mrs. William Osborne as assistant dean of Cunningham Hall.

Cynthia Clark became Oakwood's second student missionary by accepting a teaching assignment in Thailand during the summer of 1969. During the past year Oakwood became a member of a consortium of six black institutions of higher education to establish the Cooperative Library Center for joint purchasing and technical processing. The Carnegie Corporation of New York made a grant of $233,000 to the National Council of Churches for distribution to the member institutions which included Miles College (CME), Oakwood College (Seventh-day Adventist), Stillman College (Presbyterian, U.S.), Talladega College (AMA and United Church of Christ), Tuskegee Institute (Independent), and Tugaloo College (AMA and Disciples of Christ).

Sensing the need to promote the college on a broader scale outside of the Adventist community, I was, with the board's approval, able to establish the Oakwood College Advisory Council composed of leading citizens of the business, professional, and industrial community of Huntsville in 1969. The membership of the first Oakwood College Advisory Council was as follows: General J. A. Barclay, manager, Northrop Company; Mr. Burton Case, manager, Huntsville Manufacturing Company; Dr. Emerson A. Cooper, dean of academic affairs, Oakwood College; Mr. Milton Cummings, chairman of the board, Brown Engineering Company; Mr. John Frey, treasurer, Dunnavant's; Mr. John H. Goodloe, vice president and general manager, Huntsville Division, Thiokol Chemical Corporation; Dr. Frank W. Hale, Jr., president, Oakwood College; Dr. Pat Hamm, general practice, surgery, gynecology; Mr. Roy Malcolm, director of admissions, Oakwood College; Mr. O. D. McKee, president, McKee Baking Company; Rev. Harrison McMains, retired minister, First Christian Church; Mr. L. C. McMillan, executive director, Association of Huntsville Area Companies; Mr. Witnel McMillan, director of student financial aid, Oakwood College; Dr. Gaines Partridge, dean of student affairs, Oakwood College; Mr. Harry Pennington, president, Hunstville Lumber Company; Mr. Harry Rhett, investor; Mr. B. L. Sarahan, vice president and general manager, Space Systems Center, IBM Corporation; Mr. Leroy Simms, editor and publisher, *Huntsville Times*; Mr. J. P. Smith, owner, Russell Erskine Hotel; Mr. Adell Warren, business manager, Oakwood College; and Mr. F. B. Williams, Huntsville manager, Boeing Company.

Thinking that the time had come for Oakwood to seek cross-fertilization opportunities that would enable the institution to engage in productive cooperative efforts with other institutions of higher learning, I was able to persuade the board of the advisability of connecting with an interinstitutional consortium of black colleges in Alabama known as the Alabama Center for Higher Education (ACHE). The membership included Alabama A&M University, Alabama State University, Daniel Payne College, Stillman College, Talladega College, Tuskegee Institute, and Oakwood College. Several areas had been identified in which cooperative efforts could be developed or expanded. Among the collaborative prospects were faculty exchange programs, coordination of student teaching, cultural enrichment programs, audio-visual workshops, computer time-sharing and a three-two cooperative engineering curriculum.

Almost overnight Oakwood began to enjoy the impact of establishing a balance between on-campus classroom theory and off-campus community service. The Division of Education, under the effective guidance of Dr. Charles Hogan, spent a substantial portion of their time and talent in rendering services to school systems, individual schools, professional organizations, parent and community groups and to conference workers' meetings.

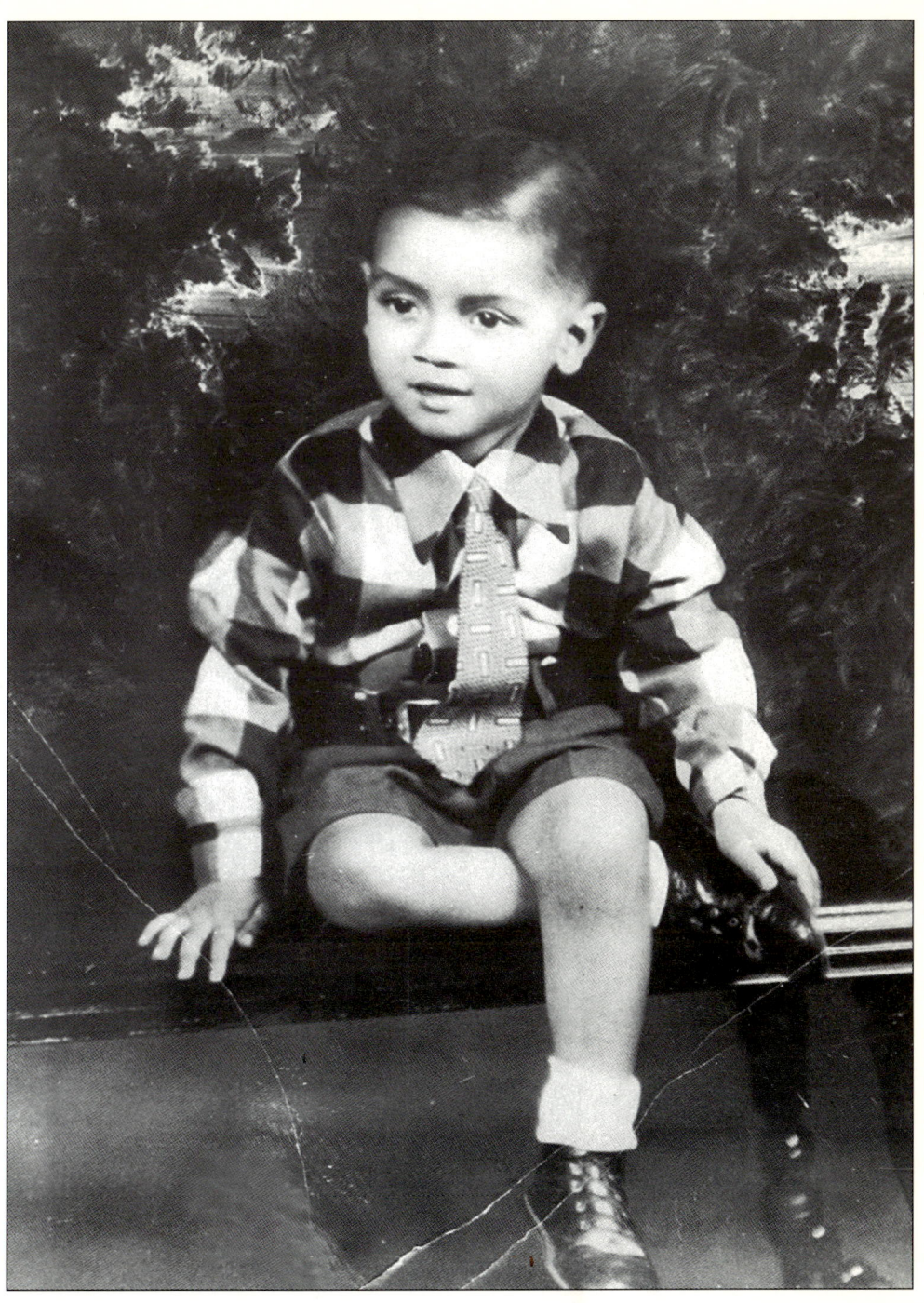

Frank W. Hale, Jr., at 2 years and 8 months of age.

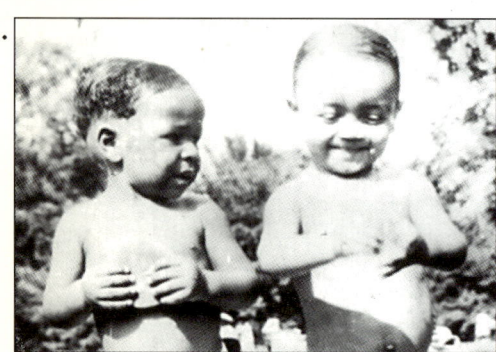

1. In Campbell, Ohio, at age 6.
2. 18 months old, with Vertis Barnes in Swope Park, Kansas City, Missouri.
3. The Harmony Four of Topeka High. (l-r: James Cathey, baritone and arranger; Frank Hale, Jr., first tenor; Eulis Cathey, second tenor; Fred Holmes, bass.)
4. Topeka High School, a magnificent, gothic structure.

All photos this page: Some of the students of Oakwood College, 1944–1945.

1. "Mother" Cunningham, an Oakwood College fixture.
2. Dr. and Mrs. O. B. Edwards exchange greetings with Elder and Mrs. Beale.
3. Dr. Eva B. Dykes on the Oakwood College campus.
4. Elder and Mrs. J. T. Stafford. We affectionately called him "Churchill".
5. Elder and Mrs. John Beale and son.

1–3: Union College students.
4. The Hub of Harmony Quartet, begun at Union College, 1945. (l-r: Clarence Schmidt, baritone; John Davis Butler, second tenor; Frank Hale, Jr., first tenor; Roy Matthews, bass.)

1. Courting days. With Ruth Saddler, Lincoln, Nebraska
2. On their wedding day. Frank and Ruth Hale, Jr., June 16, 1947.
3. Frank with his 1929 Nash on the Union College campus.
4. The Hub of Harmony Chorus. (l-r: Milton Woodson, Leroy Bookhardt, Andrew Donnelly, Charles Seard, LeCount Butler, Frank Hale, Jr., Bertrand Nunley, John Washington, Jimmy Valentine, John Frank Bookhardt, Herbert Alexander.)
5. In front of the Union College Annex, 1946.

With wife Ruth, Ruthie (age 4), and Frank III (3 months), at the end of the first year of teaching at Oakwood College, 1952.

1. Ms. Joyce Mathis accompanied by Dr. Oscar Henry, Central State University professor, 1964.
2. Central State University students at the 1963 March on Washington.
3. President Charles Wesley of Central State University prepares for commencement exercises with faculty members, 1965.
4. With Dr. Charles Wesley, leading the inaugural procession at Oakwood College in 1967. Dr. Wesley was the keynote speaker.

1. On the *Queen Mary* en route to study at the University of London as the recipient of a post-doctoral fellowship, 1960.
2. Discussing the schematic plans for a new million dollar college center on the Oakwood campus. (l-r: Mr. Alfred G. Adams, manager of Sears; Dr. Frank W. Hale, Jr., president of Oakwood College; Mr. H. H. Schmidt, chairman of the Oakwood College Executive Board.)

1.

2.

3.

1. (facing page) With members of the Oakwood College Board of Trustees.
2. (facing page) With Earl Calloway and Shirley Verrett, internationally famous mezzo soprano. Oakwood College Alumni Banquet, Chicago, 1966.
3. Lifting the first shovel at the groundbreaking for the college center on the Oakwood campus, November 6, 1967.
4. With Dr. Gaines Partridge, then dean of students during Dr. Hale's presidency, on the Oakwood College campus, 1967.

4.

1.

2.

1. (facing page) Meeting with President Lyndon Johnson at the White House.
2. (facing page) A family gathering (standing, l-r: Frank Hale, Jr.; Frank Hale, Sr., (father); Ruthie (daughter); Novella Hale (mother); Aunt Gladys Bankett; Aunt Isy Young; Dr. William P. Young (uncle); Ruth Hale (wife); Frank III (son)—seated, l-r: Uncle James Banks; Sherilyn (daughter); Aunt Georgette Green.)
3. Addressing an audience of scholars, faculty, and community leaders at the annual Graduate and Professional Schools Visitation Days Program at The Ohio State University, 1975.

1. Speaking with Alex Haley after his having given an address on *Roots* at The Ohio State University.
2. (facing page) Dean O. B. Edwards presents a special achievement plaque to Elder Louis B. Reynolds during the Oakwood College Homecoming in 1969.
3. (facing page) Preparing to debate the need for a black cultural center during a campus forum at The Ohio State University, 1972. (l-r: Dr. William Nelson, chairman, Department of Black Studies; Dr. Frank Hale, Jr., associate dean of the OSU Graduate School; Dr. William Holloway, vice provost for minority affairs.

2.

3.

1. With his book about OSU graduates who have succeeded in their fields.
2. (facing page) Greeting Dr. Karl Menninger, internationally renowned psychiatrist, at the 65th anniversary of Harding Hospital in Columbus, Ohio. Dr. Menninger was a patron of Hale's Bookstore in Topeka, Kansas in the 1940's.
3. (facing page) At a ceremony saluting Archie Griffin, two-time Heisman Trophy recipient, and Cornelius Green, OSU's football quarterback.

2.

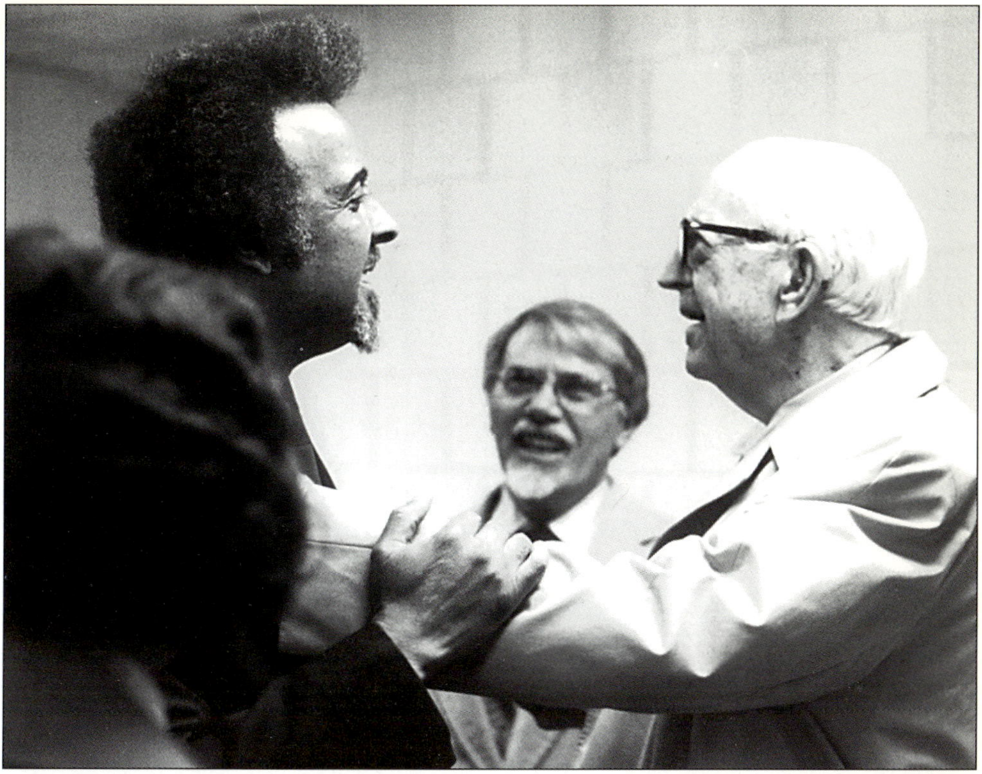

3.

Photo courtesy of the OSU Dept. of Photography

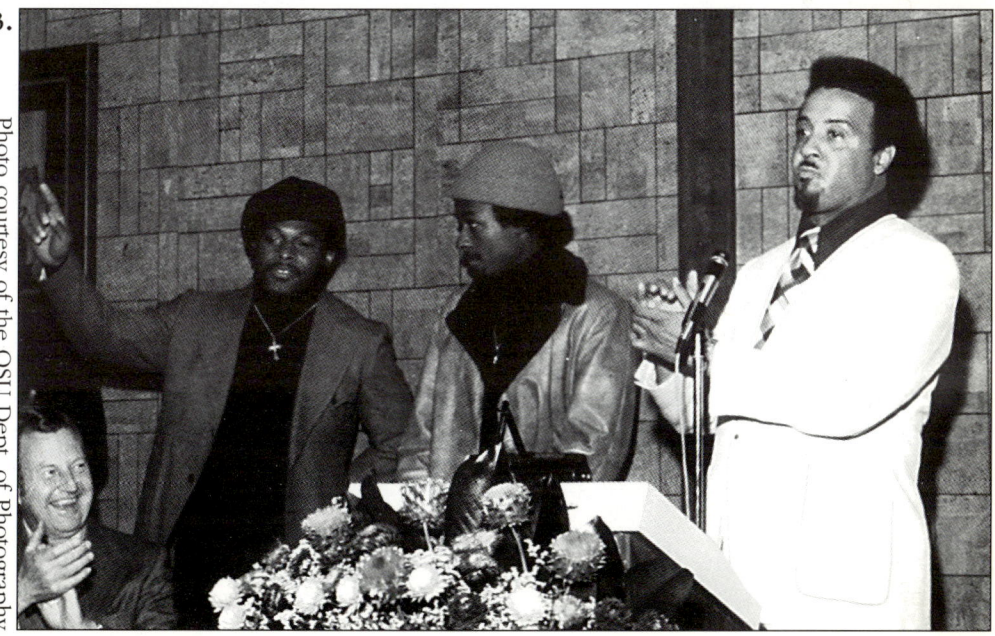

1.

2.

3.

1. (facing page) Rev. Jesse Jackson, flanked by students and Dr. Hale, leaving the Columbus Airport on his way to OSU to announce his candidacy for president in the 1984 election.
2. (facing page) With Ron Brown, secretary of the U.S. Department of Commerce, after his speech at OSU, October 20, 1995.
3. With Dr. Samuel DuBois Cook, president of Dillard University. Dr. Cook and Dr. Hale began a lasting friendship when both were doctoral students at The Ohio State University, 1953–1955.

1. Dr. Arliss Roaden, dean of the OSU Graduate School, welcomes new graduate students, 1973. (seated, l-r: Dr. Frank W. Hale, Jr.; Dr. Albert Kuhn, provost; Bill Cofield, graduate student and president of the Black Graduate Caucus.)
2. Jesse Jackson addresses the OSU student body in 1984 to kick off his presidential campaign. Governor Richard Celeste, Elder Wintley Phillips, and Dr. Frank Hale, campaign coordinator for Columbus, Ohio, analyze audience reaction.

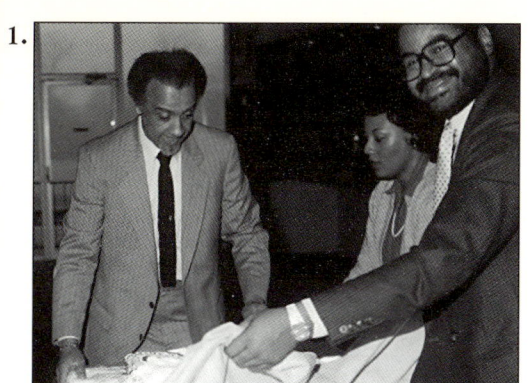

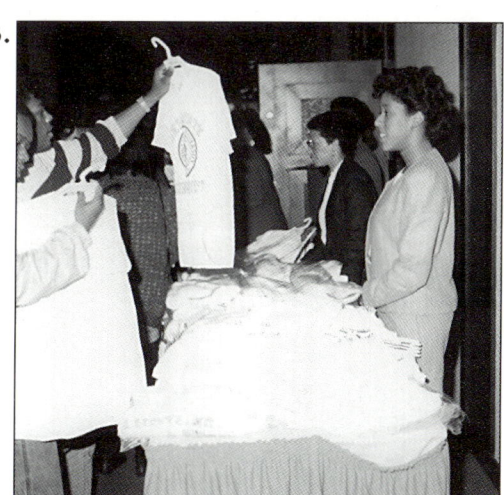

1. With Ms. Wanda White and Dr. Lester Morrow arranging a table of gifts for visiting scholars.
2. Dr. Ruth Russell, director of recruitment and placement at OSU, gives valuable information to visiting high school students.
3. Karen Reynolds and Cynthia Zachary Smith give away Hale Black Cultural Center sweatshirts to high school scholars.
4. Ms. Karen Reynolds, OSU recruiter, informs visiting high school scholars of the opportunities available at Ohio State University. (seated: Ms. Linda Jackson, program coordinator.)

1. With Ms. Rose Wilson-Hill at an event in honor of his retirement.
2. Dr. Samuel D. Proctor (seated far left) was the keynote speaker for the Minority Scholars Program. Also in this photo (seated, l-r: Rev. Tyrone Crider, Dr. Ruth Russell, Dr. Lester Morrow—standing, l-r: Dr. Joseph Stranges, Ms. Linda Jackson, Provost Myles Brand, Dr. Frank W. Hale, Jr.).
3. Ms. Linda Jackson speaks with visiting high school scholars about the programs and opportunities at Ohio State University.
4. Dr. Anne Pruitt presents Dr. Hale a book of testimonials from presidents of black colleges at an event in honor of his retirement.

1. Dr. Hale with staff members of the Hale Black Cultural Center at The Ohio State University.
2. With Larry Williamson, director of the Hale Black Cultural Center, and other center staff members. (Mr. Williamson is pictured to the immediate left of Dr. Hale.)

1.

2.

3.

1. Dr. and Mrs. Jon Robertson on their wedding day. Dr. Hale first became acquainted with Dr. Robertson this same year in the 1950s.
2. Dr. Roy Malcolm, Ohio State University alumnus and dean of college relations at Oakwood College.
3. Dr. Jon Robertson performs at the piano as Frank W. Hale, Sr., and SDA Conference officials observe, 1971.

1. Elder and Mrs. Walter Wright. Elder Wright was pastor of Ephesus Seventh-day Adventist Church in Columbus, Ohio, (1984–1990).
2. Elder Willie Lewis, president of the Allegheny Conference of Seventh-day Adventists, speaking at a church camp meeting.
3. Dr. and Mrs. Buford Griffith. Elder Griffith is the pastor of the Ephesus Seventh-day Adventist Church in Columbus, (1990–present).

1. The Ephesus Seventh-day Adventist Church, Columbus, Ohio, completed July 1987.
2. Founding members of the Peterson Society of the Adventist Men at Ephesus Seventh-day Adventist Church present the organization's National Man of the Year Award to Rev. Jesse Jackson, December 1987. (l-r: Dr. Frank Hale, Jr., founding president; Walter Gravely, Otis Vaughn, David Hill, Lucius Sullivan, Joseph Mitchell, Wesley Hawkins, Rev. Jesse Jackson, Ernest Padgette, Elder Walter Wright, Mario Broussard, Dr. Lester Morrow, Eugene Miller.)
3. (facing page) President Jennings of The Ohio State University with three generations of the Hale family, after Dr. Frank Hale, Jr., received the university's Distinguished Affirmative Action Award.
4. (facing page) Speaking to assembled guests after being inducted into the Topeka High School Hall of Fame.

3.

1. Mr. and Mrs. Frank W. Hale, Sr.
2. Mrs. Isy D. Young, Dr. Hale's 97-year old aunt, is the matriarch of the Hale family.
3. Mrs. Sherilyn Hale-Thomas, Dr. Hale's youngest child, sings at the wedding of James and Renene Price in the Hales' backyard.
4. Christina and Charles Thomas, Dr. Hale's grandchildren.

1. Mr. and Mrs. Frank Hale, Sr., at their 50th wedding anniversary gathering with (l-r) Ruth Hale, Sherilyn Hale, and Renene Carey.
2. Granddaughter Renene Carey at Ohio State University commencement ceremonies, 1990.
3. Dr. Hale's paternal grandparents, Paul and Maude Hale, and their two sons, Harold (back) and Frank (front). Taken in Athens, Ohio, in 1909.

1. Mr. and Mrs. Frank W. Hale III and their son, Frank W. Hale IV.
2. Eldest daughter, Pastor Ifeoma Kwesi, and her husband, Jim Roseboro, enjoy their wedding anniversary cake in 1992 with niece Christina..
3. The family in the Hales' backyard. (l-r: Irene Hale, Frank Hale IV, Ruth Hale, Ifeoma Kwesi, and Jim Roseboro)
4. Pastors Robert Bushner and Ifeoma Kwesi lead the wedding ceremony of Mr. and Mrs. James Price. Pastor Kwesi is the mother of the bride.

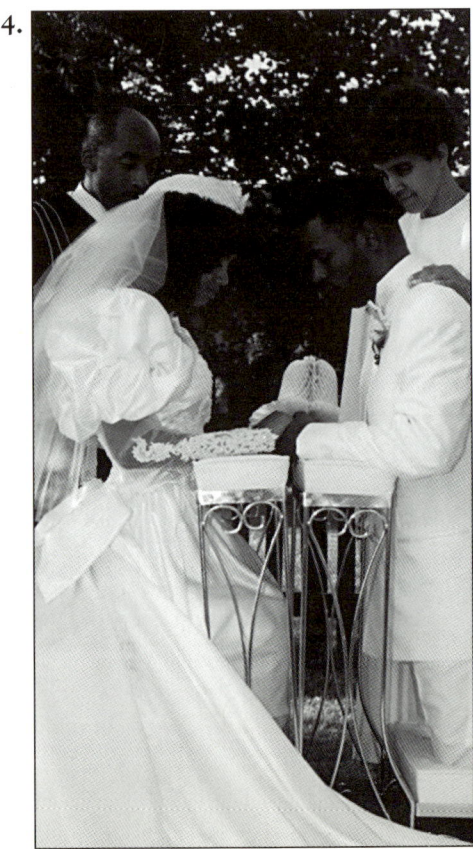

1. The Hales' A-frame cabin and 57-acre *getaway* in Hocking Hills, Ohio.
2. Dr. Frank W. Hale, Jr., addresses the faculty and student body at Kenyon College. President Phillip Jordan is seated on the far right.

Dr. Frank W. Hale, Jr., delivering the commencement address at The Ohio State University's 305th Commencement Ceremony, September 1, 1988.

The Division of Behavioral Sciences which had taken a substantial lead in the number of students who were majoring or minoring in sociology and psychology, through a program in field instruction, engaged in a variety of direct service and consultative activities in Huntsville and in nearby areas. The Division of Natural Science and Mathematics saw ten of its graduates over a decade go on to earn doctorates at some of the most prestigious institutions in America and Europe. The Division of Religion and Theology continued to serve as a point of contact for various churches in the northeastern Alabama area that sought pastoral assistance from young religion majors. Among the Alabama communities served were Huntsville, Athens, Decatur, Florence, Birmingham, Bessemer, Mobile and Montgomery. Nashville, Fayetteville, and Murfreesboro were among the Tennessee cities served.

Within the campus proper, there was a good deal more to underscore the extent to which the college provided professional growth and development for its ministerial students. Elder W. R. Starks, stewardship secretary of the General Conference, coordinated the Pastoral Ministry Workshop, emphasizing the principles of stewardship. Elder E. E. Cleveland conducted his twentieth annual evangelistic workshop.

But even in our most optimistic moments, those of us in administration at Oakwood could not have anticipated that a year earlier the college would be selected as the best college program in the "Campus Spotlight" radio broadcast series sponsored by the Collegiate Broadcasting Group of Atlanta, Georgia. The "Campus Spotlight" was a series of fifteen minute radio programs which was targeted toward high school students in an effort to recruit them to the institution broadcasting the program.

Oakwood students have made a substantial contribution to the image of the college through the years. I was proud that year after year a number of students made such stellar contributions in various areas that some of them received singular national or international recognition because of their intellectual prowess. Alvin Jackson, a biology major, won the English Speaking Union Luard Scholarship as the most outstanding black male student in attendance at a black college. After twelve finalists were selected and interviewed from among four hundred competitors, Jackson was declared the winner. The Luard Scholarship entitled him to spend his junior year in an English university with a $4,000 stipend to cover the cost of tuition, plus transportation expenses to and from the university, incidental expenses, and vacation money for travel during the Easter and Christmas holidays.

Amos Okrah, a chemistry major, was one of ten students selected nationwide to participate in a Summer Research Program sponsored by the University of Florida College of Medicine.

A group of Los Angeles physicians and professionals invited the seventy-voice Oakwood College Choir and the fifty-piece Huntsville Civic Orchestra to perform Verdi's *Requiem* under the direction of Jon Robertson at the Shrine Civic Auditorium on Sunday, March 22, 1970, in Los Angeles. Nearly four thousand enthusiastic patrons responded with a standing ovation to this cultural highlight in Oakwood's history.

It was my splendid privilege to open the program and introduce the magnificent musical groups to the Los Angeles community! Oakwood's Department of Music helped to create an abundance of friends for the college. Music-minded citizens received much inspiration from both student and faculty musicians who periodically made noteworthy public performances in the Huntsville community. A growing number of students were studying music, and a number of them were invited to appear with the Huntsville Civic Opera Company. Mr. Michael Harris, instructor of violin, was a member of the Huntsville Symphony Orchestra, and he along with Mr. Alvin Dreger, first cellist of the symphony, and Mr. Jon Roberts, pianist and chairman of Oakwood's Department of Music, formed the Oakwood Chamber Trio. Thus, Oakwood's musicians played a significant role in helping to elevate the local area's musical taste. Robertson caught the musical mood of the Huntsville community by storm. Through his fresh, vibrant, optimistic, and self-confident personality, along with his excellent musicianship, he influenced and enriched countless hundreds who received much inspiration from both his conducting and his piano performances. He gave a strong boost to the emergence of such European musicians as Beethoven, Chopin, Schubert, Verdi, and Mendelssohn.

As the college gained in reputation, the number of its benefactors increased. My contacts with the outside sources began to pay off, so much so that, by the end of 1970, our development fund donors list included these friends of the college: Brown Engineering Company; Campbell Tomato Soup Company; E. I. duPont de Nemours and Company; Endeavor Foundation; General Electric Foundation; Human Resources Foundation; IBM; O. D. McKee Baking Company; NASA; Northrop Company; Readers Digest Foundation; Texaco; 3M; Thikol Chemical Corporation; and the United Negro College Fund

Alumni Homecoming Weekend had mushroomed to the point of attracting over three hundred alumni in 1970. Mrs. Maude Bookhardt was selected as Parent of the Year. Her children, all former Oakwood students, are Dr. John Frank Bookhardt, Dr. Leroy Bookhardt, and Mrs. Lois Bookhardt Robinson. Mrs. Myrtle Murphy, president of the Washington, D.C., Oakwood Alumni chapter, was recognized as the Alumna of the

Year. Dr. Stuart Taylor, class of 1960, named White House Fellow and special assistant to the secretary of Housing and Urban Development (Secretary Romney), received the Special Achievement Award.

Oakwood continued to fulfill with flying colors her lofty mission in the field of Christian education. And I knew that angels were watching over me and the institution.

The year 1970 was not totally unlike the years that I had served as president of Oakwood College. I arrived at the college on the heels of my predecessor who had felt the full blunt of the rage of the '60's. There were those who felt that he was more wedded to the status quo than to change. As a consequence, politics took its toll on him after he had served as president for only two and a half years. Even though he left, most of the discordant elements, though in the minority, remained. So I was anointed to stand in the gap. From the very beginning I was aware that I suffered a serious political handicap. First of all, I followed and was immediately out of step with the long-standing tradition of having a clergyman elected as president. As a consequence I was not a member of the *in crowd* of ruling pastors and regional officers who, at least for a time, had my career destiny in their hands. The board was loaded with standpatters "who were like trees standing in the water" on many matters, in that they would not be moved too easily on new initiatives for the simple reason that things had not been done that way before. In fact, sad to say, some of the white board members were more open to progressive ideas than some of their black counterparts. This was particularly true of Union presidents who, in their administrative capacities, chaired the college boards in their respective areas. They were aware of what was required to meet minimum accreditation standards and to provide for quality education.

While some of our men were open to new and creative ideas, others were downright reactionary. I sometimes felt that some of them suffered from hardening of intellectual arteries. As I am not one who easily recoils from the clatter of controversy, I often found myself at odds with my board chairman and several of his ingrained allies who believed in government by laws, traditions, and policies rather than by human beings. I went to Oakwood with the fire of reform in my bones. While I had no zest for fray or conflict, I certainly did not side-step any issue that I felt was germane to the growth and development of the college. Every now and then my mother had to remind me, "Junior, unity is more important than perfection. You can be one hundred percent right, but if no one is following you, what difference does it make?" In all candor, she did not want me to suffer from foot-in-mouth disease, particularly since the board was not in the least dominated by persons whose academic preparation was similar to mine.

Nevertheless, I still seemed to find a way of stepping on certain people's toes over time. I tended to be more conservative on social issues than my youthful years might have foretold. I was contemptuous of faculty who either ignored the behavior of those students who showed dangerous signs of betraying long established standards of dress, music, and social standards or who responded lamely, if at all, in pointing out their indiscretions.

There were a few faculty who, though personally charming in every aspect to student constituents, found it to their advantage to be arrogant about their responsibilities relative to their role as supporters of faculty and administrative policies. The whole unsavory situation widened the growing rift between the president and a minor group of dissidents who were becoming increasingly insufferable from my point of view.

As tensions grew, certain board members were drawn into the underground grumblings to the point that some came to campus to conduct their own private witch hunt and prolonged probe on unsupported allegations. I took whip in hand, called a college convocation, and shocked the campus with a flaming speech, calling my detractors to put up or shut up. Refusing to flounder, I stirred up a hornets' nest with my phillipic and threatened to resign on the spot if that was what the community wanted. I had no other choice but to apply the whip and the spur in such a highly charged atmosphere. Following my speech, hundreds of students gathered in perspiring exertions of support, leaving behind them a trail of bruised and confused perpetrators. On May 3, 1970, there was a called emergency meeting of the faculty by Dr. E. A. Cooper, at which time I was given a vote of confidence by the overwhelming majority of the faculty and staff. However, in a terse and caustic statement to the board of trustees, I resigned on May 12, 1970.

How I wished I could have impressed upon my detractors the fact that my love for Oakwood had been bubbling up in my heart and mind from the very first day that I had set foot on the campus as a college freshman. My decision to accept the presidency of the college had not been a rash one. I did not permit anyone to push me into the presidential prison, especially since my salary was to be cut in half from the $17,000 per year that I had been making as chairman of the English Department at Central State College in Ohio to the sum of $8500 a year as president of Oakwood College. I felt compelled to return to Oakwood because of the prayerful call that had been extended to me and because of the opportunity to engineer greater strides for the advancement of the institution. It was a straight-up, non-hand-wringing judgment and decision based on what I believed to be God's will.

After considerable discussion and persuasion, I agreed to reconsider my decision and bestirred myself to weather the storm. The decision took unusual restraint on my part, considering the situation, and also because I was constantly being courted by attractive offers at other institutions. The school year ended with some degree of calm, but not before dissidents had firebombed the college store and had hurled a Molotov cocktail bomb through the window of the president's office on one Friday evening during the vesper services. The bomb, though detonated, died on the ledge of the windowsill inside the office. At the time, the president's office was housed in the W. H. Green Library. The admissions office was also housed there. What might have been a tragic disaster with the loss of college records and the contents of the library was curtailed because of providential protection. I knew then that the angels were watching over the institution and over me.

After prayerful consideration, I abandoned my decision to leave the college at that time and agreed to remain at the institution. It was at the quadrennial session of the World Conference of Seventh-day Adventists in early July of 1970 in Atlantic City, New Jersey, that I was elected to a second five-year term as president of Oakwood. During that session, Elder Frank L. Bland was elected as acting chairman until a permanent chairman could be elected.

The academic year 1970–71 produced a number of significant changes as a result of the college self-study that had been recently completed. Among the major recommendations presented to the board were the following ones:

> It was recommended that there be a reorganization of the college to reduce the number of seven academic divisions from seven to four so as to improve the coordination of the instructional program, enhance delegated authority and to make it more economically feasible for division chairmen to have adult secretarial help. The proposed divisions were these: Humanities and Religion, Behavioral Science and Social Science, Natural Science and Mathematics, and Education and Applied Sciences.

> That the board of trustees secure a director of counseling to replace the faculty system that was employed.

> That study be given to incorporate into the curriculum course that would provide varied vocational programs to meet student needs and to perpetuate one of the original objectives of the institution.

That the remedial programs and other compensatory courses be increased in every discipline to help students with deficiencies.

That recruitment personnel be increased in order to boost student enrollment.

That each department of the college examine its curriculum offerings to determine how best they can be improved to meet the objectives of the institution and made relevant to the needs of students and of society at large.

That a standing committee on the improvement of instruction be constituted (1) to develop in-service training for new and inexperienced teachers; (2) to prepare an agenda for inter-departmental conferences and faculty meetings to discuss the aims of education, curricula-objectives, and teaching problems and methods; (3) to conduct at a regular faculty meeting an open discussion of current national or local trends in educational methods, philosophy and experimentation; (4) to encourage departmental self-studies; and (5) to seek new and additional methods of improving instruction.

That the possibility of offering a general education major leading to a bachelor of general studies degree be thoroughly explored to permit upper classmen to work in some detail in a number of disciplines.

That studies be conducted to determine the effectiveness of the general education program in preparing students for graduate work, or business and professional careers; further that a coordinator of general studies be appointed from the teaching faculty to integrate the various education programs.

That a supervised study program be established to help students who have not been able to meet the usual achievement expectations of the college.

That the counseling service be authorized to conduct a series of workshops and seminars on how to prepare to take standardized tests, and departments provide the needed coaching services to make Oakwood students more competitive in GRE and NTE examinations.

That budgetary provisions be made for updating instructional equipment and audio-visual media, so as to improve the quality of classroom instruction.

That the college administration give serious study to the feasibility of expanding and upgrading the teaching staff through (1) in-service training, (2) refresher courses, (3) advanced study, and (4) the replacement of out-going faculty with competent scholars holding doctoral degrees.

That an office of institutional research be established.

That a positive stand be taken in support of those federal aid programs that would not sacrifice or compromise the principles and beliefs of the Seventh-day Adventist Church.

Although serving as a college president was, on occasion, overburdened with a litany of details, the lighter side of life had its humorous moments as well. Sister Anna Knight, known for her pioneer work as a missionary in India and among rural blacks in Mississippi, responded to the lure of springtime at Oakwood by cultivating and tending beautiful flower beds. She had been raised with the puritan values of the old school of hand work as she proceeded to keep her little patches of well-manicured petunias, pansies, zinnias, and snapdragons well-watched and watered with the sweat of her own indefatigable energy. Well in her eighties, she, nevertheless, got an early start each day, long before high noon signaled that it was time to go in from the heat. One morning as I was rushing to an eight o'clock meeting in my office, she underscored her commitment to Mother Earth by boldly exclaiming, "Help me dig up some of these petunias that I need to transplant over here," as she pointed to some far off corner of the area. I hesitated and paused just long enough in my attempt to explain my urgency to get to a meeting on time, whereupon she delivered a broadside that should go down in Oakwood records as perhaps the most vigorous retort in the school's history. Without ever raising her head to monitor my reaction, she bellowed, "You may be the president, but I'm the boss!" The quip was terse and acrid enough to bring me to a screeching halt and to perform her mandate in my well-tailored suit before gathering whatever resilience remained in me as I collected my composure in time to make a plausible explanation to those who awaited my late arrival. Oakwood was always alive with the commitment and spirit of veteran voices like Anna Knight, Eugenia "Mother" Cunningham, Trula Wade, Otis B. Edwards, Calvin E. Moseley, Jr., Robert Reynolds, Henrietta Emanuel, and Natelka Burrell. Oakwood's history cannot be properly understood unless it is viewed in the light of those who have stood in the trenches of early hardships—experiences that now are nearly a century long and soul-searing. Those giants provided the frontier cradle that contributed to the youthful and robust development of those who later came on the scene to give a distinctive flavor, incurable optimism, resilient toughness, and zestful eagerness to whatever their hands found to favorably and effectively do. Earl Cleveland, Charles Galley, Emerson Cooper, Jannith Lewis, Ernest Rogers, Gaines Partridge, John Blake, Inez Booth, Otis Edwards, Clarence Richards, Mervyn Warren, Murray Harvey, Calvin Moseley, Henrietta Emmanuel, James Roddy, Ruth Davis, and Ruth Stafford were steadily stellar in their commitment and contributions over the long haul. Their spirit still endures in the appeal of those who seek their guidance and counsel, whether of tender or adult years.

I was more than blessed to have had the opportunity to serve as president of Oakwood College. It continued to make giant boot-strides during my administration because of God's splendid and excellent direction. It was during these yeasty years of Oakwood's development that I gained a substantial portion of experience that was to be later used to advance opportunities for Oakwood youth who aspired to unrealized horizons in education, in the laboratory, in industry, and in frontiers yet unconquered. Because Oakwood had opened doors for me, I looked forward to having the opportunity to open additional doors for Oakwood students and Oakwood graduates. My experience as president of Oakwood college is a compelling account of how, once again, angels were watching over me. This is quite obvious in the highlights of my Oakwood administration as evidenced below:

Highpoints During the Presidency of Dr. Frank W. Hale, Jr. (1966–1971)

I. Regarding the President
- Voted the fifth president of Oakwood College at the General Conference Session in Detroit in 1966.
- Assumed presidency June 1, 1966.
- Was the second Oakwood faculty member to earn the Ph.D. degree in June of 1955. (Dr. Eva B. Dykes was the first)
- Was the first faculty member to earn the doctorate while serving on the faculty at Oakwood—1955.
- Was the first president with a professional background and preparation in higher education (the others were members of the clergy).
- As president, it was my third exposure to Oakwood, after having first been a student (1944–45), later as a teacher (1951–59), and finally as president (1966–71).
- Was the youngest president to assume the office at the age of thirty-nine.
- Authored *Sunlight and Shadows*. Southern Publishing Association, Nashville, 1967.

- Authored *The Cry for Freedom*. A.S. Barnes Co., South Brunswick and London, 1969.
- Elected to a second five-year term at the General Conference Session in Atlantic City in 1970.

II. Significant Events and Milestones
- Elder R. H. Pierson, president of the General Conference, visited and spoke to the campus community—October 17, 1966.
- Diversified the board by adding the first four lay representatives—1966.
- Added twenty new faculty and staff members—1966.
- Received board approval of a five-year capital expansion plan—1966.
- Established office of student affairs—1966.
- 70th Anniversary observed—1966–67.
- Carter Hall completed—1966.
- Operating budget doubled—1966–67.
- Inaugural ceremonies for the installation of the president (first Oakwood inauguration)—1967.
- College population increased from 433 in 1965 to 670 during the 1966–67 academic year—approximately fifty-five percent.
- Dedicated Symington Reading Development Center—1966.
- The old sanitarium building was renovated to house the Behavioral Science Center—1967.
- Oakwood given initial participation in *Who's Who Among Students in Colleges and Universities*—1966.
- United Student Movement Presidents—William Frazier, '66; William Niles, '67; Pierre Hunt, '68; David McCottry, '69.
- Oakwood's first student missionaries were Barry Black('68) to Peru and Cynthia Clark ('69) to Thailand.
- Added performance faculty in Music (Lee, Robertson, Harris, and Thompson)—1967–69.
- Co-founded the Alabama Center for Higher Education (ACHE)—1967.
- Visited the White House as a guest of President Lyndon B. Johnson to discuss higher education issues along with other college presidents—1967.
- Established a community advisory council of prominent Hunstville citizens—1967.
- First recruitment initiative to Bermuda—1967.
- First Alumni Homecoming Celebration off campus (Carriage Inn)—March 5–7, 1968.
- W. J. Blake Memorial Center constructed—1968.
- Office of Development established—1968.

- Oakwood won annual UNCF campaign competition by raising $21.95 per student, or $10,700.00—1968–69.
- Alumni association provided office space in Blake Center—1968.
- Revised *Faculty Handbook*—1969.
- Established P. W. Ridgeway Artifacts Collection—1969.
- O. B. Edwards Hall constructed—1969.
- Co-founded the Cooperation College Library Center in Atlanta—1969.
- Oakwood was first place winner in annual UNCF competition of thirty-six colleges and universities—1969.
- Oakwood College Choir and Huntsville Civic Orchestra in concert at Shrine Auditorium, Los Angeles (Verdi's *Requiem*)—March 22, 1970.

III. Innovations and Trends
- Arranged for bronze seal of Oakwood to be crafted and placed on the wall in the president's office.
- Sponsored student missionaries to South Africa, Thailand and Japan—1967–1971.
- Promoted advanced education opportunities for the faculty, resulting in a thirty percent increase in the number of teachers with doctorates—1966–71.
- Advocated for faculty increases which resulted in a ninety-seven percent gain over the period from 1966–71.
- Arranged for the Oakwood College Choir to be featured on ABC's Negro College Choirs radio broadcast series—1967–68.
- Contracted with wholesale and retail stores, restaurants, hotels and Alabama A & M College to supply bakery goods from the Oakwood bakery on a continuing basis—1967.
- Contracted with Redstone Arsenal to provide laundry services and clean six thousand uniforms a week for service personnel—1967–71.
- Pursued and received foundation and corporate financial support from the Ford Foundation, Sears-Roebuck Foundation, Harris Pine Mills, Thikol Chemical Corporation, College Placement Services, Inc., Sperry Rand, DuPont Foundation, Brown Engineering, NASA, the Alabama Center for Higher Education, Campbell's Soup Company, and the Association of Huntsville Area Companies—1966–67.
- Student members were included on all faculty and administrative committees except the president's cabinet—1968–71.
- Proposal presented for the degree, bachelor of general studies—1971.
- Contracted with Vulcan Materials Company to lease Oakwood's rock quarry to provide materials to surface Alabama's highway system—1967–71.

- Commissioned Hugh Miller and Don Davis, Redstone Arsenal technical artists, to paint murals to depict the history of Oakwood College from 1896–1969 to adorn the Blake Center upstairs lobby—1968–69.
- Promoted non-denominational graduate and professional educational opportunities for graduation seniors which resulted in:
  - Edward Cartwright (chemistry major) receiving a four-year scholarship to the Yale University School of Medicine—1968.
  - Alvin Jackson (biology) winning a English Speaking Luard Scholarship to study abroad during his junior year—1969.
  - Amos Okrah (chemistry) earning a four year scholarship to the University of Pennsylvania School of Medicine—1970.
  - Raymond Winbush (psychology) acquiring an $18,000 fellowship to the University of Chicago for doctoral studies in Psychology—1970.
  - Joyce Cordell (English) accepting a $15,000 fellowship from The Ohio State University to pursue a doctorate in speech pathology and audiology—1970.
  - LaJean Martin (education) obtaining a fellowship to pursue the master's degree in library science at the University of Illinois—1970.
  - Four music majors were awarded scholarships at the Juilliard School of Music to pursue graduate studies—(Freeman Davis, Edwina Humphrey, and Stanley Ware)—1970.
- The Oakwood College Choir and the Huntsville Civic Orchestra traveled to Los Angeles to Present Verdi's *Requiem* at the Shrine Auditorium on Easter Sunday—1970.
- Architects were selected to design plans for the construction of a new library—1971.
- Proposed the construction of a Religious Education Center to include a church sanctuary and classrooms as a training ground for prospective ministers—1969.
- Oakwood College became a member of the "Campus Spotlight" radio series sponsored by the Collegiate Broadcasting Group of Atlanta and was selected as the college having the best presentation of that year—1969.
- In 1965, there were forty graduates. From 1968 through 1970, the graduating classes averaged eighty-five.
- Regional Conference capital appropriations rose more than one hundred percent from $245,000 in 1965 to $500,000 in 1968 and 1969.
- Regional Conference operating appropriations rose more than one hundred percent from $91,818.52 in 1965 to $184,134.72 in 1969.

- Support (capital-operating) for each full-time student or the equivalent increased from $929 in 1965 to $1,519 in 1969.
- A restudy of the college objectives was undertaken because of changing social conditions. As a result, the *social* area was revised and renamed *cultural*. Another area, *personal adjustment*, was developed and added to the list of objectives to be included in the 1969–70 college bulletin.
- The college cooperated with the Academy for Educational Development in projecting the trends of Oakwood College in the future (enrollment, income and expenses, curriculum growth, physical plant expansion, student personnel services and faculty competence—1967–68.
- Purchased two eight passenger stagecoach limousines for *Musical Showcase* tours with a $25,000 Christmas gift from Mrs. Ethel DuPont at the recommendation of Senator Sparkman—1969.
- Requested and received a gift of one thousand cases of food products from Campbell's Soup Company—1968.

Chapter 13

The Ohio State University: My War Against Underrepresentation in the Graduate School

The Ohio State University first burst into the headlines of my experience when I was accepted into the Ph.D. program in communication and political science in 1952. This gigantic university with an enrollment approaching nearly thirty thousand students at the time had a virtual monopoly on my psyche then because it was studded with some of the top names in the field of communication. Among those who emerged with high distinction from my perspective were Franklin Knower, William Utterback, W. Hayes Yeager, John Black, Paul Carmack, Ruth Irwin, Harold Luper, Earl Wiley, and Wallace Fotheringham.

But things were quite different in December of 1970 when I was presented the Distinguished Alumnus Award from The Ohio State University Alumni Association during the annual convention of the Speech Communication Association which was holding its meeting in New Orleans. The presentation was made by Dr. Keith Brooks, chairman of the OSU Department of Communication, on December 28, 1970. The recognition was given for outstanding achievement in black collegiate education and in speech education as author, administrator, and professor. Little did I realize that less than a month later I would be invited to visit Ohio State to be interviewed for the position of associate dean of the graduate school, a position for which I had not applied. It was my understanding that I was the last among more than a half dozen candidates who had already been interviewed. It was indeed a time of serious soul searching for me. I had just been elected to a second five-year term at Oakwood College. I had received an inquiry from Howard University to determine whether or not I was interested in the deanship of the School of Communications. My name had been recommended as an assistant for higher education in the U.S. Department of the Navy. All of these remarkable contacts and considerations had come to my attention within a brief thirty-day period. As gratifyingly satisfied as I was with such appreciation and attention, I still found it difficult to even deal with the possibility of severing my connection with the institution that I loved so very much. Yet, I had to admit to myself that new and knotty problems continued to rise that infringed on my ability to function at my very best. I was too independent and self-reliant to let anything interfere with my usefulness and my happiness. Furthermore, recent events demonstrated that new frontiers were open to me. It became quite apparent to me that as long as there is an open mind, there will always be an open frontier. After sifting and weighing some of my options, I decided to accept an invitation to be interviewed at The Ohio State University for the position of associate dean of the graduate school.

January 27, 1971, was a grueling day of meeting with President Novice Fawcett, Provost James Robinson, several committees of the administration and of the faculty, an ad hoc committee of the graduate school, and finally with Dr. Arliss Roaden, dean of the graduate school. The ad hoc committee consisted of four black students (Estelle Baskerville, Amos Martin, Jr., Herbert A. Scott, and Harry N. Seymour), two black faculty members (Professors Lonnie Wagstaff and Howard Williams), and three members of the graduate council (Wallace Fotheringham, Saad Nagi, and John Schmitt). At the end of the day, I was the dinner guest of Dr. Arliss Roaden, vice provost and dean of The Ohio State University Graduate School. There was something about Roaden's warm and gentlemanly manner that inspired confidence. He lost little time in getting to the point. He stated rather forthrightly, "You have made a most positive and overwhelming impression on all the committees you visited with today, and I am pleased to offer you (from among sixty candidates) the position of associate dean of the graduate school and the rank of professor of Speech, subject to the action of the board of trustees which will be meeting on March 5, 1971." My heart almost stopped as I had not anticipated that I would be getting feedback from my visit so soon. His progressive spirit, his reputation as a scholar, and as

256

a fair and honest administrator were more than sufficient to make me comfortable as a prospective colleague and associate of his; nevertheless, I indicated that I needed time to discuss the matter with my family before making a decision. Other considerations also clamored for my attention: job possibilities for my wife, housing considerations, and whether I would be able to have Rose Wilson, my administrative secretary at Oakwood, to be hired as my administrative assistant or secretary in the graduate school.

On February 1, 1971, Dean Roaden formalized his offer to me in a letter offering me the position at a twelve-month salary of $26,208. Even before receiving his letter, I (after having conferred with my family) sent Dean Roaden a letter of acceptance on January 31, 1971. My prompt reply expressed my deep appreciation in these words:

> Your offer to join the team at The Ohio State University is a definite challenge, and I accept my new assignment with the desire to make a meaningful contribution to the advancement of higher education, to the university, and certainly to the wonderful young people whom we shall serve.

I shall always remember the appeals of the young black graduate students whom I encountered in a number of situations while on the campus at Ohio State. Although I had responded to the invitation to be interviewed for the position which I later accepted, I had not visited the campus with a predisposition to accept or reject the position were it offered me. While I was pleased that I was being considered for such a lofty position at the nation's largest university, I had not abandoned my endearment to Oakwood College; nor was it easy for me to forego the second five year extension of my contract which had just been voted at the World Conference of the Seventh-day Adventist Church in Atlantic City. I was deeply impressed by the petitions of the black youth at Ohio State who indicated that there were so few black mentors or role models to whom they could turn for help when they had difficulties. So great was their desire for support that one of them remarked, "Dr. Hale, if you decide to leave Oakwood to join us, the students at Oakwood will still have significant numbers of black faculty and staff with whom they can touch base when critical situations arise." Isolated as they were in an enormous sea of whiteness, their pleas were not lost on me. I sensed their bewilderment amid what appeared to be indescribable loneliness for what had become alien territory to some of them.

My wife and I spent a weekend in March searching for a house to our liking, and we were able to settle on one at 1351 Kirkley Road on my birthday, March 24, 1971. Mrs. Melissa Day, a local realtor was very helpful in our search and in arranging for the closing on April 18, 1971. Even though we had no plans to move to Columbus before May 31, 1971, we proceeded to have the house painted and wallpapered according to our tastes. With the meager limitations of our financial resources, having worked for missionary wages at Oakwood College, we were still able to add some very beautiful cabinetry to our family room and library den. The Miller Cabinet Company, a superior Amish group out of Plain City, Ohio, proved a special blessing because of their superior workmanship, dependability and their modest charges.

My memory of my personal and professional relations with Dean Roaden is a very satisfying one. I shall always remember him as a very bright and progressive dean. From the very beginning of my tenure in the graduate school, he was an arch supporter of my every effort and achievement. I found him to be a Christian and a professional of the highest integrity. Though a southerner by birth, he appeared to be especially free of prejudice, sham and exhibitionism. It was a real privilege to work for him, and he did everything possible to make my new venture a successful one. Always available for counsel, I felt free to engage him about any problems that I faced. He was always open, attentive, and unhurried whenever I approached him for any reason.

Within a short span of time, Rose Wilson joined the graduate school staff as my secretary. Soon I received a letter from Alfred E. Diamond, secretary of the graduate school, advising me that I had been approved to serve in Category II of the graduate faculty in the Department of Speech. This new status entitled me to advise graduate students and to serve on certain committees dealing with comprehensive examinations and with the defense of theses and/or dissertations. The right opportunities continued to come that would be contributing to my professional growth and advancement.

Dean Roaden, sufficiently secure within himself, generously gave me the greatest possible latitude and freedom to explore how best to develop programs within the graduate school that would both promote and sustain diversity. Initially, I requested leave to visit a number of Big Ten universities to explore what programs they had underway. I knew that I wanted to have a blueprint in readiness by the beginning of the academic year; therefore, I would have to move thoroughly and expeditiously in order to have a proposal in readiness by the end of the summer of 1971.

During the months of June and early July, I visited with Dr. Robert Cash at the University of Michigan, Dr. Herman Hudson at Indiana University, Dr. Robert Green, Dr. Thomas Gunnings, and Dr. Joseph

McMillan, and Dr. Ralph Bonner at Michigan State University, and Dr. Antonio Zomora at Purdue University. I was especially impressed with the layout that was available to black students at Indiana University, as well as the programmatic initiatives that Dr. Hudson had underway at the time.

Dr. Zomora had done a very fine job in establishing a black cultural center at Purdue. A few years later I was able to profit from the wisdom of Dr. Elaine Copeland and Dr. Richard Barksdale who were availing themselves of the best opportunities afforded them at the University of Illinois.

Upon my return to Ohio State, I organized my thinking, in so far as possible, to include the consideration of all the assets and liabilities that I had found in the institutions I had visited. It was apparent to me that not a single Big Ten institution had a comprehensive minority affairs program to deal with the various aspects of minority life on campus. There also appeared no all-encompassing program to recruit prospective minority graduate students or to provide those who were recruited with adequate financial resources such as fellowships and assistantships to maintain them. The situation was no better at Ohio State. In fact, the presence of black graduate students at the university was abysmally low. I felt both discouraged and encouraged by that fact. Discouraged because of the reality; encouraged because of my conviction that something could and would be done about it. My best judgment prompted me to seek solutions out of the fundamental fabric of my own experiences. I could not only hope; I was determined to use my new position to make a difference in the lives of a black youth who would be graduating from college in the future.

Anyone knowing the record of historically black colleges and universities is aware of the fact these institutions have always been in the forefront of addressing the needs of black students. It is also significant that these institutions can claim outstanding alumni who are making major contributions in the nation and in their communities in a variety of fields. As I began to make plans on how to best attract black students to pursue graduate education at The Ohio State University, I was captured with the notion of targeting students who were enrolled in the historically black colleges and universities. I had been intimately associated with the presidents of the United Negro College Fund and the consortium of historically black private colleges and universities.

So it was during the summer months of 1971 that I developed a whole design that would create a partnership between Ohio State and black institutions of higher learning. I felt certain that the intellectual life of the students as promoted and stimulated in the black institutions was more than adequate to make them competitive as students were they admitted into the graduate programs at Ohio State. I knew, however, that it would not be enough to have them admitted into the institution. Financial assistance is a key factor in facilitating persistence to the point of completing degree requirements. This is a fact of life for both undergraduate and graduate students of color. Therefore, I was aware that to admit black students into the graduate school without providing them with adequate financial support would be a shocking denial of reality and would fatally undermine their progress even before they got started.

Both the forward and backward look helped me to understand that, if we were going to increase the presence of black students among the pool of students to be admitted to The Ohio State University, we would also have to increase the pool of resources to accommodate the added numbers. There was no question that a very large percentage of black students came from low income families. As a consequence, I took it upon myself to urge Dean Roaden to expand the graduate school fellowship program to the point where two hundred graduate fellowships could be offered each year, with one half of them going to minority students. While I knew that the idea was a revolutionary one, I also knew that the face and composition of the graduate school student body was nearly all white. Fortunately, it was at a time when there was some consensus that some special programs needed to be put into place to address the special needs of the disadvantaged and underrepresented at the university. After all, the campus disruptions of 1968 and 1970 at Ohio State had made the significant point that business as usual could no longer be tolerated.

Understanding this, the university agreed to fund the bank of fellowships which I had requested, appointed me to serve as chairman of the Graduate School Fellowship Committee, and approved an annual Graduate School Visitation Days Program which I designed and which was instituted and became operable during the autumn of 1971. Having full faith in the tenets of my belief that each student has a right to the most extensive basic opportunities and liberties that an institution can offer, Dean Roaden was tremendously supportive in every effort that I made to open and advance opportunities for students of color.

The Graduate School Visitation Days Program is a two-day event in which fifty colleges and universities are invited to send their five highest ranking seniors along with a faculty representative to The Ohio State University campus on the first weekend in November. This program, now The Graduate and Professional Schools Visitation Days Program, is an important tradition, an annual event sponsored by The Ohio State University Office of Minority Affairs and the Graduate School.

The Visitation Days Program always includes an opening convocation attended by 250–300 honor seniors who are informed about admission procedures, housing, financial aid opportunities, and student services. On the first evening of their visit, the student guests are always treated to a program designated as "The Gospel Extravaganza" which has featured such artists as the Edwin Hawkins Singers, Walter Hawkins, Tremaine Hawkins, Andre Crouch, and the Winans. This musical attraction has also been an effective public relations vehicle in drawing a large representation of black people from the local community. It has been highly successful in demonstrating the institution's sensitivity to the interests and yearnings of the African-American community. Students tour academic departments of their interest on the morning of the second day of their visit to confer with faculty, to see departmental facilities and resources, and to receive some indication as to the prospect of their being admitted into the graduate school or professional college with financial support. Following a luncheon with members of the graduate faculty, the students participate in a *rap session* with currently enrolled graduate students while their faculty representatives meet with faculty of color from OSU to gain insights into what life is like for students of color at the university.

The capstone of the two-day visit is the Visitation Days Banquet which is held the evening of the second day and where 650 guests, including the student honorees and their faculty representatives, OSU faculty members and administrators, fellows-in-residence, and community leaders, are in attendance. The governor of Ohio and the mayor of Columbus or representatives from their offices are always present to welcome the visiting guests. On this occasion, the university presents distinguished alumni awards to noted and celebrated alumni. The very presence of these eminent leaders has been a major catalyst in motivating many of these scholars, who were among the best and the brightest in the country, to pursue their graduate and/or professional studies at Ohio State. National leaders such as Congressman Louis Stokes, Attorney Vernon E. Jordan, Jr., Dr. Samuel D. Proctor, Reverend Jesse L. Jackson, Mr. Lerone Bennett, Jr., Ms. C. Delores Tucker, Attorney Patrick Russell-McCloud, Attorney Benjamin L. Hooks, Mr. Julian Bond, Dr. Franklin G. Jenifer, and Dr. Calving O. Butts III, have served as keynote speakers.

Minority enrollment in Ohio State's graduate school rose dramatically in a very short period of time. A year after the initial drive began, The Ohio State University Graduate School awarded fifty-five doctoral fellowships with a value of $1,500,000 to black students who had been participants in the Visitation Days Program. Recognizing that a large number of minority undergraduates wish to gain employment as soon as possible after graduation from college, I recommended that the University begin awarding One-Year Minority Master's Fellowships. This made it possible for students to pursue and complete the first graduate degree within a year after completing the requirements for the baccalaureate degree. As a result, the university began offering one hundred fellowships a year to minority students, and many students who were anxious to get a job and pay off their undergraduate indebtedness found the new fellowship program to their liking. The plan ultimately gave us a better range of students and gave the students an opportunity to gain a graduate degree in short order without having to commit themselves to a four-year doctoral stint in order to be eligible for fellowship support. Of course, most of them intended to pursue the doctoral degree at some point in the future after settling into some career slot. Nearly two thousand fellowships have been awarded since the program's inception, and approximately 1600 students of color have earned master's and/or doctoral degrees as a result. The university has expended more than twenty million dollars in this most successful effort. For the first six or seven years of the program, Ohio State had a running head start on graduate schools nationwide. The positive side effect of our success was that other Big Ten schools, as well as other major universities, began to offer similar programs. Even though the competition became fierce, as the founder forerunner of minority graduate recruitment on a massive scale, the OSU program was perceived and labeled as the best, and many of my colleagues at other institutions referred to me affectionately as the *dean of minority graduate education*. Such a response reflected a recognition of what our efforts had been able to accomplish.

I certainly cannot fail to acknowledge the endorsement which I received from the presidents and academic deans of black colleges who sent us their best students, the support which I received from OSU college deans and department chairs, the cooperation which I received from the graduate school personnel, and the ongoing assistance I received from senior faculty who served as members of the Graduate School Fellowship Committee during my seven-year tenure (1971–1978) as chairman.

As a new dean on campus, I endeavored to keep intimately in touch with the power brokers on campus—senior administrators, deans, department heads and faculty. I felt it also important to work with faculty of color, and especially those who worked in minority-oriented programs. So often they are isolated from the institutional mainstream and, as a consequence, have little opportunity to influence institutional policies and practices. I made every effort to learn of their concerns so that I could be in a position to represent their points of view at meetings where important decisions were made.

Many persons contributed to the successes which I enjoyed during my tenure as the associate dean of the graduate school. Elmer Baumer, also an associate dean, taught me the ropes—the many details of how the graduate school worked, giving excellent advice and encouragement; Mildred Chavous' sense of history and excellent facilitation on numerous matters was valuable in terms of her technical assistance; Jean Girves shared stimulating and informative data that was invaluable; Joy Wittenaur was a jewel in helping to plan and organize materials for the fellowship committee; Rose Wilson was my right arm and alter ego as she left no stone unturned in our pursuit of excellence in all areas; Jules Lapidus, who succeeded Dean Roaden as dean of the graduate school was an essential ingredient in keeping the program afloat after Roaden's departure; and, once again, Arliss Roaden's vision, many courtesies and high level amenities gave me the space and opportunity to conceptualize and to create the programs for which he found the essential resources to finance and underwrite.

But there were also persons not associated with the graduate school whose wisdom and cooperation I enjoyed and appreciated. Dr. William J. Holloway, vice provost for minority affairs and professor of Education, was committed to working for the ideal of expanding equal educational opportunities on campus. Holloway was appointed the first vice provost for minority affairs in 1970, and he was responsible for establishing the Freshman Foundation Program (FFP) at Ohio State. The program provided financial support for students from student aid sources, including state and federal grants, loans, college work-study and private scholarships. During Holloway's administration over fifteen million dollars were awarded to several thousand students of color. Two major Office of Minority Affairs programs were approved and funded by the federal government while Holloway was at the helm. A four-year Pre-college Social Development Program was funded by the National Institute of Mental Health "to help minority and economically disadvantaged students in becoming socialized (adjusted) to the university." During the four-year funding period, 243 students were able to take advantage of the non-credit, five-week summer program that provided the students with a series of workshops, intensive personal and career counseling, and residence hall living experiences.

The Summer Tutorial for Readiness to Enter Training for a Career in Health (STRETCH) was funded by the National Institutes of Health for a three-year period. The name of the program was changed to Health Opportunity Program (HOP) in 1975. HOP students received intensive counseling, tutorial assistance, a practicum in a health field, and were enrolled in regular university science and math courses. While Dr. Holloway was a remarkable man who had held prominent positions in the U.S. Office of Education dealing in the area of equal opportunity, he had a very supportive staff that included William B. Johnson as director of administration; Joseph F. Stranges as director of financial aids; and Maureen Black, Tina Cade, Dora Mitchum and Gary Young, who at different periods, served as director of program development research and evaluation.

Many were my friends and colleagues at Ohio State, but I would have to single our Dr. Holloway as one so rich in integrity and so kind that I never hesitated to reveal to him my inner most thoughts and concerns about any issue, however fragile or formidable it might have been. I always cherished the high quality of his counsel.

Similarly, I had a high regard for Dr. William E. Nelson, Jr., chairman of the Department of Black Studies. It was common knowledge that Nelson had dedicated himself to seeing that the black community on campus—both students and faculty—would receive their just dues from the university's major decision makers. Nelson could become irritated and indignant at a moment's notice if he recognized that black people on campus were targets of unfair treatment. His sense of history made him intensely suspicious of the university's commitment to equal educational opportunity. A powerful defender of justice, Nelson is commanding in presenting his point of view. He has an argumentative style that can cut through complex issues like a knife through butter. When embittered, he can unleash invectives so powerful that his opponents are left squirming and shuddering with uneasiness in the face of certain defeat. Because he was adamant about what he believed in the areas of civil rights and equal opportunity, there were few on campus who were willing to challenge him head-on. I found him to be a willing and faithful ally when things got tough, and we had to contend with conservatives who were content with the status quo regarding the well-being of black people on campus.

As the demands justified it, I always called upon certain people of color for encouragement and support. They included the following: Dr. Robert O. Washington, dean of the College of Social Work; Dr. Mac A. Stewart, associate dean of University College; Robert J. Stull, associate dean of the College of the Arts; Dr. Robert A. Carter, assistant dean of the College of Law; Dr. Elson Craig, assistant dean of medical student affairs; Minnie McGee, assistant dean of the College of Engineering; and Ms. Barbara Rich, assistant dean of admissions for the College of Law.

The outcry for racial reform on the campus had been so overwhelming that the university undertook a vigorous recruitment effort to increase the presence of black faculty and staff. The clamor for broad-based representation had produced some substantial results in a relatively short period. Fortunately, these forward steps had been responsible for attracting some very capable and scholarly black personnel. Their presence and participation was a redeeming feature to the institution's image when viewed within the context of its conservative history. Though the administration had taken some praise-worthy steps to keep pace with the rhythm of the times, there were still pockets of conservatism on campus that were contemptuous of the new directions that were underway in the area of diversity. Some vented their frustrations with the way that things were going with an arrogant display of provincialism by questioning whether an institution could be equal and excellent, too. On one occasion I joined several hundred students in protest as they aired their grievances in front of the administration building, later designated as Bricker Hall. At the next meeting of the Dean's Council, Dr. Roy Kottman, dean of the College of Agriculture, openly and boldly denounced my participation in what he viewed as an unsavory episode. What had been a grass roots, spontaneous reaction by black students and black faculty, as they attempted to highlight issues and concerns that affected them, was met with insufferable disdain and clumsy rhetoric by certain elements who wanted things to remain as they had always been.

In the meanwhile, black graduate students saw the need to organize themselves into a meaningful structure, so that they could have a stage for pushing their own agenda, for negotiating representation on important committees, and for having the kind of leverage that would carry weight, both on the Council of Graduate Students and within the hierarchy of the graduate school itself. Among the most active students in the Black Graduate and Professional Student Caucus during my tenure as associate dean were William Cofield, Rhunette Curry, Carolyn Hagey, Ernestine Green, Chris Jones, Jeanette Jones, Dorothy Rainey, Troy Simmons, and Cleavonne Singleton. Bright, active and vocal, they threw their support squarely behind the various programs which I undertook to advance the interests of students and faculty of color. They were especially effective in promoting our efforts to attract students who were our guests during the November Visitation Days Program. United behind our campaign to diversify the campus, their testimonies, as students already in residence at Ohio State, made a tremendous impression. Consequently, their participation was a needed and valuable stimulus to our fruitful experiences in helping the university to be among the foremost institutions in the country in its ability to attract black students into its graduate programs. The caucus was also constructively engaged in helping to establish the Graduate School Orientation Conference (GSOC). GSOC was established to provide vital information to new graduate students of color to enable them to cope with confidence as they attempted to adjust to the uncertainties of their new situation.

Shortly after I arrived at Ohio State, some of the black graduate students requested that I design and teach a course dealing with the rhetorical strategies that black Americans had used to make significant gains in the area of civil rights. By the end of my second year (1972–1973), I had developed a course entitled "The Rhetoric of Black America." It began with the anti-slavery movement and emphasized those periods in American history where the issues of race had an alarming impact upon the stability of the country. Scores of students, black and white, have taken the course as it is usually offered during the spring quarter of each year. The tragic state of racial tensions in the country point unerringly to the need for better understanding among the races. I have used two texts in teaching the course: *The Rhetoric of Black Americans*, by James L. Golden and Richard D. Rieke, published by the Charles E. Merrill Publishing Company of Columbus, Ohio, and my own anthology, *The Cry for Freedom*, published by A.S. Barnes and Company of South Brunswick and New York and Thomas Yoseloff Ltd. of London, England.

My experiences as a dean in The Ohio State University awakened me to the sometimes discouragingly complex of factors and circumstances that contribute to the pressing problems in the field of graduate education. The importance of graduate education as a vital frontier in the expansion of knowledge should be obvious. American scientists have often wrought marvels in their respective fields only because research has been heralded as a major function of the university over the past forty years or so. Without strong graduate schools, we cannot train our students to be sufficiently competitive in the international marketplace. Thus graduate education has become the heart of the educational enterprise at the most reputable academic institutions of higher learning.

Too many African-American youth postpone their education beyond the completion of an undergraduate degree for a variety of reasons. The impact of heavy undergraduate indebtedness, the pervasive concern of students and their parents to get some return on dollars already spent, and the desire to be relieved of the fatigue brought on by the need to be involved in a rather heavy work schedule while completing their undergraduate requirements all combine to limit the enrollment of African-Americans into graduate education. Nevertheless, the situation at Ohio State during the 1970s was considerably less pessimistic in terms of its ability to attract students of color into its graduate programs. Fortunately, the Visitation Days Program, the growth and expansion of fellowships specifically designated for students of color, and the recruitment excursions of Rose Wilson throughout the South in beating the bushes for unusual talent helped to bolster the enrollment of minority youth, particularly black youth who were graduates of historically black colleges and universities.

It was my cherished dream that more and more black students would pursue graduate work in mathematics, science, and other technical fields. Most black students were concentrated in a few majors, principally in education, the humanities, the social sciences, and in business. While enrollment in some of the more technical fields was growing slowly, it became apparent to me that this situation was not due totally to the disinterest of black students. Their exclusion from some of these fields was also due, in part, because of the rigid way in which some departments used the Graduate Record Examination scores as a selective means of reducing the admission of potential candidates. Even those who designed the Graduate Record Examinations suggested that they be used as diagnostic rather than as selective instruments for minority and international students. The argument that tests should be used in admissions because they predict performance has been questioned and challenged by numerous noted scholars. Thus, the usefulness of certain qualifying tests in forecasting the success of students in the pursuit of graduate education or in their success in certain careers is often weak and pointless. Nevertheless, I had some success at convincing graduate committees to complement their testing with other criteria such as non-cognitive factors and structured recommendations. We also encouraged departments to enhance their awareness of the underrepresentation of people of color in certain specific fields.

When I became aware of the underrepresentation of blacks in the field of psychology, I immediately sought an opportunity to converse with the chairman of the Department of Psychology, who, at that time, was Dr. Rains Wallace. Unfortunately, Dr. Wallace became very ill before we ever really had the opportunity to discuss those factors which might have inhibited the growth of the pool of eligible blacks for consideration as prospects for the graduate programs in psychology. Shortly thereafter, Dr. Samuel Osipow was appointed to serve as the new chairman of the department.

Once a scheduled conference had been arranged between Dr. Osipow and myself, I apprised Dr. Osipow of the fact that few historically black institutions of higher education offered majors in psychology, as there was only a limited number of black persons who held the terminal degree. I challenged him to undertake a comprehensive effort to encourage black students to enroll into graduate programs in psychology and provide the kind of fellowship/grant financial support that would make the university and the Department of Psychology attractive to students of color. I also urged that he consider some special strategy or vehicle to heighten faculty awareness of the value of an affirmative approach that would facilitate the admission and graduation of students of color within a reasonable period of time. Few faculty and administrators, up until that time, with whom I had discussed these issues seemed to appreciate the nature of the problem as did Dr. Osipow.

He took immediate steps to rectify the situation. He established an affirmative action committee within the department and appointed Dr. Paul Isaac to serve as its chairman. The result was that the department took advantage of an unparalleled opportunity to affect the status of black women and men in psychology. For whatever reasons that formidable barriers had existed prior to that time, things began to change, and change dramatically. Whatever the assumptions were that had created the barriers that for all practical purposes had made it almost virtually impossible for blacks, in any appreciable numbers, to pursue graduate work in psychology, there appeared to have been no consensus that these barriers should have been removed prior to my discussions with Dr. Osipow. I cannot applaud Drs. Osipow and Isaac too much for their role in creating a climate of willingness and expectation that ultimately translated itself into a series of self-fulfilling successes that resulted in the recruitment and enrollment of a substantial number of black graduate students. Although we belatedly realized what can happen when people are awakened to the opportunities that await them when given the opportunity, we also learned that achieving equality for underrepresented groups involves not only specific institutional changes, but also delicate attitudinal changes on the part of institutional personnel as well. I will never forget the invitation that I received from Dr. Isaac to come to his home one Sunday evening to meet with some of the new students who had been recruited by the department. My pleasure was redoubled when I observed the full impact of the department's commitment as I had the opportunity to meet and converse with about twenty-five bright and very capable black graduate students who were enrolled within the various areas of the department in pursuit of masters and doctoral degrees. What a brave beginning I thought to myself. I was extremely excited to see that one of a number of institutional innovations was already exhibiting positive dividends. In a few short years, the Department of Psychology could boast of a number of black students who earned the doctorate and who had begun to establish successful career profiles because of the enriching experiences which they had at The Ohio State University. Among those who successfully completed the doctoral requirements in earning the Ph.D. degree were Tina Garrett, Devon Stokes, Dennis Alexander, James Stewart, Vickie McCreary, Magna James, Robin Hailstorks, and Kristen Davis.

Another bright side of the university's efforts to attract students of color into its graduate programs was the fact that a number of departments were widely recognized for the quality of their doctoral programs as documented by the surveys and evaluations made by A. M. Cartter's *An Assessment of Quality of Graduate Education* and the popular volume, *A Rating of Graduate Programs*, authored by K. D. Roose and C. J. Anderson. I took advantage of every opportunity to highlight the strengths of the university—its comprehensive programs, its highly capable faculty, its successes in recruiting top notch students of color, its commitment of financial resources in the form of grants, fellowships and associateships for graduate students, and its recognition that graduate students should have voice in their own programs and in having some substantial input into the decisions that have some impact on their daily lives. I felt that these were compelling factors that would serve as a magnet that would continue to draw students of diverse backgrounds to the university. I was extremely mindful that, although our minority initiatives were the envy of many of our graduate school counterparts throughout the country, I was anxious that we would not become apathetic and risk the possibility of losing the limited gains in diversity that we had gained. It was quite apparent to me that there were numberless shortcomings that were persistent barriers to equal educational opportunity in various areas within the university, but they were obscured because of the institution's ability to promote and market the dazzling successes that had been achieved in the graduate school.

In my judgment, with God's help and the support of numerous colleagues—black and white—I can rightfully claim some share of responsibility for four important changes during the 1970s at The Ohio State University: first, the emergence of a philosophy that insisted that the presence of students of color would enhance rather than erode the academic quality and climate of the institution; second, the importance of providing assistance and resources for those who might not otherwise have been able to take advantage of their opportunity for economic reasons; third, the result of our initiatives have produced, in a few years, the phenomenon of unexpected results to the extent that students of color, black students in particular, have achieved marvelous success as competitors in the arena of graduate education at Ohio State; and fourth, the solid academic performances of black graduate students, many of whom were undergraduate products of historically black colleges and universities, helped, in part, to dismiss the sweeping notions that these institutions are academic disaster areas that are lacking in their ability to prepare students to be competitive in post-graduate work and subsequently in their future careers.

The forces of change regarding the unmet claims of students of color throughout the United States were of such that, during the late 1960s (especially after the assassination of Dr. Martin Luther King, Jr.) and the 1970s, there was an explosive surge of activities that included open admissions programs, recruitment ventures, and the establishment of ethnic studies programs. Minority issues were given high priority at state and national professional conferences. Institutions became quite collaborative by sharing their experiences with each other on how best to meet their responsibilities in facilitating minority student access and success. I was invited to address the sixteenth annual meeting of the Council of Graduate Schools in the United States at its national conference in Denver in 1976. I chronicled my experiences in minority graduate education at Ohio State. The topic was "A Five Year Experiment in Affirmative Action at The Ohio State University." The response was so overwhelming that I was invited to make similar presentations at the University of Wisconsin, University of Missouri, Iowa State University, Michigan State University, Vanderbilt University, University of Louisville, University of Maryland, Miami University, Western Kentucky State University, Mississippi State University, and the University of Cincinnati. In addition, I was called upon to address issues of diversity at a number of national conferences including the Modern Language Association; the National Association of State Universities and Land Grant Colleges and Universities; the National Association of College Deans, Registrars, and Admissions Officers; the National Conference on Racial and Ethnic Relations in American Higher Education; the National Association for Equal Opportunity in Higher Education; the National Conference on Mobilizing for Excellence in Education; the National Association of Personnel Workers; the National Association of Minority Engineering Administrators; the Council of Independent Colleges; the Association of Governing Boards of Universities and Colleges; the Association for the Study of Negro Life and History; the Association of Black Administrators in Higher Education; the Institute for Services to Education; and Operation PUSH.

In 1973, I felt compelled to begin a search to identify black Ohio State University alumni who had established successful career profiles in their respective fields. It was my understanding that no comprehensive attempt had ever been undertaken to determine the number of African-American students who had graduated from the institution, the impact that the institution had had on them, and what they had accomplished upon leaving the institution. Somehow I felt that, if they could be located, and their story could be told, their testimony of how Ohio State helped to shape their lives and their future might well serve as a motivating foundation for attracting even larger numbers of students of color to the institution. Months were devoted to researching alumni records, conversing with department chairs, combing the faculty rosters of college and university catalogs nationwide, and making one-on-one personal contacts individually and by telephone to ascertain the whereabouts of alumni and former students.

After an extensive search, we were able to identify seventy-two black Ohio State University alumni who were leading executives and officials in government, business, education, civic affairs, and in other professions. They represented a sophisticated fraction of the nearly seven hundred black alumni who had been awarded degrees from the University of Scarlet and Gray. After gaining their approval, we compiled a volume which included a biographical outline of each of the honorees who were selected as sterling examples of achievement. Below each brief biographical sketch there was a short essay, representing the unique point of view of each honoree on the importance of higher education for black youth. I entitled the book *They Came and They Conquered*. As a part of the foreword, I indicated:

> *They Came and They Conquered* is an attempt to encourage the discouraged, to challenge the disillusioned, and to reassure the skeptical. It is a volume that recounts the successes of black men and women who gave expression to their discontent by removing the shutters from the windows of their minds to pursue their educational goals and a career, so that they would not forever be condemned to ignorance or oppression.

We were blessed with an outpouring of accolades once the book came off the press. Scores of alumni requested copies for their libraries. We did not overlook the potential that this attractive publication had as a public relations windfall for the university. College and university administrators clamored for copies so that they could produce similar publications on their campuses. I recall that President Silber of Boston University ordered several dozen copies for distribution among his department heads. It was a popular item among undergraduates at colleges where we were recruiting prospective graduate students. It demonstrated that Ohio State had established a tradition of recruiting and graduating African-American students. This new volume also mirrored the fact that Ohio State was proud of its record in the area of outreach efforts for minorities and that it was both anxious and pleased to promote and exhibit that fact. We left no stone unturned in our strategy of mobilizing the minds of African-Americans to believe that Ohio State was the best place that they could send their daughters and sons to receive a higher education. Our varied approaches proved gratifyingly effective.

Because The Ohio State University Graduate School had emerged as a leader on matters of diversity, I was constantly called upon by state and federal agencies to serve as a lecturer and as a consultant. Dr. Donald Bigelow of the United States Department of Education selected me as a reader and as a consultant for government programs for five successive years. I was also a member of the original group of consultants who met in Hershey, Pennsylvania, to discuss the pros and cons of having portable or institutional fellowships as part of the Title IX Graduate and Professional Opportunities Program. Once the program was approved, Ohio State became one of the major beneficiaries of the GPOP grants. For a number of years, it was among the top five institutions receiving the largest grants to provide doctoral fellowships for minorities and women. I was pleased to have had the opportunity to have written the first proposals that were funded by the federal government to Ohio State for this forward-moving program.

The groundswell of the new wave of interest in minority programs in academia became steadily more intense. Ohio State was admittedly better off than many institutions of higher education, at least in my area of graduate education. My presentations and consultancies took me before such state groups as the Ohio ACT Assembly, the Ohio Association of Equal Opportunity Personnel, the Ohio Association of Student Personnel Administrators, the Ohio Society of Professional Engineers, the Ohio Department of Administrative Services, the Ohio Baptist Ministers Association, and the Ohio Department of Education.

Anyone knowing the history of the university for some thirty years prior to the establishment of the Office of Minority Affairs in 1970 and the establishment of a minority affairs component in the Graduate School in 1971 may very well understand the reluctance of earlier black alumni to rid themselves of the doubt and suspicion which they registered when they were approached and requested to be supportive of certain institutional programs. It was difficult for them to discard the feelings they had concerning indignities—real and perceived—which they had experienced while attending Ohio State in earlier years. Despite all that we shared in terms of progress that was being made along racial lines, some remained in a vengeful mood, believing that historically the university had been engaged in a lawless conspiracy against the interests of black people. The emphasis on *blackness*, with the celebration of such terms as *black power*, *black is beautiful*, *black consciousness*, and *black solidarity*, had become widespread since the late 1960s. This heightened sense of cultural nationalism made it rather easy and fashionable for many blacks to decry any gains as strategies of tokenism and as means of keeping blacks appeased while still holding them in a subordinate position.

I, too, had feelings of ambivalence about the university's overall intentions regarding blacks and other people of color. While it was not my assertive nature to accept discrimination and injustice with a shrug of the shoulders, I was too much of a realist, having been reared in an environment of disfranchisement and segregation, to be casually callous or frivolous to the advancing status (slow as it is) of blacks in America. I am not sure how long it will take for it to become obvious that America is serious about its promise of "freedom and justice for all." Nevertheless, that does not relieve people of color from spending unconscionable time in assuming the initiative in campaigning for the dignity and opportunities which most Americans expect at birth.

Thus, while it was clear that the relationship between The Ohio State University and its black alumni was grim, I decided we could and would change all that. There was nothing dramatic about the way in which our office went about recognizing alumni of color who had gained considerable stature in their respective fields, but who had received no commendations from the university. We simply and ruthlessly cut through the red tape like a knife through butter, bypassing the University Alumni Office procedures, as we made plans to seize the initiative and present distinguished alumni awards to renown alumni at the time of our Visitation Days Program in November. It was always a climactic moment at the Visitation Days Banquet when distinguished alumni are given their place in the university's sun, as they are exhibited as living evidence of what happens to those who are accorded just a half of chance even when limited by the forbidden tradition of a contradictory culture.

It was during the years from 1971 through 1978 that we broke with tradition and honored such eminent scholars and leaders as The Honorable Robert M. Duncan, justice, U.S. Court of Military Appeals; Dr. Samuel DuBois Cook, professor of Political Science, Duke University; Mr. Henry Parks, president, Henry Parks Sausage Company, Inc.; Dr. Jacqueline Jackson, associate professor, Medical Sociology, Duke University Medical

School; Coach Alonzo "Jake" Gaither, Florida A&M University; Dr. Frederick D. Adams, vice president for student affairs, University of Connecticut; Dr. Charles A. Lyons, Jr., chancellor, Fayetteville State University, North Carolina; Dr. George M. Willis, director, Tumor Biology Program, Division of Cancer Research, National Institutes of Health; Colonel Clotilde Dent Bowen, special assistant for neurology and psychiatry, Office for the Civilian Health and Medical Program of the Uniformed Services, Department of Defense, Denver, Colorado; Dr. Willie Turner, chairman, Department of Microbiology, Howard University, Washington, D.C.; Dr. Henry Ponder, president, Benedict College, Columbia, South Carolina; Dr. Joseph S. Himes, professor emeritus of Sociology, University of North Carolina at Greensboro; and Ms. Faye Wattleton, president, Planned Parenthood Federation of American, Inc., New York.

Our appreciation and recognition of those illustrious alumni was more than confirmed by the brilliant contributions of each of them, but the measure of our admiration of them was reciprocated as most of them turned our goodwill gestures into accepting some meaningful assignments that supported the programmatic efforts of my office.

The issue of affirmative action stimulated intense debate from the moment that it was designated as a consideration for people of color. My first impressive recollection of it being defined as a race conscious remedy to compensate for racial inequities was when President Lyndon Baines Johnson declared that, "Equal Opportunity is not enough; we must have equal opportunity of results." There has been constant warring among conservatives, liberals and radicals in debating both the concept and justification for affirmative action. Typically, white males, in particular, have expressed very condemnatory and negative attitudes toward what they have been led to believe is preferential treatment for women and people of color. They have taken vigorous exception, with great frustration and discouragement, to programs that make adjustments to offset the inequities of slavery, segregation, and racial discrimination. I have found it more than a little interesting that many who demonstrate such a profound interest in propounding doctrines of egalitarianism and meritocracy are generally Johnny-come-latelys. They have come to the forefront only lately to stand up for the rights of white males. Where were their democratic voices when the oppressed were denied such basic rights as education, voting, access to public facilities, and residential housing unencumbered with restrictive covenants? Where are these voices even today when members of the dominant group bypass the requirements of *achieved* status (grade point average, qualifying test scores, competitive exams, etc.) and gain *ascribed* status based on political favors, affluence, membership in certain organizations,

274

alumni status of parents, and connections in the *old boy* network. They are cultural heirs of a system that has been based on wealth, prominence, and influence for centuries. As they have sat in the seats of power, they have catered to their families, friends, and former students. Suffice it to say that the impact of affirmative action, a concept introduced to help make the playing field level for people of color and women, has been greeted with scorn and derision for the most part by the very people who have been beneficiaries of special favor, patronage, and partiality. Historically, white males have found a welcome ally in affirmative action. They are not against the concept; they are just against who's getting it! They control enough resources in the media industry, so they have little difficulty in getting the reactionaries to tilt their pens at the new kids on the block who have come to compete, challenge, and try to scoop up some of the goodies that had been an unchallenged prerogative of their invisible empire for centuries.

Thus, I have had no qualms in putting my weight and influence behind the fight to provide people of color with certain advantages—yes, certain advantages that would enable them to overcome and reverse the accumulated inequities of generations. But I also know that the call to eliminate affirmative action programs is pregnant with hypocrisy. The elimination of the vestiges of slavery, segregation and discrimination calls for a national resolve and a period of time comparable to the period of time that sustained slavery and segregation. If this country is to ever move forward and demonstrate that it is willing and able to provide legal and constitutional guarantees or equal opportunity for all of its citizens, it must commit itself to accept seriously the profound heritage of its Christian and democratic ethos.

There is no reason to suppose that my activities were confined to The Ohio State University Graduate School. The impact of God's blessings relative to the graduate school's decisiveness in dealing with the consequences and concomitant effects of racial segregation and discrimination bubbled up on individual college and university campuses. For a period of time, I became a part of a country-wide crusade in helping higher education institutions to develop goals and strategies that would enable them to realize those unfulfilled promises of equality that have eluded them since the founding of this nation. Even before I was appointed the associate dean of the graduate school, the higher education community was already convulsed by a race reform movement brought on by the assassination of Dr. Martin Luther King, Jr. King's name was inevitably connected with a wave of civil rights agitation that also included among its stellar witnesses Vernon Jordan, Whitney Young,

James Farmer, James Lawson, Daisy Bates, John Lewis, C. T. Vivian, Fred Shuttlesworth, Ralph Abernathy, Fannie Lou Hamer, Stokeley Carmichael, Imamu Baraka, Sonia Sanchez, Haki Madhubuti, Gwendolyn Brooks, Bayard Rustin, Asa Phillip Randolph, Otis Moss, Jesse Jackson, Vivian Malone, Medger Evers, James Meredith, Hamilton Holmes, Charlayne Hunter, James Baldwin, Ossie Davis, Ruby Dee, Harry Belafonte, Hosea Williams, Andrew Young, Wyatt T. Walker, James Bevel, Adam Clayton Power, Malcolm X, the Little Rock Nine, Eldridge Cleaver, Earl E. Cleveland, Charles Bradford, Mylas Martin IV, A. Leon Higginbothan, Jr., Charles Houston, Thurgood Marshall, Viola Liuzzo, Michael Schwerner, Andrew Goodman, James Chaney, and James Reeb.

But the fact remains that the foundation of that new wave went far back—to David Walker, Frederick Douglass, Henry Highland Garnet, Harriet Tubman, Alexander Crummel, W. E. B. DuBois, Ida B. Wells, Sojourner Truth, James Weldon Johnson, Marcus Garvey, and many, many more. The nation's account on race continued to yield a damning indictment of her incontrovertible sins. Just as hope had sprung eternal as white allies like William Lloyd Garrison, Charles Sumner, Theodore Weld, Elijah Lovejoy, John Brown, and Salmon Chase began to associate themselves with the aspirations of black people during the nineteenth century, it was refreshing to observe that similarly during the civil rights crusade of the 1960s and 1970s there were white individuals who were defenders of the rights of people of color. Some of whom charged head-long into the daring fray were John Howard Griffin, Harry Golden, Lillian Smith, Ralph McGill, Ann Graden, Lyndon Baines Johnson, Winton Beaven, Sakre Kubo, Eugene Carson Blake, Theodore S. Hesburgh, James McBride, Dabbs and Sarah Patten Boyle.

On the academic front, I was able to ride the synthesis of civil rights ferment and equal educational opportunity into a model for establishing and managing diversity in higher education. As a consequence, institutions that were interested in the possibility of launching initiatives in the pursuit of progress in this arena invited me to visit their campuses as a lecturer, as a consultant, and as a facilitator in conducting numerous workshops and seminars. Well before the decade of the 1970s had concluded, I had made presentations at institutions like Ferris State College, Northern Illinois University, Shippensburg State College, University of Southern Illinois, Ohio Northern University, Denison University, Vanderbilt University, Mississippi State University, University of Louisville, University of Delaware, University of Missouri, and the University of Wisconsin. One important capstone during that

276

period was the commencement address which I delivered at Loma Linda University on June 12, 1977. It somewhat foreshadowed the more numerous and more challenging opportunities that I would have in the decade of the 1980s.

In 1976, Dean Arliss Roaden accepted an offer to become the president of Tennessee Technological University in Cooksville, Tennessee. He had been a welcome ally in the pursuit of equal educational opportunity, and he must take high rank among the ardent supporters of that cause at Ohio State. While he deliberately gave me the room and freedom to develop the programs to remove the undesirable effects of the problems of race that had perpetuated themselves over time, he was clearly one of the moving forces at the university that had helped to clear the path of the past and smooth the way for the future by bringing to public consciousness the need to challenge and uproot those racial inequities and tensions which strike at the very foundations of a free and democratic society.

Dr. Jules LaPidus, a pharmaceutical chemist from the University of Illinois, was selected as Dr. Roaden's successor as dean of the graduate school. While LaPidus moved with the flow of what had already been established in the arena of equal educational opportunity, I never felt that he exhibited the urgency and the kind of vigorous and affirmative effort that I had experienced under his predecessor. Nevertheless, I think it fair to temper my assessment of Dean LaPidus because he had not been the beneficiary of a tidal wave of the kind of reform resources that had become available to Roaden and to me when I was first appointed to the position of association dean of the graduate school.

By any objective assessment of our achievements in the seven years under the administrations of Dean Roaden and Dean LaPidus, I was virtually able to do anything that I wanted to do to advance the programs which I had initiated. This was possible because of the secure relationship, based upon mutual understanding and respect, that I had with each dean.

In the meanwhile, the campus as a whole was facing a real choice. It could move far beyond its initial affirmative efforts that had been put in place in 1970, or it could go to commit itself to a vigorous campus-wide effort to explore ways in which sufficiently powerful solutions could be found to make the gift of diversity a permanent and ever-growing part of its future. There was no middle way. It seemed evident that prompt and decisive action was imperative. Whatever action the university would take to defy the alternative of indecision relative to the elimination of discriminatory practices, I wholeheartedly wanted to be a part of the solutions. Not one given to underrating my own capabilities, I prayed for greater opportunities to expand and reinforce some of the programs that I had designed and developed in the graduate school. I also envisioned new programs and creative avenues that could make a difference in the lives of students of color if adequately coordinated, focused and financed. As I looked to the future, I felt angels watching over me at every turn.

Chapter 14

Moving On Up
in Administration at
The Ohio State University

⋙∘∘∘⋘

It was on October 1, 1978, that I was officially installed as vice provost for minority affairs at The Ohio State University. After an extensive nationwide search over a period of more than a year, I was selected to succeed Dr. William J. Holloway, a remarkable gentleman who had served the Office of Minority Affairs with distinction from 1970 to 1978.

From the very beginning of my assignment, I had a good working relationship with the staff of the Office of Minority Affairs (OMA) and with the members of the campus community generally. We had already established very cooperative and highly professional relationships during my seven-year tenure in the graduate school. There was no reason to suppose that I would not enjoy the wonderful and wholesome cooperation that I had come to appreciate and expect as I undertook my new challenge.

The Office of Minority Affairs was very short on physical arrangements that would lend to comfort, maximum productivity, and high morale. The arrangements were chopped and scattered, with offices located on several different floors in Bricker Hall and in Lincoln Tower. What was most despicable was the condition of the furnishings, which were scarred, scratched, battered and outdated. Just being a part of such surroundings was more than enough to dim staff morale. I immediately arranged for Provost Albert Kuhn and myself to tour OMA facilities, and I came out irrevocably for a new location for the support staff. We agreed that additional space would be made available to us on the tenth floor of Lincoln Tower, and the entire area was to be occupied by Minority Affairs and would be renovated; new furnishings would be purchased, and a kitchen would be added. I had no doubt that this beginning approach would add convenience, color, luster, and an environment that would be conducive to staff morale and productivity. It was also important that the office and its mission reflect the university's determination to advance minority interests with the same attention and quality that it gave every other unit on campus. It was a powerful statement that needed to be made. Dr. Kuhn moved expeditiously on the project and within a few weeks Minority Affairs received a remarkable face lifting that gave an incredible shot in the arm to our staff and our program. We planned an open house introduction to our new facility that was packed with wide-eyed students, faculty and staff. The exhibition gave us the initial momentum that was bound to give us the head start that we needed to establish a reputation for setting goals and getting things done. I had already learned to never recoil from taking on problems that needed to be resolved head-on.

From the very beginning, the Office of Minority Affairs had been established as the recruitment arm of the university for minority students. As the demands justified, we added full time staff members to serve as directors of major areas. Rose Wilson, who had been my administrative assistant in the graduate school, was appointed director of special programs. Special programs was a new unit which I established in OMA immediately upon my being appointed vice provost. The sponsorship of the Visitation Days Program of the graduate school was transferred to the Office of Minority Affairs at the time of my new appointment. Because of the broadened participation in the program by professional schools at the university, the program was renamed the Graduate and Professional Schools Visitation Days Program (GPSVD). The area of special programs coordinated several new activities which had not been a part of OMA sponsorship in the past. They were Martin Luther King Week activities, OMA Artist and Lecture Series, OMA Film Series, and the Minority Graduate and Professional School Orientation Conference. The area was also responsible for organizing and scheduling recruitment appointments at historically black colleges and at colleges and universities having high concentrations of students of color. While we had very little difficulty contacting black students because of our linkages with historically black colleges, it required special efforts to target Latino students. Early on in my administration, I had accompanied Ms. Wilson to a number of eastern institutions as we attempted to identify capable Latino and Native

American students. Among the institutions we visited were American University, George Washington University, Howard University, Catholic University, University of Maryland, Federal City College, and D.C. Teachers College in the Washington, D.C., area. Further east, we made recruitment visits to Hunter College, Columbia University, New York University, St. John's University, Queens College, New York University, and City College of New York.

Over time, we were able to add a small, but impressive list of Latino recruits who were admitted into a number of our graduate and professional programs. Because we desired to expand our outreach efforts in these areas, we felt confident that Ms. Wilson offered the kind of commitment and valuable experience necessary to advance our efforts in the areas to which she was being assigned. Additionally, she was given the responsibility of designing, revising and updating the minority alumni promotional book, *They Came and They Conquered*. Ms. Wilson is a regal and imposing figure. Attractive, efficient, and congenial, she continued to serve with distinction and earned the respect of her colleagues for her consistent praiseworthy achievements from year to year.

Dr. R. Timothy McDonald was appointed director of program development, research and evaluation. I had known Dr. McDonald from my years at Oakwood College, and I was aware of his gifts in the area of proposal development and grantsmanship. I recall with pleasure his interest in wanting to help us get an Upward Bound Program underway at Ohio State. It was obvious to me that he could make important contributions in helping us to establish meaningful network contacts with governmental and private funding agencies. It was also important that we have a person who could develop and maintain data on the Freshman Foundation students who represented the core of OMA's student constituency.

Because the majority of minority students come from low-income families, they are ofttimes extremely concerned about financing their education, while, at the same time, attempting to survive the rigors of a demanding academic program. The university has attempted to alleviate the difficulties associated with rising educational costs by directing minority students to take advantage of certain federal assistance programs who, without such opportunities, might not be able to pursue their education.

Thus, in 1970, the Freshman Foundation Program (FFP) was established at The Ohio State University. Under the sponsorship of the Office of Minority Affairs, students had been awarded over fifteen million dollars by the time that I had assumed my position in 1978. The financial support came from student aid sources, including state and federal grants, loans, college work-study and private scholarships. The university's contribution had exceeded four million dollars in the form of FFP grants, approximately one-fourth of the total amount of the funds that had been awarded. FFP students are awarded a full financial aid package for four years, based on need analysis guidelines established by the College Scholarship service. A formula of three-fourths grant and one-fourth self-help for FFP financial aid awards was established by OMA in 1971. The grant portion includes all state and federal grants and private scholarships and is supplemented by the FFP grant. The self-help portion includes all loans, work-study earnings, and savings from summer employment.

I felt that Dr. McDonald, who was a stickler for administrative efficiency, would fulfill the requirements of his new position with considerable success. And that he did. He was given a free reign to program proposals that would facilitate the recruitment and retention of minority students. In a few short months, McDonald designed a sound Upward Bound proposal which was funded and which served students from six Columbus high schools. Spearheading OMA's initiatives for external funding, McDonald was responsible for helping OMA to widen its influence among the funding communities, and as a consequence his well-oiled approach helped OMA and the university to garner hundreds of thousands of dollars.

Another very important staff member was Ruth S. Gresham, who was appointed director of recruitment and staff development. Blessed with a warm and congenial personality, she had enormous talent that was valuable in accelerating OMA's efforts to recruit and retain minority undergraduates. She was particularly effective in recognizing the importance of collaborating with key faculty in various disciplines. The collaborative efforts involved joint recruitment activities, the development of weekend and summer programs for high school students, and outreach programs to high school counselors and parents to inform them of opportunities available to them at Ohio State and how to take advantage of them. She confidently assumed her role, and was responsible for a number of pioneering efforts statewide that attracted minority students to the university.

The other administrative director who was a maximum force in OMA's successful efforts was Dr. Joseph F. Stranges, Jr. To be sure, I could always point with pride to his very detailed and accurate reports concerning the aggregate financial assistance package of awards for the Freshman Foundation Program. Keenly aware of the financial difficulties that minority students faced, he was especially concerned about their welfare, and left no stone unturned in providing each student the best package possible to meet his or her special needs. Dr. Stranges was loved and

282

respected like no other person I have ever known who worked in a similar capacity. The students knew that he was their friend and was very understanding of their concerns. One had to know Dr. Stranges to really know that he had moral obligations that superseded the requirements of his job description. He was always willing to go to bat for deserving students and exert some behind-the-scenes influence in their behalf. Even when he was not able to give a student the assistance that she/he needed, no one could ever cast doubt on his endeavors, which at times may have had an unhappy conclusion.

When I came to OMA, Dr. Stranges was rendering sixty percent of his time to our office and the other forty percent to the Office of Financial Aids. As a result of his serving two masters, he spent an inordinate amount of time cajoling and arm-twisting his superiors in financial aids. The process was cumbersome, and it created a monumental waste of time. The arrangement bastardized the process and throttled our plans to move expeditiously on the swarm of applications that came to our office during the critically important recruiting season. I was especially pleased when my request, that Dr. Stranges be allowed to work full time for OMA as director of financial aid, gained ready acceptance as the offices of financial aids and minority affairs arbitrated what obviously was in the best interests of minority students. I was pleased that we were able to work things out without creating any bad feelings. It was one of my early scenarios in *Buckeye diplomacy*, but it wasn't the last.

Louise Phillips, who had carried the weight of the office as business services officer since the inception of OMA, was replaced by Pamela Clark. Behind the scenes, Clark brandished a big stick, seeing to it that those who were responsible for dispensing funds, were held accountable. She was efficient, pure and simple. She was always available when I needed information and never showed the slightest reluctance to being helpful; I managed to get along unusually well with her, primarily because of our common commitment to OMA and its mission. Thus, we were correspondingly strengthened and motivated by each other's dedication to a magnificent cause.

Julia Smith wrote another important chapter in the emergence of OMA as perhaps the most comprehensive program in minority affairs in the United States. Mrs. Smith created the happy and open atmosphere that drew students to her as the counselor of the Freshman Foundation Program. Completely candid, she earned the respect of those students who came to her for help. Possessing a soul of dignity and a soft measured manner, she made even the most obscure and awkward student feel at home in her presence. Her sincere interest in behalf of students made it easier for them to rush down the thorny path of their problems to seek her assistance when they had no place else to turn. With hundreds of FFP students enrolled in the university at any one time, and with many of them singularly shortsighted because of their youth, she became an indefensible hostage, as it were, to their ongoing problems. Nevertheless, she achieved gratifying results and is deserving of unstinted praise.

The splendid pioneering recruiting work of Normando Caban cannot be overlooked. Often at a numerical disadvantage because OMA came about as a result of the crusading challenges of black students, he, nevertheless, sallied forth and championed the rights of Hispanic students in the early stages of OMA's development. He used his strong personal influence to launch outreach efforts in areas where there were high concentrations of Hispanics in Cleveland, Lorain (Ohio), Chicago, Toledo, and Puerto Rico. Ever sensitive to the needs of Hispanic students on campus, he kept a carefully-attuned ear to the ground, and responded to their concerns as each situation required.

Following James Copeland's brief stint as a recruiter with OMA, Keith Troy was appointed to take his place. His exhilarating new spirit suffused the recruitment component of OMA. One of the happiest results of his appointment was that he was laid-back, masterly organized, and with a quiet and witty flair that captured the popular imagination of his youthful prospects. His focused interest and commitment brought windfalls of student applications to the university. His highly effective and direct approach was extremely useful in helping to break the stranglehold of monopoly that the University of Cincinnati and Central State University had had in recruiting black students in earlier years.

The day-to-day operations of the Office of Minority Affairs could never have been properly cared for without the consistent and valuable support of the secretarial/clerical staff, graduate associates, and student assistants. I could never turn my back upon those who gave yeoman service to the issue-fraught rhythm of everyday life in OMA. No administrator, however capable and talented, can be effective without the frontal support of those who daily stand in the trenches to promote their programs, resist their detractors, and cover for their blunders and ineptitudes. So much of whatever I have been able to accomplish in my professional life has been due, in large part, to competent administrative assistants, secretarial staff, and student workers. Without them, I would have been immeasurably incapacitated. In this vein, I cannot take a deep breath without including the monumental impact that a number of persons in that category have had on my professional growth and advancement: Rose Wilson, Ellen Banks, Wanda Montgomery, Joyce Ford, Leona Smith,

Diane Coscarelli, Karen Waugh, and Audrey Thompson as administrative assistants and secretaries; and JoAnna Williamson, Elizabeth Chan, Zelda Holcomb, Chandra Cox, Alvin Hailstorks, Raymond Zamudio, Ronald Johnson, Kathleen Bailey, Lenora Barnes, Gloria Smith, Phil Mason, David Wang, Levonne Williams, Linda Jackson, Gwendolyn Garvin and Doron Maniece, as graduate associates.

Believing that it was extremely important to establish a strong link between the Office of Minority Affairs and the Columbus community, I established the Office of Campus and Community Relations and appointed Linda Jackson to serve as its director. Keenly aware of the mounting impact of the role of the larger community in helping to promote a positive image of the institution, we made a conscious effort to enlarge our vision in this area. Our reach was extended to include alumni, churches, civic and social organizations, representatives on the city council and the school board, professional groups, as well as local, state, and national politicians. This approach enabled us to make a major move toward improving relations between the campus and community.

Additionally, we established a community advisory council, and Reverend Isaiah Pogue, the pastor of Bethany Presbyterian Church, served faithfully and effectively as its chairman. Our vigorous efforts in this area paid off as we were fortunate to have a diverse group of representatives from the local area who added the weight of their prestige, their energy, and their expertise to our council. Among those who gave notable cooperation and assistance to our endeavors were Paul Cash, employment manager, AccuRay Corporation; Robert Freid, personnel manager, Kal Kan Foods; Mary Glascor, retired educator; Earl Harris, director of human relations, Schottenstein's Stores, Inc.; Marie Jones, administrative assistant, Social Security Administration; Dr. Shuh-Chai Lee, research engineer, Ohio Department of Transportation; Bruce Merrill, branch manager, IBM; Rev. Irvin S. Moxley, associate on ethnic affairs, Synod of the Covenant; Earl Murry, corporate director, employee relations, Anchor Hocking; Mickey Pheanis, branch manager, City National Bank; James Roseboro, manager, minority purchasing, Borden, Inc.; Rev. Leon Troy, pastor, Second Baptist Church; Rev. Samuel Varner, Advent Community Church; and Charles Wallace, director, Columbus Child Care Center.

Their presence not only added luster to the causes which the Office of Minority Affairs espoused and promoted, a number of the council members successfully petitioned their organizations for financial support for our various programs and activities. This was particularly true for AccuRay, Kal Kan Foods, Schottenstein's Stores, IBM, and Anchor Hocking. Thus, once again, the force of their diverse leadership qualities supported and dramatized our day-to-day operations and, as consequence, aroused positive public opinion in our behalf. I endeavored to keep intimately in touch with those wonderful volunteers whose very presence and participation gave lavish testimony to the crusading strides which were underway in our office.

From the very beginning of my tenure as vice provost, I knew that it was important to develop a comprehensive plan in order to increase minority enrollment on campus. I had to look backward before I could look forward. Numerous studies had already been undertaken and completed to determine the extent of minority presence on the campus. I consulted with Dr. James Leitzel, who for a number of years had chaired the Senate Committee on Minorities and Women. I reviewed tons of reports and recommendations that had been developed over the years concerning all aspects of minority involvement at the university. I gathered minority data profiles on departments, colleges, and other units of the institution. It was also useful to assess the extent of the institution's commitment to issues of diversity and equal opportunity. While the literature of the institution was rather loaded with statements of policy and procedures, statedly designed to increase minority presence on campus, I, however, was cautiously suspicious of how valid those pronouncements were in view of what appeared to be the gross underrepresentation of people of color on the campus. One could walk down halls and look into classrooms and laboratories, and would have to labor to catch a glimpse of a person of color—particularly an African-American—now and then.

I soon decided that we were going to have to take an integrated approach that would involve broad campus and community participation if we were going to change the complexion of the institution. I immediately pounced upon the idea of designing a revised *3R* strategy not reading, 'riting, and 'rithmetic, but recruitment, retention, and release (with a diploma and degree). Based on this 3R concept of recruitment, retention and release, we designed a schematic which was entitled *The Educational Pipeline for Minority Students at The Ohio State University*.* Under the heading of *recruitment*, we identified the precollege, undergraduate, and graduate professional outreach strategies that constituted our overall recruitment plan. Under the heading of *retention*, we listed the various components and support areas that assisted minority students in their academic and social adaptation to the institution. These components included the categories of administrative policies, counseling, cultural heritage and recognition programs, financial aid, personnel office and

* See Appendix H, page 418.

286

organizational support mechanisms, technical support, and college/departmental units. Under the heading of *release*, we listed the categories of placement, graduation, and alumni networking. This schematic received widespread distribution among students and faculty, so that the campus community would be knowledgeable concerning the services that were accessible to all minority students.

In the early 1980s, the Office of Minority Affairs moved steadily toward defining and refining its goals, chiefly through the mechanism of off-campus retreats during the summer in preparation for the approaching academic year. The retreat strategy was a gratifying challenge where the OMA staff was able to gather tremendous momentum in preparation to meet the demands of the new year. The spirited give and take of discussion and problem-solving became a yeasty laboratory of new ideas and reform. The retreats also gave us the opportunity to know and appreciate each other more, and they offered a refreshing interlude, which included some opportunities for recreation before plugging into the full-time pressures of our professional responsibilities. The natural and colorful surroundings of Mohican State Park and Deer Creek State Park served as ideal locations for a number of our staff retreat workshops.

During the fired-up sessions of those retreats, we worked through and tackled head-on a series of *goals* and *strategies for action* to meet those goals. We prepared and adopted some forward-looking documents that, in essence, served as road maps into the future, as we were attempting to define both our direction and our destiny.

Among the goals which we specified were the following:

- To initiate articulation between the university and two-year colleges to attract capable minority students who have already demonstrated their ability to perform well beyond high school.
- To allocate extra resources to create a bank of merit scholarships for the most capable students in order to outbid other competing institutions.
- To promote a closer articulation among OMA, departments, schools, and colleges at OSU so that all units will be working together to promote the recruitment and retention efforts for minority students.
- To encourage graduate and professional school admissions committees to complement qualifying test scores and grade point averages of students with other criteria in the assessment of students of color in the selection process.
- To identify institutions with high concentrations of Hispanics/Latinos and contact key faculty and administrative personnel in those institutions to facilitate the recruitment of Hispanic/Latino students.

- To collaborate with the university development office to design a consistent fund-raising program to assist OMA in the programmable efforts.
- To seek opportunities for OMA representatives to inform minority constituencies of OMA program opportunities.
- To develop a viable minority faculty/staff organization.
- To collaborate with the Ohio Department of Education to identify those high schools throughout the state with high concentrations (fifty percent and above) of black and Hispanic students.
- To sponsor staff development workshops and seminars for university personnel, exposing them to consultants and seasoned scholars who have had successful track records in dealing with issues of diversity.
- To compile and publish brochures and booklets on programs and opportunities for students of color at OSU.
- To contact minority community organizations (civic, social, religious, professional) to assist in the support of minority programs.
- To develop an early hands-on stepladder program (beginning in junior high school), designated PRELUDE, to recognize and recruit talented students of color.
- To cooperate with local churches in sponsoring *Education Day* programs in their churches involving OMA personnel and OSU students as a means of establishing a vital link between the university and local churches.
- To develop a brochure entitled "Power Through Education" that would underscore OMA's mission, goals, academic and cultural enrichment programs, table of organization, financial aid opportunities, recruitment and outreach efforts and its role in the coordination of campus and community councils designed to promote the activities of the office.

By the early 1980s, The Ohio State University Office of Minority Affairs was generally being heralded as one of the most effective offices of its kind in the nation. The administration of Dr. William J. Holloway, which had preceded my administration, had exerted a stimulating influence on the campus community by its knowledge, its forthrightness, and its spirit of cooperation.

It was refreshing for me to note that finally, after a decade, the higher education community across the nation was beginning to take initiatives here and there that it had found repulsive in earlier days. While the black clergy and a few liberal politicians had spoken out vehemently during the 1960s, the voice of the academy had been weak, ambivalent, and tardy. In short, the academy had trailed most sectors of American life until, under the pressure of coercion, they were driven to establish the creative ground that would enable them to produce a breath of fresh air by taking some responsibility for contributing to the struggle for gaining equal opportunity for all of the nation's citizens.

While the landscape of diversity had improved at The Ohio State University in the early 1980s, the concept of equal access was yet to be demonstrated, as it still was more of a myth than a reality. The proportion of students of color at the university was moving in the right direction, but it did not come close to parity as measured by the minority proportion of the general population within the State of Ohio.

One of the pleasant features of those years was the substantial impact that the Freshman Foundation Program (FFP) was making in its recruitment of students of color and economically disadvantaged students. It was in 1971, one year after the establishment of FFP that the provost authorized the Office of Minority Affairs to enroll four hundred new students of color each year so that, by the time that I took over the reins of leadership in OMA in 1978, nearly 3400 students had been enrolled in FFP. I learned quite early that the success of recruitment efforts cannot be facilitated by full-time recruiters alone. Just as the African proverb asserts that, "It takes a village to raise a child," it takes initiative and cooperation at every level throughout the institution in order for recruitment efforts to be effective.

Through the mechanism of the Coordinating Council of Minority Affairs, OMA was active in assisting various departments, schools, colleges, and administrative units within the university in developing recruitment/retention programs for students of color. Commitment, cooperation and coordination are the minimum essentials to successful recruitment efforts. As impressive and as charismatic as individual leadership may be, effective recruitment, in order to be sustained, must have vigorous across-the-board support university wide.

It is extremely difficult to gain such support when there is no reward mechanism in place for those who take the time to make a meaningful contribution to advancing the cause for diversity on campus. Far too often, achievements in this area of university life go almost unheralded. There are numerous incentives for faculty to become engaged in various university activities. Consequently, rather than to be locked into a cocoon of isolation and invisibility, some choose to focus their efforts in areas where they will be appropriately recognized, rewarded, and hailed as *conquering academics*. Often there is a perception that those who are involved primarily in issues of diversity are on the doorstep of the institution rather than inside where the coveted territory of respectability is sought by all.

I felt convinced that OMA was ready to emerge and take on heightened significance in the years ahead. My strategy was to bring people to the planning table from units across the university to serve on the Coordinating Council of Minority Affairs. My initial council, which remained unchanged for the most part in succeeding years, was composed of Dr. Georgiana Bowman, coordinator of black student programs in Student Affairs; Ms. Carmen Breckenridge, coordinator, Office of Hispanic Affairs; Ms. Bernadine Butler, counselor, College of Administrative Science; Dr. Elson Craig, assistant dean, College of Medicine; Dr. Larry Eskridge, assistant director, Office Financial Student Aid; Dr. Norma Gilliam, counseling psychologist, Counseling and Consultation Services; Dr. Willie C. Glover, counseling psychologist, Counseling and Consultation Services; Mrs. Ruth Gresham, director, recruitment and staff development, Office of Minority Affairs; Dr. Frank W. Hale, Jr., vice provost, Office of Minority Affairs (chairperson); Dr. William J. Holloway, professor, College of Education; Mr. Terry Jordan, director, minority recruitment, College of Pharmacy; Dr. Richard Kelsey, assistant professor, College of Education; Mr. Robbin Kirkland, manager, Drake Union; Dr. Timothy McDonald, director, program development, research and evaluation, Office of Minority Affairs; Ms. Minnie McGee, assistant dean, College of Engineering; Dr. William E. Nelson, Jr., chairman, Department of Black Studies; Dr. Charles Nesbitt, assistant professor, Department of Black Studies; Dr. Cynthia Pace, coordinator, minority recruitment, College of Dentistry; Mr. Richard Payne, assistant to the vice president; Dr. Anne Pruitt, associate dean, Graduate School; Ms. Barbara Rich, assistant director, academic studies, College of Law; Ms. Loyce Scott, BSSW Program, College of Social Work; Dr. Mac A. Stewart, associate dean, University College; Ms. Betty Story, project director, School of Nursing; Dr. Joseph F. Stranges, director, financial aids, Office of Minority Affairs; Ms. Tina Sullivan, assistant coordinator, Office of Black Student Programs; Ms. Willie Sullivan, assistant professor, School of Music; Dr. Robert O. Washington, dean, College of Social Work; Dr. Howard Williams, assistant professor, Department of Veterinary Physiology and Pharmacology; Ms. Peggy Wilson, assistant professor, Medical Technology Division; Ms. Rose Wilson, director, special programs, Office of Minority Affairs.

I still recall vividly how well the coordinating council worked together. We gained a great deal through the gradual development of the importance of common interests. We developed a common agenda, not just from choice, but from necessity as well. It didn't take us long to recognize that minorities, who are quantitatively limited in numbers, find it necessary to be disciplined enough to be unified in developing goals and strategies that they can agree upon. I had an underlying assumption in strongly supporting the need for a united front by those units, interest groups, and individuals who lack the resources, the organizational structure, and political clout of some of the more dominant interests in campus. It was the assumption that unanimity is a most important factor in determining whether minorities will be successful in their efforts to bring about institutional change. One reason for this is that senior administrators often demand total agreement be exercised among the principal minority personalities within the institution. So power becomes most evident among minorities when they are on one accord. The council's actual performance was most effective in bringing together a diverse array of personnel who were open to each other, and as a consequence they kept at the center of their agenda those concerns and problems that most seriously they pledged among themselves to resolve.

It was the coordinating council's interest in establishing more positive public and community relations that led to the establishment of the Community Advisory Council within OMA. This action was key to keeping both the campus and community informed concerning those activities and programs that were mutually beneficial. The council initiated a series of visits to the campus by minority community leaders. Over time, representatives from the Columbus Board of Education, Columbus City Council, the mayor's office, the Ohio General Assembly, as well as business and professional leaders addressed the Community Advisory Council. While the council was composed of a number of community persons, it also included key minority personnel at the university. Their presence provided orientations for community members who learned about the programmatic opportunities and the resources that were available to minority students. They also were made aware of those special events that were open to the public throughout the year, particularly those occasions that featured lectures and artists of color. It was always refreshing to observe people of color brimming with pride when such celebrities as Benjamin Hooks, Vernon Jordan, Julian Bond, Shirley Chisholm, Mary Berry, Jesse Jackson, Louis Stokes, Leontyne Price, Shirley Verrett, Edwin Hawkins, Walter Hawkins, Louis Farrakhan, Stokeley Carmichael, and a host of others came to the campus.

Recognizing that only a few persons from the dominant group in the campus community had had any real or meaningful experience in areas of diversity, our staff sponsored an annual Minority Faculty and Staff Colloquy which was designed to expose the campus community to some of the nation's leading authorities on how best to remove the remaining barriers facing minority groups to full participation of education, in American life.

Practically every unit of the campus was invited to send representatives to attend these all-day sessions which were always held the week prior to the beginning of the academic year. With the support of the president and provost, even the most conservative among deans and department heads found it difficult to ignore our request to participate and/or send a representative from their area. For some, it was a bothersome intrusion on their routine and their persistent bias. For others, the colloquy became a beacon of enlightenment, and as a result, it generated a spirit of cooperation and collegiality. Understanding that the struggle for equality in academia would be a protracted one as in every other area of American life, the colloquy served multiple purposes. In addition to serving as an information mechanism on issues of inclusion, we also used the colloquy as a means of campus networking and encouraging some sense of community and civility. As a forward-looking strategy, we assumed that it would instigate some humanitarian advances that were desperately needed within the institution. We were not disappointed as a refreshing spirit of communion began to suffuse these encounters more and more with each passing year. As it turned out, participation grew from about fifty participants in 1978, the first year the colloquy was established, to more than three hundred in 1987.

The campus community enjoyed a priceless cement of common cause as the colloquy became fashioned into a marvelous channel in creating an informal confederation of allies who came together to deal with common problems. We were recipients of the most recent scholarship studies by stellar academics who came armed with incredible credentials and expertise. We were delighted to reap the fruits and share in the farsighted creations of visionaries like Dr. Shirley Vining Brown, a project director with the National Academy of Sciences; Dr. Gail Thomas, professor of Sociology at Texas A&M University; and Dr. Therman Evans, CIGNA corporate medical director when they addressed the subject, "The Minority Pipeline: Factors that Contribute to the Underrepresentation of Minorities." Dr. William C. Parker, vice chancellor for minority affairs at the University of Kentucky, and Dr. Valora Washington, vice president and dean of the faculty at Antioch College, helped to accelerate our efforts in mobilizing the mind of the campus toward dealing with the snarls of the slow pace of diversity as they addressed the theme, "Beyond Racism: Strategies for Coping as Minority Students and Minority Professionals in Predominantly White Institutions of Higher Education."

As a part of mobilizing the mind of the campus to focus on issues of diversity, we were especially fortunate in having two champions of equality to participate in one of our colloquies, Dr. Lawrence E. Guy, professor of Social Work and Urban Studies at Howard University, and Dr. Edwin

J. Nichols, a clinical and industrial psychologist who has held major positions with the National Institute of Mental Health. They made peerless presentations in providing solid strategies for "Challenging the Barriers to Equality in the Higher Education Community." Dr. Mary F. Berry, professor of History and Law and a senior fellow in the Institute for the Study of Educational Policy at Howard University, and Dr. Philip G. Hubbard, professor of Mechanics and Hydraulics Engineering and vice president for student services and dean of academic affairs at the University of Iowa, proved to be a powerful tandem in a colloquy which focused on "The Equalization of Opportunity—Negotiating the System in Higher Education—Affirmative Action: Myth or Reality."

Continuing to tackle the problems of equal opportunity in higher education, our office sponsored a series of staff development workshops during my final year as vice provost. Our calendar of events included the following academic personalities and their topics:

> Dr. Howard G. Adams, executive director, National Consortium for Graduate Degrees for Minorities in Engineering, Inc. (GEM)
> Topic: "Successfully Negotiating the Graduate and Professional School Process"
>
> Ms. Sara E. Melendez, associate director, minority concerns, American Council on Education
> Topic: "The Teacher Education Reform Movement and Its Impact on Minority Students and Minority Professionals"
>
> Ms. Linda Bates Parker, director of career development and placement, University of Cincinnati
> Topic: "My Experiences in Working with Minority Programs: Successes and Failures"
>
> Dr. Janice Hale-Benson, associate professor and director of Early Childhood Education Program, Cleveland State University
> Topic: "Facilitating the Intellectual Development of Black Children"

All in all, my leadership in The Ohio State University Office of Minority Affairs was passionately preoccupied with serving as a *drum major for equality*. The campus community generally exhibited a lukewarm, *standputtism* approach to minority concerns. Eager to grapple with issues of color and diversity, time and time again I was involved in high-pressure sessions, and I labored valiantly even to gain the most simple victories that would advance the status of people of color. At times, my victories were clean and clear-cut; at other times I was forced into the acceptance of a compromise as an alternative between a naked outright loss and some lofty goal I wanted to achieve.

Recognizing that is a symbiotic relationship between the presence of faculty of color and our ability to attract students of color, I was amazed at the indifference, insensitivity, and downright resistance that was demonstrated in certain university quarters to the appointment of representatives of color on search committees. The inner sanctum exclusivity was inevitable and would be preserved so long as no special efforts were made for heterogeneous groups to be represented in important decision-making bodies. One such memo dealing with this issue was as follows:

To: President Harold Enarson
From: Frank W. Hale, Jr., Vice Provost
Subject: OMA Participation in High Level Administrative Searches
Date: 1/16/80

Dear Harold:

I am aware that the university in recent months has sought to fill certain high level administrative posts such as a vice president for health services, a vice president for development, a director for the Mershon Center, and a dean for student services.

I feel that it is extremely important that our office be represented on search committees for these nationally visible administrative slots. I also feel certain that every effort should be made to attract able minority candidates for such positions. These approaches are extremely vital to any positive affirmative action thrust and to the integrity of our affirmative action commitment at this university.

Thank you for your response.

My files do not indicate that I ever received a response, and if I did, I saw no consistent or measurable indication that my recommendation was ever given any priority consideration. The fact remains that senior central administrators, deans, department heads, and senior faculty are far more eager to remain loyal to the tradition of the *old boy* network for recommendations than to carve up the territorial spoils of ownership for the sake of equity considerations.

I was acutely dissatisfied with the way in which minority programming was decentralized throughout the university. Even a superficial analysis of the organizational arrangement made it apparent that such a loose structure was an obvious betrayal of what the university had described as its commitment to equality of opportunity and results. One of the chief weaknesses of the arrangement was that so much of what the institution had determined as goals and strategies fell through the cracks because there was no central office of authority to whom the scattered offices which focused on issues of diversity had to report. Minority recruitment efforts, for example, were housed in the Office of Minority Affairs. Minority retention efforts were housed in the Office of Student Affairs. Each office had its own unchallenged authority. Almost everything that was shared between the two offices depended on the good faith of those who headed those offices. In many ways, the left hand did not know what the right was doing. We were clearly vulnerable to duplication, wrangling over goals and strategies which should have been of equal interest and concern, and openly and underhandedly sabotaging the programs of each other as we attempted to hammer out the survival of our own units in a madhouse of conflicting ambitions. Likewise, almost every area on campus had its little piece of minority programming. Apparently, central administrators thought it too harsh for academic units to be accountable to a nontraditional unit such as the Office of Minority Affairs, as I certainly knew that such an approach was too soft to accomplish the most-cherished objectives which we sought.

Earlier, I had written a memo to Provost W. Ann Reynolds to express my concerns. It was as follows:

To: W. Ann Reynolds, Provost
From: Frank W. Hale, Jr., Vice Provost for Minority Affairs
Subject: Integration of Minority Services
Date: November 19, 1979

Dear Ann:

Given Ohio State's comprehensive efforts to increase and support the presence of minority students, some thought should be given to consolidating certain support programs that are now scattered throughout the university. Because of declining resources, some institutions have attempted to accommodate minority programs by relying more and more on outside financial support. Such approaches, based on an institution's own sense of priorities, give recognition to minority programs as nothing more than an adjunct to an institution's full complement of what it has already established as valid or legitimate. We cannot afford to take such a course. As financial stringencies become more urgent, we will need to address concerns of coordination, resources, duplication and decentralization.

In order to present a set of unified services to students—(1) recruitment, (2) academic counseling, (3) tutoring, (4) personal counseling, (5) career counseling and placement, (6) workshops (study skills, reading, test-taking), (7) cultural and social enrichment, (8) financial aid, (9) coordination of black, Hispanic, Asian, and Native American programs, and (10) the Freshman Foundation Program—a single minority administrative structure within the Office of Academic Affairs would seem beneficial. Such an approach would create more visibility for the overall program, and greater access to central decision-makers. Resources, both monetary and human, would be more concentrated.

In the end, I felt that the law of divide and conquer was at work, as my efforts in this area were frustrated by those whom I presumed would not be happy partners to any proposition that would endorse a cohesion of minority input and power on campus. Such an arrangement, designed to deal forthrightly with the intolerable neglect and indifference, as exhibited in certain corners of the campus when dealing with matters of equity, caused senior offers to come face-to-face with political reality. Torn by conflicting aims of academic freedom and affirmative action, the perspective of the Office of Minority Affairs was expendable. As among the newest, frailest and most controversial units on campus, we could be thrown to the wolves in order to save the more mature and reputable entities in the academy. Provost Reynolds' response was not at all surprising:

To: Frank W. Hale, Jr.
From: W. Ann Reynolds
Subject: Future Progress of Minority Programs at Ohio State University
Date: November 27, 1979

As I have indicated to you in verbal conversation, we want to offer a complete set of positive services and offerings to minority students as possible. However, it is also impossible to set up a mini-university within Ohio State University only for minority students. This would not achieve the goals that you and I both hold dear. Let's continue the conversations and the memos to work toward the best possible sets of services and educational experiences for our minority student and make sure that you, as vice provost of minority affairs, are playing an important role in coordinating them.

I was well aware that Dr. Reynolds was in an uncompromising mood on giving central authority and jurisdiction to the Office of Minority Affairs when dealing with global issues affecting students and faculty of color. Such potent power would upset the applecart and create chaotic circumstances for those bastions of authority on campus whose uninterrupted ascendancy was assumed unassailable. The argument contesting the setting up of a mini-university within the university was a fallacious one. The idea was one of setting up a one-stop location and organizational structure where the needs of minority students could be met without having to suffer the cumbersome experience of having to sort out a disturbing distribution of services all over the campus. The centralization of services was proposed in order to remove the yoke of isolation and alienation from the experiences of students of color and, at the same time, to provide a model of sturdy accountability for those units who needed to be made keenly aware of the injustices in their areas and then, in turn, would be compelled to do something about it.

All of our battles, however, did not result in grim results. Borrowing a chapter from the successful operation of the Graduate School Visitation and Fellowship Program, I proposed the establishment of a Minority Scholars Program to award scholarships to academically talented Ohio minority high school graduating seniors to attend Ohio State. The proposal was based on the fact that significant numbers of talented minority Ohio high school graduates were attracted to institutions of higher education outside of the state to pursue their collegiate education. Thus, the state was losing much of its minority *cream talent* to institutions outside of the state. With the support of Provosts W. Ann Reynolds, Diether Haenicke, and Mylas Brand, the proposal was established, funded and strengthened to the point of it becoming one of the premiere programs in the country. In a short period of time, we were able to identify and successfully attract several hundred honor student applicants every year. Established in 1982, the program has consistently and effectively achieved its objective. While making fantastic gains in the recruitment of minority high school scholars, the program, at the same time, put the brakes on the good fortunes of Ivy League-type institutions that earlier had pretty much had their own way in raiding the state of its prize college candidates. Well over five hundred minority scholars had been able to take advantage of the Minority Scholars Program during my tenure as vice provost.

Dr. Diether Haenicke, dean of the College of Humanities at Ohio State, succeeded Dr. Reynolds as provost and senior vice president for academic affairs. Provost Haenicke and I had a genuine, warm, and respectful relationship with each other. Dr. Reynolds had tried my last nerve as a staunch and stubborn egotist who remained an everlasting blight on my spirit during the entire reign of her narrow-visioned tenure. Her administrative style was a baffling ghost that I could never quite grasp. At every turn, she attempted to stifle my initiative and self-respect, but my own sense of rugged individualism prevailed even in the presence of a burden that was overwhelming. As a humanitarian of philanthropic impulses, Haenicke was profoundly concerned about those factors that disturbed and weakened the morale of students and faculty of color within the institution. It was during his tenure that the idea of a black cultural center was resurrected.

As early as 1972 a proposal for a black cultural center had been presented by the Department of Black Studies to the senior administrative staff at Ohio State for their consideration. Even though the rationale for such a center grew out of the negative effects that institutional racism, underrepresentation, social isolation, and cultural disorientation can have on black students, the issue was hotly debated both within the black community on campus and between the proponents of the proposal and the white campus power structure. The campus patriarchs viewed the proposal as promoting a separatist (segregated) concept. Black constituents on campus had supported the center concept generally but were caught up in the issue of control. Some wanted the center to be under the auspices of the Department of Black Studies. Still others wanted the center to be under the auspices of the Office of Student Affairs. A forum was held where proponents representing Black Studies, Student Affairs, and Minority Affairs held forth their views relative to the administrative locus of the proposed center. At the forum's conclusion, the vote was overwhelmingly in favor of Minority Affairs as a compromise decision. A committee of black faculty and administrators also voted 14–2 in favor of Minority Affairs. Even though the black constituency on campus had spoken loud and clear concerning its wishes, the central administration (desiring to have the center under Student Affairs) held the decision of the majority hostage by refusing to release funds for the center (Royer Commons) unless the black community supported the administration's point of view. The black community on campus, except for a very small fraction, stood united and refused to be bought. Consequently, the proposal for a black cultural center remained in limbo for approximately a decade.

After this extended hiatus and also realizing that both the national and campus commitment to equality and access had faltered somewhat, I dared to revisit the history and need for a black cultural center, first with Provost Haenicke and then with President Edward H. Jennings. I contacted each of them, however, only after I had discussed this new initiative with Dr. Russell Spillman, vice president for student affairs;

Dr. Mitchel Livingston, dean of student life; Dr. William E. Nelson, Jr., chairman, Department of Black Studies; and Dr. Mae A. Stewart, associate dean of University College. We had all agreed that the center would be under the auspices and direction of the Office of Minority Affairs. In 1985, President Jennings, encouraged by the performance of what the Office of Minority Affairs had already been able to accomplish, made the ultimate commitment to establish and fund a black cultural center on The Ohio State University campus.

$350,000 was allocated for the renovation of Bradford Commons. Soon I received a list of architects from whom we were to select our first choice. None on the list were African-Americans. I made a call to Mr. William Sykes, the director of Ohio's Department of Administrative Services, and asked him to prepare me a slate of African-American architects who could be added to the list of prospective candidates who would be capable of designing, drawing up plans, and supervising the renovation of the building. In a short period of time, he sent me the names of Curtis Moody, John Coke, John Spencer, and Howard Nolan, all of whom were added to the list of prospects. As things worked out, a magnificent gesture of generosity and maneuver took place when these African-American architects won the contract; whereupon, they agreed to contribute their earnings to be set up in a scholarship fund for African-American students in the College of Architecture. It was a stroke of racial pride and unity that seldom is afforded the kind of attention that reaches the headlines for far more undesirable exploits of people of color.

The black cultural center was designed to serve as a *family room* or a *home away from home* on campus. The center was to serve as an antidote to the perceived impersonality of administrative structures, the indignity of suffering instances of racial prejudice, and the lack of precollegiate experience and preparation that created a variety of anxieties and apprehensions. Those of us who proposed the center considered the initiative a pluralistic approach, underscoring the fact that America takes pride in granting diverse groups an opportunity to preserve their identify and to develop independent associations. White students have their fraternity and sorority houses and residence halls for athletes, honor students, etc. Evidence of this is seen everyday in the composition of our ethnic neighborhoods, our ethnically and racially focused celebrations, and in the history and development of those religious and educational institutions that have an ethnic or racial orientation and emphasis. Additionally, the center was designed as an opportunity for older and more experienced students to assist entering students on ways to negotiate the system. It also served as a major vehicle for bringing students of different backgrounds together to gain an understanding and an appreciation of the richness and diversity of various cultures and to learn of their profound impact on the development and advancement of western and global civilization. The center officially opened on October 11, 1989.*

Perhaps one of the happiest opportunities which I had was that of co-founding the minority scholars honorary, the Alpha Kappa Mu Honorary. Originally established at Tennessee State University, a historically black university, OMA organized a chapter (Mu X) at Ohio State in 1986. Serving as co-sponsor and advisor to the organization, Linda Jackson planned and implemented a program for the honorary that recognized the academic accomplishments of students. Undergraduates must have a cumulative grade point average of 3.3 in order to qualify for membership, and graduate students must have a 3.7 in order to qualify for membership. Ohio State was the first Big Ten university to have an Alpha Kappa Mu Chapter. Linda Jackson and I were recognized as honorary members of the honorary at its installation of officers which occurred on February 20, 1986. The national office sent a delegate from Kentucky State University to conduct and validate the establishment of the chapter and the installation of its officers. Michael Bailey, a doctoral student in political science at the time, was the honorary's first president.

About three years prior to my retirement, my consultantships began to mount. From the time I was first appointed as associate dean of the graduate school, my opportunities as a consultant steadily grew. I engaged in far-flung experiences of addressing state and national conferences and institutions of higher education on issues relative to defining, managing and evaluating diversity. My ventures carried me to address such national bodies as the Association of Governing Boards of Universities and Colleges; Association of Graduate Schools; Council of Independent Colleges (President's Institute); Modern Languages Association; Council of Graduate Schools; National Association of College Deans, Registrars, Admissions Officers; National Association of Equal Opportunity; National Association of Personnel Workers; National Association of Land Grant Colleges and Universities; National Conference on Racial and Ethnic Relations in American Higher Education; Association of Black Administrators; National Conference on Mobilizing for Excellence in Education; Southern College Placement Association; Speech Communication Association; Operation PUSH; Ohio Association of Student Personnel Administrators; Ohio Society of Professional Engineers; and the Ohio Association of Equal Opportunity Personnel.

* See Appendix J, page 423.

300

Likewise, colleges and universities also demonstrated interest and enthusiasm in my visiting their campuses for lecture and consultant services. There was an unprecedented outpouring of interest in my services over the decade from 1978 to 1988. There was the opportunity that I had to meet with fifteen vice chancellors from throughout the University of Wisconsin System on the main campus in Madison to discuss and plan long-range goals for access and retention in October of 1987. During the same month, I conferred with the president, central administration officers, deans and department heads to plan minority programming options for the future at the University of Southern Colorado in Pueblo. Because of my successful experience in The Ohio State University Graduate School and in the Office of Minority Affairs, my consultantships continued to expand to the point where much of my energy was channeled into accommodating the surging interest of the academy's feverish preoccupation with issues of diversity and affirmative action. That rising, ever-expanding interest manifested itself with a resounding impact as I was involved in a series of encounters of giving professional device on a number of campuses including the University of Missouri at Columbia, Rutgers University, University of Louisville, University of Oklahoma, University of Georgia, University of Maryland, Mississippi State University, Denison University, Kenyon College, University of North Florida, West Chester (Pennsylvania) State University, University of Illinois, University of Texas, University of Kentucky, Vanderbilt University, Hampton University, Kent State University, Virginia State University, University of Cincinnati, Andrews University, Columbia Union College, Western Michigan University, College of William and Mary, University of Delaware, University of Southern Illinois (Carbondale), University of Tennessee, Kennesaw State University, Loma Linda University, College of Holy Cross, Cleveland State University, Saint Paul's College, Hope College, Morgan State University, State University of New York (Oneonta), Ohio Northern University, and scores of others. My consultantships for federal agencies included the U.S. Air Force, U.S. Department of the Army, U.S. Department of Education, U.S. Central Intelligence Agency, and the U.S. Military Academy (West Point). Additionally, my state educational consultantships have included the University System of Georgia, Ohio Department of Education, Virginia Council of Higher Education, and the Tennessee State Commission on Higher Education.

The marvelous adventures that I experienced during my tenure as vice provost stand as achievement without parallel in the history of minority affairs programming in higher education. Starting as a frail struggling unit on campus, the Office of Minority Affairs emerged as a comprehensive, vital, and productive arm of the university, with its influence stretching from coast to coast.

Why our magnificent success? First, we were blessed with a mission whose major potential and resources had barely been tapped. Second, we developed into a remarkable team of tough, dedicated, energetic, resourceful, and efficient people. I cannot say enough concerning the bright and committed leadership of directors like Ruth Gresham, Timothy McDonald, Linda Jackson, Rose Wilson, Danny Boone, Lester Morrow, and Joseph Stranges. They needed only a minimum of administrative guidance as they took effective steps in streamlining and decentralizing the programmatic aspects of the office. The goals of the office would have been seriously undermined had it not been for the day-to-day activities of Keith Troy, Normando Caban, David Harrison, Karen Reynolds, Cynthia Harris, Aldrick Gore, James Copeland, Dwight Hollins, Angel Morales, and Malikah Faquir—all of whom criss-crossed the state, beating the bushes for students wherever they could find them. Our supporting staff, in many respects, while behind the scenes, were noteworthy in the consistency which they gave to detail without infringing on the focus which was required to master all aspects of our mission. Ellen Banks, Pamela Clark, Patricia Knox, Wanda Barnett, Julia Smith, Diana Coscarelli, Joyce Ford, Esperanda Morgan, Audrey Thompson, Carla Moody, Vicky Braddy, Juanita Rispress, and Leona Smith were stellar off-stage notables in the gifted contributions which they made to the office. While some were, as administrators, forced to the center stage of OMA's operations, it was the strong support of the hands behind us that was responsible for our successes. Along this line, we are not shy to admit that graduate associates contributed heavily to the growth, development, and progress of the enterprise—Larry Williamson, Gwendolyn Garvin, Yoon Kim, Myra Crouch, Jose Arevalo, Ora Spann, Joni Lawson, Raymond Zamudio, Chandra Cox, Alvin Hailstorks, Milton Matthews, Ronald Johnson, Kathleen Bailey, Elizabeth Chan, Zelda Holcomb, and Doron Maniece laid bare the nuts and bolts of the qualities that were required to keep our office at a uniformly high standard of efficiency.

Because of the pioneering phases of so much what took place in OMA, my role in the successful operation of the office was, at times, overemphasized. On the one hand, I found that the high atmosphere can become chilling when at the helm—at the top of an organization. The strenuous demands and strains of having to produce at a high level on an ongoing basis can rattle the nerves, unsettle the stomach, and torment one's mental faculties. I fretted increasingly, if not openly—at least inwardly—as my career advanced, sometimes drifting into confusion and at other times into apathy. The physical and nervous exhaustion of it all resulted in the emasculation of my vitality and sending me into the high-standing territory of hypertension even before I had turned forty years of age. That was a category into which I had been imprisoned even before I had assumed the challenges of Ohio State. It should have been no surprise to me when physical tragedies unfolded in my life in 1981, and then again in 1986 (six-way heart bypass surgery).

For a period of ten years after coming to Columbus, Ohio, and connecting with The Ohio State University, I had been engaged in a sweep of activities—in season and out of season—that kept aflame my zeal for bringing meaning and enhancement to my educational aims. I continued to respond to calls for addresses and consultation services at colleges and universities, at state and national conventions, and before church, civic, and social organizations. I received more calls than I could possibly accept, and I accepted more calls than I possibly should have.

I was invited to speak at a NAACP banquet in Kokomo, Indiana, on one Saturday night in early March of 1981. It was clear from the response that I received from the nearly five hundred guests who were in attendance that the Lord had once again blessed my ministry of challenging the community to come together to promote better educational opportunities for their children. I reminded them of how excessively conservative the climate of the country had become, and how important it was for them to motivate and nurture the enormous potential of our youth. Well aware of the chilling impact of the Reagan years on people of color, I felt that it was time for African-American people to take the offensive in encouraging our young people to be serious about their studies early on—in elementary, middle schools, and high schools, so that more of them would be better able to make their way into and through college and into academic, managerial, and professional careers.

Once the banquet was over, at about eleven o'clock that night, I got into my car and proceeded to make my three hour trip back to Columbus. Although it was in the month of March, I had incredibly good fortune because the roads were clear and unencumbered as the hand of winter had not blanketed the area with its typical implantation of snow. My major problem in meeting the challenge of the highway was not to buckle under the weight of fatigue and fall asleep during the midnight and early morning hours. After conquering the horrors of the highway, I fell victim to a freak occurrence that nearly cost me my life; but God sent his angelic reinforcements to undergird me just when I needed it most.

Arriving at home at about two o'clock in the morning, I was exhausted after having clawed my way through the isolation and loneliness of the night. Although my energies had been seriously depleted, I received a magnificent burst of vitality as I was greeted at the front door by my lovely wife. She seemed to have always been right there at that precise and crucial moment when genuine love and warmth gave me the surprising capacity to seize some degree of success with a bold hand even in the midst of the most acute crisis. And that early morning hour was no exception. She had just prepared me a small bowl of slaw salad with a slight accompaniment of pecans for a light snack when tragedy cocked its head and struck a deathblow in my direction. While cracking a pecan, I had inadvertently overlooked the fact that a piece of pecan shell had fallen into my salad. As I took the next spoonful of salad and swallowed it, I experienced the most devastating trauma of my life. I almost suffocated on the spot as the lights nearly went out in my head. Darkness quickly descended in my physical sky, and I could see nothing but stars as Ruth and I raced to the car and headed to Riverside Methodist Hospital which was approximately one mile northeast of us. I insisted on driving myself because I sensed that, if I had relaxed only for a moment, I would have succumbed. There was not the slightest trace of air evident, as I had not even a trivial indication that air was available to me. The cycle of inhalation and expiration was closed, it seemed to me. My body jerked with involuntary rhythms of trauma as we sped toward the hospital with a determination founded on faith, will, and power in the hands of an Almighty God whose name I called upon in the silent eloquence of my seemingly hopeless predicament.

It was in the emergency room on March 15 of the year 1981, that the pecan shell was dislodged with a scoping instrument that ruptured my esophagus in the process. I was sent home that same evening. Because no X-rays were taken, the rupture was not discovered until after I was back to the hospital and readmitted the next morning. I had become delirious overnight and had developed a temperature of 105°.

Emergency surgery was necessary to save my life because chemical pneumonia had set in my lung cavity, as well as in the area around my heart which was full of infection and poison. My situation remained critical for two weeks, and the care which I received at the hospital did little to either relieve or to improve my situation. On March 30, I was transferred to the Thoracic Division of The Ohio State University Hospital where the second major surgery was performed on that very day by Dr. John Vasko, as infection once again had invaded my lung cavity. It was necessary for the surgical team to remove three ribs in order to rid my body of the poisons that penetrated that vital area. I will never be able to forget the unusual amount of tender professional and inspirational support that Dr. Vasko gave me during my confinement. In addition to visiting me during his daily rounds, he always made my room his last stop in the evening—usually around eleven o'clock, before he headed for his country home in Ashville, Ohio, about twenty-five miles away. He proved to be a professional of the highest order, as I observed the marvels of his day-to-day pursuit and progress of my condition. He left no stone unturned in providing me with the best counsel and technical assistance that was available. When it appeared that any staff person was not performing up to the high standards of his expectations, he was, at times, ruthless and relentless in his demand for excellence. Nurses and technicians alike took special care to function appropriately when they were under his supervision.

I went from 215 pounds down to 160 pounds during a very short period of time. For eighteen weeks, I could not eat or drink anything by mouth. All nutrients were given intravenously. After about the first twelve weeks, the miracle of improvement and recovery began to occur. I had not been aware that only about ten percent of all operations on a ruptured esophagus are successful. Even as my abdominal and thoracic capacities were housing a variety of about fifteen different life-saving tubes, I was able, through the help of God, to manage certain aspects of my precarious situation. Initially, I was faced with an inundation of pain-killing drugs that had me figuratively floating through space, as I experienced awesome imaginary exhibitions of flight, spangled with fluorescent colors of every variety. It was as if I was given a private viewing to a magnificent fireworks display in mushrooming splendor. At the same time, I felt out of control— unable to think, act, or have any management over my own destiny. I had never felt so helpless. As the effects of the drugs began to wane at one point, it seemed as if I had been the victim of an awesome exhibition of unchained fury; whereupon, I took the occasion to advise my doctor and the medical staff that I would rather endure the pain than to be a hostage or prisoner of drugs which forced me into the torture of total dependency upon others to direct my affairs. And from that day, unconscionable pain notwithstanding, I was a free spirit. Amazingly enough, in a few days thereafter, mind ruled over matter, and pain was no longer my enemy. It had been conquered with a determined will that was wedded to the will of an Almighty God. I knew that angels were watching over me.

I owe so much to God's sustaining hand in my behalf and to Ruth, my beloved and beautiful wife, who stayed, who cared for me, and who kept the doctors and staff alert to my every fluctuation, who kept a record of medical transactions that occurred (weight, blood pressure, blood samples, radiological reports, intravenous intakes, etc.), who monitored visitations and the lengths of stay, who responded to all letters, telegrams, and telephone calls, who gave loving attention to my every need, and who constantly encouraged and loved me every step of the way—night and day—never leaving the hospital at all during the first ten weeks of the twenty-one weeks of my confinement. She was a mighty rock of overall love and support that enabled me to conquer what appeared unconquerable. It was her spirit of undaunted faith and love, that far exceeded the lurid prospects of self-defeating nihilism, that enabled me to become a conqueror through the blessings of Jesus Christ.

I was also especially blessed to have had my mother and father who traveled two hundred miles round trip daily from Findlay, Ohio, to be at my side. My children (Ifeoma, Frank III, and Sherilyn) kept daily watch like sentinels over me, unstintingly sharing their courage and concern. I also owe a great deal to Dr. Samuel DeShay, at that time head of the medical work for the World Church of Seventh-day Adventists, who came to Columbus and who, along with Dr. George Harding and my wife, had helped to arrange for my transfer to The Ohio State University Hospital because of its highly competent thoracic team of surgeons; and to Dr. George Harding, Jr., again, who never missed visiting me daily for a period of over six to eight weeks during the initial stages of my hospitalization; to Dr. Harold Enarson, the president of The Ohio State University, who led the way in arranging for my transfer to The Ohio State University Hospital and who made it possible for me to be placed in a VIP apartment suite that would also accommodate a place for my wife to reside, so as to be at my bedside at all times; to my dearest friends and relatives who came from afar and spent days to be at my bedside—my aunt Isy Young, my cousins (Dr. And Mrs. Saunders Thompson, Dr. Cephas Jackson), Dr. William DeShay, Vertis Barnes, Jr., Florence Robertson, Dr. Gaines Partridge, Jannith Lewis, Elder R. Hope Robertson, Sr., Edith Taylor, Dr. and Mrs. Clarence Schmidt, and Dr. Calvin Rock; to members of my staff who kept the office running smoothly during my absence; to the members of my church (Ephesus S.D.A. Church) who shared their time and resources in my behalf; to the workers and administrators of the Allegheny West Conference who manifested their sentiment through visitations and generous gifts of love; to Dr. and Mrs. Timothy McDonald, Dr. Joseph Stranges, Rose Wilson, Otis and Marion Vaughn, Elder Stephen Lewis, Elder Jethroe Lester, Elder Kenneth Schelske, Cordell Newton, Jackie Smallwood, Jim Ross, Brenda Hinkle, Karen Stockling, and Sam Martin, who gave their consistent support through visitations, counsel, and encouragement; to the hundreds who sent food for the family, flowers, letters, telegrams, tapes (sermons and music), cards, and made telephone calls as expressions of their love and tender emotions; to those who called long distance—on a daily and weekly basis, like Dr. Jon Robertson, Elder Edgar

Mims, Dr. Matthew Kates, Elder Herman Vanderberg, Eunice Vanderberg, Samuel Rashford, Dr. Samuel Cook, Dr. Talbert Shaw, Dr. Andrew Billingsley, Elder Charles L. Brooks, Elder Dunbar Henri, Elder Shelton Kilby, Lerone Bennett, Congressman Louis Stokes, Helen Beckett, Sherman Brown, John Pitts, Elder David Trusty, Frank Jackson, Elder Michael Bernard, Wayne Humphrey, and to family members, Tommy and Thea Saddler, and Corloyd and Gloria Thomas; to scores of others who made local and long distance inquiries concerning my health; to members of The Ohio State University community of faculty, students and administrators for prayers in my behalf; to the clergymen of Columbus who shuttled in and out of my hospital room like watchmen on the walls of Zion; to the corps of medical personnel at Rhodes Hall who adopted me as their own, professionally and personally; and last, but not least, to Dr. John Vasko, my surgeon, and his able staff, who directed and guided by God, saved my life because of their caring and competent surgical procedures and subsequent treatment that led to my recovery.

In the word of Andre Crouch's "My Tribute," "How can I say thanks" for the many things that God has done for me through His Providence and through all of my family and friends whose lives became bound inextricably with mine? Beyond a doubt, it was the transfusion of their faith, prayers and confidence that sustained me during my weakest moments.

Obviously I was spared to perform a greater work. "To God Be the Glory," and for angels watching over me.

At the end of four tormenting months—March 15 to July 20, 1981—I was weak and weary, but undiscouraged. Nevertheless, I was forced to adopt what was to be a more measured pace on my road to recovery. I early foresaw that reducing and slowing up on my activities would not be easy for me to accomplish. In the meanwhile, the Republican Party continued to be a formidable barrier to the advancement of women and people of color. The party's obvious opposition to affirmative action reinforced the polarization that had already dominated the public mood. Even as I experienced an uphill struggle to literally get back on my feet, I was more than anxious to return to the bare-knuckle daily battles of tearing down those barriers that had been erected against the advances of people of color in higher education. Given the general political outlook in the early 1980s, I knew that any opportunity for a smashing success was less than auspicious.

It was not until October of 1981 that I returned to full time duties in the Office of Minority Affairs. My hands were full as I seized the opportunity to create a Minority Scholars Program to attract top caliber high school seniors of color. I was eager to establish a program that would keep our most academically talented students within the state, hoping that we would be able to attract a large percentage of them to Ohio State. In November, Dr. Charles V. Willis, professor of Education and Urban Affairs at Harvard University, was the keynote speaker for the Eleventh Annual Graduate and Professional Schools Visitation Days Program. Late during the year, we were well on our way to completing the second edition of *They Came and They Conquered*, a directory of alumni who had significant profiles in their various professions.

Burning with sincerity and commitment, I began to give attention to strategies that would increase the retention of students of color on campus. Recognizing the financial needs of students, our staff was successful in creating financial assistance programs in meeting the needs of students who needed tutorial assistance, who required travel support to professional conferences, and who needed assistance in getting their theses and dissertations typed and bound. OMA also contributed to the support of student minority departmental organizations who desired to bring in visiting lecturers and consultants for professional development. It was less costly at times to bring a professional to the campus to serve a significant number of students than to assume the costs of sending a substantial number of individual students to the same professional meeting where the costs of transportation, housing, and per diem would be prohibitive.

The 1982–83 academic year got us off to a triumphant start as twenty-one high school seniors from Columbus, Ohio, were awarded $1000 renewable scholarships. It was the initial effort that opened the door to making the Minority Scholars Program one of the model programs of its kind in the nation. It was during that same year that Dr. Josue Cruz was appointed to serve as assistant vice provost to coordinate Hispanic recruitment and retention programs in OMA. Reverend Jesse Jackson, national president of Operation PUSH, was the keynote speaker for the Twelfth Annual Graduate and Professional Schools Visitation Days Program. On that occasion, distinguished alumni awards were presented to three illustrious alumni: Dr. Herman F. Bostic, professor of French and associate dean for educational affairs in the Graduate School of Arts and Sciences at Howard University; Dr. Helen G. Edmonds, professor emeritus and former chair of the Department of History and dean of the Graduate School of Arts and Sciences at North Carolina Central University; and Dr. Michael A. Olivas, associate professor of Education and Law and director of Institute for Education, Law and Governance at the University of Houston. Distinguished service awards were given to Mr. Elijah Pierce, a ninety year old internationally acclaimed wood carver from Columbus, and Dr. Margaret Roberts, chief of Speech Pathology and Audiology for Columbus Children's Hospital.

In the realm of scholarship philanthropy, the Columbus chapter of Links, Incorporated, began to serve as co-sponsors of minority scholars in the autumn of 1982 with the inception of the Minority Scholars Program. During that year the Links committed themselves to supporting five scholars over the four years of their undergraduate studies at Ohio State. The Links scholars were Zina Hamilton, Karen Hill, Sheryl Jackson, and Thomas Reed. Two of the scholarships were sponsored by Links members: The Vashti D. Taylor Memorial Scholarship was funded by Mr. and Mrs. James K, Jackson in memory of the mother of Mrs. Linda Jackson, and the Carl M. Basnett Memorial Scholarship was funded by Mrs. Roberta Basnett in memory of her husband. In their ongoing commitment to educational, cultural and civic activities, the Columbus chapter of Links, Inc., also hosted "An Evening with Nancy Wilson" at the Hyatt on Capital Square before a sellout crowd of nearly five hundred patrons who purchased tickets to the dinner-musical for $50 each. This festive scholarship program was under the auspices of the Links for students of color at The Ohio State University. A number of the Links scholarship recipients have graduated and have gained influence and standing sufficient to make them distinguished by any professional measure of competence and accomplishment. The Links officers during that monumental year were Shirley Mann, president; Linda Taylor Jackson, vice president; Elizabeth Evans, corresponding secretary; Dr. Maureen Black, recording secretary; and Yvone Ruffin, treasurer.

One of my major concerns at Ohio State was the fact that the recruitment, promotion and tenure of faculty of color did not even keep pace with the limited recruitment and enrollment of students of color. This was especially true of African-Americans, Hispanic-Americans, and Native Americans. It was evident to me that special measures had to be taken to attract and hold personnel (faculty, administrators, and staff) of color. Yet all of the warm and bold statements concerning the institution's intentions in this area concealed weak and faulty implementation strategies. I remember well how I urged senior administrators and faculty chairs to pursue the following strategies in order to achieve a more balanced racial balance within the faculty:

1. Identify bright undergraduate and graduate students of color and fund them for graduate work before assigning them to teaching (administrative responsibilities as part of a *grow your own* initiative).
2. Make time for teachers of color to pursue research beyond the requirements of the classroom.
3. Assign senior faculty as mentors to junior faculty of color.

4. Provide funds to faculty of color for professional development.
5. Create administrative internships to personnel of color who wish to gain skills that will prepare them for administrative opportunities.
6. Seek employment for the spouse of a prospective faculty member that the institution seeks to employ.
7. Recognize and give credit to faculty and staff of color who go beyond their required duties to serve students of color.

It must also be understood that there are certain institutional factors that historically have impeded the promotion and tenure of faculty of color. It is not uncommon for faculty of color to:

- Serve as arbiters and negotiators in resolving problems of racial conflict and misunderstanding.
- Assist in the recruitment of students and faculty of color.
- Promote the institution, serving as an unofficial public relations agent of the institution.
- Respond to students of color who seek them out for special help.
- Perform as *experts* because they are called upon to advise on issues that are common to people of color.
- Take the lead in promoting and advocating for changes that improve the conditions of people of color within the institution.

Since there is a symbiotic relationship between the presence of faculty of color and the presence of students of color, it is very important that the recruitment and retention of faculty of color be a major factor in improving the environment for diversity on a college or university campus.

As early as 1979 Dr. Michael A. Olivas, an OSU alumnus (Ph.D. '77) stated that, "Ohio State is an underachiever when one considers its potential to meet the academic needs of Hispanics... " He challenged the university to make existing minority programs "more sensitive and representative." By 1983, the university had appointed an assistant vice provost for minority affairs and had included Hispanic students as a major target group in its overall strategy of recruiting talented youth of color to pursue graduate education at Ohio State. Assisted by OMA recruiters, Dr. Cruz, the newly-appointed assistant vice provost, set out to recruit Hispanic students on both the undergraduate and graduate levels. Several colleges and universities were contacted and visited in Texas which resulted in the largest single attendance of Hispanic students in the history of the Graduate and Professional Schools Visitation Days Program. Dr. Cruz was also successful in having a proposal for a grant of $40,000 being approved by the Campbell Soup Company to support the migrant student component of the Minority Scholars Program. The initial grant made it possible for five scholars to be awarded scholarships totaling $7600 each, or $1900 a year for four years. Administrative costs were also covered by the grant which was presented to OSU President Edward Jennings by Mr. Jeremiah O'Brien, vice president of the Campbell Soup Fund, Inc. In order for a student to meet the definition of *migrant*, his/her parents had to be migratory agricultural workers who had worked in Ohio for at least three months in each of the immediate past three years.

It was during these years that I continued to have hopes for an enlarged future in the area of scholarship support for promising students of color. I personally assumed the responsibility of contacting community-based civic and social organizations, businesses and corporations with offices in Ohio about entering into a partnership pact with the university and the Office of Minority Affairs (OMA). I sought to persuade these groups to provide scholarships for talented Ohio youth. Increasingly, these organizations began to realize that, by supporting these students and urging them to remain in Ohio to pursue their education, they were also making an investment to insure future vibrant and productive communities throughout Ohio.

Among the generous supporters to the Minority Scholars Program was Kal Kan Foods, Inc. Initially, it provided support for six annual scholarships to students of color. As the third largest pet care company in the United States, Kal Kan operates a plant in Columbus. This facility is one of four in the nation owned by Kal Kan producers of Kal Kan canned dog food, Mealtime dry dog food and Crave dry cat food. The company is privately held and is a part of Mars, Inc., a worldwide company which pioneered the pet food industry in Europe.

I remember how grateful I was after the Lambda Boule Chapter of the Sigma Pi Phi Fraternity added their philanthropic voice to the expanding chorus of organizations that began to focus their attention and direct their resources for the advancement of minority youth at Ohio State. As one of the co-sponsors of the Minority Scholars Program, the Columbus chapter of the fraternity (Lambda Boule) contributed $1000 to the Minority Scholars Program. At the time the local officers were John H. Rosemond, M.D., immediate past sire archon; Marvin Green, M.D., sire archon; J. Harold Thomas, grammateus; William "Cy" Butler, thesauristes; and David D. Hamlar, D.D.S., chairman, social action committee.

In the development of this healthy drive to attract Ohio's top scholars of color to Ohio State, Marathon Oil Company, with its corporate headquarters based in Findlay, Ohio, came on board as a contributor to the Minority Scholars Program in 1983, providing a $5000 annual gift for four years to fund five scholars with renewable commitments to the students who maintained a satisfactory academic standing.

If one were to be asked what were the factors that contributed to the almost immediate success of the Minority Scholars Program, it was fortunate for us that we had a team of committed and competent staff persons, who were so impressed by the advantages that such a program would accord the students that they were willing to endure the strains of overtime and overwork. While at times the monster of unfortunate friction would raise its head among staff members, they, nevertheless, generally set aside their egos and formed a closely-allied and unified effort to target and attract the most capable students of color in Ohio as candidates for our Minority Scholars Program.

Rev. Keith A. Troy had an exalted reputation as a wonder-worker, as a recruiter par excellence, and as superior academic counselor. His talents shone brilliantly as he attracted students in significant numbers from throughout Ohio. Students and parents had a deep faith in his capability as a counselor as they often crowded the reception area in Lincoln Tower waiting to consult with him. Troy always encouraged students with his optimistic assessments of their potential; yet he would remain true to his role as a professional by insisting that they perform up to the level of their capacity. He was icily unsympathetic to any students who were slack in their enthusiasm or in their effort toward the goals which they were scheduled to pursue.

Although genuinely interested in his work in OMA, he was impaled on the horns of a difficult dilemma because, in addition to his university responsibilities, he was also pastor of New Salem Baptist Church. As the church grew dramatically and his church duties increased, he ultimately came to the conclusion that he would have to relinquish his post at Ohio State. Having earned the B.A. degree in education and religion at Morehouse College and the M.Div. degree from Colgate, Troy brought a delightful and disciplined, yet witty, perspective to his position. He was a hands-on, getting-things-done, forward-looking professional who was inclined to do things as much or more by intuition than by theoretical or untried measures that had little foundation. Because of his broad experience and his clever ways of getting things done, the recruitment program lost much of its early momentum upon his departure.

Mrs. Linda Jackson, too, was singularly effective in administering the Minority Scholars Program as the OMA coordinator of campus and community relations. Mrs. Jackson is a very bright professional who first suggested the idea to me of establishing a Minority Scholars

Program at Ohio State. She had had experience beyond her years in developing and implementing equal educational opportunity programs. Indeed, she had operated on practically every level of the educational system. An easy-going, happy-hearted person, who exuded graciousness and love of people, she possesses the kind of magnetic personality that engaged and brought students to her door and seeking her counsel without the slightest degree of in trepidation. Because of her genuine warmth and friendliness, she subtly and effectively swept students along, involving them in various co-curricular activities under the sponsorship of the Minority Scholars Program.

Beginning as a teacher in the Dayton Public School System, she has taught students from the fourth through seventh grades. Later, she served as a language arts consultant for seven elementary schools with the Dayton Board of Education and was a school counselor before becoming associate director of Project Echo at the University of Dayton. After moving to Cincinnati, her career took her to the top levels of higher education administration at the University of Cincinnati. She began as a counselor for Talent Search/Project Youth and was later appointed director. She then served for three years as assistant dean for student development and was assistant vice provost for student affairs before she and her family moved to Columbus. Prior to joining the staff of the Office of Minority Affairs, she was the coordinator for academic advisement in University College where she wrote the original proposal for special services that was funded for $103,000.

After the Minority Scholars Program began to take off, David Harrison became a premier professional and dominant voice in helping to propel the program to the point where it would achieve astronomical heights. Because of his star-reaching pragmatism and idealism as well, Harrison's approach to recruitment was always efficient, effective, and first-rate. In an unsparing pursuit of excellence in whatever he put his hands, he repudiated with smashing intensity anything that was mediocre or half done.

Thus, the Office of Minority Affairs, recommitting itself to the improvement of outreach to and retention of students of color, was involved in a bare-knuckled battled for the best minds of members of underrepresented groups throughout the state and the nation. It was the initiative of the *Student Reception Model* that enabled us to triumph—doubly—on our recruitment and selection of students for the Minority Scholars Program. The model, once again, focused on meeting junior and seniors in large group settings in an informal atmosphere where refreshments and snacks were provided and where comprehensive information and concerns were addressed in a timeframe covering approximately one hour. Members of the OMA staff made 5–10 minute presentations each, entertaining questions, and assisted students in completing application forms that were brought to the campus by the visiting OMA staff team to begin the application process.

It took an extremely dedicated staff to effectively engineer such a program. Among those who contributed their sparkling support and persuasive abilities to these efforts were Karen Reynolds, Cynthia Harris, Aldrick Gore, Dwight Hollins, Malika Faquir, Joyce Ford, Audrey Thompson, Myra Crouch, Angel Morales, Esperanza, and Jose Arevalo.

Of course, this exciting venture would never have gotten off the ground without the vigorous and penetrating support and commentaries of Dr. Ruth Russell, the director of recruitment placement; Dr. Lester Morrow, the director of research and evaluation; Mr. Ricardo Maestas, director of Hispanic programs; Linda Jackson, director of administration; and Dr. Joseph Stranges, director of financial aids.

While our far-visioned strategy of outreach was sorely needed and we had a sophisticated team of professionals to accomplish our tasks, it was the friendly warmth of metropolitan school administrations, principals, and counselors who willingly embraced our venture that was the key to our successes. Assistant Superintendent Ann Lane Gates of Akron organized a meeting for our team to meet with fifteen persons that included principals, administrators and counselors. Mr. Brinson Terry, director of guidance for the Cincinnati Public Schools, assembled a group of twenty-eight administrators, principals and counselors when our team shared a luncheon meeting with them at McIntosh's. Similarly, Assistant Superintendent James Williams of the Dayton Public Schools brought together twenty-two key persons who held significant posts throughout the system in our meeting at the Daytonian Hilton. Mr. Frank Huml, deputy superintendent of schools in Cleveland, gathered forty principals, administrators and counselors for our meeting at Bond Court. The result was the same when Mr. Kubic, director of guidance for the Youngstown Public Schools, convened twenty principals and counselor for our meeting at the Ramada Inn. The influential support of all of these leaders opened the doors that made it possible for us to carry our mission and our message to high schools throughout the state. Recognizing, too, that our success could not exist apart from the Ohio Department of Education, we enlisted their support in identifying those high schools who had a combined black and Hispanic enrollment that was fifty percent or more. We concentrated our efforts among those institutions.

314

In Cincinnati, we visited Woodward, Walnut Hills,Hughes, Withrow, Western Hills, Taft, and Aiken high schools. In Dayton, we recruited at Colonel, White, Dunbar, Belmont, and Meadowdale. In Youngstown, we met with students at South, East, and Rayen. Our travels carried us to Scott, Libbey, and Devilbiss in Toledo. Columbus gave the opportunity to meet with students at Linden-McKinley, Walnut Ridge, Brookhaven, East, Mifflin, and Eastmoor. Cleveland yielded the largest number of high schools with high concentrations of black and Hispanic students. We visited East, John Hay, John Marshall, Collinwood, Lincoln-West, John Adams, John F. Kennedy, Glenville, and South. We also contacted many students at Shaw in East Cleveland. Our travels also carried us to Buchtel High School in Akron and to Southview in Lorain. It was no accident that because of the wide-spread support that our efforts were receiving throughout the state, to an increasing degree, our recruitment endeavors continued to produce praiseworthy results.

Our OMA team continued to gain in confidence as it became apparent that there were no insuperable obstacles to a committed and dedicated core of people working together. I personally enjoyed the opportunity of crisscrossing the state with members of my staff. It was a solid demonstration of teamwork and that our victories were not by any means a one-man show.

Our successes did make a tremendous impression on leaders at many institutions who were seeking to advance the cause of diversity on their campuses. As a consequence, I was constantly being called upon to share our success stories on college campuses and at state and national conferences throughout the country. These multiplying opportunities enabled me to develop a vast reservoir of goodwill for The Ohio State University as well as an unbelievable degree of prestige that enhanced its reputation as a pioneer and forerunner in the areas of minority affairs and diversity.

Few African-American educators have enjoyed the large number of appearances that my positions as associate dean in the graduate school and as vice provost have offered me. My professional life has been one of the most active and positive opportunities to enjoy the give-and-take of cross-fertilization on issues of race and equal opportunity that one could ever imagine. In demand as a public speaker and as a consultant, I often felt that I should own stock in the major airlines, as I was constantly airborne in meeting certain professional assignments. While I feel certain that I have given more than five hundred speeches during my professional career before churches, civic groups, and a variety of other groups, nearly one-half of these assignments have been before educational groups and assemblies.

I will never forget the opportunity that I had to be the commencement speaker at Loma Linda University on June 12, 1977. Originally established as the College of Medical Evangelists (CME), it became incorporated into Loma Linda University in 1961 and, since that time, has won an excellent reputation as a medical school and for its standard of health care. Over the years several members of its staff have made significant breakthroughs in the medical fields; consequently, the institution achieved international recognition, establishing its place as a highly regarded medical school among its peer competitors. Thus, it was a noteworthy honor for me to be selected as the commencement speaker.

Nevertheless, aware that the institution was making monumental efforts to continue to gain coveted prestige within the medical community I challenged the graduating class and the institution to remain true to its moorings in an address which I entitled "Up Front, and Without Apologies." I warned that the institution should not lose its distinctive Adventist focus nor divorce itself from the fundamental beliefs of the church. It was my focus that the medical school could promote and use the latest scientific techniques in its teaching and research, while at the same time unapologetically taking on those national interests that undermine the health of the nation. I attempted to make this point in the statement below:

> Our concern for human potential and preservation as a denomination should challenge our brains and hearts to take on the alcohol, tobacco and drug industries, for example, as they continue to plague our society with every conceivable ill—making slaughterhouses of our homes and highways, as well as addicts, derelicts, and cancer victims of our families and friends.

I felt that some aspects of denominational influence and tradition were beginning to escape the institution for the sake of professionalism and a creeping independence of the medical community within the church from the church's administration.

It was obviously impossible for me to respond to all of the invitations which I received to address various groups, but as I could spare the time, I took advantage of those occasions that enabled me to boost the needs of people of color. While American society has always pledged to make reforms relative to equal opportunity and justice, its hands have continued to build up menacingly powerful practices to the contrary. The momentary satisfying victories which African-Americans have gained have only come as a result of frustrating battles to overcome the status quo. These battles have generally been initiated by black leaders who were supported by the

316

black masses. While some white allies have accompanied our brothers and sisters in these great crusades for justice, the initial moves and leadership were the result of having learned the harsh lesson that those in power do not give it up voluntarily or graciously. Our gains have come, largely, as the result of considerable pressure from among such giants as Frederick Douglass, Sojourner Truth, Booker T. Washington, W. E. B. DuBois, Marcus Garvey, A. Philip Randolph, Thurgood Marshall, Adam Clayton Power, Jr., James Farmer, Martin Luther King, Jr., Malcolm X, Fannie Lou Hamer, Harriet Tubman, and Jesse Jackson—among many other stalwart, everyday folks in the trenches.

As The Ohio State University chalked up significant gains in the area of diversity, I continued to be involved in telling the story of how we were making long strides in the right direction toward our goal of equal opportunity. It has been my privilege to deliver addresses or serve as a consultant at many of our leading colleges and universities, including Howard, Dillard, Hampton, Kenyon, Rutgers, Oakwood, College of William and Mary, Denison, Oberlin, Wilberforce, University of Wisconsin, Spelman, University of Maryland, University of Missouri, University of Kentucky, College of Holy Cross, University of Nebraska, University of Tennessee, University of Texas, University of Illinois, University of Michigan, Vanderbilt University, West Point Military Academy, and many others.

Faced with a growing assertiveness among various organizations to focus their energies and discussions on issues of diversity throughout the higher education community, I have been invited to address some very prestigious organizations. I was the speaker for the Sixth Annual Conference of Ford Foundation Doctoral and Post-doctoral Fellows that was sponsored by the National Academy of Sciences in Washington, D.C., on November 6, 1987. Earlier that year, as mentioned before, I was invited to meet and consult with fifteen vice chancellors of the Wisconsin System of Higher Education to discuss and plan long-range goals for the access and retention of students of color. We met on the main campus of the University of Madison.

I have always enjoyed the fervor and festiveness of luncheon and banquet settings. There is a spirit of warmth, aliveness, and expectation that marks such occasions with limitless sparkle and ardor. I'm especially reminded of the great enjoyments that I experienced when speaking for the Jefferson Awards Luncheon at the Hyatt Regency in Columbus, for the annual Graduate School Banquet at Michigan State University, for the Oklahoma Achievers Banquet, for the Ohio Department of Education Statewide Conference, for the University of Western Kentucky's Spring

Conference, for the Council of Graduate Schools National Conference Luncheon, for the Southern College Placement Association's Annual Luncheon, for the Ohio Baptist Ministers Association Annual Banquet, for the Ohio Society of Professional Engineers, for the Ohio Association of Student Personnel Administrators, for the Ohio ACT Assembly, for the CIL Annual Conference of Graduate Education, and for the Fiftieth Anniversary UNCF Banquet, among others. These highly publicized and highly spirited occasions seem to generate a lofty sense of keen focus and inspiring delivery that captured my imagination as in other settings. I am always amazed and somewhat embarrassed when I see a crowd jumping and standing to its feet in exuberant and enthusiastic applause at the conclusion of one of my speeches. I have never quite figured our the formula that brings such electricity to such occasions. Quite often, amidst such applause, I stand stunned as I mentally recount the fact that I had failed to mention some of the key points that I had planned to say.

Nevertheless, I am always thankful for God's blessings at such times. I have often felt drained and empty following such presentations. But God is so good, and I can only thank Him for filling in the gaps, standing in the breach, and giving me the gift of speaking from the deep recesses of my soul what I feel, what I believe, and what I know to be the truth in my heart of hearts.

I learned early in my professional life that there is no substitute for organization in the preparation of a speech. Once one decides on the specific purpose of his/her speech, then it is important to organize the speech into certain main ideas or principal divisions that will enable the speaker to achieve his/her objectives. These main ideas are the framework for the building that the speaker intends to erect during the process of giving the speech. These main ideas must always be adapted to meet the needs of the audience and the occasion. But when all is said and done, it is the supporting materials that are used in the speech that will determine how effective that speech will be. Audiences are not moved by vague generalities. They are convinced of a point of view through the use of examples, comparisons, testimony, illustrative stories, poetry, statistics, and personal experiences. These content variables must, however, be married to a style that includes enthusiasm, sincerity, audibility, clarity, coherence and a well-paced delivery.

I have always tried to be so full of my subject in terms of its content, and so convinced of its value that I can make my address interesting and believable to the audience to which I am speaking. When I am speaking, I make it a point to establish contact with individuals in the audience, speaking as if I am conversing with them in private conversation. In this

318

way, I can get a barometric reading on how the presentation is being received. The best time to get a hold on the audience is at the beginning. If they are lost at that juncture, it is difficult to regain their attention after that.

The ebb and flow of enthusiasm during a speech feeds both the speaker and the audience. There is a circle and cycle of communication that begins with the speaker setting goals, and to set goals requires planning, and planning requires analysis. To implement, one must organize. To organize, one must develop ideas that meet the needs of the audience. To communicate those ideas, one must motivate. To motivate, one must share one's sincerest beliefs. To share, one must care; and to care, one must believe in the value of each person. And to believe in the value of each person, one must present oneself in such a way, and with such warmth, congeniality and tact, that it will inspire belief in the person who is speaking and in what the person is saying.

Next to the luncheon and banquet circuits, I prize the opportunity to challenge youth in commencement settings. It has been my privilege and delight to address graduating classes at Alabama A&M University, Columbus Union College, Albany (Georgia) State University, Wilberforce University, Loma Linda University, Topeka (Kansas) High School (my high school alma mater), Howard University, Shaw University, Tennessee Technological University, Barber Scotia College, Atlantic Union College, Oakwood College, and The Ohio State University. It is no wonder that on such pulsating occasions such a sophisticated group of graduates are not always quick to grasp the essential points that are being addressed. They, too, like the members of the audience, can let their minds wander as the fanfare and loftiness of the moment can become so intoxicating.

Most noteworthy among my many commencement addresses were the opportunities that awaited me in addressing the Ph.D. graduates at Howard University on May 6, 1987, and the Oakwood College graduating class on June 2, 1991. The exercises connected with my address at Oakwood were held in the Oakwood College Church, a magnificent edifice that is the crown and glory of black Seventh-day Adventists. The sanctuary that accommodates more than three thousand people was packed from top to bottom as I challenged the class to "Remember"—to remember the sacrificial contributions of their parents, guardians, relatives and friends toward their educational pursuits, to remember the counsel and instruction of their dedicated teachers, to remember their African heritage and historical roots, to remember their social responsibility to champion the causes of the less fortunate and those who are dispossessed in our society, and to remember their religious and spiritual moorings—making Jesus Christ the center of their lives. Of all the speeches that I have ever given, I somehow felt that this particular one fulfilled its promise of blessing on all who were assembled. God had moved in a most remarkable way, as His spirit lifted me into realms unimaginable as my brain, heart, and soul exploded with a succession of inspiring ideas that had not been a part of my preparation. Once again, I was indebted to God for His towering presence on that occasion. I was not slow to learn that angels had been watching over me. I sought seriously to exempt myself from any personal vanity as the audience stood and rendered spontaneous and thunderous applause for an extended period of time. Their response was a ringing avalanche that underscored the reality that it is no secret what God can do!

I have introduced some of my experiences and successes on the public platform—not to snub the major focus of my activities at The Ohio State University—but to indicate my response to the outstretched hands of those who invited me to share my experiences and efforts at Ohio State, distinguished once again for its willingness to begin new initiatives in the difficult and politically sensitive area of racial diversity. Nevertheless, Ohio State, like other four-year institutions of higher education began to experience a severe drop in the enrollment of African-American students in the latter part of the 1980s. Additionally, the retention and graduation rates of African-American undergraduate students began to decline appreciably. In an attempt to reverse this very negative trend, a university-wide committee was formed to correct the situation. As a result, a strategy was proposed, and it was called " Action Plan: Recruitment and Retention of Black Students at The Ohio State University." Dr. Barbara M. Newman, associate provost, served as chair of the committee, which included Dr. James Bishop, special assistant to the provost; Dr. Sue Blanshan, director of the Office of Human Relations; Dr. Anne Simpson, director of the Center for Teaching Excellence; Dr. Franklin Simpson, director of the Office of Affirmative Action; Dr. Russell Spillman, vice provost for student affairs; Dr. Mac Stewart, associate dean of University College, and myself.

The plan was developed because of the clear and unmistakable commitment of President Edward Jennings to affirmative action. He, beyond a doubt, wanted the university to continue its role as a national leader in the recruitment and retention of black students. The action plan was a comprehensive team effort involving faculty, staff, students, alumni, and administrative input. The plan was discussed with the Council of Deans, with black faculty at a special meeting, with over a hundred student leaders, and at four open meetings where comments and suggestions were

320

encouraged and welcomed. Hundreds of copies of the plan were distributed throughout the university to the various colleges on campus and to the executive committee of the American Association of University Professors.

President Jennings opened the university Senate's first meeting of the 1987–88 academic year and challenged the assembled group in these words during the final and climactic point of his speech.

> The final but no less critical issue for this university in the coming year is affirmative action. This issue is fundamental to advancing one of our greatest strengths—our diversity. Diversity is central to our mission as a land-grant university. It is central to our identity as a major research university. It is central to our potential as a preeminent institution. It is central to our goal of having the very best faculty, staff, and students in our midst. And it is absolutely essential to the creation of educated women and men.

Jennings pulled no punches in admitting that the university had been inept in its approach to improving diversity on campus. He underscored his point in severe terms:

> I need only to look around this room and note that this university Senate is essentially a white organization. Indeed, as I review my own staff or as I review the Council of Deans, I see the rare exception; but those areas also remain too much white male preserves.

One of the happiest results of the action plan was the implementation and development of a pioneering Young Scholars Program which would target sixth and seventh graders from around the state who would be admitted to Ohio State if they pursued and completed an appropriate college preparatory curriculum. This program was designed so that the students would have continuing contact with the university and attend summer programs at Ohio State. To date, the Young Scholars Program has successfully involved nearly two thousand students from the major metropolitan areas of Ohio.

Another gratifying result of the action plan was the fact that Dr. Jennings closed the door on those excuses that were constantly being used in order to maintain the status quo. He cut the legs out from under those who always focused on the problem without offering any meaningful solutions. He expressed his sentiments in this terse statement:

> We have all used excuses. We claim that we cannot do anything about this because these students are unprepared. But if we look at

the students at Ohio State who are in the top ten percent nationally in ACT scores, the graduation rate for black students is roughly fifty percent, compared to a graduation rate of seventy-five percent for all such students.

For those who use the excuse of pool size, he urged them to increase the enrollment of blacks at the undergraduate, masters, and doctoral levels. He also indicated that we should not hide behind the traditional academic reluctance to hire our own. He suggested that the advantages of diversity and quality outweigh the disadvantages of becoming too insular. Jennings put real teeth into the action plan by adding two million dollars to the five million dollars the university was already spending annually on affirmative action. He promised the carrot and the stick by declaring that incentive funding would be available to those units that demonstrated recruitment and retention results of students and faculty. He also stated that concomitant sanctions would be developed and applied to those units that failed to reach affirmative action goals.

The Action Plan had three major goals:

- To increase the pool of qualified black youth who would be admissible to a four-year college after completing a college preparatory curriculum.
- To increase the accessibility of The Ohio State University to black undergraduates, to black graduate and professional students, and to black faculty and staff through creative and effective recruitment and retention strategies.
- To create a university environment, enhanced by its diversity in which each member of the community feels welcomed, respected, and appreciated, and is encouraged to develop to the fullest of his/her talents and potential.

During the year, Dr. James Bishop was appointed as a special assistant to the provost to develop the Young Scholars Program. Extremely well-qualified and as an articulate spokesman for higher education, Dr. Bishop was extremely well-suited for the position. As a Massachusetts Institute of Technology Ph.D. recipient in the field of Inorganic Chemistry, Dr. Bishop had served as associate dean of student affairs at MIT, as dean of students at Amherst College, and as vice provost for university life at the University of Pennsylvania before coming to Ohio State.

In order to attract Dr. Bishop to Ohio State, he was offered an annual salary that exceeded mine by approximately $13,000. I had no quarrel with what they were offering him, but I took the occasion to parlay my salary to the level that was equal to his. I challenged both

Provost Myles Brand and President Jennings to set my salary on the basis of what I had already accomplished if they were going to set his on the basis of what they expected him to accomplish. With emphatic forthrightness, this was the one time during my career when I felt that my terms were non-negotiable, and I was unwilling to budge, considering the sixteen years of untiring and pioneering service that I had rendered the university in the area of affirmative action. To their credit, both Jennings and Brand deserve unstinted appreciation for supporting my requirement without the slightest debate or hesitation.

I gave full-hearted support to the initiatives and strategies proposed in the action plan over the next year. As I plunged into my work with all the enthusiasm and vigor of past years, the steady and prolonged waging of engagement to advance programs of diversity began to take its toll. I began to recognize the need for safeguarding my health. After all, I had had two major operations; and the results in each case might have been disastrous, except for God's grace. Good sense suggested that it would be counterproductive to remain tied to a twelve- to fifteen-hour daily grind of activity. I had no intention of wearing myself out on the job before I could accomplish some of creative interests that I assumed that the future had in store for me. I simply did not want to squander my remaining years by pushing papers and fighting daily battles to jostle the consciences of those in power to do for people of color those things that most Americans expect to be accorded to themselves at birth.

Once I had made the decision to retire, I felt free as a bird. I had no intention of developing a rocking chair existence. I simply wanted my schedule to be my own, to go and come as I pleased, rather than to be the tool of someone else's scheme or agenda on a daily basis. So on May 17, 1988, I sent the following letter to President Jennings:

Dear Ed:

This communication is to formally announce my retirement to be effective December 31, 1988. It was on June 1, 1971 that I first connected with The Ohio State University as associate dean of the graduate school, and I have never regretted my decision.

This university is one of the most progressive institutions of higher education in America today. It is alive with new academic challenges, revitalization and growth as well as maintaining some of the treasured traditions that have contributed to its reputation as an ideal quality institution.

I have appreciated so much the support which your administration has given the Office of Minority Affairs during my tenure, and because of that fact it has become a national model. Given that distinction and the taut tenor of the times in the area of affirmative action, it is essential that the university accelerate its pace in the arena of minority programming, and, of course, the action plan speaks to that commitment.

Finally, permit me to urge you to move expeditiously in the search for my successor. The OMA staff is eagerly concerned, as I am, about the future direction of the Office of Minority Affairs. Early in the year, I indicated to them that the search would commence during winter quarter. You should understand their apprehensions, not having been apprised of any developments at this point. Once again, I urge you to conduct a national search. We need to put to rest the various rumors floating about. It is important that the immeasurable gains of our rich history in the Office of Minority Affairs have your reassuring touch.

With best wishes, I am

Sincerely yours,

Frank W. Hale, Jr.
Special Assistant to the President and
Vice Provost for Minority Affairs

One of the happiest results of my decision was the great and gracious response which I received from many of my campus colleagues. Such irony! It was interesting to note that the very one who had stirred up such a storm of controversy over the years was now receiving ringing declarations of applause. Whether those reactions were sincere or not, I knew that, with God's help, I had left an enduring imprint on the university community. Even though Ohio State was in the heart of middle America with all of its ingrained conservatism, a distinctive flavor of hope remained within my psyche. There lingered a kind of incurable optimism that silences doubt even in the face of inexplicable circumstances.

Just the very thought of retirement caused me to reflect upon all of the blessings that I had enjoyed over the nearly four decades of my profession as a teacher and as an educational administrator. I could never escape the profound contributions that so many have made to both my personal and professional progress. Many influences have contributed to the thrilling saga of my life. My parents, Novella Esther Banks Hale and Frank Wilbur Hale, Sr., contributed powerfully to my upbringing. They played such an indispensable role in helping me to develop the confidence that was necessary to deal with the adjustments that I would have to make in society because of the color of my skin. They superbly equipped me to recognize the importance of self-reliance, that kind of intellectual stamina that rises to the top with instinctive courage when the chips are down. Life was never a humdrum experience around our home. Both my mother and father had marvelous powers of the mind. They were great planners. Nothing was left to chance. Whatever task was before them caught the full impact of their focus with no waste of energy. I never knew them to be second class in anything, and that passion for quality and excellence was never lost on me.

Having decided to retire from the boundless details of full-time administration, I began to pursue opportunities that would offer me engagements as a consultant. It was my intention to intersperse my retreat from around-the-clock commitments and part-time consultancies with some volunteer activities, the satisfaction derived from lecturing and writing, and a measured degree of traveling and merry-making. Other diversions beckoned for favored attention, and they were put on hold until I could sift even more concerning future activities. I was certain, however, that I was far too energetic, creative, ambitious, and resourceful to be confined to a life of laborless drudgery.

Once I had announced my retirement, it seemed as if a torrent of activities engaged my time and attention. President Jennings invited me to give the summer quarter commencement address on September 1, 1988. Every year, in its four commencements, one for each season, Ohio State graduates more than than ten thousand students at each of its ceremonies. That first day of September is a day that I shall never forget. It was full of pageantry with colorful regalia, extended processions and untempered exhilaration and excitement. The graduates marched with heads held high as parents, guardians, relatives, and friends cheered lustily. St. John's Arena was packed to capacity with thirteen thousand cheering witnesses. It was a glorious moment for the graduates and glorious moment for me as well, as I challenged them to understand that they were on "Borrowed Time." I reminded them that, "From the moment you were born, the clock began ticking away the seconds, the minutes, and the hours—time that was subtracted from the time you have allotted to do what you need to do to make a difference in the world." Thus I challenged them to:

> Step into life and harness it. Step up in life by ever advancing yourself to reach your full potential. Step over the obstacles in life that people would place in your way; and step out of the crowd, and be your own person—challenging what must be challenged—staking your claim on what is right and what is reasonable.

As the end of the year approached, a retirement committee was formed to plan a festive event in my honor. It had never occurred to me that such a swan song ceremony as the committee had in mind would be in the works. After thirty-eight years in higher education, I knew that it was time for me to unload the load that had already begun to compromise my time, my health, and other interests that were just waiting behind stage to emerge.

The committee was an exceptional one, as it was composed of forty-three community and campus leaders who were known for doing things right. Mr. Lewis R. Smoot, Sr., the president of the Sherman R. Smoot Construction Company, was the honorary chairman; Ms. Linda Jackson, director of administration for The Ohio State University Office of Minority Affairs, and Mr. Clifford Tyree, retired youth services administrator for the city of Columbus, were co-chairpersons. The committee roster included Mr. James Allen, Ms. Wanda Barnett, Attorney Otto Beatty, Jr., Attorney Napoleon Bell, Dr. Wilbur C. Blount, Ms. Shirley Bridges, Dr. Mary Claytor, Ms. Marcia Conley, Mr. Bob Cunningham, Attorney Jackie-Souel Downey, Ms. Shirley Duncan, Attorney Ben Espy, Ms. Kathy Espy, Rev. Phale Hale, Dr. David Hamlar, Mr. Jerry Hammond, Dr. George T. Harding, Mr. Earl Harris, Ms. Loretta Heard, Rev. Luther Holland, Ms. Betty Howton, Mr. James K. Jackson, Ms. Linda Jackson, Mr. Amos Lynch, Ms. Connie Mayfield, Rep. Ray Miller, Mr. Curtis Moody, Dr. Lester Morrow, Mr. Gerard Mullins, Dr. William Nelson, Jr., Ms. Loretta Patterson, Dr. Margaret Roberts, Dr. John H. Rosemond, Ms. Linda Sanders, Mr. Lewis R. Smoot, Sr., Dr. Mac Stewart, Mr. Roger Street, Ms. Charleta Tavares, Mr. Clifford Tyree, Mr. Lawrence Williamson, Dr. C. Dexter Wise III, and Elder Walter Wright.

This very fine group of people began their task with a high degree of unity and enthusiasm. It is my understanding that, from the very beginning of their planning, they caught the spirit of a religious revival as they stirred the community into action in support of their efforts. The date for the celebration-retirement program was set for December 4, 1988, at the Aladdin Temple Shrine. Strategies of various kinds were used to promote the affair. Mobilizing the mind of the community to participate in such a major undertaking was the urgent task facing the committee. Headed by Linda Jackson and Clifford Tyree, the committee was gifted with zealous and imaginative leadership. As the date of the occasion drew near, an exhilarating wave of excitement swept the community and the $25 tickets began to sell like wildfire.

I will never forget the electricity that was on the evening of that special event. Hundreds of people converged on the Aladdin Temple Shrine

326

even before the doors were open to the public. It was a cold but clear December evening as 1200 patrons ignored the chill of the wintry air to catch the exuberant contagion of an event which many called the largest and most colorful retirement gala that had ever occurred in Columbus. Tables lined with the most beautiful arrangements of poinsettias created a decorative pattern of crimson and green. I stood open-mouthed and in optic fixation as I felt totally enveloped by the charm, beauty and glow of an exquisitely decorated ballroom. Its very aesthetic essence reminded me that the world does not consist only of asphalt, concrete, wood and steel. The table settings, augmented by candlelight, were delicate, elegant and provocative. To all of this must be added the choice assortment of fashionable people who appeared to be enjoying themselves immensely and nodding, speaking and exchanging greetings all around the hall before settling at their designated tables for the evening. The corsage business had to have been booming that day as the ladies were laden with the most luxurious and most colorful assortment of blossoms that I had ever seen to accompany their gorgeous dinner dresses, evening gowns, and attractive attire. The men weren't taking a back seat either, as many were remarkably handsome and decked to the tee in superbly tailored suits, tuxedos, and African regalia. The men were uncommonly dapper, and the ladies were uncommonly beautiful and of sweet disposition as the banquet program got underway.

While I did not know or recognize all of the personalities who were present, I could tell by the remarkable turnout that the evening would be luminous with the tinsel and frills of Christmas decorations and with the gaiety that summons the most effusive expressions of enjoyment on such occasions. Ruth, my lovely wife of forty-one years at the time, was overwhelmingly beautiful for the occasion. She was too natural and too honest to be anything else. My oldest child, Ifeoma Kwesi (christened Ruth), glowed with unpretentious radiance. Sheri, my youngest daughter, seemed transfixed by all that was taking place as almost everything and everybody caught her wondering eye. Frank, my son, followed his normal routine—saying nothing, but taking in everything. My dad was enjoying every moment. He was so proud that the occasion was in my honor that he whispered in my ear at an appropriate moment, "Frank, oh, if Mother could only be here to witness this." She had passed on three years earlier, but she had played no small part in whatever flashes of success had been mine.

As the program began, several hundred would-be ticket purchasers were turned away because the place was filled to capacity. The Honorable Ray Miller, general assemblyman of House District 29, served as master of ceremonies. Elder Walter Wright, the pastor of Ephesus Seventh-day Adventist Church, gave the invocation. The very best in music was provided by "Oasis," a magnificent choir of young adults under the direction of Dr. James Stewart, Pastor Wintley Phipps, Pastor Shelton Kilby, Sherilyn Hale-Thomas, and Clifton Davis.

Reverend Jesse Jackson, the president of the National Rainbow Coalition, gave a stirring keynote address and lauded me for my contributions to American higher education. He added that many of his speeches reflect the philosophy and input of our discussions. "Dr. Hale has beat back hatred and indifference with love and care... through it all he has not negotiated his soul," he continued. He further acknowledged our relationship with Wintley Phipps when he said, "When you hear Wintley Phipps at the Democratic National Convention, you hear Frank Hale, because I would not have known Wintley if it were not for Frank Hale."

Presentations were made in my behalf by Dr. Philip Jordan, the president of Kenyon College; Dr. Calvin Rock, vice president of the General Conference of Seventh-day Adventists; Elder Delbert Baker, editor of *Message* magazine; Dr. Roy Malcolm, dean of college relations at Oakwood College; Dr. Carolyn Hagey-Mayo, executive director, West Tennessee Area Health Education Center; Dr. Mylas Brand, vice president for academic affairs and provost at The Ohio State University; Dr. William E. Nelson, Jr., professor of Black Studies and Political Science; Dr. Amy Riemenschneider, chairperson, University Senate on Women and Minorities; Mrs. Shirley Duncan and Mrs. Gloria Jefferson of the Columbus Links; and Mr. Lewis R. Smoot, Sr., president of the Sherman R. Smoot Construction Company.

Among the representatives from Oakwood College and Huntsville, Alabama, were Mrs. Inez Booth, Mrs. Anne Galley, Mr. and Mrs. Lynn Ross, Mrs. Clara Rock, Dr. Jannith Lewis, Dr. Francis Bliss, Dr. Lucille Lacy, and Mrs. Gladys Lacy.

I was especially blessed to have my father, Frank W. Hale, Sr. (Chief), my children—Ifeoma Kwesi, Frank Hale III and his family, Sherilyn Thomas and her family, my ninety-one year old aunt, Mrs. Isy Young of Youngstown, Ohio; my cousin, Dr. Marian Patterson of Los Angeles, California; and my dearest friends, Vertis and Francis Barnes of San Diego, California—all joining in supporting Ruth and me on this very illustrious occasion.

In my farewell response, I savored a special tribute in this passage:

> I want to dedicate this very special moment to that vast army of
> black, brown, red and yellow diamonds yet unborn who will some day
> enjoy the full fresh air of freedom. I want to dedicate this moment to

328

our allies in the struggle—black, white, red, yellow and brown, who know that we can never stop marching until racism is conquered and the entire surface of the world can bear the triumphant footprints of freedom.

At the conclusion of the program the sponsoring committee encouraged Ruth and me to take a vacation as they presented us with a check for $5000. What a send off! Reverend Phale Hale, pastor of the Union Grove Baptist Church, gave the benediction.

It was less than one month prior to my retirement ceremony that I was shocked and happily amazed beyond belief when I went to my office on the morning of November 7, 1988. One of my colleagues approached me with a hearty, "Congratulations, Frank," as he pointed to a *Columbus Dispatch* newspaper clipping from the morning newspaper. The headlines read, "Student Center Named to Honor Hale." It was an action that the board of trustees had voted at the recommendation of President Edward H. Jennings. At the same time, I was voted vice provost and professor emeritus, and an endowed scholarship fund was established in my name. I had not had the slightest hint that such recognitions would be coming my way. It was a humbling conclusion to certain contributions that were made possible by the sacrifices of many—so many who had come before me in tougher times—and who sparkled like bright stars in the dark skies of a system that either denied or distorted their existence. It has always been my objective to employ education as the vehicle for liberating our people from those beliefs and actions which make them less than human and more subject to the deadening effects of oppression. As educators, it is our privilege to blow into flame the dying embers of those whose humanity has become disillusioned and disaffected by the more profane, more profligate, and more racist aspects of society. If any way, my life has helped to make even the slightest degree of positive difference in this regard, then **to God be the glory!**

Chapter 15

Preparation for Retirement
and Beyond

———————◦◦◦◦———————

I retired from The Ohio State University effective December 31, 1988, and I joined the staff at Kenyon College in Gambier, Ohio, as the executive assistant to the president for multicultural affairs on January 1, 1989. It had never occurred to me that I would give up my position at Ohio State and suddenly take up another within twenty-four hours. Since June of 1988, I had been serving as a part-time consultant at Kenyon College, and President Philip Jordan had encouraged me to become a part-time member of his staff once I completed my requirements at Ohio State. Kenyon College, founded in 1824, has an established reputation as one of the strongest academic private colleges in the country. In general, it admits only those students whose high school grades and qualifying test scores are among the highest. It is often referred to as the *little Harvard* among colleges and universities in Ohio.

President Jordan indicated that he wanted me on board to promote cultural diversity among Kenyon's campus constituents. I had earlier prompted him to be aware that the institution needed to develop programs that would recognize the contributions and achievements of the various ethnic groups that make up the mosaic of America. When I arrived at Kenyon, there were fifteen African-American students enrolled on campus among fifteen hundred students. Their presence represented a paltry one percent of the student population. I immediately set out to focus on the recruitment of students of color, concentrating in Cincinnati, Cleveland and Columbus.

Recognizing that room, board and tuition amounted to nearly $20,000 a year, I knew that it was necessary to increase the package of financial assistance if we were to have any success in the recruitment of African-American and Latino students in particular. With President Jordan's support, I arranged to have a luncheon meeting with John McCoy, the president of Bank One in Columbus. I apprised him of the need for the campus to become more diverse and that we would need more grant and scholarship money in order to attract students of color. He was open to the idea of providing ten $15,000 scholarships to highly capable students; consequently, he contributed $150,000 to establish a scholarship fund for students of color. As a consequence of his contribution and solid recruitment endeavors, we were able to enroll a total of forty-five African-American students for the 1990–91 academic years, raising their percentage on campus from one percent to three percent.

I discovered to my discomfort that senior administrators assumed that the student body was thoroughly integrated then. It was during my first year at Kenyon that I put the issues of diversity into high gear. As the college administration appeared ready to hoist the banner of inclusiveness near the top of its agenda, I moved expeditiously to capture the positive mood which the merits of this new vision offered. I invited two top-notch professionals to address the faculty on the subject of diversity in two separate colloquiums. Dr. Valora Washington, vice president for research and grants administration at Antioch College, spoke to the faculty on August 23, 1989, on the topic, "Creating a Campus Community of Substance and Spirit." On October 10, 1989, Dr. Reginald Wilson, senior scholar with the American Council on Education, addressed the campus community on the topic, "The Status of American Minorities in Higher Education: Where Do We Go From Here?"

The 1989–90 academic year kept me very busy, hammering out in a whirlwind of various activities, programmatic plans for the black student union and Adelante, the Latino organization. I was clearly vulnerable to the criticism of conservative elements on campus as I became involved in an assortment of multicultural activities:

- Developing and implementing the refurbishing of the black student union.
- Organizing a campus-wide effort in preparing Christmas boxes for community families.
- Conducting luncheon diversity workshops.
- Planning a black/Latino scholarship luncheon.
- Co-sponsoring Dr. Jack Shaheen's lecture on "The Arab and the Muslim in American Culture"—April 6, 1990.

- Sponsoring the all-campus convocation featuring Reverend Jesse Jackson—April 26, 1990.

It was during that same year that I proposed and designed a program of eminent ethnic scholars and performers to visit the campus during the 1991–92 academic year. The proposal was an attempt to make multiculturalism meaningful and useful in aiding the campus community to understand and appreciate the contributions of people of color to American society. The proposal was designed to do this in the following ways:

- To increase campus and public knowledge, sensitivity and awareness of the various individuals and groups that have contributed to the American culture.
- To review the historical and sociological problems of ethnic minority groups.
- To humanize the campus community against racial and ethnic polarization that has the potential to be divisive and destructive.
- To listen and interact with those eminent persons of color who have been victims of racism in order to provide balance to the testimony of those persons who have been members of the powerful and dominating groups.
- To engage the expertise of faculty and staff scholars as provocateurs who can encourage discussion among visiting lecturers, the campus community and members of the public from communities that are contiguous to Kenyon College.

The proposal was approved for funding, and the calendar of events identifies the guest participants who visited the campus.

August 21, 1991—Dr. Samuel D. Proctor
professor emeritus, Rutgers University

September 17, 1991—Dr. Carlos E. Cortes
professor of History, University of California, Riverside

October 15, 1991—Dr. Asa Hilliard III
Fuller E. Callaway Professor of Urban Education, Georgia State University

October 24, 1991—Dr. Molefi Asante
chair and professor, Department of African American Studies, Temple University

January 16, 1992—Dr. Mary F. Berry
Geraldine Segal Professor of Social Thought and History, University of Pennsylvania

February 8, 1992—Attorney Patricia Russell-McCloud, J.D. president, Russell-McCloud and Associates

April 4, 1992—Women of the Calabash (concert)

Even though I had retired from full time duties at The Ohio State University and was willing to accept some limited responsibilities at Kenyon College, the telephone calls and mail continued to mount, requesting my appearance as a speaker or as a consultant around the country. I was quite willing to accept many of these appointments, because I still felt inclined to bear some sense of responsibility for preparing our youth, in particular, to face the inexorable realities of life.

Only a brief look at my calendar indicates that the lecture circuit placed a high demand on my time and energy. My lectureship schedule at one point approached marathon proportions over a nine-month period:

- "Reading Maketh a Full Person," September 24, 1989
  Oakwood College (Alabama)
- "The African American in Academia in the 21st Century,"October 4, 1989
  University of Cincinnati
- "The Christian in the Academy," October 14, 1989
  Columbia University, St. Paul's Chapel, New York City
- "Assessing Institutional Commitment on Issues of Diversity," November 3, 1989
  Virginia Council on Higher Education, Richmond, Virginia
- "Know Then Thyself," November 14, 1989
  Honors Convocation, Union College, Lincoln, Nebraska
- "Black History—What About a Black Future?" February 5, 1990
  Shawnee State (Ohio) University
- "Affirmative Action—Making It Work," February 8, 1990
  University of Louisville
- "Give It Your Best Shot," March 11, 1990
  Pillsbury and the University of Minnesota, Minneapolis, Minnesota
- "Building Minority Programs," March 29, 1990
  University of Tennessee, Knoxville, Tennessee
- "Establishing and Maintaining Institutional Commitment," April 11, 1990
  Columbus College (Georgia)
- "The World is Yours," April 13, 1990
  Graduate Education Conference, CIC, University of Illinois, Chicago
- "Changes, Challenges, and Opportunities," April 29, 1990
  Ohio Association of Equal Opportunity Personnel Conference, Columbus

- "The Black Male: An Endangered Species," May 4, 1990
  National Rainbow Coalition Regional Conference, Hotel Westin, Atlanta
- "What's Happening in African American Education?" May 4, 1990
  Third National Conference on Blacks in Higher Education, Mariott Marquis Hotel, Atlanta
- "Keep on Stepping," May 12, 1990
  Commencement Address, Shaw University, Raleigh, North Carolina; awarded the Honorary Doctor of Humane Letters degree

It was during that same school year, on April 22, 1990, that I was elected as the nineteenth member of The Topeka (Kansas) High School Hall of Fame from among more than 25,000 of its graduates. Shortly thereafter, on May 5, 1990, Ruth and I were flown to the University of Nebraska where I, along with four others, was the recipient of the Alumni Achievement Award. It was a year full of pleasant surprises as I was also appointed to the Advisory Council of the College of William and Mary.

All was not peaches and cream or perfume and roses during my tenure at Kenyon College. The college was immersed in a tradition of conservativism that colored so much of its image, its curriculum, and its selection of faculty and students.

By the end of my second year at Kenyon, I began to sense that President Jordan's approach to diversity was little more than window dressing. He began making cuts in my budget, and freezing my travel to those professional conferences where vital contacts were made for recruiting students and faculty of color. I was not restrained in letting him know that to include such an infant office in the across-the-board cuts to which more mature departments were subjected was not fair or equitable. I knew that my days were numbered because I could not face or accept the sterile approach that was beginning to take place in an institution where the record for attracting and accommodating people of color was historically shabby.

Had it not been for the warmth and congeniality of the African-American students and the comraderie of Mila Collins, the assistant dean of students; Michelle Gilliard and Matthew Davis, assistant directors of admission; Ric Sheffield, assistant professor of Sociology and Legal Studies; and William (Bill) Brown, assistant director of Physical Education and Athletics, as well as head basketball coach, life would have been far less tolerable. I too enjoyed the dedicated collegial association of certain white allies who were also committed to the struggle of equal opportunity. They included John Anderson, Howard Sachs, Andrew Foster, Peter Rutkoff, Miriam Dean-Otting, Juan DePascuale, Susan Spaid, Vernon Schubel, and my wonderful secretary, Juanita Newman.

It was the African-American and Latino students who were so open and hungry for learning who captured my attention and who responded to sound advice and counsel. Among the noteworthy of them who were solid and stable activists were April Garrett, Stephanie Garrett, Princess Hogue, Kendra Stamper, Rebecca Vasquez, Evelyn Ortiz, and Asha Ragin.

I found them so alive and articulate and not at all content with verbal solutions to either real or hypothetical problems. They would shuttle in and out of my office with regularity, seeking my judgment on sundry matters and savoring the widest possible freedom which I gave to their convictions and challenges. They were a great bunch. I have found that bright young people provide me with an indispensable laboratory for keeping abreast of the contemporary issues of the time. They keep you thinking and working intelligently and energetically if you only take the time to listen. All in all, my experiences at Kenyon were sweet and sour, rich and demanding. In the meanwhile, Ruth and I had purchased a lovely A-frame cabin and fifty-seven acres of virgin rustic woods right off Highway 33 on Highway 180 in Hocking Hills. This happy location among the undulating hills provided us with a serene atmosphere of country and rural life in pastoral settings. We had been richly blessed to purchase this lovely acreage from Representative Michael Stinziano of the Ohio General Assembly. The odor of towering pines, flowering shrubs, and the songs of birds offered us the kind of weekend tranquility that was so badly needed after being involved in a substantial schedule of assignments and involvement at Kenyon College and out-of-town assignments as a lecturer/consultant.

While I found the searing impact of conventional conservatism at Kenyon College disheartening, I gained a great deal of respect for President Jordan whose leadership style was tremendously energetic, and as a result he helped to create an invigorating academic climate. As a person, he was confident, buoyant, and optimistic—a born booster, a great storyteller, and a scholar par excellence. Although he professed to be essentially democratic, as a creature of his ultraconservative environment, he gave me the very distinct impression that he didn't believe that an institution could promote a full measure of equality and still be excellent too. While I am sure that we were both somewhat skeptical of each other's meaning of democracy, we, nevertheless, respected the intensity of each other's viewpoints. We operated on similar terms when it came

336

to the rhetoric of diversity, but Jordan's cautious approach to promoting and implementing racial diversity on campus convinced me that he could not be comfortable with the kind of elbow-rubbing equality, unheard of in institutions where the compounded trappings of elitism, rank, position, titles, and honorific offices are so commonplace. And to a great extent, that is the type of institution that Kenyon College is. It is a citadel of retreat from the real heterogeneous world of people—small and great; rich and poor; black, white, red, brown and yellow; educated and uneducated; dignified and undignified; good-humored and mean-spirited; and of the stable and unstable. There was a homogeneity of culture and spirit that could easily make one feel exclusively indebted to the status quo.

When I first joined the staff at Kenyon College, the task force on diversity had already laid the groundwork for the strategies that I would undertake to advance the concept of pluralism on campus. I must give credit to President Jordan for his initial boost and support in addressing issues of equity and inclusivity.

Among the things that my office was able to accomplish during my three and a half years at Kenyon were the following:

- Established Martin Luther King Week as a tradition, and established an annual Martin Luther King Award.
- Organized the Multicultural Affairs Advisory Council as a permanent body to address issues of diversity.
- Initiated an annual faculty/staff colloquium on diversity.
- Supported Black History Month with funds for lecturers and artists.
- Planned and implemented the furnishing of the Black Student Union Ujima Imani Lounge.
- Served as mentor and role model for students and faculty/staff of color.
- Wrote the original proposal to provide merit (honor) scholarships for African-American and Latino students and presented the same to the board of trustees, which was approved by them.
- Spearheaded the efforts of the Multicultural Advisory Council that culminated in the acquisition of a multicultural center and the development of guidelines to deal with student discrimination and harassment.
- Assisted various organizations financially in their efforts to promote multiculturalism.
- Provided sponsorship and financial support for students to attend professional conferences.
- Prepared and distributed a suggested bibliographical entries on people and issues of color to be purchased by the library and the college bookstore.

- Collaborated with and supported Adelante and the Black Student Union.
- Prepared an annual calendar/brochure, highlighting the Eminent Artist and Lecture Series sponsored by the Office of Multicultural Affairs.
- Arranged to get complimentary tickets for students to attend Les Ballet Africans, Ballet Folklorico, and the Columbus Symphony Orchestra.

This chapter would be lacking if I did not express my appreciation to President Jordan and the Kenyon College family for its efforts in assisting me to provide the campus with a greater, yet limited, understanding and appreciation of cultural history and tradition of people of color. I do hope that these initiatives will be sustained. I would hope that my observations—some positive and others not so positive—will be received in the constructive manner in which I intended them relative to my experiences at Kenyon. I do, however, close this chapter of my life with the quiet mix of contentment and measure of fulfillment knowing that I gave the institution the best of what I had to offer.

On May 5, 1992, a group of Ohio State University students called A.C.T.I.O.N. (Afrikans Committed to Improve Our Nation) submitted a list of twenty-two demands to President Gordon Gee and demanded a response by May 12, 1992. In the intervening time between May 5 and May 12, President Gee invited me to the campus to discuss the possibility of a new assignment that would help him to calm racial unrest on the campus. Dr. Gee and I had discussed the possibility of my serving the university in a consulting capacity several months earlier; however, the pressure of the A.C.T.I.O.N. group placed him in the position of offering me the opportunity to serve as a senior counselor/consultant to the president immediately. I accepted his offer on May 12, 1992, and immediately sent a letter of resignation, effective immediately, to President Jordan the next day.

To my great frustration and bewilderment, I discovered on the morning of May 13 that the president had not consulted with the A.C.T.I.O.N. group concerning my appointment. Though it was a tactical and procedural error, certain members of the group felt that Dr. Gee had gone over their heads by not discussing the appointment with them. They insisted that they had no quarrel with me as a person, but with the process of the president not seeking their input in determining who would be the consultant to the president. I resigned the appointment immediately, rather than be caught between the rock and a hard place. Once I had left the president high and dry, it left me outdoors without a position at either OSU or Kenyon. Knowing that, "All things work together for good to them that love the Lord… " I distanced myself from the total situation.

It wasn't long before I established my own consulting firm, TIPS (Technical, Instructional and Professional Support Services). The range and scope of my consultancies have carried me from coast to coast and to high schools, colleges, universities, and to state and national conferences on education, religion, leadership and race relations. It was during the 1960s and 1970s that the nation was on the verge of experiencing a phenomenal boom in the diversity industry. Such phrases as *equal opportunity* and *affirmative action* were in common vogue, and the doors of corporate America and higher education were open and initially receptive to aspiring people of color. By the late 1970s and early 1980s, the mood of the country turned conservative and sour. Creative and inventive programs of equality which had flourished in earlier years became dismantled during an economic climate that brought government spending for human needs to a virtual halt. The private sector, for so long a sanctuary for white entitlement programs, accentuated profit over people. Blacks, who had their foot in the door, found themselves locked into a system where whites only had the keys to promotion. Faced with factors of disillusionment and retrenchment, many blacks withdrew from a chilly climate of locked-in careers. Others were displaced in the face of economic realities. Still others never learned to cope with the competitive corporate or university culture and received their pink slips after the affirmative action surge had lost its initial appeal and momentum.

Conspicuous among the giant consultants in the diversity industry is Dr. Edwin Nichols. With fine presence, flashing eyes, a pleasing voice, and masterful teaching, he has made a thriving livelihood in helping corporate and university executives to achieve employee and student diversity in their organizations. The principal stimuli that have rekindled managerial interest in diversity have been projections of *Workforce 2000*, a report prepared by the Hudson Institute and sponsored by the U.S. Department of Labor. The report indicates that the American work force will become increasingly diverse. The corporate community has concluded that readiness is the key to competition. Mylas Martin, a communications consultant in corporate America, has indicated to me on more than one occasion that a corporation's ability to tap the potential of its employees—regardless of their race, gender, or background—will be a critical determinant of its well being. He, like William Wilson, underscores the declining significance of race, if those seeking job opportunities are able to bring experience, expertise—in short, competence—to the table.

Long before establishing my own consulting firm, as early as 1979, I had waded into the cold waters of attempting to resolve complaints of racism on college campuses. I had been a member of a team of consultants that had attempted to sensitize the Denison University campus community to the effects of institutional racism. I had joined Dr. Robert O. Washington, dean of the College of Social Work at Ohio State University, and Minnie McGee, assistant dean of the College of Engineering, in carving out a three and a half day consultation project (September 20–22 and October 1, 1979) to ascertain as broad a perspective as possible concerning problems of racism at the institution. Our final report was entitled "Matters of Inter-group Relations at Denison University."

It was in 1980 that I got into the full swim of consulting when I was invited to join a team of consultants to visit the United States Military Academy at West Point, New York, to evaluate its commitment to affirmative action and its approach to the principles of social equity and social opportunity. The perception of the Academy's response to black cadets within the student body was not encouraging. I discovered that the black cadets, like black students on most white campuses, reacted to their institution with frustration, defensiveness, and mistrust. As one black cadet remarked, "When I leave the academy and go out to the community, I feel very proud that I'm a cadet at West Point—It feels good to be identified with such a prestigious service academy—My friends and associates are impressed. But, when I return, the minute I hit the gates, I get a sinking feeling in my stomach, because I know once I'm on campus, I'm a nothing again."

Black cadets reported that they were made acutely aware that *black* was not *in* those days. They perceived that there was declining support for the needs and concerns of black cadets. They cited the lack of availability of black social and cultural activities as a case in point. "There is no attempt to meet the needs of the black cadet socially," remarked one cadet. Another offered, "The Dialectic Society (a group that promotes entertainment at West Point) is a clique that has no interest in our welfare." Still another cadet reflected, "It has been four years since the 'B.T. Express' was at the Academy, and no one has been concerned enough about our wishes since, to bring other black groups."

Black cadets felt that the role of the tactical officer was crucial in determining whether or not black cadets got a fair break. They were critical of the rigid and inflexible way in which it appears, in the eyes of some, that the academy responds to misconduct on the part of blacks while being much more lenient on similar cases involving white cadets. They cited the case of a white cadet, who, though having three major violations (drinking on the post, sleeping on the post, and having a female in his room after taps) was retained and was graduated in the Class of 1979. On the other hand, there was a consensus that a black cadet, who had bounced three checks (due to certain mitigating circumstances according to the cadets) and taken unauthorized leave, was given the shaft by being dismissed from the academy. In two other incidents cited, black cadets were incensed over the fact that a white cadet was retained after failing two courses, and a black cadet was dismissed for similar academic deficiencies. The cadets felt that the only thing that made the difference was the fact that the white cadet's tactical officer recommended his retention and the black cadet's tactical officer did not. They were bitterly critical of a system which they felt allowed for too much subjectivity from their point of view.

The black cadets, as a group were totally disconcerted over the fact that a white plebe of Company F-2 wrote a "Role Reversal" pamphlet ("100 Nights"), a book of black jokes which was humiliating and demeaning to black cadets. When he was asked why he wrote the book, the plebe was alleged to have said, "I hate black people." It was reported that the plebe received twenty demerits and twenty-five area tours which, according to black cadets, was only a slap on the wrist.

Verbal abuse of black cadets by white cadets was considered commonplace according to the testimony of black cadets. It took the form of racial slurs, intimidation, *nigger jokes*, or other racial epithets. Some cadets reported that some white cadets, complete with southern drawl, would poke fun at black cadets by using phrases while passing such as *"Hallelujah," "Right on, Brother," "Give me five," "Sho 'nough,"* etc.

Others thought that the military academy's attitude on race was such that it affected both assignments and promotion. "Now that the academy has had its one black brigade commander (Cadet Captain Vince A. Brooks, Jr., Class of 1980), it appears to be back to business as usual," remarked one discouraged cadet.

"John Taylor certainly qualified this year because of his overall academic record, strong leadership, and his superior physical skills. However, he was given a token position on a brigade staff as an athletic officer," deplored one cadet.

The comments of black officers mirrored those of the black cadets. They indicated that there had not been a concerted effort to recruit black officers. In fact, they indicated that there were only two black tenured professors at West Point, Major James Stith and Major Jerome Adams. There was a sweeping consensus among the black officers that they were being systematically excluded from policy-making decisions affecting the lives of black cadets. "No effort has been made to even receive informal input from us," a concerned officer complained.

Administrators at West Point, by and large, felt that the institution's commitment to improving the racial presence and climate at the academy was evidenced by its willingness to develop programs and services for minorities as well as the specific commitment of administrators, faculty and blacks. In our final debriefing session, Commandant Franklin stressed the elasticity of West Point's admissions program in determining a prospective candidate's admissibility. Yet, there was little evidence that the commandant was aware of the extent of the apprehension and unrest that existed among black cadets and black officers with respect to their assessment of the commitment and the atmosphere of the academy with respect to minorities.

Brigadier General Smith, dean of the academic board, indicated that national and responsible efforts were being made to undergird the retention of minorities and women. He indicated that West Point had increased the number of women and minorities on the faculty, had taken more *risk* cases, and had instituted an Underloading Program which permits cadets to take a lighter load when necessary. Lieutenant General Godpaster, superintendent of the academy, indicated that he felt that there were no financial limitations that would hinder the academy from meeting its short-range affirmative action goals.

It was very obvious to me and to other members of the consulting team that the admission and assimilation of minorities and women into the United States Military Academy had not been a simple matter. It was apparent from our investigation that, although blacks were involved in higher education for the same reasons as their white counterparts, they exhibited greater dissatisfaction with the collegiate experience. We listened and recorded the impressions of those who have been involved in both the recruitment and retention of students of color. The crucial test, of course, of an institution's commitment to anything is whether it continues past the initial spurt of its own rhetoric, conviction, enthusiasm, and strategy.

As consultants, we raised a series of critical questions which could be applied to most any campus situation. Among them were the following inquiries:

1. How has the institution responded to its new clientele—people of color and women?

2. Were new departments, committees, positions, established?

3. Did goals change?

4. How was the institution affected?

5. How do majority students and faculty feel about students and faculty of color, and vice versa?

6. How do they actually interact—in class, in meetings, in informal situations, in barracks (residence halls)?

7. Were there new curricula or courses?

8. Did teaching practices change?

9. Did new forms of information gathering begin to appear?

10. Have explicit goals or targets been set to increase people of color and women?

11. Have identifiable programs focusing on people of color been initiated in such areas as recruiting, admissions, and selection, supportive services, and in academic and cultural programming?

12. Are there separate programs for different racially ethnic groups or are they multi-ethnic in focus?

13. Are programs by people of color given broad institutional support and presence by administrators, faculty and students?

14. Are there mechanisms for distributing student activities funds to organizations of students of color for coordinating their activities?

15. Is there an attempt to collect and analyze data on the needs and concerns of students and faculty of color? Of the racial climate on campus?

16. Are there adequate mechanisms for dealing with interracial problems?

17. Is there a minority advisory board?

18. Is the counsel of officers (faculty) of color sufficiently sought and utilized?

19. Is the institution willing to make significant changes to meet the needs of personnel of color, or does it seek changes primarily from them as a *mainstreaming* effort?

Finally, based on all that we had heard and observed at West Point, we were aroused to the point of making certain suggestions and recommendations, and they were as follows:

1. A mechanism should be created by which black and white cadets can meet to air grievances without rancor and retribution.

2. The academy should create a vehicle, such as a minority advisory council, by which the concerns and needs of people of color are addressed.

3. Some study should be given to using alternative admissions approaches to improve opportunities for applicants of color.

4. A booklet should be designed that would include biographical sketches and portraits of West Point graduates of color who have established successful career profiles in their respective disciplines.

5. The academy should adopt policies and procedures to ensure that academic and tactical officers are sensitive to the emotional and academic needs of the cadet of color. An apparatus should be established to monitor the effectiveness of these personnel in dealing with personnel of color.

6. The central administration should foster a positive climate that promotes affirmative action within all units at West Point.

7. Institutional seminars and workshops should be conducted with faculty and staff to reduce racially prejudiced attitudes. Further, the academy should take immediate and summary action when instances of prejudice have been identified.

8. West Point should expand its student entertainment and activity programs to include programs that feature entertainers, artists and lecturers of color which reflect the interests of students of color.

9. The academy should conduct periodic research to determine the attitudes of its cadets of color concerning the institution's affirmative action program.

10. Central administration should give black officers informal and formal access to the institutional heads as a means of facilitating those problems unique to people of color.

11. Consider having an annual visitation day program at the academy to invite large numbers of prospects of color to the academy for a one or two-day program which stresses the quality of education and the advantages of the West Point experience.

12. The military academy should make sure that organizations of students of color at West Point are given the kind of legitimacy that will assist their functioning both on and off campus.

13. A black chaplain should be appointed to meet the religious, personal, and emotional needs of black cadets.

14. The cultural traditions of Black History Week should be given high priority as a special event to be supported by the academy.

15. Develop a list of prominent civilian leaders of color in order to establish points of contact among persons and organizations who can assist the academy in its recruitment efforts for students of color.

16. Design a long-range *grow-your-own* program to increase the number of black officers in the army and on the United States Military Academy staff.

My first extensive consulting assignment at West Point drew my attention to the importance of an earlier comment that Paul Wisdom and Kenneth Shaw had made concerning the problems of black students on the white college campus:

> The problem is that only when they arrive on campus and realize how totally white it is (do) black students become reformers and revolutionaries. The problem is that black students found whites with control over every element of the university to the total exclusion of blacks; the blacks had nothing of their own. The inequity of the system paired with irrelevance to them of the education it offers, sows the seeds of reform or revolution. The result of this combination—the white establishment, the white curriculum, the white social environment, the white cultural standards, plus the discovery of hostility, apathy, misunderstanding, and experience in the other world in which they find themselves—is dissatisfaction, bitterness, and the determination to change the system.

It was Dr. Gordon K. Davies, director of the Virginia Council of Higher Education, who invited me to address the topic "Diversity on the College Campus of the 21st Century: Your Role in Increasing Black Faculty and Student Participation" at a statewide retention conference at the Omni Hotel in Richmond on April 24, 1989. About five hundred leaders from the higher education community were in attendance. Among the interventions that I proposed were those listed below.

- Begin a tracking system to identify people of color with high potential.
- Establish mentoring programs to enhance and advance people of color who are already in the system.
- Create educational and training programs to enhance and sensitize faculty and administrators to cultural differences.

- Identify prospects early on as candidates for faculty positions by funding them for advanced educational opportunities so that they can return to their respective institutions on amortized arrangements that are beneficial to all parties concerned.

Perhaps, one of the most challenging consulting opportunities that I had was when I was invited by Dr. Russell Garth, vice president of the Council of Independent Colleges, to address and consult with 150 college presidents on the subject of minorities on campus at their 1991 Presidents Institute at the Pointe of South Mountain in Phoenix, Arizona, on January 3, 1991. I covered such basic topic areas as policy and institutional procedures, enlarging the pool, screening the candidate pool, recruiting, professional development, and campus climate.

As the demand for my services as a consultant began to mount to address the issues of diversity on college and university campuses, I decided to publish an inventory to assist institutional personnel and units (faculty, administrators, departments, colleges and universities) to evaluate various aspects of the institution (traditions, policies, practices, goals) to determine their effectiveness in providing a dynamic pluralistic environment on their campuses. Thus in 1991, *Hale's Inventory for Assessing an Institution's Commitment to Multicultural Programming* became a reality. It has been used by scores and scores of institutions as an instrument to develop and implement strategies to facilitate diversity. The *Inventory* is divided into eight areas: administrative leadership, admissions and recruitment, financial assistance, student support services, curriculum, campus environment, graduate and professional programs, and multicultural hiring. The *Inventory* spans a comprehensive schematic for assessing, implementing and improving the environment for diversity on a college or university campus.

Among the positive initiatives which the *Inventory* documents that should be encouraged are the following:

- Formulating a forthright vision and commitment to diversity by the president and chief administrative officer.
- Developing a team of deans, departmental chairs, faculty, staff and student leaders who are jointly committed to achieving diversity.
- Creating a climate for discussion, dialogue and debate on issues of diversity.
- Setting admissions criteria that include factors other than quantitative ones for admissibility.
- Providing priority consideration and financial support in areas that have been traditionally been underfunded.

346

- Placing a high value on establishing retention strategies that will enable members of underrepresented groups to persist and graduate.
- Recognizing the unique experiences and contributions of people of color to the extent that they are reflected in the institution's curricula and its invitations of scholars and artists of color to participate in campus events.
- Encouraging the social bonding of students from a common culture in affirming their right to be drawn to each other and to have some campus space as a family room or center set aside where they can engage in social and educational exchanges.
- Developing strategies to identify capable undergraduates as prospective graduate and professional students, so as to provide them with funding support and mentoring opportunities that will ensure their success as students and as future faculty members.
- Hiring faculty of color and establishing mentoring programs for junior faculty to facilitate their requirements for promotion and tenure.

I have spent considerable time on the campuses of large public comprehensive universities. They generally have the advantage of being located in the proximity of large metropolitan urban areas with significant concentrations of people of color. The smaller private colleges have much greater challenges because of their location, selective admissions procedures, and high tuition costs. They also have borne the image of elitism which often flies in the face of those who come from low-income families and whose existence has been tooth and nail. A number of these private institutions began vigorous and impressive programs of diversity, and began to focus on multicultural perspectives in the early 1990s. I had the privilege of responding to consulting invitations at some very prestigious institutions during this period. They included Oberlin College (April 10, 1992), Columbia Union College (August 20, 1992), Albion College (August 22, 1992), and Hiram College (September 16, 1992). I conducted similar workshops and seminars on multiculturalism at Mt. Union College, Andrews University, Hope College, Loma Linda University, Ohio Wesleyan University, Columbus (Georgia) College, and Boston College.

I certainly have appreciated the opportunity to familiarize myself with the problems and challenges of so many colleges and universities. I can never forget the wonderful and warm personal and professional relations that I had with members of my own consulting team. Dr. Valerie Lee, associate Professor of Women's Studies and English at The Ohio State University, was especially effective in making presentations on "Global Issues in the Liberal Arts Curriculum." Winner of several teaching awards and author of numerous scholarly publications, she has had two decades of teaching canonical and non-canonical literature, including fifteen years at Denison University. Dr. Antoinette Miranda, assistant professor of Education at The Ohio State University, is in demand as a consultant to conduct workshops on multicultural teaching, multicultural counseling, cultural diversity, and multi-ethnic perspectives in the curriculum. As a nationally certified school psychologist, she, too, has won several teaching awards. She is a specialist in cross-cultural competence. Dr. Winfred Stone, associate dean and director of graduate administration at Bowling Green State University (Ohio), is highly regarded nationally as a leader in graduate education and in multiethnic education. His emphasis in consulting has been on "Multicultural Education: Stages of Development." Ms. Linda Jackson, former director of administration for The Ohio State University Office of Minority Affairs, has an established reputation for her creative activities in "Pre-college Multicultural Initiatives." The scope of her services has benefited Ohio State, the University of Dayton, and the University of Cincinnati, as well.

Less than one year after I had retired from The Ohio State University, I enjoyed the great opportunity of experiencing the grand opening of the Frank W. Hale, Jr., Black Cultural Center on October 11, 1989.* Little did I realize that such a moment would occur when I, along with others, participated in earlier protests and demonstrations in the early 1970s as we expressed our need for such a center on campus. We had an absolute imperative to provide, in some measure and through whatever means within our grasp, for the intellectual and emotional comfort of African-American students.

The Hale Black Cultural Center, a component within the Office of Minority Affairs, has as its principle goals to:

> Plan, develop, and implement a diverse offering of activities having a distinct emphasis on African–American culture.
>
> Foster an environment of cultural growth, sensitivity and awareness.
>
> Serve as an educational, social, and cultural support unit for the campus and extended communities.
>
> Enhance the understanding and appreciation of the richness and diversity of African-American culture and its impact on Western civilization.

* See Appendix J, page 423.

The grand opening of the Hale Black Cultural Center introduced a program with a broad group of representatives from various organizations. After the invocation by Elder Walter Wright, pastor of the Ephesus Seventh-day Adventist Church, Dr. Edward H. Jennings, president of The Ohio State University, gave the official welcome. Attorney Linda Ammons, executive assistant to Governor Richard Celeste, extended greetings in his behalf. The Honorable Ray Miller and Attorney Otto Beatty represented the Ohio General Assembly. The Honorable Dana G. Rinehart, mayor of Columbus, joined Attorney Ben E. Espy, city councilman, in representing the city of Columbus; and Mrs. Loretta Heard gave greetings as a member of the Columbus Board of Education.

A series of speakers from student organizations including David Straub, president, Undergraduate Student Government; R. Luke Evans, president, Council of Graduate Students; Kimberly Frazier, president, Association of Black Students; Stephanie McIver, president, Black Graduate and Professional Student Caucus; Charles Dobbins, president, Black Greek Council; and Rick Iverson, convener, "Just Us." Dr. William E. Nelson, research professor of Black Studies and professor of Political Science, gave a sketch of the rationale and history of the center. Dr. William Parker, vice chancellor for minority affairs at the University of Kentucky, was the keynote speaker. He was introduced by Linda Jackson, acting vice provost for the Office of Minority Affairs. Special salutes to Dr. Hale were rendered by Ms. Gloria Jefferson, the president of Columbus Links, Incorporated, and by Dr. Mary Ann Williams, associate professor of Black Studies. Dr. Barbara Newman, associate provost, gave the dedication remarks; Captain and Mrs. Nelson Barnett, Jr., were present as the first donors of personal mementos of Captain Barnett's father (diplomas, certificates, and a saxophone which he had used to work his way through Ohio State). Special music was rendered by Kaelyn CoCrott, journalism major, and Lee Jones, graduate student in higher education. Lawrence Williamson, the assistant director of the Hale Cultural Center, introduced and acknowledged local artists who had contributed their works to the center. The architectural firms of R. M. Harpham, Moody/Nolan, Ltd., and Spencer and Spencer, Inc., were recognized for their generous and expert contributions to making the renovation of the center a reality. The program was concluded with the audience singing "Lift Every Voice and Sing."

The center includes two handsome galleries—The Richard Barthe and Elijah Pierce galleries—both of which display the considerable and equally handsome permanent collection. Williamson has been very effective in increasing donations for the already substantial permanent collection and in planning for a series of ongoing rotating exhibits featuring local and national artists. Its 8800 square feet will soon double when it takes over the other half of what was once designated as Bradford Commons, a single story building, sandwiched between OSU residence towers and an academic building.

The center provides meeting office space for twenty-nine African-American student organizations and offers its facilities for cultural programs, classes, and film screenings. It has two conference areas (The Sojourner Truth/Frederick Douglass Conference Room and the Harriet Tubman Conference Area), an extensive student lounge (Martin Luther King Lounge), a hall of fame multipurpose room, and a bank of computers to assist students in their research in meeting class assignments. All works in the Hale Center's permanent collection were donated. One of the premier pieces in the collection is large mixed-media work, "Blossoms," by internationally-known artist Sam Gilliam, from his 1989 tulip series. Other prominent contemporary black artists represented include Elizabeth Cutlett, Meta Vux Warick Fuller, Paul Goodnight, and John Riddle.

Historical African art objects representing the Ashanti, Dan, Dogon, Benin, Yoruba, and Zulu ethnic groups were donated by art historian and art educator Dr. Samella Lewis, an OSU Ph.D. who is editor of *The International Review of African American Art* published by the Hampton University Museum.

Glass cases along the wall of the Martin Luther King Lounge house historical objects. Artists who have pledged their support through donations of their works include Queen Brooks, Smoky Brown, W. T. Bruce, Barbara Chavous, Jeffrey Clark, James Kwame Clay, Larry Winston Collins, Benjamin Crumpler, Ed Colston, Roman Johnson, Paul Harper, Bill Harris, Charles Hollingsworth, Joe Howard, J. D. Jackson, Kojo Kamau, Terry Logan, Watt Neil, E. Okechakwu Odita, Baba Olugbula, Leon Page, Pheoris West, Aguaetta, and the late Robert Stull and Beverly Turner.

The center also serves as a Thanksgiving Day alternative for students who have too many miles to encompass or too little money to make it home. The center serves free dinners to nearly two hundred students as a part of the holiday festivities each year. Kroger stores have traditionally donated all of the food already cooked, and members of the center staff serve the students who have remained on campus during the holiday period. Many of the students are international students who don't have to feel left out during the holiday season.

Further, the center provides seminars, lectures, workshops, and group discussions throughout the year. Already, it has become an oasis rich in history, culture, art appreciation, and cultural exchanges that are creative and supportive of the university's mission to promote cultural diversity.

Chapter 16

My Partnership with Jesse Jackson

It was in the spring of 1975 that I joined the Columbus, Ohio, chapter of Operation PUSH, headed by Reverend Cameron Jackson of the First Zion A.M.E. Church. Early Martin Luther King ideals were withering before the smudgy blasts of a rising conservatism throughout the country. I felt that America could no longer aspire to be a free nation, so long as it remained extravagant in flaunting its racist practices. Because I had the impression that Reverend Jesse Jackson was an unbought leader, I decided to cast my lot with the local PUSH chapter. Reverend Jackson, at the time, served as the national president of Operation PUSH located in Chicago, Illinois.

History had already taught us as black people that we were powerless to battle single-handedly against the system. The Montgomery Boycott and the series of cases that culminated in the *Brown* decision demonstrated that the best defense that those who are oppressed can use is to organize and fight for their rights, even when the dice are loaded heavily against them. We have used the legislative branches of government to enact laws, the federal courts to issue injunctions, state and federal authorities to bring in troops to protect our people, and executive orders to eliminate segregation and discrimination and to create equal opportunities in the armed services and in employment practices.

When Reverend Cameron Jackson was not able to attend the Fourth Annual PUSH Convention in Philadelphia, Pennsylvania, during the month of August, the Columbus chapter elected me to attend the meeting to represent the local chapter as a delegate. I was pleased now to be a part of an organization that was setting broad goals to meet the needs of black people. I saw no hint that Jesse Jackson was, even to the slightest degree, inclined to tilt his lance in order to enjoy favor with the big boys. He campaigned for economic and social reforms and was fully representative of the interest of little people no matter what their color or gender.

And so when I arrived in Philadelphia, I was anxious to meet Reverend Jackson. In fact, I had the happy occasion of meeting him and Reverend William Gray at the same time. Reverend Gray was a local pastor who also headed the local chapter of Operation PUSH. Both gentlemen greeted me warmly, and each one invited me to participate in the programs that were scheduled over the following few days. Reverend Jackson manifested a vigorous excitement about him as he asked me to be especially attentive to the program on education that was listed in the conference bulletin. Just in a short period of observation, I was confident that Reverend Jackson was one of the most articulate orators that I had ever heard. At the same time, Reverend Gray gave wide currency to the philosophical concept of pragmatism, which emphasizes the practical side of thinking. Whether in conversation or on the public platform, Reverend Gray goes straight to the point, demonstrating with precision the essence of truth as he presents it. He was the embodiment of that proverb which states that, "In the great race of life, common sense has the right of way."

Fortunately, the overall influence of that PUSH convention was excellent. It championed many causes—for the homeless, the poor, the unemployed, and a host of others. The persistent crusade for the rights of black people filled the air, the discussions, the planning sessions, and the agendas for future meetings. I was inspired by the astute thinking and quick-triggered strategists who were prepared to do battle until unrestricted freedom was granted to all Americans. Deeply involved in the PUSH momentum were stellar spokespersons such as Reverend Otis Moss, Reverend Clay Evans, Mrs. C. Delores Tucker, Mr. Ernest Green, and Dr. Alvin Poussaint. The Board of Directors of PUSH for Excellence, Inc., included Dr. Mary F. Berry, vice chairwoman; Attorney John H. Bustamente, general counsel; Mrs. Camille Cosby, Dr. John Hope Franklin, Dr. Benjamin Alexander, and Mrs. Lucille Conway Loman. These stalwart pioneers added immeasurably to the reputation and successes of the organization.

The black Baptist Church played no small part in the growth, development, and operation of PUSH. To this day the leadership of local PUSH chapters throughout the country often rests in the hands of Baptist pastors who have enjoyed a desirable and durable friendship with

Jesse Jackson over the years. The Baptist Church was more than a place in the organizational history of PUSH; it was also a state of mind and a symbol of battle and survival. Even before and during the days of Martin Luther King, it was on the front lines of battle as a base for mass rallies, where many black Americans have always felt secure and rooted in the spiritual soil of their ancestors.

The PUSH Convention of 1975 was on the whole informational, inspirational and creditable. It focused on those national priorities which were wrong. It chided the national politicians for a housing bill, a jobs bill, for enacting a two billion dollar highway bill, and for raising the war budget in peacetime. Reverend Jackson, in his keynote address, challenged the present generation to become more enlightened:

> Too many of us, marry but divorce… Too many of us, get a job, but won't produce… Too many of us, get a healthy body, but destroy it… Too many of us, get the right to vote, but won't register to vote… There are reasons for it, but there can be no seasons for it.

It was shortly after the Philadelphia PUSH Convention that Reverend Jesse Jackson envisioned a student-motivation program that would challenge students to accept a life-style of discipline and sacrifice that would enable them to achieve high goals and avoid the impediments to educational excellence—drugs, alcohol, violence, absenteeism, vandalism, and sexual experimentation. His program, designated PUSH-EXCEL, was designed to be a mass-oriented, grassroots effort involving students, parents, educators, clergy, business persons, and representatives of the media. It was about distributing responsibility so that it created a process of total community involvement.

Reverend Jackson sought my services as an educational consultant and asked me to develop some guidelines that would address the philosophy, the basic principles, the goals, and the objectives of PUSH-EXCEL. An epidemic of enthusiasm swept the country for this program after Reverend Jackson gave it a remarkable boost and showing on national television. I had hardly seated myself as vice provost for minority affairs at The Ohio State University in October of 1978 that Reverend Jackson had invited me to come to Chicago to serve as his assistant and to serve as national director of the EXCEL program for two years. In fact, he contacted President Harold Enarson at Ohio State, seeking his approval to grant me such a leave. While I was anxious to explore ways in which Project EXCEL could be woven into the fabric of American education at all levels, I did not feel comfortable giving the whole loaf of my talents and experience at that time to the project. After all, I was just getting my foot into the door of a new assignment at the university; I had no stomach for setting myself up for failure by biting off more than I could reasonably chew.

Even before Reverend Jackson's invitation to me to join his full time staff, I had flown to Chicago on certain weekends to plunge myself into Friday afternoon, Saturday night, and all-day Sunday sessions to be involved in the preparation of PUSH-EXCEL materials, as well as in discussions with Reverend Jackson and members of the PUSH staff about ways and means of implementing the concept on the national basis. I was involved in these activities during the summer and autumn of 1977.

I enjoyed working with some very able Operation PUSH staff persons to get the program underway. Dr. Charles Warfield, executive director of Operation PUSH; Dr. Donald Thompson, executive assistant to the president of Operation PUSH; Dr. Cordell Richardson, national EXCEL director; Mr. Sam Tidmore; Mrs. Frances Davis; Reverend Frank E. Watkins, Mrs. Lynette Lewis, and Reverend Willie Barrow were formidable hardworking and dedicated members of the staff.

On my own, I prepared a draft entitled "A Handbook for Understanding and Implementing PUSH for Excellence." It was a forty-four page document which was later distilled, parts of which were used in the publication of a primer which served as an introduction to the National PUSH for Excellence Program.

By the winter of 1977, we began making plans to do what we could to involve the federal government in coming on board as a partner in the PUSH-EXCEL program. Through the good offices and influence of Dr. Mary Berry, assistant secretary for education in the United States Department of Health, Education and Welfare, we were able to get funding. Project EXCEL was awarded a contract for $400,000 to strengthen EXCEL programs in Kansas City, Missouri; Chicago, Illinois; and Washington, D.C., to fund projects in three additional cities, and to support an NIE evaluation of ongoing EXCEL programs.

Meanwhile, Reverend Jackson deputized me to serve as program coordinator for a national conference on Mobilizing for Excellence in Education which was to be held at Howard University May 16–19, 1978. The conference was to serve as a convocation of national, community and educational leaders to identify strategies for achieving excellence in education. The objectives of the conference were:

1. To define the EXCEL proposition in broad terms so that the black poor and others may share equally and fully in the mainstream of American life.

2. To provide a participatory forum where representatives from selected cities could obtain information, skills, and the appropriate orientation to return to their cities and more preliminary plans to begin Project EXCEL programs in their communities.

3. To bring together scholars, educators, community and national leaders to discuss the methods by which students of all races and ethnic backgrounds could achieve basic skills and attain academic excellence.

The conference was a partnership arrangement among PUSH for Excellence, Inc., Howard University and the U.S. Department of Health, Education and Welfare (HEW). Dr. Mary Berry deputized Ms. Sandra T. Gray as the coordinator for HEW. Dr. Eunice Newton was the coordinator for Howard University, and I was the coordinator for Operation PUSH. We had the respective endorsements of Joseph A. Califano, Jr., secretary of HEW; Jesse Jackson, national president of Operation PUSH; and Dr. James E. Cheek, president of Howard University.

As program coordinator for the conference, it was my responsibility to notify prospective attendees across the country of the conference and to solicit suggestions from community leaders for participants on panels, workshops, or as presenters in plenary sessions. To the delight of conference registrants, there was a prominent class of major league presenters who succeeded admirably in helping the conference to achieve its ends.

Our fortunes were enhanced when the staff of the prestigious periodical, *Phi Delta Kappan,* agreed to include a special supplement to its November 1978 issue, featuring the key conference presenters. The supplement was pounced upon by a swarm of conference participants following the meetings so that they could take full advantage of the information that would provide them with a heaping helping hand as tools in their efforts to promote the education of youth in their home communities. The leading presenters whose messages were carried in the special *Phi Delta Kappan* edition were Jesse L. Jackson, Kenneth B. Clark, Mary F. Berry, Robert L. Green, Samuel D. Proctor, Frank W. Hale, Jr., Bernard C. Watson, Alvin F. Poussaint, Edythe J. Gaines, Otis Moss, Rosetta Taylor Moore, Elias Blake, and Faustine C. Jones.

More than 1200 participants from twenty-four states and sixty-one cities attended the conference. Among other key program participants were Dr. Arthur Jefferson, superintendent, Detroit Public Schools; Mr. Jack Valenti, president, the Motion Picture Association of America; Mr. Robert Maynard, chairman, Institute for Journalism Education; Dr. James

Comer, director, Child Study Center, Yale University; Ms. Charlayne Hunter-Gault, correspondent, Public Broadcasting Service; Mr. Ben Bradlee, executive editor, *The Washington Post*; Dr. Andrew Billingsley, president, Morgan State University; Dr. Prezell Robinson, president, United Negro College Fund; Dr. Kenneth Tollett, director, Institute for the Study of Educational Policy, Howard University; Mr. Tony Brown, president, Tony Brown Productions; The Honorable Richard Hatcher, mayor of Gary, Indiana; Dr. Charles Lyons, president, National Association for Equal Opportunity in Higher Education; Mr. Lionel Bordeaux, president, National Indian Education Association; Mr. Tony Gonzalez, president, Association for Mexican-American Education; Dr. Joseph E. Hill, president, National Alliance of Black School Administrators; Dr. Manford Byrd, deputy superintendent, Chicago Board of Education; Dr. Garland Millett, associate director, Department of Education, General Conference of Seventh-day Adventists; Dr. Rebecca Carroll, deputy superintendent, Baltimore City Schools; and Bishop H. H. Brookins, Fifth Episcopal District, AME Church, Los Angeles, California.

The conference was thrilled to the masterful musicianship of the Woodson Senior High School Male Chorus; Mr. Leroy Dorsey, bass, Howard University; Mr. James Holliday, tenor, Howard University; Shaw Junior High School Concert Choir; Ms. Nelda Ormand, soprano, University of the District of Columbia; D.C. Youth Chorale; Morgan State University Choir; and Mr. Wintley Phipps, bass, Andrews University.

It was a splendid conference which made the point that the education of our youth cannot be left solely to professional educators. It was designed to define *community educators* more broadly to include ministers, parents, the media, business persons and others to accept the responsibility of forging and reinforcing positive educational values. The outcome was a smashing victory for the apostles of Partnership Education.

During those days when I was serving as a consultant for Operation PUSH, I had the opportunity to speak at a luncheon sponsored by the organization. I invited the magnificently talented bass-baritone, Wintley Phipps, to sing on that occasion. I had wanted both him and Reverend Jackson to meet, as each one was making a spectacular contribution in their respective fields. Phipps' overpowering performance was an electrifying discovery for Reverend Jackson, and since those early days, Reverend Jackson had had the Elder Wintley Phipps (now an ordained minister in the Seventh-day Adventist Church) to sing when Reverend Jackson keynoted the Democratic National Convention and when he

356

toured a number of African countries to meet with heads of state. It is no secret what God can do!

Our growing friendship and fellowship continued to blossom as I began to appreciate more and more Jesse's (friends do refer to each other and about each other on a first-name basis) continuing quest and pledge to fight for a just society and a peaceful world. From time to time, I began to send him tidbits of information for his speeches on such issues as the Equal Rights Amendment, economic equity, the reproductive rights of women, affirmative action, U.S. policies in Central America, environmentalism, and an assortment of others. There were even times when I dared to hew and hone complete passages for him to include in his speeches, and he has often used some of them. Then, too, I encouraged him to become a presidential candidate and to develop a functional base that included the dispossessed, the disfranchised, the disillusioned, and the despondent.

While I cannot claim credit for his decision to seek the Democratic nomination for president of the United States in 1984, I was among the twenty or so persons who sat with him in his Chicago home to discuss that possibility in the autumn of 1983. With his mind made up, some of us discussed the lurking dangers that stood in the way of his ever even completing such a campaign. I will never forget his response. Without the slightest hesitation, he declared, "Jackie (his wife) and I have considered those possibilities, but my commitment is to justice. We want to test the moral character of America, whether white America can put character over color and reason over race." His demeanor was serious, unadorned, and to the point. At that moment, my respect for his wisdom and unwearied will soared.

His response gave me the zeal to be willing to charge into the fray and support his candidacy, knowing that he would press the full weight of his prestige, his energy, his determination, and his sensitivity for the downtrodden into the arena of competition. It was a new day in the history of my endeavors when I urged the university administration to invite Reverend Jackson to appear on campus during his 1984 campaign, and I had forewarned Reverend Jackson that I was going to do so. I was eager to do something to generate enthusiasm among college and university students for Jackson's candidacy. It was my sense that if Jackson seized the opportunity to capture the mood and attention of this group, especially on a major university campus early in his campaign, the spin-off might produce the kind of momentum that would arouse public opinion in his favor.

Reverend Jackson took full advantage of the invitation and came to The Ohio State University in early November on the very eve of the day that he had made an earlier announcement in the nation's capitol to launch his campaign for the presidency. Serving as his host, I met Jackson at the Columbus Airport as he was greeted and followed by an entourage of reporters and national media personalities who descended upon Columbus and Mershon Auditorium on The Ohio State University campus. Jackson was greeted by an enthusiastic standing room only crowd in excess of three thousand who had packed the auditorium, chanting and waving posters which read, "Run Jesse Run."

With his usual dynamic, crowd-pleasing and thought-provoking delivery, Jackson's message was simple, clear, and to the point. Stressing the need for young people, particularly black youth, to register to vote, Jackson gave the example of how President Ronald Reagan won several states in 1980 by only a fraction of the number of unregistered black voters in those same states. In addition, Jackson pointed out that just as Reagan had his "perverse coalition of super-rich, right-wing conservatives and racists," there must be a rainbow coalition of the oppressed: blacks, Hispanics, American Indians, poor whites, young people, women and all of the rejected to "put Reagan out of the White House."

During a short question and answer session following his speech, Jackson did reveal that, if he won the Democratic Party's nomination, his running mate would probably be a woman. Sharing the platform with Jackson was Dr. William E. Nelson, chairman of the Department of Black Studies; Dr. Herbert Asher, special assistant to OSU President Edward Jennings; about twenty undergraduate and graduate student leaders; Mrs. Jacqueline Jackson, Jackson's wife; and myself.

The evening on that occasion was anything but tame. When it comes to creating extraordinary excitement and evoking spontaneous enthusiasm, Reverend Jesse Jackson is unrivaled as the most gifted orator in American politics. Savoring his decision and announcement, his youthful audience gave evidence that Jackson did indeed become the first black to attain both the credibility and political impact to be a genuine presidential contender.

While the media attempted to portray Jackson solely as a champion of American blacks, Jackson underscored his concern for women, Hispanics, senior citizens, the young, the poor and others who were dispossessed. He was at his articulate best during the public press conference which followed his address. Especially deft and skilled in extempore, he parried question after question with the quality of a fencer and with the exuberance and charm of the "country preacher" which had become his distinguishing trademark.

Categorical in his desire to have a woman as his running mate, Jackson quipped, "If Indira Ghandi can govern six hundred million persons in

India, and Margaret Thatcher can rule Great Britain, and we can survive Ronald Reagan, then Americans should be ready for a woman to serve as vice president of the United States."

Jackson finally had injected some fireworks into what had been a dull Democratic campaign. Following his address at Ohio State, I then accompanied him to East High School where he addressed nearly two thousand members of the Columbus community. Many contributions were made to his campaign there by local businessmen, civic leaders, clergy, and members of the public. His popularity, always high in the black community, went soaring lustily to the cheers, chants and applause of a welcoming audience. It was a glorious and personal triumph for Jackson at the very beginning of his campaign.

Jackson returned to Columbus on Sunday, April 29, 1984, at a mass rally which was sponsored by the Central Ohio Citizens for Jackson Committee at the State Fairgrounds (Lausche Building). Mr. Jerry Hammond, member of the Columbus City Council, was the state convening co-chairperson, and I continued to serve as the chairperson of the Jackson Campaign for Columbus and Franklin County. Nearly ten thousand people turned out for the rally which was co-sponsored by many groups including the Black Elected Democratic Officials (BEDO), the Baptist Pastors Conference, the Baptist Ministerial Alliance, the Interdenominational Ministerial Association, the Ohio Baptist General Convention, the Young Black Democrats Association, the Nation of Islam, the Columbus Campaign for Arms Control, the Federation for Progress, the Arab Anti-Discrimination League, the Students for Peace and Disarmament, the Arab American Coalition, the National Alliance of Political and Federal Employees, the Ohio State University Students for Jackson, the Ohio University Students for Jackson, and the 29th Democratic Citizens Caucus.

Special music attractions included the James Cleveland Gospel Workshop Choir, the Crawford Singers, the Five Gifts of Song, His Own Youth Chorale, Spirit Song, the Union Grove Angelic Choir, the Imperial Clefs, the Claire United Methodist Church Jubilee Choir, and soloists Ruby J. Wood, Vivian Walton, and the nationally recognized baritone, Mr. Wintley Phipps.

Jackson eloquently made the point that national security must be defined in broader terms to meet the needs of the sick, ill-housed, unemployed, illiterate, poor, and malnourished. It was a long, long journey for Jackson to the Democratic National Convention where he had hoped to capture the presidential nomination of his party. He was a mighty ebony whirlwind as he streaked across the country—challenging, debating, preaching, persuading, and pleading with people at every step of the day. Grabbing hands, slapping backs, and kissing babies, he thundered forth with new vigor and confidence. Jackson could count on his network of black Baptist clergy, a rather sophisticated assortment of black middle class advocates, and a swelling tide of poor blacks who felt left out or jilted by a system that they felt had absolutely no regard for them. White folks, even so-called well meaning white folks, felt threatened and vulnerable when they considered their historical advantages. Jackson's resounding challenge of "Our Time Has Come" did nothing but send chilling fears up and down their spines.

Even as powerful white politicians, as well as grassroots whites, retreated from this candidacy, the embers of black hope were fanned into flames as black registration soared in eleven southern states to nearly 5.5 million, compared to 4.3 million in 1980—a 1.2 million registration increase over the four year period. It is no secret that many black candidates for office in local communities rode Jackson's coattails to their own personal victories even as Walter Mondale had little difficulty in wrapping up his party's nomination.

Jackson was witheringly sarcastic toward those of which he was contemptuous. Case in point: "I'd rather have Roosevelt in a wheelchair—than Reagan on a horse," he would always assert to the unchallenged applause of his partisan advocates.

But as devastating and as effective as Jackson could be in attacking his adversaries, he had in his wife, Jackie Jackson, a chocolate-covered beauty of creative intellect, indomitable strength, and unbridled individuality. I've marveled at the way in which she possesses the maternal and visceral understanding of what it takes to be a sterling wife and mother. It doesn't take a moment of discernment to recognize that this woman was seldom, if ever, ambivalent about anything. On the numerous occasions that I have observed her, she has never given any visible sign of insecurity. In fact, I have observed that she has jacked up the price of noble womanhood, as she is completely at home with the unaltered pace of her husband's almost full-time travels, while at the same time going full steam ahead to the rhythm of her own contemporary and cultural interests. It became very obvious to me why Jackie and Jesse loved each other. Neither of them gave any evidence of wanting to change the very innate qualities of the other. They worked together—as in the campaign—when they wanted to, and they worked apart as the occasion required. Theirs was a love that obviously was deep, respectful, and fully integrated. It was bright with sunlight when their fingers were interlaced with hands that were dexterous and supple in a partnership that was obviously resolute and unmovable as they stood on their porch in Chicago bidding me farewell one moonlit April evening.

Their heroic sacrifices in the 1984 campaign had not gone for naught. Jackson was proud of what they had accomplished, and he had a right to be. Because Jackson was no staunch apostle of the status quo, even though at times he needed to take a hands-off posture and reassess his vision of the future, he never even had the thought of letting storm clouds become any part of his agenda. Awakened by the reality of the national climate, he, nevertheless, refused to give in to any spirit of disillusionment that might have stalemated a lesser competitor. Despite the moans of those who expected that he might well have justifiably retreated from future political skirmishes, he retreated from the grim philosophy of F. Scott Fitzgerald's philosophy as expressed in his novel, *This Side of Paradise*, that, "all gods dead, all wars fought, all faiths in man shaken." While nevertheless disappointed and restless, he was determined to fight national cynicism and intolerance and their by-products head-on. Thus even as his 1984 campaign for the presidential nomination by the Democratic Party ended, he started his 1988 campaign for the presidency even more resolute and with a broader base of support.

Because the Ohio Primary was scheduled for May 3, 1988, I felt it important to set the appropriate stage for Reverend Jackson to receive the highest visibility and notoriety possible just before that date. I was a little worried too about what we might be able to do in terms of pulling the right people together who could add to his campaign coffers. Those of us who were Jackson supporters struck upon the idea of having him to come to The Ohio State University campus again as he had done in November of 1983. Instead of having him appear and speak at the 3100 seat Mershon Auditorium, we wanted to bring him to the fourteen thousand seat St. John Arena on May 2, 1988, the evening before the primary. Aside from all of the stimulating politicking that was required to gain approval for the event, the preparation for such a gigantic event seriously strained every fiber and nerve of those of us who were down in the trenches performing the everyday tasks of preparations.

The field was wide open, and Gary Hart, Al Gore, Richard Gephardt, Paul Simon, and Michael Dukakis became the major contenders. Ronald Reagan was a formidable foe who stood unflinchingly at the helm of the Republican Party. With the press, the pundits, the pollsters, and the doomsday prophets counting Jackson out even before he began his campaign, he, notwithstanding, simply wanted an opportunity to present his case to the American public. And that he did, becoming a strong alternative to the Democratic Party's fragmented leadership, as well as a prophetic voice of reason to the nation. He attacked the linen and lace traditions of the Republican Party with its protracted support for business and wealthy interests. He also appealed to the vital American values of family, community, morality while confronting the scourges of teenage pregnancy, substance abuse, crime, poverty, homelessness, unemployment, and racial divisions.

So many of the political power brokers turned a deaf ear to the man and his message until they were shocked into reality when Jesse Jackson won sixteen first or second place finishes on Super Tuesday, while Dukakis won twelve and Gore eleven. After Jackson ran a strong second in Illinois, surprise victories in Puerto Rico and Alaska, and winning a landslide victory, out-polling Dukakis two-to-one in the Michigan caucuses, terror gripped the power brokers, and a strategy was devised to call on the super delegates—those who were chosen by virtue of their party office rather than by popular vote—to join in a stampede to derail Jackson's campaign train that was moving full steam ahead. Even after Mayor Koch helped to sabotage Jackson's campaign in New York, Jackson would have been in a virtual tie with Dukakis had Al Gore and Paul Simon dropped out of the race, because he had placed second in the states that they had won, and he would have had access to their delegates. So in a very real sense, they helped to ravage his campaign at a critical point by contributing to the *stop Jackson* crusade.

Interestingly enough, Jackson attracted his largest crowds after New York. He drew twelve thousand people to a rally on May 2, 1988, on the evening of the primary at The Ohio State University where thousands were turned away after St. John Arena was filled to capacity.

Fundraising was intimately bound up with the effectiveness of Jackson's campaign as it was in the case of the other candidates. There was absolutely nothing in Jackson's campaign message about corporations exploiting the poor that would make Jackson's appeals for funds attractive to them. His proposal for a progressive tax which would impact on the wealthy left him highly unpopular in their community. For the most part, he received his contributions by passing the plate at church rallies, from those of low and middle income status, and representing, to a relatively minor degree, the contributions that were generated by his rivals on the campaign trail. Fortunately, an honorary committee which I, along with several others, formed called "Friends for Jesse Jackson," decided to have a reception in his honor on the Sunday afternoon (May 1, 1988) prior to his speech at Ohio State University the following day.

Dr. and Mrs. Alfred Jefferson agreed to host the occasion at their magnificent million dollar home on the Scioto River in Columbus, Ohio.

Over three hundred guests, each contributing a minimum of $100, attended the festive affair. The Planning and Coordinating Committee was composed of Ben and Kathy Espy, Frank and Ruth Hale, Jim and Linda Jackson, Alfred and Gloria Jefferson, Amos and Geri Lynch, and Vernard and Margaret Roberts. It was a resplendent afternoon as those who gathered enjoyed the contagion of the atmosphere that included unescorted tours within the lavishly bedecked interior of a home where elegance reigned supreme throughout every inch of its quintessential quarters. Painted a bright white, the Jefferson mansion is grounded in spectacular plantings of every variety, with permanent sunshine on the rear terrace that slopes ever so gently to the flowing Scioto. It provided a welcoming social environment to the many who had come to visit with Reverend Jackson in a setting that was informal, congenial, and clearly an extraordinary experience into the world of make-believe.

At the appointed time, the mingling crowd gathered on the magnificently manicured lawn below the upper balcony in the rear of the mansion where Reverend Jackson was poised to speak after my introduction of him. Faces of the crowd beamed upward, each recognizing Jackson as one of the chief moving forces of our generation. Uncommonly handsome, intelligent, and articulate, he held preeminent sway before ever uttering a word. As a non-conformist who is gifted with fascinating ideas, he had already set a new high standard for political oratory. His remarks, however, on this occasion, were far more conversational and well-tailored to the sophisticated ambience of the moment. After addressing us on key issues of his campaign, we lustily applauded his cries against inhumanity, injustice and intolerance.

Some remained outside after partaking of the delectable cuisine that was embellished and embroidered with American and Continental delicacies—the freshest of vegetables, meats, seafoods, cheeses, desserts, salads, sandwiches, pastries of every variety and sundry beverages. Others relocated inside, enjoying the music provided by Bernard Edwards at the Steinway piano while reveling in the reflection of handsome mirrors that accentuated the images of gorgeous furnishings, crystal chandeliers, as well as the immaculately tailored clientele of those who were present. At the conclusion of this masterfully orchestrated reception, we presented Reverend Jackson with a check for $30,000 as a contribution to his campaign.

The next day was destined to be a day dominated by the fact that The Ohio State University community and the Columbus community as whole would be focused on the appearance of Reverend Jesse Jackson who would be at the point of having completed a three-week series of successive primaries in large northern industrial cities. The Ohio Primary was preceded by New York's on April 19, and Pennsylvania's on April 26. Jackson's candidacy was buoyed up by the knowledge that his impact on youth in Ohio was seen in his appearances at several high schools and where they expressed their sentiments for his candidacy most emphatically by leaping to their feet and cheering him with a passion, as they did no other candidate.

It almost seemed prophetic that twenty years after the assassination of Martin Luther King, Jr., a civil rights disciple and colleague of his was now one of the Democratic front-runners for the highest office in the land.

Although The Ohio State University Office of Minority Affairs, along with nearly twenty-five student organizations, co-sponsored the occasion, this major event would never have gotten off the ground without the supporting cast of representatives from various campus offices: Joan Peaks (special events), Caleb Brunson (traffic), Dean Ramsey (grounds), Charles Smith (maintenance), James Chisman (public safety), Dan Meinert (Red Coats), Mal Baroway and Steven Sterrett (university communications), and Jim Zimmer (printing). Dr. Herb Asher, special assistant to President Edward Jennings, and Dr. Russell Spillman, vice provost for student affairs, were very cooperative and supportive.

Throughout all of the planning and preparation, I also enjoyed the consistent and committed support of key community persons: Jacqueline Souel, who had served as the executive office coordinator in our 1984 Jackson campaign; James Evans, who engineered our delegate selection procedures; Gerard Mullins, who keyed our voter registration drive; Robert Cunningham, Jill Frost and Ann Walker, who were our communication consultants; Attorney Donald Conley, legal counsel; Clifford Tyree, vice chairperson, Citizens Committee; Marsha Conley, house parties; Linda Jackson, administrative coordinator; James K. Jackson, treasurer; George Sloan, secretary; Ako Kambon, staff aide; Michael Gruber and Charles Ross, consultants; Reverends Charles Booth, Odell Waller, and C. Dexter Wise, pastors in residence; and Jerry Hammond and myself serving as state convening co-chairperson and Columbus and Franklin County chairperson, respectively.

As in all of his appearances, Reverend Jackson instinctively knew how to work his audience. He was able to give his hearers the kind of psychological uplift they needed. It was impossible to be a passive listener when Jackson was in motion. Nothing about his presentations were ever frail or anemic. He was incredibly spectacular as he reeled off facts and figures with the acumen and accuracy of an IBM computer. He stayed on course, spelling out the misery of the underclass contrasted to the succulence of the upper class. He pounded the podium declaring, "We must fight for good jobs in America." He indicted American corporations for exploiting the poor at home by taking their business abroad and capitalizing on near slave labor overseas. He tackled the drug problem on both the supply and demand sides. He proposed cutting military spending and increasing our real security by giving greater attention to the needs of the poor and under-privileged in America. He proposed that the federal government should aid states in equalizing funds for all school districts, so that all of America's children could receive an adequate education. Strong, determined and uncompromising, he never stopped declaring war on the issues that under-mined the respect and well-being of the little people. His goal was constant: "Take it to the titans of power."

Jackson had already demonstrated his prowess in his drive to make corporate America responsible to citizens of color. In the late 1970s and early 1980s, he had pushed, promoted, and executed far-reaching eco-nomic covenants with some of the nation's largest corporations, industries and financial institutions. These covenants concentrated on economic reciprocity, investing in those black communities where companies had built their economic base. It was a policy that insisted upon a fair and equitable return on the black consumer dollar. It was a covenant that con-centrated on institutional development in the black community—that corporate American invest in black banks, savings and loan companies, insurance companies, newspapers, radio and television stations, advertis-ing agencies and more. It insisted that blacks be represented on the board of major corporations.

And Jesse Jackson settled for nothing less when negotiating with Sears, Seagram, Coca-Cola, Pepsi, Heublein, Kentucky Fried Chicken, Uniworld, and many others.

Jackson went for the jugular in pushing for the Voting Rights Act, for one standard in admitting people to our country, for full employment, for an aggressive peace campaign, for disarmament, for a consistent and humane policy in Latin America, for quality education for all children, and for equal rights for women. He was among the very first to advocate for a strong drug rehabilitation and training program.

Behind all of Jackson's vibrato, hit and run style of dealing with issues, he has left a monumental imprint on the American scene. Bold and often arrogant beyond belief, his sense of love and caring shines through. I have seen his eyes water and his hands tremble when coming face to face with a forlorn senior citizen who unfolds her tale of hardship. I have seen his eyes glow and a full blown smile lighten his world of expectations when surrounded by young people who seriously seek his counsel. I have seen him sacrifice the comforts and conveniences of his own needs—and the isolation of being distanced from his own family to promote a better way for those who have no hope, nor hope of hope—and stretch himself beyond accepted limits to make things happen for those who seem not to know what has happened to them. Like many of us, Jackson is a man of curious contradictions—so lovable, and yet so volatile—so sensitive and yet at times, so insensitive—so tolerant, and yet at times so intolerant of points of view not his own. Nevertheless, his legacy is clear. He keeps on marching for justice.

I am indebted to him, as we all should be, in sharing in the partnership of his vision.

Chapter 17

I Love My Church

————⊃○⊙○⊂————

I was born into a family of Baptist believers in Kansas City, Missouri. Little did my parents know as dyed-in-the-wool Baptists that they would ever take a turn which had profoundly affected the thinking and character of generations on mother's side of the family (the Banks') as well as the Hales. The Baptist theology had been ingrained in mother from her early days when she was baptized in the James River into the membership of Mt. Nebo Baptist Church in Surry County, Virginia. It was also the creed of most of the farming families in the area who played an influential role in the moral and spiritual life of most of the black people in neighboring communities such as Smithfield, Hopewell, and the Isle of Wight, among others. Dad, on the other hand, found his religious haven at Mt. Zion Baptist Church in Athens, Ohio. It was a church that his uncle, Edward Berry, had built, paid for, and given to the congregation. His mother, Maude Hale, had rendered indispensable service there as a teacher, youth leader, and faithful member. It was quite natural, then, that Mom and Dad undertook to pursue the religious route of their early childhood days.

The Bible and Bible study were early mainstays in our family. Mom and Dad were, for the most part, self-taught biblical scholars. Dad was singularly blessed with a retentive mind, so much so that he could quote long passages and even some chapters of the Bible from memory. Mom had the power of deep religious conviction to the extent that, if the Bible said so, that was sufficient for her.

My parents were active members of the Paseo Baptist Church where Reverend D. A. Holmes, considered by many to be the dean of black Baptist preachers in America, pastored the congregation. Though faithful and loyal supporters of their church, and always motivated by spiritual considerations, they remained open to new truths as they were unfolded to them in their study of the Scriptures. One day, Mrs. Mary Barry visited them, and offered to give them Bible studies. Mrs. Barry was a faithful member of the Beacon Light Seventh-day Adventist Church, and as she looked deep into the eyes of Mom and Dad, they felt something spiritually special and agreed to have weekly Bible studies under her tutelage.

Mrs. Barry's visits were always initiated with prayer followed by a thorough study of such topics as "The Word of God," "The Second Advent," "The State of the Dead," "A Healthy Body," "Christian Stewardship," "The Sabbath," "The Spirit of Prophecy," and "Baptism." Mrs. Barry in her own quiet way was an extremely strong and terribly knowledgeable woman when it came to the Bible. At each step of the way and with each lesson, my parents were accepting of truth as it was revealed to them. It was not long before my parents had the opportunity to sit under the powerfully instructive sermons of Elder Calvin E. Moseley, Jr., the young minister who had been appointed pastor at Beacon Light Seventh-day Adventist Church in Kansas City. Soon their desire to become Seventh-day Adventists and to become members of that church were overpowering. Consequently, they became members while still in their mid-twenties.

I do not recall my direct exposure to the Adventist Church prior to my return from staying with my aunt and uncle in Campbell, Ohio, at age nine. It was at the church school that I got a healthy dose of Adventist Christian education while in the fourth grade under the direction of my teacher, Ms. Luvada Lockhardt. My earlier discussion of my experiences at that school should have included the extent to which Ms. Lockhardt involved us in all sorts of activities: writing contests, spelling bees, memorizing Bible texts, book reports, and taking us on field trips. It was in that setting that the truth and relevancy of the Bible were affirmed. I never had to go to extraordinary lengths to believe in Christianity or in the tenets of the Seventh-day Adventist Church. My kinship with what I was taught was reinforced by the incredible love and warmth of those who were devoutly practicing Christianity around me—my parents, Ms. Lockhardt, and the wonderful family of church members whom I encountered each Sabbath.

Through the coming years, I enjoyed similar experiences at the College Avenue Seventh-day Adventist Church in Topeka, Kansas, in the early 1940s; at Allon Chapel in Lincoln, Nebraska, in the middle and late 1940s; at Ephesus Seventh-day Adventist Church in Columbus in the early 1950s; at Tekoa Temple in Springfield, Ohio, in the late 1950s and early 1960s; at Oakwood College in the middle and late 1960s; at the Worthington Seventh-day Adventist Church in Worthington, Ohio, in the early 1970s, and at the Ephesus Seventh-day Adventist Church in Columbus, Ohio, again from the middle 1970s through the 1980s and 1990s.

My very first contact with the Ephesus Church of Columbus took place when I began my doctoral program at The Ohio State University in June of 1953. The two pastors who faithfully served the congregation during those days were Elder J. Milton Thomas and Elder Jacob Justiss. There was a strong core of faithful members who undergirded the church program at every turn. Mother J. Estelle Barnett was an unfaltering pillar of strength, as was Sister Bertha Crawford, who was her right-hand associate in promoting the Christian Benevolent Association. "Shep" and Maxine Robinson, Calvin and Dorothy Patterson, Gene and Celeste Miller, James and Thelma Bradley, Warren and Louise Neil, George and Theresa Birden, Henry and Sally Hope, William and Viola Boyer, Joseph and Alma Jones, William and Aletha DeShay, Otis and Marian Vaughn, Robert and Martha Watkins, Lillie Dunlap, Fannie Morgan, Edna Smith, Minnie Hudson, Joseph Rhyne, John and Sarah Ruth Pitts, and James Ross—all of these saints were passionately involved in one way or another in keeping the church moving upward toward being prepared to be in that number "When the Saints Go Marching In." Many of them are now gone, while some still faithfully remain, never lost courage, hope, virtue, cheerfulness, and the self-respect that the life of a true Christian exhibits and commands.

It was in 1971 that my family and I returned to Columbus as I had been invited to serve as associate dean of the Graduate School and as professor of Communication at The Ohio State University. Although I was very heavily involved in my new professional assignment, I nevertheless kept my mind and heart upon the pulse of what was happening within the Seventh-day Adventist Church. I wanted to get a taste of what life was like within the walls of the white Adventist church, as my total church life had been circumscribed to the black experience as far as church matters were concerned. Once our family was settled and situated on Kirkley Avenue, approximately half the distance between downtown Columbus and Worthington, Ohio, a suburb city just north of Columbus, we decided to attend the Worthington Seventh-day Adventist Church, which was considerably closer than the black church which was much farther away. Always a student of human nature, I was determined to learn a little more about how worship was conducted on the other side of the racial divide. So as a family, we immediately got into the swing and swim of things at the Worthington Seventh-day Adventist Church.

It was a typical Adventist Church, throbbing with a variety of interests and activities. I observed that it was probably not the typical white church, as it was loaded with upper-middle class and several affluent parishioners. In fact, the church reflected something of an institutional image because many of its members were associated with and held significant posts at the Harding Hospital, a private psychiatric medical facility with an excellent national reputation. In fact, many members of the Harding family, descendants of the founder and also of President Warren Harding, were actively involved in the church. A number of members were also employees of the Worthington Foods Company, a thriving industry that was known for its vegetarian food products. While our family became passionately involved in the services of the church from week to week, it was not difficult for me to observe that most of the people there had really seized the salient points of what it means to be practicing Christians. They were honest, straightforward, thoughtful, courteous, and attentive without being patronizing. They opened their hearts and the doors of their homes to us on numerous occasions. Their cheerful, warm and welcoming behavior stamped an impression upon us that we shall never forget. There were a few, of course, who were never comfortable in our presence. Prejudice creates a poverty of the spirit that dwarfs the marvelous possibilities that human beings can gain from each when they are open to one another's humanity.

One could not escape the fact that certain members had a powerful influence in the workings and operation of the church. Their opinions were highly valued, and as issues arose, their experience, wisdom, and community standing were brought to bear in weighing, balancing, calculating, evaluating, and determining the appropriate decision. Dr. George Harding, Dr. Herndon Harding, Mr. Allan Buller, Mr. James Hagel, Mr. Warren Hartman, and Dr. John Whieldon were principal pioneers in this regard.

We were privileged to enjoy some very find preaching while in Worthington. It was obvious to us that the church leadership had had a very direct hand in the selection of some very bright and young clergymen as pastors of their learned congregation. I will never forget the spirited and picturesque sermons of Don Winders. He would nail his points to your heart with simple stories and the colorful conviction that left your senses pulsating with new life as you departed the doors of the sanctuary to begin a new life. His sermons were full of beautiful pictures—flush with the records of God's wonderful creation—flowers, babbling brooks, towering trees, entrancing sunrises and sunsets—all intermingled with the spiritual lessons that lifted us out of our failures and discouragements. Once again, we were sent home winging, ready to take on the challenges of another week.

The ages of our children, Frank III, Ruth, and Sherilyn, played a part in our decision to transfer our membership to the Ephesus Seventh-day

Adventist Church on East Fifth Avenue in Columbus. Its membership was historically and predominantly black. Many of their closest friends and associates were there, young people they (Ruth and Frank III) had known from the days when I was there as a doctoral student at Ohio State.

Absolutely nothing was lost in terms of the spiritual ardor that was marvelously present in our new church home as well. We had the blessed privilege of enjoying the ministries of Elder Henry M. Wright (1972–1976), Elder J. H. Lester (1978–1979), Elder Stephen Lewis (1979–1984), Elder Walter Wright (1984–1989), and Elder Buford Griffith (1990–the present).

Elder Henry Wright possessed an unrivaled eye for getting to the heart of a text, a parable, or any biblical experience. He saw lessons and mined gems of truth from well-worn biblical stories that no one had ever presented before. Even the smallest detail would not escape his keen mind—a mind that outstripped the ordinary and penetrated to the heart of things. His experienced spiritual eye drew a conclusion from the slightest evidence. He would have made a powerful trial attorney. I found his messages disturbingly priceless when I applied them to my own life, as he extracted the meaning of everything that came within his mind's range. His weekly Sunday telecast, "Yours for the Asking," was the premier local religious telecast in the city. Elder Charles Drake was a Baptist styled preacher who could bolster up your spirits with an early knockout. He came out firing, and lost little time in making his point with canon-like zeal and effectiveness. Elder Jethroe Lester was the pastor's pastor. He knew how to counsel and how to pray. He had a ready tonic for the half-starved despondent member. He was a bedside wonder who could lift your spirits as he called every member of your family by name, entreating heaven's outpouring on each one of them. He made remarkable things happen with his simple and unadorned approach to everyday matters. Elder Stephen Lewis was a boyish package of spiritual dynamite. He was crammed and stuffed with enthusiasm. There was no doubt among the members about his commitment. He knew how to magnify the power of God in his every sermon. He was possessed with superhuman and irresistible power to be a man of such small stature. It was he who appointed me to become the building fund chairman in 1980, a position that Brother Otis "I'm on Fire" Vaughn had held since 1976.

It was during Elder Lewis' administration that Evangelist Earl E. Cleveland came to Columbus and conducted his fiftieth evangelistic crusade under the Canvas Cathedral at the corner of Broad Street and Ohio Avenue. The average attendance at the nightly meetings was two hundred, and on Sunday evenings, nine hundred people would show.

Evangelist Cleveland made no apologies for presenting scriptural interpretation in a straight-forward *Thus saith the Lord*-approach. He captured the imagination of his audience who was often unfamiliar with such subjects as "The Seventh-day Sabbath," "The Mark of the Beast," "Clean and Unclean Meats," "The State of the Dead," or "The Five Laws that Govern the Universe." Much of his terminology and teaching was couched in everyday situations and experiences which were meaningful to his listeners. It explains, in part, and certainly not to exclude divine inspiration and revelation, why the messages of truth which he shares are indelibly imprinted and long remembered by those who have been fortunate and blessed enough to sit at his feet.

The power of the fifty-three year ministry and evangelism of Earl E. Cleveland had earned him a place in the front ranks of church evangelists of our generation. No description is adequate to reproduce the dynamic impact of this preacher of righteousness. His unadulterated witness provides a clear exhibition that a disciplined mind and a willingness to be amenable to the will of God are just the human qualities, be they ever so rare, that are more than sufficient with God's accompanying power to use sincere vessels of clay. Cleveland has preached a gospel for more than six decades that has been uncompromising, uncluttered by fad and fashion, and uncontrolled by those would be prophets and priests who find his *thus said the Lord* an anathema to their *thus saith I.*

Here in Columbus, Ohio, night after night he asked the assembled guests to search the dusty corners of their lives. And what we saw did not permit complacency. He is equipped as are few men with wisdom, experience, a knowledge of the Bible, a consecration of self, a mastery of the mechanics of communication, a sense of humor, and an understanding of human psychology to testify to God's goodness and care for His children. Earl Cleveland has never lost sight of the whole mission of the gospel and of the church, within or beyond its walks, and because of that fact, it can be said of him as it was of the early apostles, that he is among us who helped to turn the world upside down.

I will never forget Elder Walter Wright's first sermon after he was installed as our pastor in February of 1987. He vehemently declared in his opening statement, "I have come to build a church!" The real impact of his message became evident by the fact that considerable discussion took place over: (1) whether the old church should be renovated, (2) whether a new church should be erected on the site of the old church, or (3) whether a new church should be built at a new location.

Once the church decided to follow the latter course, I went into action to begin fund raising efforts that would expedite the process. Early in the year, I challenged members to be prepared to make great sacrifices during the approaching holiday seasons. On Thanksgiving Sabbath alone, members turned in $57,000 in actual funds, and they contributed an additional $30,000 on the following Sabbath. On the third Sabbath in December another generous gift of $27,000 was placed on the *Jesus Tree.* The wholesale emergence of sacrificial giving over the next two years led to the most striking and significant occurrences of unselfish generosity in the history of the church. Some members mortgaged their homes, others cashed in retirement and insurance policies, and still others depleted their savings.

Within a short period of time, the church purchased 11.7 acres of land on the corner of Sunbury and McCutcheon Roads. The property was owned by Schottenstein's, Inc., and Brother Earl Harris, Sr., served as the intermediary to facilitate the transaction. Pastor Wright used his knowledge of buildings to oversee the building of a beautiful edifice that officially opened July 18, 1987. God had given us a dream that we had never expected would happen so soon after Elder Wright had announced his intentions. Once again, we learned that, "If God be for us, who can be against us?" It was also helped that we had in Elder Wright the confluence of a creative mind and a strong backbone to withstand the pressures of some warring personalities.

Elder Buford Griffin's ministry has blessed the congregation over and over again. Through powerful, spirit-filled preaching, he has served as a unifying force in harmonizing the membership. Since becoming pastor of Ephesus in April of 1990, the church has continued to grow. Because of his outreach efforts—revivals and revelation seminars, he has added to the church membership on the average of fifty new members each year. God, too, has blessed the efforts of Ruth and me as we have given Bible studies to Anthony Burgess, Audrey Dixon, Cynthia Everhart, and members of the family of Betty Jones. Burgess, Dixon, and Everhart have been baptized and are now members of Ephesus. During this period, our hearts have been especially lifted as our daughter, Ifeoma Kwesi (christened Ruth Hale) was rebaptized and pursued religious studies at Oakwood College and Andrews University before earning the M.Div. degree at the latter institution. She is now pastor of the Oak Park Seventh-day Adventist Church in San Diego, California. Our son, Frank W. Hale III, has served as the First Elder of Ephesus for the past five years. "To God Be the Glory!"

During the middle 1980s, the Ephesus Seventh-day Adventist Church in Columbus, Ohio, began to buttress its weekend Sabbath services with a number of programs designed to promote individual growth, group fellowship, and spiritual and intellectual growth. Examples of courageous actions to foster these included the founding of the Frank

Loris Peterson Society of Adventist Men, the children's choir, and the learning center.

The Peterson Society was founded in December of 1987 when I convened a group of fifteen men who committed themselves to using their influence to motivate and serve as role models for young African-American youth, sharing with them the knowledge, resources, and experiences of the group throughout the year. The society, too, felt the need to provide an opportunity for the men of the church to become involved in meaningful well-coordinated events to support the overall activities of the church. It was apparent that the men of the church had no structure in place comparable to the Dorcas Society or the King's Daughters that afforded them a base of mutual support. Since its inception, the organization has sponsored a variety of programmatic activities, including lectures, recitals, spelling contests, oratorical contests, classes in manhood development, value-focused retreats, and excursions to athletic functions at The Ohio State University, the Columbus Clippers baseball games, and to the pre-Olympic trials which were held in Indianapolis, Indiana. Each year the organization sponsors an Anniversary Weekend during the first week of December, at which time it invites a prominent teacher within the denomination to give the Sabbath sermon. This occasion has become a major community event as many guests join us at this time, along with many visiting ministers who share the platform with our pastor, the guest minister and Peterson Society officers.

We have already been blessed to have experienced the dynamic inspirational preaching of Elder Charles Bradford, Dr. Calvin Rock, Elder Earl Cleveland, Elder Walter Pearson, Dr. Benjamin Reaves, Dr. Barry Black, Elder Randolph Stafford, and Elder Jack Morris. On the Sunday evening which follows, the society sponsors a scholarship banquet, at which time it honors and recognizes outstanding local students (20–25) who have demonstrated superior qualities in the areas of academics, leadership and character. The honorees are given monetary awards and medallions at this major event which is always keynoted by a prominent national leader. Our speakers have included Congressman Louis Stokes, Dr. Samuel Dewitt Proctor, Dr. Benjamin Carson, and Dr. Arthur Thomas.

The Children's Choir, composed of approximately forty young harmonious voices, has blossomed into a significant arm of our musical ministry at Ephesus. Elaine Crawford, the director, and Jacqueline Parris, the pianist, have spent long hours of dedicated and sacrificial service to prepare the choir for their appearances. The counseling support of Crystal Adams and her husband, M. C. Adams, has borne many fruits, not the least of which has been the recognition that the children's choir has gained stature as a legitimate and responsible musical group within the active church life of the congregation.

Typical of the excellent music that historically has been so much a part of the services at Ephesus is the major role that the Oasis Chorale Ensemble has played. This group composed of young adults, many of whom are college trained, is unrivaled in terms of their musicianship, their enthusiasm, their consecration and their constant support to the church that has now extended over a period of nearly two decades. Their repertoire is both comprehensive and eclectic; thus, they are in demand and have made public appearances throughout the United States at youth conferences, evangelistic meetings, and for various church anniversary celebrations.

Most recently, Ephesus has undertaken a pioneering effort in establishing a learning center for pre-school aged children. This initiative promises to offer the community a God-centered educational development program that will ultimately expand to meet the academic and spiritual needs of our youth at higher levels. Currently, nearly sixty children are enrolled in this program that had its rich beginnings under the direction and guidance of Ms. Yvette Cooper.

All in all, the members of Ephesus still work in a fury of passion so that the great day of the Lord's Second Advent will not take us unaware.

So much of what we have gained in our religious journey as a family is due, in large part, because of our Christian parents. Even though I lost my mother on April 12, 1985, and my father on April 27, 1991, their religious maturity and lives left us examples that will never be lost on us. It is unfortunate that we generally do not understand the value and indispensability of our parents as much while they are living as we do after they are no longer with us. We are products of our homes where our parents are powerful influences in our lives. While my home was a sanctuary of love and serenity, my parents, nevertheless, opened my mind to a world of balance, of good and evil, of successes and failures, and of pitfalls and snares. One of their great gifts to me, however, was their opening up the doors of opportunity for me to live my life independent of them, and even independent of their desires and ambitions. Yet, all the while, their spiritual map never left me without a sense of direction. During and even since their departure, their greatest gift and blessing to me was their spiritual philosophy of life which they themselves affirmed by the way they lived.

Even prior to my parents' departure, I had long before come to confront my own sense of verities and values. I have always had a problem of dealing with morality based on expediency. Semanticists would have us believe that *nothing is*, that everything is relative, situational, and that truth is based only on one's notion of what is right and wrong. I happen to believe that some things defy syrupy subjectivity; they are either irrevocably good or bad, right or wrong, just or unjust. I know that such a point of view doesn't sit well among those of the philosophic breed who are contemptuous of absolutes.

Although I have spent so much of my time in academic circles where, for some, religious faith receives the rawest kind of cynicism, I find it appalling that so few acknowledge and note the correlation between the steady erosion of religious standards, as a basis of morality, and the unprecedented wave of crime and social pathologies so pervasive in our society today. I feel blessed that I am a member of a denomination that does not debate the authenticity of the Bible and is precise and untentative in its doctrines and teachings relative to biblical claims and commands. It takes no imagination to discover that obedience to God's directives relative to marriage, temperance, stewardship, diet, family values, and racial equality are indispensable factors that contribute to the harmonious interplay of our physical, mental and spiritual powers. To deny the truth and promising potential of the Bible as the Word of God without any preconditions is to open oneself to a larger misunderstanding of one's own role in this one grand opportunity that we call *life*. Attempts to confine the truth to traditions, practices, and trends of humanity's dwarfed and exhausted insights is to both trivialize and insult the integrity and omniscience of God who started us on our way in the first place.

It is quite apparent that too many denominations and religious orders boldly respond to contemporary practices. They have devalued many of the missions and moorings that gave birth to their churches, temples, synagogues and houses of worship. The shaky platform on which their tenets rest have neither shape nor focus. Their anchor is attached to a kind of faddism that gains its staggering influence from the street rather than *thus saith the Lord*.

My church, using the Bible as its road map, has provided me with a blueprint for living. Even during my weakest moments of failure and moral deafness to God's will for me at significant points in my life, I have always known where the compass was and how to reclaim my moral direction through faith, forgiveness, and the promises of a loving God.

Epilogue

Reflections and Projections

I have experienced an intense and overwhelming joy in life, certainly with my family and very obviously in my profession. I have possessed a vigor and a drive in my pursuit of possibilities in higher education that has been inexhaustible. I have reveled in my role as an administrator, shouldering the responsibilities of multiple tasks simultaneously and, with God's help, with more than a modicum of success. Strong in opinions and beliefs, I have always relished a good debate as such encounters are indispensable to quick thinking and to a genuine analysis of the issue being argued. I am extremely grateful to God for blessing me with communication skills that have enabled me to be a competent teacher, administrator, consultant, and public speaker.

While some may have thought that it has been my nature to itch for a fight, I have always been more forthright in coming to the defense of others than fighting to project my own interests. I can truthfully say that I do not and have not ever hated anybody, but I have had no difficulty in being relentless in attacking those whose wanton greed and inhumanity seek to take advantage of others. My sense of fellowship with the sufferings of my people has gotten me into serious scraps with folks in very high places. Faced with certain uncomfortable situations, I have not hesitated to use whatever techniques and maneuvers that were appropriate to take those I thought guilty of oppression and cowardice to the mat.

Nothing has had more of a bearing on my professional life, generally, than my love of books. I learned to appreciate so many things at an early age, and reading was one of them. Newspaper reading was a daily challenge during my childhood, because my parents expected me to be able to summarize the contemporary issues of the day at the dinner table. I learned to read quickly, surveying the newspaper for its major stories, and then assimilating its content in order to be prepared for the evening's question and answer period. My parents were always pleased and sometime astonished about how well I remembered in great detail most everything that I read.

To be sure, it was the experience that I received in my parents' bookstore in Topeka, Kansas, that extended my appreciation for books, and enabled me to embrace things literary as a way of life. Books have, in so many ways, added to the richness of my life. It is practically impossible for me to pass a bookstore, new or used, without indulging myself of getting a measure of relief and serenity, only after venturing and then purchasing a quantity beyond my means. It is a simple preoccupation that underscores my vulnerability for love for learning. My extensive library of more than ten thousand volumes includes such seminal thinkers and scholars as Shakespeare, Myrdal, Marx, Einstein, Woodson, Mays, Douglass, Malcom, Tolstoi, DuBois, Wells, Asante, Hooks, West, Gates, Churchill, Morrison, Baldwin, Thoreau, Ellison, Milton, Pushkin, Homer, Angelou, Plato, and Fanon. It contains the heroic efforts of major crusaders for justice as Garvey, Garrison, Tubman, Brown, Truth, Sumner, Johnson, Brooks, Marshall, Hamer, King, Malcolm, and Jackson.

It was my marriage to the literary tradition that enabled me to produce scores of articles for professional journals and which was responsible for my having attained the rank of full professor in each of three institutions— Oakwood College, Central State University (Ohio), and The Ohio State University.

One of the most heart-warming aspects of my life has been my relationship with special people who have added so much to my life and happiness. My closest friendships have grown and developed beyond any class or political requirements. Vertis Barnes, Jr., and I have been best friends since our mothers met in the maternity ward in preparation of giving delivery to us. It is a friendship that has expanded over the durability of sixty-eight years. Outside of my family, he and Gaines Roland Partridge have been my fondest of friends over the years. During my boyhood days in Topeka, Kansas, it was Milton Woodson who was always there, at play, at church, and at singing in the church and Hub of Harmony Quartet. The intricate structure of personal and friendly relations grew at Oakwood with Jannith Lewis, Jon and Florence Robertson, and Roy and Edrene Malcolm. During the most heated days of racial controversy within the church, it was Burrell and Bonnie Scott, as well as Mylas Martin IV, who were sources of amicable friendship and support. In later years after moving to Columbus, I met an astute young puppy by the name of Henry Griffith in the field of school administration, and we hit it off because of mutual interests and

378

respect for each other. As far as I can remember, he is the only man alive who has called me out of my name to my face and gotten away with it. Griffith's brilliant and fluent writing has landed him articles in some of the nation's most prestigious journals. Time and time again, he, as we have baited each other, has intruded his keen intellect on some of the most controversial issues of the day. I cherish his friendship because of the depth of his integrity and the scope of his unshaken intellectual inquiry.

The whole litany of my professional life has been augmented by certain women who have been extremely devoted and dedicated to my professional growth and development. I have had a distinctive advantage because of their exceptional support. Several student secretaries gave major assistance to me when I held administrative assignments at Oakwood. They were Eunice Vanderberg, Helen Smith, Carol Moore, and Pauline Orme. Maxine Crump and I had great rapport when she was my secretary during the time that I was chairman of the English Department at Central State University. Rose Wilson had almost complete authority in arranging the affairs of my office when I served as president at Oakwood College. She continued her effectiveness as my administrative assistant in the graduate school at The Ohio State University. It goes without saying that Linda Jackson, Ellen Banks, and Wanda Barnett, Patricia Knox and Pamela Clark were my mainstays in the details of office and financial management ventures at Ohio State.

Over the years, I learned so much from the expert skills and collegial relationships that I had with such superior professionals as Arliss Roaden, Edward Jennings, Frank L. Peterson, Joseph Stranges, Barbara Newman, Eva B. Dykes, Albert Kuhn, Harold Enarson, Diether Haenicke, Prince Wilson, Garland Millet, Emerson Cooper, Talbert Shaw, William Nelson, Anne Pruitt, Elmer Baumer, William Holloway, Carleton Lee, Lenora C. Lane, Charles Wesley, Clara Henderson, and Manny Tzagournis.

I have always been interested in travel. While early in my professional life, I did not like to fly; it later became in fact a way of life during my presidency at Oakwood and during my administrative years at Ohio State. Nevertheless, I have had only two close calls in my air travel over the years: one was in 1971 when I, along with forty-two other passengers on a twin-engine prop jet owned by the North Central Airlines, landed at St. Joseph County (Michigan) Airport with only one engine. I had been on my way to Andrews University for a Black History Week speaking engagement when the plane began to experience engine difficulties midway between Chicago's O'Hare Field where the flight originated and South Bend. You can imagine our anxiety and fear as we finally landed among several fire department companies, aerial and aircraft units, and emergency and ambulance units. I knew that we had touched the ground safely only because angels were watching over us.

It was on December 29, 1980, that my son Frank III and I were special guests of the university when we flew to Phoenix, Arizona, as a part of the university's presidential party to witness the Fiesta Bowl football game between Ohio State and Pittsburgh. Upon our return takeoff two tires blew out on the United Airlines charter flight at Sky Harbor International Airport. We heard a loud pop, similar to a shotgun, and the plane began to fill with smoke. Both tires and the number two engine were on fire. My son and I escaped through the emergency door exit over the plane's wing, and we had to jump about ten feet to the ground. Some passengers suffered ankle, leg and arm fractures in their escape attempts. Frank and I suffered no fractures, although it was necessary for me to have ultrasound treatments for nearly a month because of a back strain. Fortunately, an explosion did not occur. We were able to praise the Lord again, as angels were watching over us.

I have so much for which to be grateful. I think of the larger than life opportunities that I have had to address great assemblies, particularly during the commencement season. My engagements at Topeka High School where I was graduated, Oakwood College on two occasions, Loma Linda University, Howard University, Wilberforce University, and Shaw University were remarkable milestones in my professional life. They offered gigantic settings to explore gigantic issues.

I have always had a perceptive eye for those whose quality of life and experience taught me valuable lessons. Among those who had a penetrating religious and/or professional influence on my life were Elder Louis B. Reynolds, Elder Frank L. Peterson, Elder Calvin E. Moseley, Jr., Elder Walter Wright, Elder Buford Griffith, Dr. Charles Wesley, Dr. Winton Beaven, Dr. Arliss Roaden, Dr. Albert Kuhn, Dr. William J. Holloway, Dr. Edward H. Jennings, Dr. Eva B. Dykes, Ms. Luvada Lockhardt, and Dr. Jannith Lewis.

The focus of my presidency at Oakwood College was on creating a vision for the future by doing what I could to promote that vision among all the constituents of the Oakwood community—students, faculty, staff, administrators, and alumni. I am very pleased and proud of the many programs which God enabled me to introduce at Oakwood. I was always looking beyond the moment—seeking to upgrade the faculty and the curriculum at every turn, urging the board to view Oakwood with the same eye and commitment for academic quality as had been the case for historically white Seventh-day Adventist colleges, encouraging students, upon their graduation, to be more compassionate toward human pain and suffering and more intolerant of social injustices and inequities, and challenging faculty to understand that there is no substitute for spiritual and academic excellence as they went about their work.

The opportunities for positive leadership continue to skyrocket, and Oakwood College has been so fortunate in having Dr. Calvin Rock and Dr. Benjamin Reaves as very able successors to my tenure in office. The face and complexion of America is changing, and accordingly, it is inevitable that the substance, shape and style of higher education will change as well. The year 2000, already imminently upon us, offers us a challenge in terms of Christian and secular civility.

Hopefully, on the issues of diversity, institutions of higher education will begin to provide a more realistic view of American life, daring to create a climate that will encourage discussion, dialogue and debate about racial and cultural perspectives. Such an approach would be both constructive and revolutionary, though a distinct departure from traditional practices that refuse to acknowledge that racism and society's willingness to ignore it are endemic to our culture. The post-Rodney King period and the worrisome disruptive aspects of the O. J. Simpson trial and its aftermath highlight the importance of the need for institutions of higher education to accept their responsibility for promoting a pluralistic world view as an essential core of higher education. Such an approach will be an inevitable direction in the future to meet the exploding demands for recognition and inclusion by people of color as they become unprecedentedly concentrated, vocal, and more powerful on the American scene.

Because of the wider range of abilities and skills that are required in our technological society, it will become necessary to develop curricula that will complement the sophisticated world of science and technology into which they will be ushered upon the completion of their college requirements. In order for the quality of instruction to be enhanced, the academy will need to consider the advantages of hands-on instruction by engineers, scientists, technicians and computer experts whose expertise can offset the imbalance created by current faculty whose methodology is often limited to theoretical blackboard instruction devoid of practical experience. That limits their ability to master the relevant information that is required to make their students imaginative and competitive for the twenty-first century.

It should not seem ridiculous that I am very much concerned about the role that educational institutions should play in addressing those problems that cast an enormous dark shadow on the state of myopia in the academy relative to meeting the needs of urban America. Again, the recent Million Man March focused on the cluster of pathologies that plague and undermine the vitality of our inner cities—homelessness, unemployment, poverty, crime, racial tensions, gang warfare, homicides, drug abuse, air and water pollution, health hazards, police brutality, teenage pregnancy, traffic congestion, as well as other negative conditions. Most institutions of higher education cater to agricultural, legal, financial, and medical interest groups, but they have done little to respond to the deteriorating needs of the most distressed areas in America. With the shift in our demographic profile as increasing numbers of America's newcomers invade the central cities of our country, every college and university in the nation will need to develop strong and distinctive relationships with their neighboring communities who are often dangerously out of the loop of the interests and priorities of academic institutions. Such challenges may very well help the institution to discover its need for having a soul as well as a brain.

My travels, too, have affected my growth immensely. Always keenly interested in new discoveries, I along with my family members have enjoyed the natural beauties of the Rockies, the Grand Canyon, Yosemite, Niagara Falls, Lake Tahoe, Mt. Rainier, the Ozarks, the mesas of Arizona, as well as cruises to the Bahamas, Puerto Rico, Bermuda, St. Thomas, and fantastic automobile excursions throughout Canada. My overseas travels have carried me to London, Paris, Honolulu, Cairo, Jerusalem, Amsterdam, and Scotland.

I have never ceased to enjoy the great cultural outlets of life—the London Symphony Orchestra under the direction of Sir Malcolm Sargeant, the Kansas City, Cleveland, New York and Philadelphia Orchestras, and the matured and superior voices of such great artists as Marian Anderson, Paul Robeson, Roland Hayes, Dorothy Maynor, Lily Ponds, Leontyne Price, Maria Callas, Beverly Sills, Todd Duncan, William Warfield, McHenry Boatright, Jessye Norman, and Shirley Verrett.

But it has been my family, most of all, that has set its stamp on my life, my work, and my successes. They, each of them, have been at the central core of my life. Always obsessed with making a better life for me than they had experienced, my parents were determined to kindle within my breast a love for learning. They did everything they could to encourage in me a fondness for all that was good and profitable. They were extravagant in praise when I did something praiseworthy, and extravagant as well in punishment when I dared to enter into the intolerable world of indifference or indolence. It was my crowning fortune to be born to Godly parents who knew where they were going even when I didn't.

My wife, too, of forty-eight years has been a precious treasure and resource. She possesses marvelous powers of intuition, mind, and purpose. My life in many ways would have been a miserable failure, but for

382

the spiritual stability, mental discipline, and emotional stamina of this special angel from high and heavenly places. My life has been successful to the extent that it has confined itself to much of her counsel, insight, and direction. She has been a monument of common sense throughout the years of our marriage.

My children, likewise, have given sublime support to my every effort. I have been able to give wholly to my profession because of their indescribable loyalty to all that of which I've been a part. They always recognized that, as a family, we are all a part of one piece. They knew that with my success or failure, theirs was at stake as well. Their honor, their careers, and their future successes also rested with mine., So all of them helped me to make the most of myself with their encouragement, their suggestions, their comprehensive attention to what I was about, their indelibly fixed focus on their own future, and their gift of persistence, honesty and excellence in whatever their hands found to do.

Ifeoma and Frank III have been genuinely supportive. Jim Roseboro, Ifeoma's spouse, while battling with Lou Gehrig's disease, has a formidable spirit that defies the agony of pain which he daily endures. Irene, Frank III's spouse, plays a vital role as wife, mother, and as administrative secretary to Elder Willie Lewis, the president of the Allegheny Conference of Seventh-day Adventists. My granddaughter, Renene Price and her husband James, pursuing careers in teaching and nursing, keep in constant and loving touch.

The quality of excellence characterizes other blood members of my family. This quality has given them preeminence, respect, and success in their respective fields. Mrs. Isy O. Young (my aunt), and my cousins, Charlotte Walton, Susie Brown, Marian Patterson, Elfleda Tate, Georgette Thompson, Corinne Harris, Claudine Pinson, and Mary Bebbs are all infinitely successful people in their own right, and they all have been lovingly consistent in their support of me years on end.

Of course, I know that angels had been watching over me after my two critical bouts with a ruptured esophagus in 1981 and after six-way bypass heart surgery in 1986. Thank God for the gifted hands of Dr. John Vasko and Dr. David Myerowitz, who, under His guiding direction, sent sunshine through the gloom in these critical surgeries respectively.

Over the years, I have been very active as a volunteer with the United Negro College Fund (UNCF). As president of Oakwood College, I had been a member of the National Board of Trustees of UNCF, so when my family moved to Columbus, Ohio, in 1971, I was happy to have the opportunity to renew my long-standing personal commitment to the college fund. I offered not the slightest resistance when James Allen invited me to serve as a member of the Central Ohio Board of UNCF. I remembered Mr. Allen from many years before, when I had pursued doctoral studies at The Ohio State University in the early 1950s. He has always maintained a fundamental allegiance to the fund and, more than any other person, has been responsible for creating a texture of substantial support for the fund throughout the business and corporate community in central Ohio. My experience in working with him, Ray, Adams, and the other board members has been a delightful one. I was the recipient of one of the finest honors ever bestowed upon me when I was presented the Frederick Douglass Patterson Award, the UNCF's highest award, at the organization's fiftieth anniversary banquet in 1994.

Perhaps, the one experience that has captured more than any other of my experiences in higher education was the success that God gave me in establishing the Graduate and Professional Schools Visitation and Fellowship Program at The Ohio State University. While approximately two thousand students of color benefited from that program, I was particularly pleased that so many Seventh-day Adventist youth could also take advantage of this treasure of opportunity. While many of those students were graduates of historically black colleges, a significant number of the students who were admitted were from Virginia State University, Dillard University, Hampton University, Morgan State University, and North Carolina A&T University; Oakwood College also had an impressive list of students who were admitted and who were fellowship recipients. Some Oakwood alumni glowingly refer to Ohio State as the Oakwood Annex.

Among some of the successful Adventist graduates of that program were Dennis Alexander, Ph.D., Psychology, '94; Brenda Black, M.A., English, '73; Paul Brantley, Ph.D., Education, '75; Joyce Cordell, Ph.D., Communication, '73; Leslie Crichlow, Business Administration/Law, M.B.A./J.D., '83; Henry Fordham, M.A., History, '74; Ephraim Gwebu, Ph.D., Chemistry, '79; Judith Hawkins, M.S., Home Economics, '77; Patricia Holness, Ph.D., Horticulture, '85; Ricky Little, D.M.A., Music, '84; Valerie Gray Lee, Ph.D., English, '76; Sandy Robinson, J.D., Law, '79; Anthony Sims, D.D.S., Dentistry, '83; Devon Stokes, Ph.D., Psychology, '83; Beverly Vaughn, D.M.A., Music, '82; Karen Warren, M.S., Nursing, '76; Delvius Wagner, M.A., Communication, '78; Angela Stovall, M.A., Education, '84; Patricia Scott, M.A., M.P.A, City and Regional Planning/Public Administration, '76; Roy Malcolm, Ph.D., Education, '74; Charles Miller, M.Acc., Accounting, '76; Judy Montford, M.A., Journalism, '80; Charlotte Osterman, M.S.W., Social Work, '75; Linda Ammons, M.A., J.D., Communication/Law, '80, '84; Ronald Campbell, M.B.A., Business Administration, '76; Kristen Davis, Ph.D., Psychology, '85;

Carleton Galley, M.A., Physical Education, '79; William DeShay, Ph.D., Education, '75; James E. Hawkins, Ph.D., Communication, '79; Allen Hackley, M.D., Medicine, '79; James Stewart, Jr., Ph.D., Psychology, '84; Joseph Warren, Ph.D., English, '82; Teni Garrett, Ph.D., Psychology, '84; and Anthony Mayo, O.D., Optometry, '86.*

I was especially blessed to have been invited to address the Twenty-fifth Anniversary Banquet of the Graduate and Professional Schools Visitation Days Program at The Ohio State University on October 30, 1995. As the founder of the program, I was delighted that the program had been sustained at the institution of Scarlet and Gray over the years to the point that more than two thousand students of color have been accepted, admitted, and awarded graduate and professional degrees. Their successes have registered a plus for the dint of indomitable and inflexible purpose. They speak to the triumphs of faith and fortitude over seemingly impossible circumstances.

My challenge to the six hundred assembled scholar-guests was to "Remember"—to remember the contributions of their families and friends, to remember the support of their teachers of the past and present, to remember their ancestral roots—those who were magnificent models of survival in a hostile environment—to remember their responsibility to society by seeking to remove the shutters of hopelessness from the minds of those who seem condemned to life's deflating inequities, and to remember God who had brought them this far by faith. This, of course, represents only a condensed version of my speech; nevertheless, it was a hallelujah evening! My address was received with exhilaratingly warm applause, and scores of students remained afterward for me to autograph their banquet programs. It was an evening that I shall long remember. Once again, Rose Wilson-Hill did a magnificent job in planning and implementing the two-day event. Ms. Wilson-Hill is director of administration for The Ohio State University Office of Minority Affairs. Truly, even after twenty-five years, angels continued to watch over me and the program which I had established.

In the spring of 1994, Dr. Keith Parker, an associate professor of Sociology at the University of Nebraska in Lincoln, Nebraska, arranged for me to come to the university to keynote a statewide conference on designing and managing programs of diversity in higher education. While the program was under the auspices of the College of Education, Dr. Parker's counsel had been sought in the preparation of the program because of his reputation as a scholar and because of his effective leadership as a catalyst

* See Appendix M, page 432, for additional listing of graduates.

in developing outreach initiatives relative to the recruitment of students and faculty of color.

As a consequence of my appearance and presence on campus, I was invited by Dr. William Seiler, chairman of the Department of Communication, to return as a visiting professor of Communication during the summer of 1995. Fortunately for me, it was an opportunity to return to the campus where I had earned the B.A. and M.A. degrees in Communication, English and Political Science in 1950 and 1951.

The five week summer session was filled with gratifying opportunities and results for me. I had the privilege of teaching a class on the "Rhetoric of Black America," a course I had designed and taught at The Ohio State University going back as early as 1972. My class was one that could be taken for undergraduate as well as graduate credit, offering me the challenge of keeping in tune with the interests of both sophisticated students as well as those who were less experienced in terms of having met the competitive challenges of their graduate counterparts. That cross section of academic background was reflected in the fact that there were graduate students whose potential was quite evident by that fact that a number of them were serving as teaching or research assistants in the departments of their major discipline. At the other end, there were undergraduates in my class like Tom Frazier, Nebraska's celebrated football quarterback, who also demonstrated potential for high academic achievement. It was a mix that provided a classroom environment of give and take that was refreshing and rewarding.

My professional contacts were also extended as my visit to the campus gave me the opportunity to meet with some very well-grounded young African-American professionals. There were two bright young women who had been recently appointed as faculty members in the Department of Communication, and they already had students eating out of their hands because of their scholarly resourcefulness and personal warmth. They were Drs. Veronica Duncan and Venita Kelley. Then, too, there was a young graduate student by the name of Stacy Webster who I feel is destined to make her mark as she exhibited uncommon enthusiasm for her classroom assignments as a teaching assistant.

I am fully aware, as are most African-Americans, that American democracy has yet to live up to its creed, and it will not fulfill its promise of the dream of most citizens of color until its blessings reach every citizen. While I know that, over the nearly seven decades of my life, certain steps have been taken to improve the lot of people of color, energetic steps have yet to be taken to eliminate so many of the conditions that impact negatively on those who are members of the dominant group.

Special programs continue to glare as disturbing indications of the misfortunes that have victimized too many of our citizens. Disgraceful problems related to unemployment, poverty, crime, substance abuse, homelessness, and racial inequalities undermine opportunities for many to achieve a better life.

From the very beginning of my career, I have been dedicated to motivating those youth who are young, gifted, and people of color. As Americans, we could be awakened to what our true potential could become, if we were willing to admit and express openly our scandalous and treacherous attitudes on matters of race. Such attitudes are very apparent both individually and in institutions; they are reflected in their composition and the administration of their policies.

Here is a picture that is dark and gloomy, except for one's own soul force, a force which enables one to distinguish the fictitious from the real—a force disciplined by suffering, ennobled by pain, and redeemed by the historical triumphs of perseverance and heroism.

The central characters in this drama have been the *minds* and *hearts* of those who by the dint of indomitable will and inflexible purpose have triumphed over seemingly insuperable difficulties. The grand catalog of the experiences of people of color has yet to be written. When it is written, it will be a volume of the most fascinating romances of struggle and achievement under unconscionable difficulties and of obscure beginnings and triumph, and above all, determination, disarming the darkness by proclaiming it.

Redoubled attention must be given to the education and moral and academic development of our children. Without solid support and direction, they cannot protect themselves against the wiles of the unsanctified streets and the dangerous self-seekers who lurk there. There was a time, in my youthful days, when most of my peers really valued the possibilities inherent and available in a sound educational pursuit. It is no secret that a good many African-American youth today exhibit contempt for education as a *white man's game.* We must not hesitate to take on those forces of any ilk who are anti-intellectual and anti-achievement in their orientation. The concept of *achievement and power through education* includes a fully-developed, personal power strategy that flows from education and job training into equal opportunity and full employment. People may be discriminated against because of their color even if they are competent and qualified and, as a result, lose out on certain job possibilities. But all doors of opportunity will not be closed to them. The door will never be cracked in the first place for those who have not taken the advantage to improve themselves educationally.

Unfortunately, some youth have grown so frustrated and deflated that, in their desperation, they view life as defeating and futile. They are totally cynical, if not hysterical, about the possibilities for their achievement because society and their own lack of personal responsibility has made them that way.

America likes to boast that she is the champion of the free world. We are so obsessed with defining strength in terms of the atomic, hydrogen, and cobalt bombs that we are able to store that we undervalue and undermine some of the most precious freedoms upon which this country was founded. We cannot combat the dangerous ideologies of racism with rhetoric and guns. The best way to preserve a democracy is to practice it.

On Monday, October 16, 1995, I sat glued to my television as my heart of hearts applauded the unprecedented demonstration of black unity at the Million Man March in Washington, D.C. While I reveled in the rally's call for a spirit of atonement, I, like many others, found it difficult to salvage what might very well have been a *pure* message of unity from the inflammatory and divisive message of Louis Farrakhan. Yet, there is so much truth in what he says in terms of how the nation has been a promoter and partner in meting out severe injustices to black people and other people of color. It is the truth which Farrakhan speaks so boldly and forthrightly that makes him so attractive to African-American men. If he is to be an example, a role model, and a leader of hope, then he must temper his style—and not the truth—in order to create the healing process of which he so eloquently speaks. Demagoguery of any kind is no substitute for civility. As black people, we must come to the realization that we must wholeheartedly apply the standards of decency and morality equitably to ourselves as well as to those who have oppressed us. However unpleasant it may be, we do not have the luxury of concocting one code of ethics for black people and another for those who have repudiated our humanity and our dignity for centuries on end. Racial intolerance in any color is despicable.

I have always considered myself an optimist, and yet I hasten to add that it is extremely difficult for me to be overwhelmingly hopeful as disillusionment, discord, dissatisfaction, and division abound between and among the races. Even as we speak of unity, we are caught in the crosscurrents of the post-election politics of resentment. The debate about racial equality and affirmative action has been saturated with an unhappy combination of mean spiritedness and a poverty of vision. Our country is reeling from the exacerbated tensions and aftermath of the Rodney King and O. J. Simpson trials and verdicts. Politicians have disgracefully used negative racial images to manipulate public opinion and voter turnout, rather than incisively and vividly defining the problems facing us and offering viable alternatives and solutions that would bring us together.

As black people, we do not know whether O. J. was guilty or not. We certainly do not approve of such brutal killings, no matter who the murderers or victims are. What is puzzling, however, was the manner in which white Americans responded to the verdict. White juries make decisions on a daily basis that negatively impact on blacks who are indicted. It was only recently that the Simi Valley all-white jury exonerated the police mob who beat Rodney King so unmercifully and in full view of their courtroom cameras. It was just another instance of white America having a penchant for looking the other way, or passing by on the other side, when people of color are brutalized, particularly by a police force that represents security for whites and who rarely challenge their inhumane treatment of people of color.

Some have used affirmative action as a whipping boy to justify dismantling a positive program that has been in place only thirty years. The nation must come to challenge a system that for four hundred years imposed the devastating effects of slavery, legal segregation and discrimination on African-Americans.

Black people did not invent affirmative action, nor do they have a monopoly on it. When it was against the law for blacks to go to school and then later were confined by law to segregated schools from 1896 to 1954 under the doctrine of separate by equal, whites enjoyed the affirmative advantage of a running head start as well as a superior education. Even though the Fifteenth Amendment granted blacks the right to vote, the calculated opposition to denying them that right in the deep South made it necessary to enact a Voting Rights Act in 1965. For nearly one hundred years up until that time, whites enjoyed affirmative action at the ballot box.

When whites earned graduate and professional degrees and credentials, not available to blacks because the doors of higher educational opportunity were closed to them for the most part for nearly 175 years, it was whites who were awarded job opportunities and powerful positions of influence based on their academic preparation. They were recipients of affirmative action which not only benefited them but their progeny as well.

The reality is that the plight and blight of African-Americans as over-represented victims of unemployment, poverty, substance abuse, imprisonment, mortality and health hazards are due, in part, as a reflection of our negative record of equal opportunity. It is more than a little asinine to assume that three decades of affirmative action in behalf of black people will offset four centuries of unequal treatment and neglect.

There is another side of the coin, however, and that is the side that must speak to the responsibilities that we as blacks must shoulder to improve and enhance our own situation. While many of our difficulties can be traced to a heritage of slavery and to man's inhumanity to man, we cannot continue to brush under the rug certain problems of our own doing. Even as our experiences daily remind us that white businesses and financial institutions are prejudiced against us, that slavery devastated our families, that the criminal *injustice* system tilts in favor of whites, that the educational system inflicts more than its share of negative stereotypes on our children, we must take stock of the history of our ancestors who were survivors, and whose conditions were far worse than ours, yet who fought racism with an urgency and competitiveness that catapulted many of them into focusing on how they could change their situation rather than adjusting to it. History records the spectacular successes of more than a few blacks who overcame the hurdles of racism, who conquered insuperable odds, who went on to prepare themselves as doctors, lawyers, ministers, teachers, nurses, and craftsmen. They are representatives of that hard and historical reality that has enabled our people to survive and even thrive when those of lesser mettle might very well have become extinct.

Now that I have come to the conclusion of my chronology, I must admit that it would have been a most difficult task for me to have made an abridgement of this rather substantial record of my going and coming from birth. Fortunately or unfortunately (I'll let the reader decide), I have not had the necessary detachment of mind or spirit to abbreviate, if not short-circuit my own writing, as every stage in my life has been no ordinary journey. Thus, I have dared the risk of exposing myself to the slings and arrows of the mature and unbiased minds who make it their business to bring to light the strengths and weaknesses of those who write, critiquing their work from the vantage point of literary tradition and their own critical perspectives.

I have attempted to share some aspects of my life through the windows of my higher education and religious experiences. I, at the same time, thought it would be unfortunate if my progeny grew up without any inherited knowledge of the history of their forebearers. Yet, from the very beginning of this adventure—yes, this risky enterprise—I have been a captive to the undulating, up and down, ebb and flow, inner hauntings of the kind of self-wrenchings that one experiences in the struggle of beginning any new venture of consequence. While I did not want to suppress the blessings of God's leading in my behalf throughout my life on one hand, on the other hand I did not want my story to be dismissed as self-asserting or self-serving. As the years and decades began to unfold during my educational journey, I began to become painfully aware that America was increasingly stacking the deck against African-Americans. There was little evidence that the nation was committed to building long-range programs for the culturally different that would fit inextricably into the fabric of America's promise of equality for all Americans. The country seemed impervious to the reality and recognition of the inter-relatedness of all levels of living to developing individual and group wholeness. How is it possible for anyone to assume that the material and personal resources of the nation are equally available to all people so long as unemployment, poverty, substance abuse, homelessness, health hazards, criminality, and the interplay of destructive racist forces plague those groups that historically have been excluded from society's opportunities and advantages?

I have attempted to stand foursquare against such injustices. As the ripples of unrest orchestrated into a roar across the landscape of America in the wake of the Reagan years, I knew that we were on the verge of something that was not only unsettling but would eventually become cataclysmic in the black community if some of us did not begin to make a more serious commitment for the welfare of our youth. I thought about a statement that my longtime friend, James Cathey, made to me in a recent telephone conversation: "Frank, as middle-class black Americans, we have taken our hands off the plow. We've been too distant from our young people, and those of us who have the intellectual and experiential resources need to get on with it." Inspired by his remarks and the writings of Richard Majors' and Janet Billison's *Cool Pose* (1992), Janice Hale-Benson's *Black Children: Their Roots, Culture, and Learning Styles* (1982), Andrew Billingsley's *Climbing Jacob's Ladder* (1992), Haki Mudhubuti's *Black Men—Obsolete, Single, Dangerous?* (1990), and Molefi Asante's *Afrocentricity* (1988), I have rediscovered my own overwhelming desire to protect black youth from the ravages that threaten them at every turn.

The absurdities of racism still require a hard-hitting and implacable challenge with the truth. And retired though I be from the strains of an externally imposed schedule of requirements, I still get exercised to pursuing a whole range of actions when I read the single and myopic-focused opinions of Thomas Sowell's *Civil Rights: Rhetoric or Reality?* (1984), Dinesh D'Souza's *Illiberal Education* (1992), Patrick Buchanan's *Conservative Votes, Liberal Victories* (1975), William Bennett's *De-Valuing of America* (1992), Arthur Schlesinger's *The Disuniting of America* (1991), Allan Bloom's *The Closing of the American Mind* (1987), Rush Limbaugh's *The Way Things Ought To Be* (1992), and Jared Taylor's *Paved With Good*

Intentions (1992). I continue to ask myself the question, "How can so-called enlightened men continue to project such images of sophistication in view of all their political, ideological, and stereotypical rancor?" Racism, whether clothed in resourceful, rhetorical, or revisionist ideology, is racism nonetheless.

I am so certain that my lifelong goals as an agitator of truth will ultimately be fulfilled because there is always something that lies unseen and unforeseen in the heart of a crusader. Yet, I have been blessed to have seen a number of reforms, which I have urged, enacted into the policies of educational and church institutions. The gift of speech has been one of my potent and political and professional weapons. Unarguably, it has been a talent given by God. It has profoundly blessed my efforts in the classroom, in administrative endeavors, on the lecture circuit, in consulting activities, and before state and national conferences.

In this work, I have sought to give some balance to all that I have said in the past by sharing some of my most earnest thoughts with the help and nudge of letters, news sources, and recollections. I have attempted to blend two indispensable allies—love and learning—that one must learn to reconcile as moving power toward self-fulfillment. As I ponder and meditate upon my next possible journey into the written work, I will seek the solace of nature that has always been my catalyst for creative activity. I never tire of monumental mountains, rippling streams, spears of lightning splitting the sky, shimmering sand dunes in the desert, the incomparable and majestic fanciful fountains of the Grand Canyon, the hallelujahs of rain and wind, and the flickering shadows of sun-kissed images. All of these are a part of the great gallery of God's handiworks, and they should remind us of the wonderful and ideal relationships between the beauties of nature unaltered by man and the marginal manifestations of what we have become in our space age dog-eat-dog lusts, as we needlessly inflict wounds upon our environment—all because of greed. History has been one long struggle of people struggling to make peace among themselves, but that will never come so long as humankind makes little effort to make peace with the environment—trespassing and transgressing the rights and properties of others for selfish and profitable gain.

The challenge for us is to make sure that our children and grandchildren will not live in a withering civilization where people are unwilling to share the blessings of opportunity and earth's resources, where some struggle against the uncharted course of the legendary figures of domination and oppression, while others bask in the affluence and succulence of America's promise of equal opportunity. As long as the dreams of people of color remain unmet, I will do my best to shape the direction and future of this country in a way that will promote and address the special needs of those who have a legitimate claim to the rich treasures of an ideal society and democracy.

In the meanwhile, my final journey in life will be to encourage the discouraged, to challenge the disillusioned, and to reassure the skeptical. We owe it to our noble ancestors who paid an exacting and unspeakable price in defense of liberties which so many of them never had the rare privilege to enjoy. In the meanwhile, I would like to have the blessed assurance that Heaven's angels are still watching over me.

Appendix A

ADVENTISTS HEAR RACIAL PLEA
'Lower the Church Bars'

Article taken from the *San Francisco Call-Bulletin*, July 30, 1962.

A specter of racial segregation hovered over the Seventh-day Adventist Church's convention here today.

It was raised by Dr. Frank W. Hale Jr., a Negro and chairman of the English Department of Ohio Central State College, who demanded complete integration within the church.

Hale addressed nearly 1000 Negro men and women at a protest meeting in the Jack Tar Hotel.

Hale also is chairman of the Laymen's Leadership Conference organized last year to seek greater rights for Negroes from the church's World Conference.

He said demands to cease discrimination had been demanded last year, but that the Adventist leadership had done little to lowering racial bars in employment at church institutions.

Hale accused the church leaders of being a group guilty of "contemptuous indifference to the Golden Rule."

"Our message must embrace the simple and elementary principles of human conduct and not unwittingly proclaim to the world that we are merchants of external piety, while at the same time, we build an image that causes the world to distrust us because of our attitude and treatment of minorities," he told the protestants.

He offered a nine-point program designed to end segregation in the church's schools and places of worship.

Another speaker at the meeting was Mrs. Estelle Barnett, of Columbus, Ohio, a 73-year-old former probation officer and social worker, who said:

"We are not heretics, as has been said, nor a left-wing group, but Christians."

"The time has come when, as Christians, we must stand up life men and women and be counted."

Mrs. Barnett attacked Reuben Figuhr, world Adventist president, and Frank L. Peterson, his principal Negro adviser.

"If they are un-Christian," she said, "that is no reason for us to be un-Christian."

"When they have hatred in their hearts, they have never been converted."

Peterson was named last Friday by Figuhr to answer charges Negroes have been barred from all-white Adventist schools.

Peterson, 69, from Wash., D.C., meantime, was elected vice president of the world church organization, at a convention session in the Civic Auditorium.

A Negro, he formerly served as an associate world secretary of the church and was also secretary of the church's Regional Department, established in 1909 to look after interests of Negro church members...

Appendix B

Adventist President Denies Racial Segregation Charges

Article taken from the Oakland Tribune, July 29, 1962.

Reuben Figuhr, president of the Seventh-day Adventist World Conference, has rebuffed charges leveled at the church by minority group members that it still practices racial segregation.

Figuhr took time to discuss the charges Saturday at the Conference's Sabbath service in the Cow Palace.

"Sometimes a small group creates a situation that is not at all representative of an organization's point of view," he said. "Integration in the church is moving ahead deliberately and steadily."

Figuhr's statement referred to claims made Saturday by Mr. and Mrs. Burrell Scott, an Ohio Negro couple, that their 13-year-old daughter had been refused admittance to an academy run by the church.

Frank W. Hale Jr., a Negro professor at Ohio Central State College, also added fuel to the racial row. He charged that Figuhr's statement proclaiming desegregation within the church was merely "bold words producing little action toward segregation."

Howard Weeks, Adventist international public relations director, later charged that "Hale wants to total integration right now without regard to other factors."

The 35-year-old Hale said, "I want action now. I have a child and I know of others who have been denied admission to an all-white student Adventist school."

He said plans to make a public appeal to secure an audience with the leaders of the church over the segregation issues at a rally set for 3 p.m. today in the Jack Tar Hotel.

The rally, sponsored jointly by the Laymen's Leadership Conference organized by Hale 18 months ago and the Oakland alumni chapter of Oakwood College in Alabama, is expected to draw more than 3,000 of the 6,000 Negroes attending the church world meeting.

Hale said that he had tried, but unsuccessfully, to arrange a meeting with the leaders of his church through proper channels.

Weeks denies that Hale's request has been denied. He said that the executive committee of the Seventh-day Adventist Church invited Hale and his associates in the Laymen's Leadership Conference to Washington last fall for a complete airing of the dispute.

"Hale should first convince the leaders of his race who are members of the executive committee if he's so interested in effecting some new policy for the church," Weeks commented.

Weeks explained that in the mid-40's, at the request of the Negroes in the Adventist Church, six all-Negro conferences were formed. The Scotts and Hale belong to the Allegheny Conference.

Weeks said that Negroes in all areas, including Hale's, have a choice of belonging to either an integrated conference or their own all-Negro Conference. Each conference administers its own schools and gives priority to enrollees from its own area.

Hale admits that Negroes did request their own organizations and that the request was actually an anti-integration move on the part of the Negroes because the church was completely integrated at that time.

He said it was done because with the scattering of Negroes throughout eight conferences. Negroes were not having enough voice in the church affairs.

Hunter noted that a Negro boy, Robert T. Slaughter, has been tentatively enrolled but that the lad came from an integrated church that belongs to his conference. He explained that the boy was "tentatively admitted" pending receipt of the usual references required of all students.

DECISION LATER

Scott, a well-to-do Oberlin, Ohio, contractor, said the letter from Shull advising them that a decision would be made in August also advised them to seek admittance to the Pine Forge (Pa.) Academy which is a school run by the all-Negro Allegheny Conference.

"But that's 500 miles away and our part of our tithe goes to support the Mt. Vernon Academy," Mrs. Scott complained.

Hale, after stating that "In many American cities the only segregated school will be the Seventh-day Adventist School," added, "It is ironical that 50,000 Negro Adventists in the United States pay tithes which support 'consciously segregated' schools."

HURLS CHALLENGE

Frank L. Peterson, a Negro and associate general secretary of the Adventist Church, in charge of the Negro conferences, challenged the

Scotts and Hale at every point, but especially on the matter of the use of the tithe.

Peterson said that every cent of tithe money goes for missionary expansion. Funds for education are raised by separate campaigns and offerings, he said. Also, money given to support education in one conference is not transferrable to another conference, he explained. Whatever Scotts give for Adventist education goes to the Pine Forge school, he said.

Appendix C

The Historic March on Washington from a Personal Perspective

An essay by Dr. Frank W. Hale, Jr., Vice Provost and Professor Emeritus, reprinted from the *Columbus Call and Post*, September 30, 1993

There had been many new events which had not influenced people's daily lives enough for them to have been historic prior to August 28, 1963, but such could not be said of the impact of the March on Washington which occurred on that date. This magnificent event in American history produced a black-white coalition for the advancement of human rights on a scale that had never before taken place.

At the time, I was serving as chairman and professor of English at Central State College in Wilberforce, Ohio. Since the *Brown* decision of 1954, the dialogue and debate had become fierce concerning the African-American's rightful place within the American democratic system. The nation had been engulfed in the seething tensions that came in the aftermath of the Montgomery Bus Boycott, the Emmett Till murder, and Birmingham bombings, the venomous rhetoric of southern white militants like Governors George Wallace, Ross Barnett, and Lester Maddox, the radical terrorism of bigots who used bombs, bullets, tear gas, fire hoses, police dogs, bayonets, the murder of Medger Evers, and other vicious means to maim and kill in the name of law and order, in order to discourage and dissuade those who sought the same rights that white Americans expect at birth.

It was because of these conditions, which were occurring with increasing frequency that ignited, as if it were by spontaneous combustion, a wave of sit-ins, freedom rides, marches, legal actions, and an outburst of literary revolutionary antagonists who highlighted America's contradictions on matters of race in prose, poetry and political diatribe.

Sensing this special moment in history, I led a caravan of seven carloads of students to this massive civil rights demonstration in the nation's capital. The ebb and flow of the history of the civil rights movement had become a series of sudden forward spurts up until that time, each followed by a gradual adjustment to what appeared to be significant improvement at the moment. It was as if each phase of the movement had sprinted forward a few paces only to slow down again in order to catch its breath. There was something, however, about this demonstration that would inevitably pave the way for greater opportunities and greater discoveries for generations yet to come.

It came just at a time when Congress was debating a civil rights bill that had been initiated by President Kennedy earlier that year. It came at a time when African-Americans had gained the psychological momentum they needed after the *Brown* decision, the Montgomery Boycott, the Little Rock confrontations, the series of NAACP court challenges that had culminated in numerous victories under the legal expertise of Thurgood Marshall, and the singular leadership of Dr. Martin Luther King, Jr., to stay on the battlefield and to let nobody turn them around. It came at a time when there was a convergence of white allies—clergy, labor union leaders, members of Congress, students and the general public. It was indeed a rainbow coalition of sorts.

Our caravan of weary pilgrims arrived at the capital about 3:00 A.M. and settled at the base of the Washington Monument after travelling all night. We were not alone as scores were already stretched out on blankets and on the unprotected lawn itself, slumbering, dozing, and snoring, even as they used their suitcases for pillows in the early morning hours. As the sun began to rise against the eastern sky, the silhouetted forms of thousands could be seen streaming toward the monument against the crimson hint of dawn. They came on foot, on bicycles, in buses, cars, and trucks. They came from everywhere—north, south, east, and west. Some came by train, others by plane. They carried banners, babies, and bundles of every variety. They were invigorated and enmeshed in the crosscurrents of expectation and exhilaration. It was a monumental camp meeting scene as people sang, danced, listened to media reports of the occasion on their portable radios, and munched away at the sandwiches and other victuals that they had prepared for this golden conjuncture in history.

As the day continued to unfold, the streets were swallowed up by the masses of people who had come to enunciate their support for the first broadside offensive launched by African-Americans in a campaign for racial justice and human brotherhood. The mood and spirit of the crowd was infectious. There was an aura of righteous and joyous dignity in the air as the multitude began to swarm toward the Lincoln Memorial. It was a hot and humid day. Curls and beads of perspiration began to pour from the bodies that were caught in the flush of heat and flesh. As the mercury in thermometers rose, hairdos languished, collars drooped, and shirts and blouses were plastered against anatomies of every description. Some members of our delegation joined the rank and file of many who sat on the edge of the reflecting pool with bare feet in the water.

The crowd began to cheer as the rich and famous began to arrive and take their places near the platform—some to perform and others simply to register the fact that they were in support of the movement. There were white entertainers like Charlton Heston, Burt Lancaster, Joan Baez and Marlon Brando on one hand, and black notables like Sammy Davis, Jr., Sidney Poitier, Lena Horne, and Harry Belafonte on the other. With each appearance of a celebrity, the crowd whistled, cheered, applauded, and stomped in animated and high-spirited approval over the public affirmation of their cause. It was particularly striking that nearly one out of every four persons assembled was white. It was a testimony to the effective work of churches, synagogues, labor unions, educational institutions, and political organizations.

A gargantuan crowd of more than two hundred and fifty thousand people encircled the Lincoln Memorial. It was, in fact, the largest single gathering in the history of Washington, D.C. It was a dramatic episode made up of representatives from "more than 700 groups with diverse political and social agendas," according to the *Washington Post.* Even members of Congress and distinguished senators like Hubert Humphrey of Minnesota and Jacob Javits of New York were among the throng. The young who had accompanied me from Central State College (now university) sat transfixed as Peter, Paul and Mary sang the haunting harmonies of "How Many Times Must a Man Look Up Before He Can See the Sky?" Some of them nearly choked on their tears when Mahalia Jackson, the queen of gospel, belted out the lyrics of "I've Been 'Buked and I've Been Scorned." The occasion was much more than a demonstration. It was an active protest against *invisibility*, the infinite autobiographical metaphor of the African's quest in America.

When A. Philip Randolph, founder of the Brotherhood of Sleeping Car Porters and the key organizer of the march, introduced Dr. King as the "moral leader of the nation," there was an explosion of thunderous applause that lasted for minutes on end followed by chants of "King! King! King!" There was no doubt in anybody's mind whom the crowd had come to hear, although they had respectfully listened and applauded when James Farmer of CORE, Roy Wilkins of the NAACP, Whitney Young of the Urban League, John Lewis of SNCC, Dr. Eugene Carson Blake of the National Counsel of Churches, and Walter Reuther of the United Auto Workers made their presentations. King, who had been the dominating presence among civil rights leaders prior to the march, yielded not an inch of his moment. I had heard him several times before in Birmingham, at Central

402

State College, Wilberforce University, and the University of Dayton. Each time he was bold and venturesome in challenging the audience to adopt his vision of racial equality rather than conforming to a pattern in a society that seemed committed to the status quo.

Like never before, King spoke with a commitment and a cadence that was electrifying. On that momentous day, King transcended his role as clergyman. He marshaled the masses from the traditions of the past to the needs of the present, and the hopes of the future. He urged them to note that the Founding Fathers had signed a promissory note in the Declaration of Independence and in the Constitution to which every American would fall heir. Though it had guaranteed the inalienable rights of life, liberty, and the pursuit of happiness to all Americans, it had failed miserably and had defaulted on its obligations to people of color. Instead, King bemoaned, "America has given the Negro people a bad check, a check which has come back marked *insufficient funds*. But we refuse to believe that the bank of justice is bankrupt... so we have come to cash this check—a check that will give us upon demand the riches of freedom and the security of justice."

From the beginning, the concept of the March on Washington was formed around the idea of identifying and recruiting white allies to form a black-white coalition that would transcend the regional boundaries. King amplified this focus in his speech by warning against hate and bitterness and by declaring, "We cannot walk alone." He warned the nation that, "We can never be satisfied as long as the Negro in Mississippi cannot vote and the Negro in New York believes he has nothing for which to vote."

Then in a poetic blaze of eloquence, King lifted his eyes from his manuscript and declared that, despite the difficulties and frustrations of the moment, he had a dream. With the recurrent rhythm of his refrain, King energized and mesmerized the multitude into a frenzy of chanting, cheering, screaming, crying harmonious humanity, held riveted and swayed by the intoxicating truth and pathos of each phrase which he punctuated with the convictions of his own philosophy and personal experience.

He majestically captured the loftiness of the moment by repeating a series of symbolic refrains such as "Now is the time... ," "We can never be satisfied... ," "With this faith... ," "Let freedom ring... ," and of course "I have a dream... ." As King unleashed phrase after phrase with an impassioned intensity, unlike that which he had ever exhibited before, grown men and women of all ages, teenagers, and little children cheered, hugged each other, and wept uncontrollably. From the beginning of that day to the very last sentence of King's speech, which by any rhetorical measurement was a masterpiece, it was apparent to me that I had been a witness to a holy crusade for human dignity.

The succession of Civil Rights Acts and initiatives (1964, 1965, and 1968) that followed in the train of this commemorative and unprecedented experience provided civil rights champions with a new birth as well as a dramatic new surge of enthusiasm. The ensuing decade (1965–1975) became a decade of exploration and innovation as major gains were made in the field of higher education for example. The number of African-Americans enrolled in college dramatically increased from two hundred and sixty-nine thousand to one million and twenty-six thousand. Those enrolled in the nation's law schools nearly tripled from thirty-five hundred to nearly ten thousand. Medical school participation among African-Americans grew from sixteen hundred and fifty to nearly five thousand. President Lyndon Johnson's Great Society directives had really taken hold in the academy. His message that equal opportunity is not enough, and that there must be equal opportunity of results, so clearly enunciated in his Howard University Commencement address of 1965, had begun to flourish.

Ironically, by the beginning of the nation's Bicentennial Celebration, a decade of revisionism and disintegration (1975–1985) had already begun. America began moving backward rather than forward in its pledge to achieve full participation for citizens of color in the life and prosperity of the nation. It is not necessary to rehearse statistics because the evidence is clear and unmistakable that in education, employment, income, health, longevity and other basic measures of individual and social well-being—vast gaps persist—some even to the point of widening—between people of color and the majority population.

The reality today is the same as it was thirty years ago at the time of that famous march. If we allow these disparities to continue, we will be both vulnerable from within and without. The United States will suffer a compromised quality of life and harmony from within, a lower standard of living, and as a consequence, an endangered posture in the world of economics. We should know full well by now that, in the spirit of Martin Luther King's dream, special efforts and programs need to be implemented to meet the needs of the discordant elements in our society. We need to ask ourselves again, "Are we or are we not dedicated to the proposition that was designed to guarantee the inalienable rights of life, liberty and the pursuit of happiness to all Americans?"

We should know, too, that whether out of the altruism of our Judeo-Christian ethos or the principles of our Jeffersonian democracy, or simply out of the desire to survive, the United States, competitor that she is in the international arena, cannot afford to make any individual or race in her society expendable. The sliding scale of imponderables which may result, if we do otherwise, has left us with little choice.

Appendix D

Why Not Now?

Outline prepared as a focus for the efforts of the Laymen's Leadership
Conference (LLC)—February 1961

Statement: The present climate of Negro-white relations among Seventh-day
Adventists affects the denomination's programs adversely and is contrary
to principles of Christian doctrine and conduct.

PROBLEMS

Problem I. Our educational policies are discriminatory.
A. Our institutions too often adopt quota systems to limit members of
minority groups.
    1. Colleges
    2. Academies.
    3. Medical schools
B. Many of our local church school boards will not accept colored students.
C. There are no Negroes of professional rank now serving on the staff of the
majority of our institutions.

Problem II. Our policies and practices in the employment field are discriminatory.
A. Negroes are not employed in all departmental divisions of the work, but
are assigned only to the *colored* work.
B. Negroes are not represented in some of the larger denominational establishments which they support with their hard-earned dollars.
    1. The Review and Herald Publishing Association
    2. The Voice of Prophecy

Problem III. Our policy of racial segregation within our churches char-acterizes us as insincere in our testimony and application of Christianity.
A. Colored and white churches
B. Colored and white conferences

C. Segregated youth camps

D. Segregated vacation Bible schools

CAUSES

Cause I. We have failed to follow through on the writings of Sister White in the area of race-relations.
> Testimony of *The Southern Work*.

Cause II. We have failed to develop any sound communication forum between the Negroes and whites that would tend to harmonize the actions of the whole world.

A. The denomination has failed to register its conviction against the sin of segregation and discrimination as have other religious bodies.

    1. Presbyterians

    2. Baptists

    3. Methodists

    4. Catholics

B. We have encouraged antagonism between Negroes and whites because of our cautious approach in this area.

> We have permitted each member, more or less, to decide for himself the meaning of brotherhood.

C. We have bypassed opportunities to establish Race Relations Institutes for the purpose of discovering the grievances which seem responsible for our practices.

Cause III. We have often intimidated those who have dared to promote better relations between the races.

Cause IV. We have sacrificed the principle of *love* upon the altars of *bread and butter*.

> We have been afraid to speak the *truth*, for fear we might lose some *prejudiced dollars* from among certain conservative elements of our denomination.
>
> Testimony of our leaders.

SOLUTIONS

Solution I. We need to adopt a positive stand on social reform as we have on Sabbath reform, temperance reform, health reform, etc.

Solution II. We need to discontinue the quota systems in our educational institutions.

Solution III. We need to open the doors of our education institutions to all qualified teachers.

Solution IV. We need to open our doors of employment to qualified people in all fields.

Solution V. We need to open the doors of our churches to all bona fide Seventh-day Adventists irrespective of race or color.

Solution VI. We need to open conference office and departments to qualified personnel irrespective of race or color.

Solution VII. We need to operate interracial youth camps in order to encourage mutual trust among our young people.

Solution VIII. We need to *give ear* to and promote the teachings of the Bible and Sister White in encouraging the principles of fellowship.

Solution IX. We need to foster Race Relations Institutes which will serve as centers of instruction for developing techniques that will improve race relations among Seventh-day Adventists.

Solution X. We need to move with all deliberate speed on the solutions herein mentioned.

Appendix E

A Look Into London

An essay by Dr. Frank W. Hale, Jr.,
written the autumn of 1960 following post-doctoral study at
the University of London.

One midnight last summer I stepped off the train at the Waterloo Station in London. It was exactly three hours from the time I had arrived in Southampton from New York on the *Queen Mary*. I soon sensed that I was about to embark upon one of the most fascinating experiences of my life in the second largest city in the world. I moved rapidly to hail a taxi. London at night is so sprinkled with candles of light from her many lampposts that I felt a sense of reverence as I went riding through her streets in a sanctuary-like quiet.

The city spreads out on both sides of the Thames River like a giant fork into northern and southern halves. I was soon deposited with my luggage in the heart of northeastern London at the huge Y.M.C.A. on Great Russell Street just off of Tottenham Court Road. I had no difficulty in slumbering into eight hours of unconsciousness after lugging two suitcases, a footlocker, a *vel-pack*, and a valise up five flights of stairs to my room, for the elevator was not in operation at that hour of the morning.

When I went downstairs to catch a breath of early morning London air after I awoke, I was anxious to begin the first lap of my *acadation*. (This is the term that I coined for my summer activities which would include three weeks of *vacation* in England and France and six weeks of *academic* pursuits at the University of London.)

Tourists monopolize every corner of England and Europe during the summer holidays, and the British Museum was no exception to this cosmopolitan climate on the day that I visited within its walls. To my right as I walked in, there was a group of German students being lectured to by a Swan representative. Just ahead I observed a snappy French couple crisply exchanging remarks as they turned to enter the Egyptian and Assyrian department. I was thrilled to see an original copy of the Magna Charta and the *Codex Sinaticus*, one of the earliest known Greek manuscripts of the Bible. Although I spent an entire day viewing collections of Greek and Roman antiques, Oriental antiques, and Egyptian and Assyrian antiques, I am sure that my total impression of the museum was only a summary one. I was informed by a guide that the number of volumes in the entire library totals more than six million.

One of the most striking features of London is that there are so many rival interests which may involve a visitor. As I walked into the heart of London on one misty morning, I was immediately torn among shifting thoughts to Buckingham Palace, St. James Park, Westminster Abbey, and the Houses of Parliament. The only thing I could do approaching a general compromise of action was to elect the first three because of my limited time.

St. James is picturesquely situated in the mall the leads to Buckingham Palace. It is indented with trees, terraced lawns, flowers of every variety, and a winding lake of five acres. Pageantry and ceremony are a religion in London. One of London's most popular traditional ceremonies is the changing of the guard each morning in the forecourt of Buckingham Palace, the London residence of the queen. I was in the midst of a swarm of amateur photographers, that segment of the tourist population which has become addicted to the pattern of straining every nerve to get a picture whatever the cost.

Pausing only for a moment to study the faces of those who were worshipping at the shrine of English tradition, I then hurried my pace over to Birdcage Walk and straight east to Westminster Abbey, a church which ranks with St. Paul's cathedral as being the best known among the many beautiful and interesting churches of London. I am a teacher of English literature, and chills of inspiration shuttled up and down my spine as I stood in the *Poets' Corner*, that spot around which is gathered the tombs, memorials, and busts of the great men of letters like Shakespeare, Coleridge, Burns, Keats, Shelley, Wordsworth, and Dr. Johnson. This experience was a magnificent climax to an eventful day.

About nine o'clock the next evening, I decided to see Soho for myself. (All of the reports concerning it had been so lush!) I began to walk. I moved cautiously down Charing Cross Road with eyes as big as teacups, devouring all of the frantic innuendos of London stardust. I was first struck with the racial minglings which London's business, educational and diplomatic circles were producing. Such a blend was so evident in social intergroupings that a large segment of the rejuvenated youth population appeared to be moving in polka-dot patterns. This was specially evident as couples were at the entrance to a public dance hall.

I turned off on one of the side streets and approached the capital of frolicsome life, Greek Street. Cafes, bars, and burlesque shows lined both sides of the street and bedecked all levels of the dilapidated real estate from the basement to the top floor. Male tourists, plush with vacation pay, gazed wistfully into the pigeonholes of vice. They were choice bait for the charming serpents of feminine pulchritude that lurked behind the shadows, waiting to entice them. When the moment was ripe, these female wenches popped their beguiling faces and serpentine forms into the darkened doorways and became silhouetted against a shimmering backdrop of red, blue, and purple light. Hair styles and colors, reminiscent of the spectrum, crowned each worldly-wise profile. Colors of red, orange, and violet were the most popular among these male catchers. One of the Jezebels went so far as to catch a middle-aged executive by the arm, dragging him back into her web. A combination of financial security and sexuality was what they had to offer each other.

The next night was a study in contrast to the night before. The stage was the Royal Albert Hall. The setting was Haydn's *Creation*. The cast was composed of the Croydon Philharmonic Society, the Royal Choral Society, the Watford Philharmonic Society, and the BBC Symphony Orchestra. The director was Sir Malcolm Sargent. I sat experiencing profound emotion during the marvelous orchestration and the sweep of the chorus in the unforgettable exultation of "and there was light." On the northern part of its 635 acres, Hyde Park is a favorite place for mass meetings, popular demonstrations, and public oratory. I was party to a crowd numbering in the hundreds that listened to an old bearded and unkempt philosopher—whose roost was a flimsy A ladder—feverishly bark away on "the evils of religion." He was never wholly without distraction, for he welcomed the sporadic heckling of those loafers and idle sponges who make this sort of recreation their daily obsession.

Although to many Americans the outside educational world offers no allurement, I took full advantage of the opportunity which I had to enroll at the University of London for a six weeks' course in the "Art Literature and Music of England, 1660–1780." It was the morning of July 11 when I turned my back on the Y.M.C.A. and approached my new place of residence—Canterbury Hall—in Cartwright Gardens. Each day I excitedly walked three blocks to the School of Pharmacy Lecture Hall to get my diet of England's great giants. Lecturers from London University, Oxford, and Cambridge required but the waft of a breeze from their literary lore to fan the embers of our aesthetic experience into a flame. These scholars brought with them a love of learning, typical of the Augustans, and, thus, stimulated our enthusiasm by reviving our interest in the works of the period. Among the giants which were introduced to us were Milton and Pope in literature; Jones and Wren in architecture;

Handel and Purcell in music; and VanDyck and Reynolds in art. The Department of Extra-Mural Studies scheduled visits for us to places of interest related to the work of the course. We spent an afternoon viewing modern British art at the Tate Gallery which is located in Grosvenor Road overlooking the Thames. The next afternoon the feminine creatures in our herd sighed and swooned when we spotted the actor, Anthony Quinn, seriously studying some of the rich works of the masters at the National Portrait Gallery which has a collection of nearly two thousand portraits.

The city of the famous London Bridge has from its beginning led a stony path in its uphill march. Caesar's Roman legions invaded her borders about 55 B.C., and when the legions were withdrawn, Irishmen from the west and Scot and Picts from the north took successive turns in exploiting the unfortunate remnants of the Roman empire. London was again pillaged and laid desolate by Danish invaders at the beginning of the ninth century. When the plague visited the city in June, 1665, and claimed nearly ten thousand victims, it was the last in a series of menacing ravages of the Black Death that began afflicting London in the fourteenth century and continued through the sixteenth and seventeenth centuries.

In the course of modern history London was destined to share in the destruction of World Wars I and II. But it was in the latter that the German swastika cocked her deathly arms and hurled enough flying bombs to destroy over a million houses and leave nearly a half million people homeless. Yet when the smoke and dust had settled after the last bomb had dropped, the golden cross atop St. Paul's Cathedral was still at attention. It was a reverent postscript to England's finest hour.

London was not to lose her courage in a day. Men, women and children harmoniously dug in after the war to reestablish, reconstruct, and rehabilitate. These British people never forgot one of the great friends and companions during the war, Franklin D. Roosevelt. One cool evening I stood in Grosvenor Square across from the American Embassy and paid silent tribute at the Roosevelt Memorial which was unveiled by that president's widow in 1948. So much did the British admire this great American that, when £50,000 was asked for, with no donation to exceed five shillings, they responded and the goal was exceeded within twenty-four hours.

There is no more fascinating effort open to one who has visited London than to formulate sound conclusions. At best such an attempt at reconstructing the past can be but partially successful.

To the foreign visitor, London is a composite of many things. It is where monuments, art treasures and literature of many great civilizations have been preserved for all generations. It is Big Ben stalking each passerby. It is the fog or rain that is expected to intrude five or ten minutes each day. It is the flourishing traffic of the Thames and the *bloody* double-deckers that race to and fro in every part of the city. It is an atmosphere of conservatism and tradition. The average man inherits his religion and his politics much as he inherits the color of his eyes, and has scarcely more likelihood of changing one than the other.

On the other hand, London is a party of extremes. It pays a high price tag for sentimentality, so much so that the first lady of Buckingham Palace receives a stipend of £475,000 a year from the British government for the privilege of being the Queen of Britain's illustrious commonwealth. It is a scuffling city at night where the playgoers and music lovers converge on Piccadilly Circus while the *hypersexed* consort with the shade. It is to all men all things. It is overwhelming.

I became so profoundly attached to this great metropolis within a few months so that even now, though I have long since returned to my native America, I still take imaginary journeys through the "Chartered Streets" of William Blake's London.

Appendix F

Oakwood President Compiles Stirring Cries for Freedom

Article taken from *The Huntsville Times*, February 1, 1970, by Carolyn Callhan.

"Hererin lie buried many things which, if read with patience, may show the strange meaning of being black here at the dawning of the Twentieth Century. This meaning is not without interest to you, Gentle Reader; for the problem of the Twentieth Century is the problem of the color line." So writes W. E. B. DuBois in 1903 in the Forethought of his slender volume of essays and sketches entitled, "The Souls of Black Folk."

Today, at the beginning of the seventh decade of the Twentieth Century, the "cry for freedom" is still going up from the black soul. In the hope of finding some answers to continuing problems, Dr. Frank W. Hale, Jr., president of Oakwood College, has compiled an anthology of what he feels are some of the significant speeches and writing by key figures in the civil rights struggle since 1954. He calls it, "The Cry for Freedom."

Published last week by A. S. Barnes and Company, "The Cry for Freedom," is aimed not only at the academic market, where it will, according to Hale, serve as excellent source material for high school and college students, but also at members of industry who are attempting to solve the many aspects of "the color line problem" which have been laid bare during the civil rights struggle. The speeches themselves may even provide models for the student of public speaking.

The text runs 426 pages divided into six categories, plus a preface and introduction by Hale. A brief biographical sketch introduces each selection. The speakers represent responsible, and for the most part, moderate leadership, black and white. James Baldwin's eloquent plea in behalf of the Negro child, spoken before a group of New York City's public school teachers, opens the book and the section devoted to Men of Letters. Educators, government officials, legal officials, clergymen and civil rights activists are also heard from.

Besides Baldwin, some of the prominent leaders whose words are included are Eugene Carson Blake, Ralph Bunche, Harry Golden, Father

414

Theodore Hesburg, Sen. Jacob Javits, former presidents Kennedy and Johnson, Martin Luther King, Jr., Walter Reuther, Carl Rowan, Roy Wilkins, and Whitney Young Jr.

"It is not a mud-slinging work," says Hale. He hopes industrial leaders, many of whom, according to his publishers, have already placed orders, will find in it guidelines for solving what Hale insists are "moral, not political issues."

In expressing his views on civil rights Hale faults the church for not assuming an early role in solving the problems of integration, condemns it, in fact, for having "sanctified" segregation. "It (the church) must become involved in housing, unemployment and quality education," he says.

He thinks, however, that the days of tension for black people are over in the sense of worrying about what's going to happen. "Black people are bullet-proof," he says, "after you've been the target so many years, why flinch? The whole black experience has been conditioning black people for one rebuff after another, but they haven't given up. Constitutional guarantees are the thing which give black people hope. If they believed just what they see and are involved in, they would become paranoid or communistic overnight."

Hale admits that what he is hearing in the black community from people formerly committed to non-violence is that they don't care how change comes about, and that they are wondering if non-violence can work in a society where, they feel, political life is corrupt.

The purpose of his book, as Hale sees it, is to call on black and white leadership to get down to the business of solving these problems for the black man and anyone else in this country who is underprivileged. "This nation," says Hale, "owes it to the Negro and the Indians, and others, to bend over backwards to make restitution.

"America has the answer," he says. "It can be found in the Golden Rule."

Appendix G

A Farewell Tribute to Dr. William J. Holloway

Speech delivered at a Farewell Reception for Dr. Holloway on June 27, 1982, Drake Union Lounge (OSU), Columbus, Ohio.

Ladies and Gentlemen:

I rise to associate myself with all of you who have come to bid Bill Holloway farewell. I am grateful for the opportunity to express to him our appreciation of his character and accomplishments as scholar-statesman and his admirable and endearing qualities as a man.

For forty-two years he has served the field of education since his graduation from Hampton Institute in 1940. While I shall not recall in great detail the multitudinous services that he has rendered to this nation, you should know that he was awarded the Master of Arts degree from the University of Michigan in 1946, and the University of Illinois awarded him the Doctor of Education degree in 1961. Later, he did post-graduate work at Howard University where he was a Far East Studies Fellow.

A product of Smithfield, Virginia—the mainstream of hams and peanuts, a territory contiguous to and only fifteen miles from my own roots in Surry County, the birthplace of my mother, Holloway possesses the kind of character that appears to have been carved out of the unblemished granite of those sterling qualities of whom the prophet Micah spoke in his searching question—"What doth the Lord require of thee, but to *do justly*, and to *love mercy*, and to *walk humbly with thy God?*" He has embodied in his life the prophet's advice. Virginia gave us George Washington, Thomas Jefferson, James Monroe, Nat Turner, Booker T. Washington, and now William Jimmerson Holloway.

Time will not permit me to attempt to analyze or measure the immenseness of his intellect, the crispness of his wit, or the strength of his commitment to just causes.

Because of his power of leadership, because of his unrivaled and rare faculty of sympathetic understanding, and because of his superlative tenacity to tough ideals, we are all the better for having known and been associated with you, Bill.

We have known you—*the scholar-educator* who brought thirty years of rich experience to OSU when you first came to us in 1970.

We have known you as *the innovator-planner-implementer* who designed the structure and organization of the Office of Minority Affairs and the Nigerian Education Program and made them work.

We have known you as *the advocator* who stood your ground unflinchingly when things got tough.

We have known you as *the humanitarian*, living each day of your life for the betterment of others.

I have a family showcase in my dining room that houses special treasures and family heirlooms which I have collected over the years. They are treasures which have come down from my parents, my grandparents, and my great grandparents. Some of these items are well over one hundred years old. They include glassware, china, brass, and wood carvings. For example, I have my father's first pocket watch, dishes which my great grandmother used, a revolver which my deceased uncle, who was a physician, kept in his office, and a beautiful blue hand-painted pitcher which belonged to my wife's grandmother.

In an analogous way, there is a showcase on my mind when I think of the experiences which Bill Holloway and I have shared here at The Ohio State University.

I think of my first days at Ohio State University when I was greeted by Bill with warmth and hospitality. I recall how well he cooperated with me during the initial stages when we were establishing the Graduate and Professional Schools Visitation Days Program. He was always a big man who was never threatened by a new person bringing new ideas. In that showcase of my mind, I recall the struggle that we had over the great debate of whether or not the university should have a black cultural center. I also remember how Dr. Holloway along with several other black administrators led the way in the 1975 rally around the administration building involving nearly two thousand black students who were seeking greater opportunities for minorities at this university. Perhaps the high water mark of his career was experienced just yesterday, as a result of his Nigerian Education Program when he proudly introduced the ambassador of Nigeria to the United States and, in turn, was the recipient of a gift presented to him by the deputy governor and the commissioner of education.

It was a culmination of the experiences of a great man who came, who saw, and who conquered.

Appendix H

The Educational Pipeline for Minority Students at The Ohio State University

Outline of the 3 R's utilized by the OSU Office of Minority Affairs—1978–the present

RECRUITMENT

Precollege
Prelude
RAP
High School Visits
Career Days
Church Programs
Alumni Activities
Upward Bound
High School Visitation Days Program
Columbus Public School Collaboration
"Early Bird" Summer Enrichment
Research Apprenticeship Program

Undergraduate
Freshman Foundation Program
Minority Scholars Program
College and Department Recruitment
Campus Visitation Program
Community Organizations

Graduate and Professional
Black College Campuses
Major Universities
Graduate and Professional Schools Visitation Program
CIC Fellowship Program
G*POP Fellowship Program
College and Department Recruitment

RETENTION

Administration Policy
Affirmative Action
Affirmative Action Grants Competition
Distinguished Affirmative Action Award
Human Services Officer

Counseling
Developmental Education
Counseling and Consultation Center

Cultural Heritage
Asian American Week
Black Church
Black Greeks
Black Studies
Black Theatre
Black World Week
Black Gospel Choir
Hispanic Awareness Week
Dimensions News
Drum
Gospel Extravaganza
Martin Luther King Week

Financial Aid
College Work-Study
Government Loans
Emergency Loans
Minority Scholars Program
Minority Fellowships
Associateships
Grants
Community Partnership Pacts
Research Assistance
Travel to Professional Meetings
Tutoring

Personnel Support
Black Student Organizations

Coordinating Council
Hispanic Student Programs
Office of Minority Affairs
Developmental Education
Peer Counselors and Tutors
Minority Faculty
University Advisory Council
Minority Faculty/Staff Colloquy
Staff Development Workshops

Technical Support
Learning Resources Center
Career Exploration
Career Planning and Placement
Testing and Evaluation

Department/School/College
Academic Advisement
Department/College Tutors

RELEASE

Placement
OMA Job Fair
Co-op Opportunities
Internship Programs
Graduate and Professional Schools

Graduation
Bachelor's Degree
Master's Degree
Doctoral Degree

Alumni
Network
Partnership Pacts
They Came and They Conquered

420

Appendix I

Hale Provides Grads Options on Problems

Article taken from *The Call and Post*, Thursday, September 8, 1988

People must know themselves, know how to control themselves and give of themselves.

That was the message Frank W. Hale Jr. gave to the graduating students of the Class of 1988 at Ohio State University's summer commencement recently at St. John Arena.

Hale, special assistant to the president and vice provost for minority affairs, said that people who know themselves are comfortable with themselves, feel adequate and competent, and have a sense of being and leadership.

"People who are self actualizing… are straightforward and articulate, spontaneously simple and direct in terms of what they have to say," he said. "(They) know the value of hard work. They don't wait for things to happen: they make things happen."

Hale said at some point, one must control one's self.

"There are three ways to approach any problem. We can approach it through escape by avoiding it. We can approach it by embracing it and saying, 'I can do nothing about it.' Or we can approach a problem through encounter by saying, 'I will deal with it,' " he said.

Hale told graduates the time has come to decide to develop a resistance against overwhelming social and political patterns, noting the problems of hunger, contamination of the biosphere and what he called the rape of minerals and resources from Third World countries.

He said that there is more to education than learning and knowing.

"Somewhere our values ought to be beyond the stretches of achieving money and status and prestige. We do have responsibility and it's an opportunity for you," he said.

Hale challenged graduates to learn to give and have the courage to give. "It is good to give when asked," he said. "It is better to give unasked. You are the only generation that has the power of veto over the survival of the next generation and I hope you take that seriously."

Hale, 61, of Worthington, will retire from Ohio State on Dec. 31, after 17 years at the university. A former president of Oakwood College in Huntsville, Ala., Hale has served Ohio State as a professor or communication and associate dean of the Graduate School. The Kansas City native has bachelor's and master's degrees from the University of Nebraska and a doctorate from Ohio State.

Appendix J

Response to the Opening of the Frank W. Hale, Jr. Black Cultural Center

Speech delivered October 11, 1989, at the opening of the Frank W. Hale, Jr. Black Cultural Center, The Ohio State University, Columbus, Ohio.

You may be sure that I consider it a very great honor and a very great distinction to have the privilege and opportunity of having this significant black cultural center named in my honor. I want to express my appreciation to President Edward H. Jennings for helping to make this possible. An irresistible sense of reflection and awe well up within me when I think of the student pioneers, some of whom sacrificed their education and career, to make it possible for other black students and black faculty and staff to be recruited for this campus as a prelude to this moment. They stood tall and with unwavering patience and perseverance and met the demands of the emergency of under-representation and lack of diversity. We must place them high on the historical pinnacle of sacrifice, honor and gratitude. They deserve our applause and much more!

And so we are here today at this opening of this black cultural center; that is a good designation, because *black* is global in its designation of black people the world over. It includes the African-American experience and transcends it. In effect, it speaks to the centrality, perspectives and challenges of the black experience wherever in North America, South America, the Caribbean, in colonized nations the world over and, of course, in the Motherland, Africa.

The rationale for such a center grows out of the need for *discovering* and *rediscovering*. There was a time, not long ago—and for some even now—when we denied our African identity. We aspired toward *cultural whiteness*. As we made substantial contributions to our surrounding culture, we became more absorbed by it. As we began to seek final identification into the American mainstream, we forgot our roots down by the old mill stream and yet, we have—for the most part—remained shadowy members of society because only doors on the periphery have been slightly cracked for us.

This center today is a testimony of this institution's intent to promote pluralism within the landscape of diversity on this campus. It stands as a bridge between blacks and other ethnic groups on this campus. It should stand as an instrument to stamp out the suffocating and the destructive effects of institutional racism by conducting transracial programs and activities that will give us all an opportunity to learn more about each other.

This center can become a *family room* for black students who seek shelter from social isolation, cultural discrimination and the loneliness which small numbers create. It represents an opportunity for brothers and sisters to come together to affirm, to assert, to enunciate, to emphasize, to propose, to contend and give voice to their concerns.

Here you can meet to enjoy educational and social exchanges. Here you can determine causes for common advocacy. Here you can join hand as mentor and protege to be instructed and to learn how to negotiate the system. Here you can create bonds with allies—white, Hispanic, Asian and Native Americans who are sensitive to your needs and concerns.

Here you can come in recognition of the fact that you are your brother's and sister's keeper. This center is a monument that says that neither the university nor we as black people claim exempt status from those who seek legitimacy within the fabric of the American ideal, and whose American dream remains unmet. This center says, in effect, we cannot insulate ourselves from the problems or potentialities of black people by claiming such exemption.

This center is a serious attempt to deal with a serious need—the need to increase and expand the pool of black scholars across the landscape of disciplines from art to zoology. It stands as a co-curricular tool to enlarge the canons and boundaries of study, scholarship and to serve as a laboratory of leadership for black students here at The Ohio State University.

Make no mistake about it, while it will serve as a focal point and as a forum for us to rediscover our origins, reshape our identity, and deal in precise ways with our *Africanness*—our particular culture and history—it should not substitute cultural romanticism that denies the universality of humanity. In doing this, we would succumb to the very plague that has denied the validity of our contributions as a people.

On the other hand, we make no apologies for our focus, one that is sharpened to concentrate and converge on that which is consistent, challenging and cohesive within our culture. Oh how necessary this is. For years, for example, I taught World Literature, and I have shuddered at the extent to which an entire landscape of black literature and authors have been denied a place in corporate literature, and thus have remained shut off and shut out of national and international linguistic boundaries. Such isolation has confined the genius of such brilliant writers as Phyllis

424

Wheatley, Frances Harper, James Weldon Johnson, Paul Laurence Dunbar, Claude McKay, Langston Hughes, Countee Cullen, W. E. B. DuBois, and Ralph Ellison. Such isolation has also confined great numbers of people to unwarranted ignorance and provincialism.

Apologies are *not* in order for having such a center. Everything that is anything begins again! There is both specificity and universality in blackness. We focus on blackness to establish the authenticity of our identity which has been systematically denied. We project our universality to remind the world and ourselves of the significant contributions that we have made to humankind. We can no longer delay to define ourselves, the roles we pursue and the goals we seek. That alone is our responsibility.

And let us remind you that no one doubts the universality of Herodotus the Greek historian, who time after time celebrated the deeds of his countrymen, or Caesar who made Roman history and wrote it to vindicate himself in the eyes of the Romans, or the French writer, Rousseau, who rebelled against the social order in his country and became the prophet of the French Revolution, or the master, Shakespeare, who chronicled English history in such works as *Richard II*, *Henry IV*, and *Henry V*. Or who would deny the universality of William Faulkner in our own country who restricted his writing to the decadence of southern characters and society in *Sound and Fury*, *Intruder in the Dust*, and *Go Down Moses*.

So we, too, have earned the right to rediscover our origins and to reshape our identity. This, of course, has become a difficult and complicated matter in our country where so long the practice of separateness has been thrust upon us—pushing in and out of ghettos, in and out of blind alleys, trying to cope with the mind-boggling messages that we get on a daily basis telling us that *we have arrived, we have enough, we're denying the rights of others because we want ours, we expect too much* because we demand what others expect at birth even as we have run the gauntlets of Wallace, Bilbo, Eastland, Talmadge, Nixon, Helms, and Reagan. "It is enough to make you wonder about the integrity of your own sanity," as Samuel Butler exclaimed in *The Way of All Flesh*.

In preparing for this presentation, it suddenly came to me as if I had had a dream, to make some long distance calls to our ancestral heroes and heroines to inquire of them what to tell you, and this is what they said— I talked to Beethoven, acclaimed by many as the world's greatest musician, and a black man, and asked him what should I tell you—and he said—"Tell them, tell the music majors, that race has no place in potential. Tell them that my concertos, sonatas, and symphonies transcend color, that they are universal, and have captured the hearts of millions around the world. You may tell them, incidentally, that I am proud of my blackness. Tell them my blackness is a matter of record by Frederick Hertz, the German anthropologist in *Race and Civilization*, by R. H. Schauffler, *The Man Who Freed Music*, volume one, page eighteen, 1929, and by my famous teacher, Joseph Haydn, who too was black. Haydn's performance before Prince Esterhazy, who exclaimed in the middle of Haydn's first allegro of Haydn's symphony, was interrupted by, "What! The music is by a black moor?"

I talked with Imhotep of ancient Egypt, the real father of medicine who lived about 2300 B.C. Hippocrates, the so-called father of medicine, lived two thousand years after Imhotep. Greece and Rome gained their knowledge of medicine from Imhotep. I asked Imhotep what should I tell you—and he said—"Tell them, tell the pre-med majors, to be the best that you can be—that was my philosophy, and time will tell the truth. In Rome I was worshiped as the *Prince*. I wore many hats as prime minister to King Zoser, and I was also recognized as the foremost architect of my time. Learn all that you can about everything there is to know, and keep on stepping."

I talked to Hannibal, the Carthegenian general and the father of modern military science—a full-blooded black, who in 218 B.C. conquered territory in Spain and France and performed the outstanding feat of crossing the Alps, and who defeated Rome with only twenty-six thousand men remaining of his original force of eighty-two thousand men when Rome was the mightiest military power in the world with a million men. He defeated them in every battle for fifteen years. He said, "Tell them—tell all of them that mountains are made to climb, that rivers are made to cross, and problems are made to be solved. Tell them that my strategies are still taught in all the major military academies of the world. Tell them that their heritage is an enormous one, build on it and keep on stepping!"

I talked to several black kings about my visit here this evening—

Yusuf—king of Upper Senegal (1086), who crossed the Strait of Gibraltar with fifteen thousand blacks and inflicted a terrible defeat on Alphonso VI who was attempting to push out and eliminate the Moors. Among those who fell was Roderigo Diaz De Vivar (El Cid), the greatest figure of the heroic age of Spain.

I talked to John VI, king of Portugal, a mulatto who transferred his throne to Brazil (Rio De Janeiro in 1808)—*maker of modern Brazil*. I talked to his son, Pedro I, who became the first emperor of Brazil in 1822. Pedro's daughter became queen of Portugal and was a sister-in-law of Queen Victoria of England.

426

I talked to Jean Baptiste Bernadotte, founder of the present royal family of Sweden, a private in Napoleon's army who rose to be field marshal. In 1818 he ascended to the throne of Sweden as Charles XIV.

I talked to Askia, emperor of Songhay, who ruled an empire that stretched from the Atlantic Ocean to Lake Chad—larger than western Europe, as Capital Timbuctoo, an early democratic civilization.

I talked to King Tut and a host of Egyptian pharaohs along with the other black heads of royalty—

They told me—"Tell them that their roots are rich. Tell them their blood line is filled with the corpuscles of courage, with the antibodies of adventure to master racism, discrimination and exploitation.

I then skipped over centuries of black heroes and heroines and talked to giants of modern vintage—

I talked with the Harlem Renaissance writers—Alan Locke, Langston Hughes, Countee Cullen, Arna Bontemps—

Frederick Douglass, David Walker, Harriet Tubman, Sojourner Truth, William Edward Burkhardt DuBois, Marcus Garvey, Elijah Muhammad, Martin Luther King, Jr., Mary McLeod Bethune, and Malcolm X—

And each of them in their own way said—Tell them to keep on stepping; step into life with vigor and expectation; step up in life with your goals and aspirations; step over in life and confront the obstacles and barriers facing you; step out of life, don't be afraid to challenge the ridiculous.

Tell them that, without black culture, there is no black history. Without black history, there is no black dignity. Without black dignity, there is no black pride. Without black pride, there is no freedom. And without freedom you are at the mercy of others to tell you who you are, what your history is and what you are to become. The day will come when your history will speak, but it will not be the history which will be taught in London, Paris, Rome, Moscow, Washington or the United Nations. It will be the history that will be taught by those who have won freedom. We must write our own history, and it must begin with you!

Appendix K

No easy task
Speaker: Multicultural progress in education takes hard work

Article taken from the *Daily Nebraskan*, University of Nebraska–Lincoln newspaper, April 1, 1994, by Kara G. Morrison, Senior Reporter.

Frank Hale said progress on multiculturalism and diversity in higher education could only be achieved by aggressive and united efforts.

"When we get down to it, it's all about commitment," said Hale, who received his Bachelor of Arts and Master of Arts degrees in communications, political science and English from the University of Nebraska–Lincoln in 1950 and 1951.

"Long before civil rights legislation, long before affirmative action initiatives, there were blacks and whites who were committed to (equality) and went out of their way to make a significant difference," Hale said.

The legacy of such work, Hale said, needs to continue.

Hale was the keynote speaker for the Teachers College's annual conference Thursday in the East Campus Union. The conference theme was "Personal Growth Through Diversity."

Hale, currently vice provost and professor emeritus at Ohio State University, is credited with much progress in diversifying education.

Ohio State was one of the top institutions in numbers of African-American students receiving doctorate degrees in the late 1970s.

Although Hale said much progress had been made in terms of multiculturalism in education, he said universities had much hard work ahead of them to attract and retain minority students.

"We have to begin with administrative policy and procedures," Hale said. "There has to be a commitment from the top."

With the administration's commitment, Hale said, universities must aggressively recruit minority students and provide them with financial aid.

"I learned a lot from (Ohio State football coach) Woody Hayes," Hale said. "He was not only a great coach; he was a great recruiter.

"You don't get good athletes by sending out a letter with a little note at the bottom saying 'equal opportunity employer.' Affirmative action says, go get 'em."

428

Then, Hale said, a university must diversify its curriculum and work to assure a positive campus climate for minorities.

"Curriculum, to be global and to be reflective, needs to entertain all ideas," Hale said. "It is important for all people where they sit to understand that out of their roots, each has made a contribution."

The final test of a university's commitment to diversity, Hale said, is whether it commits significant resources to the effort. He emphasized, "Commitment without cash is counterfeit."

Hale, who arrived Wednesday and will be in Lincoln until Sunday, said he had not yet had time to assess the progress UNL has made in terms of diversity since he was a student here. But he said he was encouraged by his invitation to speak at the conference.

"I'm glad to know the university is taking this issue seriously," Hale said.

Appendix L

A Word of Greeting

Speech given extemporaneously on November 10, 1995, at the opening convocation of Oakwood's Centennial Celebration at the Oakwood College Church, Huntsville, Alabama.

By substantial numbers from many corners of geography, we have come to the Queen of Colleges. We have come for many years, always in increasing numbers, as we always will to pay homage to a great institution that has sheltered us as well as our progeny from the plague of secular permissiveness and from the malaria of materialism. Instinctively and spontaneously, we have come to applaud and to cheer the fact of this centennial. The fact is that this glorious institution has lived through the hardship, the labor, and the sacrifice which must be endured by every institution of heroic mold. Because she has struggled from obscurity to eminence, she has established an unshakable bond between her and all of us who recognize her as our champion of Christian education, trusting her unabashedly with our loyalty and our love.

But it doesn't stop there. We hope that you will go home with a new sense of vision, a vision that will enlist you as a soldier of enthusiasm, marching shoulder to shoulder toward our common objective of opening avenues of opportunity to every young person who desires to pursue a Christian education. We hope, too, that you have a marvelous time here. We know you are going to do that so that you can capsulize the spirit of what we need to do to continue to make this institution a blazing beacon on the front line of higher education in the world.

Here you are in one of the space capitals of the world where rockets are designed to reach ever so high up into the clouds, and even so also, for thee our dear Oakwood, the sky, too, is the limit. And because of that fact, it imposes an inescapable obligation for us to exercise individual attention to duty, unflagging support, unquestioned loyalty, unabashed integrity, unassailable consistency, unshrinkable commitment, unshakable optimism, undrudging labor, unparalleled love and satisfaction, and faithfully discharging all of the above with undimmed eye and undiminished vigor for the institution that has done so much with so little in providing inspiration, guidance, and service to multiplied hundreds, nay thousands, on behalf of our Lord and Savior, Jesus Christ. It is here, this paradise on earth, that has given us a foretaste and a quickened sense of what our Heavenly Home will offer that great cloud of eminent witnesses who first caught a glimpse of the hereafter at this place where loveliness keeps house.

I remain confident of this institution's historical commitment and in the quality of its performance. And now abideth the University of Alabama, Alabama A&M University and Oakwood College, but the greatest of these is Oakwood College.

Appendix M

Oakwood College Alumni Who Are Graduates from The Ohio State University

Colleges of Medicine, Education, and other Graduates

Paula Barnes, M.A., Education–Humanities	'75
Albert Dudley, M.B.A., Business Administration	'76
Gloria Samuel, M.A., Education	'76
Karen Wells, M.S., Home Economics	'76
Deidra Brooks, M.A., Communications	'77
Michelle Cleveland, M.M., Music	'77
Constance Irving, M.A., Mathematics Education	'77
Joyce Knight, M.A., Education	'77
Thompson Kay, M.A., Education	'79
Thomas Daniels, M.H.A., Hospital Administration	'80
Vanessa Blake, M.A., Music	'81
Sherrel Downes, M.S., Social Work	'83
Wellesley Johnson, M.S., Social Work	'83
Michael Mayne, M.A., Mathematics Education	'83
Edna Duncan, M.A., Human Services Education	'85
Steve Burks, M.D., Medicine	'88
Magna James, Ph.D., Psychology	'88
Alvin Jackson, M.D., Medicine	'89
James Harris, M.D., Medicine	'90
Perry Jennings, M.B.A., Business Administration	'91
Nozipho Nxumalo, Ph.D., Education	'91
Jenee Bowman, M.D., Medicine	'92
Ronald Clements, M.D., Medicine	'92
Oliver Davis, Jr., M.S.W., Social Work	'92
Marcia Douglas, M.F.A., Art	'93
Sheryl Guthrie, M.D., Medicine	'93
Kimberly Monk, M.D., Medicine	'93

Michelle Vieuxfort, M.D., Medicine	'93
Charmine Blair, M.D., Medicine	'94
Olivia Davis, M.A., Communication	'94
Michael Dulan, M.D., Medicine	'94
Del Edwards, D.O., Optometry	'94
Eileen Brantley, M.S., Education	'95
Maritza Griffiths, M.A., Family and Human Relations Development	'95
Sharhonda Martin, M.D., Medicine	'95
Charrice Wellington, M.D., Medicine	'95
Newton Andrews, M.D., Medicine	Scheduled to graduate in '96
Samuel Cort, M.D., Medicine	Scheduled to graduate in '96
Paul Monk, M.D., Medicine	Scheduled to graduate in '96
David Crump, M.A., Chemical Physics	Graduation year unknown
Alan Hackley, M.D., Medicine	Graduation year unknown
Elise Longpree, M.A., Political Science	Graduation year unknown

College of Law Graduates

Sandy Robinson, J.D., Law	'79
Leslie Crichlow, J.D., Law	'83
Lauretta Smith Roe, J.D., Law	'86
Linda Ammons, J.D., Law	'87
Ryan Chandler, J.D., Law	'87
Erica K. Jackson, J.D., Law	'91
Johnlander Jackson, J.D., Law	'92
Kendal Coes, J.D., Law	'93
Ben Swift, J.D., Law	'95

Appendix N

Danny Boone: A Eulogy

Delivered by Dr. Frank W. Hale, Jr., Ph.D., at the memorial service for Danny Boone at Triedstone Baptist Church on July 12, 1989.

Danny Boone developed his profession in a remarkable way, and we shall applaud his contributions even beyond his transition.

There is something about one's personality which sometimes eludes the photographer, which the painter cannot reproduce, the sculptor cannot chisel, and which the biographer cannot always describe effectively.

I liked the way that Danny went about his work—his profession.

Danny was committed. He was genuinely interested in the students he served. He was unpretentious in his manner, but generous in his desire to motivate and assist youth.

Danny was congenial. He possessed a graciousness of manner, cordiality of bearing, generosity of feeling, and the delightful art of pleasing. He didn't have to fake a smile; he had one—a real smile!

Danny was sharp—not in some flamboyant, ostentatious, artificial sense. He possessed a keen intellect; he was self-propelled. he was an able organizer. He was a creative programmer. He was a director who knew how to direct—consistently, imaginatively, and independently. He never called upon me to do his job, to design his program or to resolve his problems, even though he kept me informed of his modus operandi. Danny knew his stuff.

Danny was a team player. Danny maintained a camaraderie with Upward Bound directors throughout the region. He had good chemistry. He was warm, generous, and cooperative with his colleagues in the Office of Minority Affairs and on campus.

Danny got the job done! He served as Upward Bound program manager from 1983 to 1989. He developed proposals that were funded to a total of $1,146, 136. Many a youth owes their advancement or first motivating insight in life to his accommodating desire and disposition to help along wherever he could. And Danny never stopped doing and caring. He provided some invaluable lessons for all of us—Like a mighty oak, he withstood the storm.

I first became aware of Danny's illness about two years ago. It was quite obvious that he was in pain. Danny was a fighter. He never looked backward. He never pampered or pitied himself. He fought to the end. I see him making meetings, with pillow in hand, to buffer his suffering. I hear him standing his ground—holding on to his individuality even when speaking out on an issue when he was all by himself. He was no captive to the crowd. His illness did not imprison his focus, his drive, or his sense of fair play.

The Scripture says, "To every thing, there is a season and a time to every purpose:

"A time to be born, and a time to die.
A time to weep, and a time to laugh.
A time to mourn, and a time to dance.
A time to get, and a time to lose."

This is Danny's time—
And it is our time—
And a time for Danny to leave us
And a time for us to live the good things he has left us—
commitment, congeniality, courage.

O Danny Boy, the great timekeeper has called your name
O Danny Boy, we'll surely miss you just the same
O Danny Boy, you gave your all, you gave your best
O Danny Boy, you've earned the right to have your rest
O Danny Boy, you had some class
You opened your heart to lad and lass
You accepted them all—from vanilla to fudge
A lesson up front on not to judge—Your focus centered on trust and truth
This was your monument to our youth.

Vilakazi wrote a poem, "Then I'll Believe," recounting the death of his father.

"I'll believe then that you are dead
Only when the hills and flickering rivers
The wind roaring from North and South
When the cutting winter frost and dews
That lay on the grass today and yesterday
When all these are swallowed and fade away
I'll believe then that you are dead."

The spirit and contributions of Danny live on, and on, and on, and on, and on!

Autographs/Notes

Autographs/Notes

Autographs/Notes

Autographs/Notes

Autographs/Notes